Palgrave Macmillan Studies in Banking and Financial Institutions

Series Editor: **Professor Philip Molyneux**

The Palgrave Macmillan Studies in Banking and Financial Institutions are international in orientation and include studies of banking within particular countries or regions, and studies of particular themes such as Corporate Banking, Risk Management, Mergers and Acquisitions, etc. The books' focus is on research and practice, and they include up-to-date and innovative studies on contemporary topics in banking that will have global impact and influence.

Titles include:

Yener Altunbaş, Blaise Gadanecz and Alper Kara
SYNDICATED LOANS
A Hybrid of Relationship Lending and Publicly Traded Debt

Yener Altunbaş, Alper Kara and Öslem Olgu
TURKISH BANKING
Banking under Political Instability and Chronic High Inflation

Steffen E. Andersen
THE EVOLUTION OF NORDIC FINANCE

Elena Beccalli
IT AND EUROPEAN BANK PERFORMANCE

Paola Bongini, Stefano Chiarlone and Giovanni Ferri *(editors)*
EMERGING BANKING SYSTEMS

Vittorio Boscia, Alessandro Carretta and Paola Schwizer
COOPERATIVE BANKING: INNOVATIONS AND DEVELOPMENTS
COOPERATIVE BANKING IN EUROPE: CASE STUDIES

Roberto Bottiglia, Elisabetta Gualandri and Gian Nereo Mazzocco *(editors)*
CONSOLIDATION IN THE EUROPEAN FINANCIAL INDUSTRY

Alessandro Carretta, Franco Fiordelisi and Gianluca Mattarocci *(editors)*
NEW DRIVERS OF PERFORMANCE IN A CHANGING FINANCIAL WORLD

Dimitris N. Chorafas
CAPITALISM WITHOUT CAPITAL

Dimitris N. Chorafas
FINANCIAL BOOM AND GLOOM
The Credit and Banking Crisis of 2007–2009 and Beyond

Violaine Cousin
BANKING IN CHINA

Vincenzo D'Apice and Giovanni Ferri
FINANCIAL INSTABILITY
Toolkit for Interpreting Boom and Bust Cycles

Peter Falush and Robert L. Carter OBE
THE BRITISH INSURANCE INDUSTRY SINCE 1900
The Era of Transformation

Franco Fiordelisi
MERGERS AND ACQUISITIONS IN EUROPEAN BANKING

Franco Fiordelisi, Philip Molyneux and Daniele Previati *(editors)*
NEW ISSUES IN FINANCIAL AND CREDIT MARKETS

Franco Fiordelisi, Philip Molyneux and Daniele Previati *(editors)*
NEW ISSUES IN FINANCIAL INSTITUTIONS MANAGEMENT

Franco Fiordelisi and Philip Molyneux
SHAREHOLDER VALUE IN BANKING

Hans Genberg and Cho-Hoi Hui
THE BANKING SECTOR IN HONG KONG
Competition, Efficiency, Performance and Risk

Carlo Gola and Alessandro Roselli
THE UK BANKING SYSTEM AND ITS REGULATORY AND SUPERVISORY FRAMEWORK

Elisabetta Gualandri and Valeria Venturelli *(editors)*
BRIDGING THE EQUITY GAP FOR INNOVATIVE SMEs

Kim Hawtrey
AFFORDABLE HOUSING FINANCE

Jill M. Hendrickson
REGULATION AND INSTABILITY IN U.S. COMMERCIAL BANKING
A History of Crises

Otto Hieronymi *(editor)*
GLOBALIZATION AND THE REFORM OF THE INTERNATIONAL BANKING AND MONETARY SYSTEM

Munawar Iqbal and Philip Molyneux
THIRTY YEARS OF ISLAMIC BANKING
History, Performance and Prospects

Sven Janssen
BRITISH AND GERMAN BANKING STRATEGIES

Kimio Kase and Tanguy Jacopin
CEOs AS LEADERS AND STRATEGY DESIGNERS
Explaining the Success of Spanish Banks

Alexandros-Andreas Kyrtsis *(editor)*
FINANCIAL MARKETS AND ORGANIZATIONAL TECHNOLOGIES
System Architectures, Practices and Risks in the Era of Deregulation

M. Mansoor Khan and M. Ishaq Bhatti
DEVELOPMENTS IN ISLAMIC BANKING
The Case of Pakistan

Roman Matousek *(editor)*
MONEY, BANKING AND FINANCIAL MARKETS IN CENTRAL AND EASTERN EUROPE
20 Years of Transition

Philip Molyneux and Eleuterio Vallelado *(editors)*
FRONTIERS OF BANKS IN A GLOBAL WORLD

Imad Moosa
THE MYTH OF TOO BIG TO FAIL

Simon Mouatt and Carl Adams *(editors)*
CORPORATE AND SOCIAL TRANSFORMATION OF MONEY AND BANKING
Breaking the Serfdom

Anastasia Nesvetailova
FRAGILE FINANCE
Debt, Speculation and Crisis in the Age of Global Credit

Anders Ögren *(editor)*
THE SWEDISH FINANCIAL REVOLUTION

Dominique Rambure and Alec Nacamuli
PAYMENT SYSTEMS
From the Salt Mines to the Board Room

Catherine Schenk *(editor)*
HONG KONG SAR's MONETARY AND EXCHANGE RATE CHALLENGES
Historical Perspectives

Noël K. Tshiani
BUILDING CREDIBLE CENTRAL BANKS
Policy Lessons for Emerging Economies

Ruth Wandhöfer
EU PAYMENTS INTEGRATION
The Tale of SEPA, PSD and Other Milestones Along the Road

The full list of titles available is on the website:
www.palgrave.com/finance/sbfi.asp

Palgrave Macmillan Studies in Banking and Financial Institutions

Series Standing Order ISBN 978-1-4039-4872-4

You can receive future titles in this series as they are published by placing a standing order. Please contact your bookseller or, in case of difficulty, write to us at the address below with your name and address, the title of the series and the ISBN quoted above.

Customer Services Department, Macmillan Distribution Ltd, Houndmills, Basingstoke, Hampshire RG21 6XS, England

---

Regulation and Instability in U.S. Commercial Banking

A History of Crises

Jill M. Hendrickson
Associate Professor of Economics, University of St Thomas, USA

palgrave
macmillan

First published 2011 by
PALGRAVE MACMILLAN

Palgrave Macmillan in the UK is an imprint of Macmillan Publishers Limited, registered in England, company number 785998, of Houndmills, Basingstoke, Hampshire RG21 6XS.

Palgrave Macmillan in the US is a division of St Martin's Press LLC, 175 Fifth Avenue, New York, NY 10010.

Palgrave Macmillan is the global academic imprint of the above companies and has companies and representatives throughout the world.

Palgrave® and Macmillan® are registered trademarks in the United States, the United Kingdom, Europe and other countries

ISBN 978-0-230-28066-3 hardback

This book is printed on paper suitable for recycling and made from fully managed and sustained forest sources. Logging, pulping and manufacturing processes are expected to conform to the environmental regulations of the country of origin.

A catalogue record for this book is available from the British Library.

A catalog record for this book is available from the Library of Congress.

10 9 8 7 6 5 4 3 2 1
20 19 18 17 16 15 14 13 12 11

Printed and bound in Great Britain by
CPI Antony Rowe, Chippenham and Eastbourne

To my family

Contents

List of Tables, Figures and Appendix

Tables

Figures

Data Appendix

1
Commercial Bank Instability

In early 2001, a colleague of mine expressed concern that the deregulation of banking witnessed in the previous ten years would make the U.S. vulnerable to another experience similar to the Great Depression. Between 1929 and 1933, close to 10,000 commercial banks failed, costing depositors millions of dollars. Though my colleague probably did not fear another catastrophe of quite that magnitude, he was concerned that instability would follow deregulation. Similarly, students in my classes often conclude that banking systems outside the United States must be more vulnerable to crises and instability because they lack the regulation of U.S. banks. In both cases, my colleague and my students simply assume that regulation preserves or creates stability and prosperity. They are not alone. Many scholars of banking contend that periods of stability and prosperity are rooted in public policy decisions regarding the regulation and supervision of commercial banking. Indeed, the most recent 2007–2009 financial crisis has been blamed on the very deregulation that my colleague alluded to several years ago. However, it is increasingly difficult to accept the assumption that bank regulation begets bank stability because the U.S. experience clearly suggests otherwise.

Two historical themes

Reflecting on the historical evolution of banking in the U.S., two prevalent themes emerge. First, regulation has always played an important role in the development and performance of banking. Indeed, the U.S. commercial banking industry has been regulated since the first bank was chartered in the eighteenth century and the industry continues to be highly regulated today. This regulation has taken many forms. Some of it required that banks engage in certain activities while other forms of regulation prohibited certain activities. For example, during antebellum banking, the production of banknotes required the purchase of state debt. The Glass–Steagall provisions of the Banking Act of 1933 prohibited commercial banks from any corporate securities dealings. Additional provisions from the 1933 act prohibited the payment of interest on demand deposits, placed a limit on interest paid on time deposits, and prohibited interstate banking and branching. Public policy towards banks also takes the form of a federal safety net. The 1933 creation of federal deposit insurance is one example and the lender of last resort function of the Federal Reserve is another. More contemporarily, the Community Reinvestment Act of 1977 requires that commercial banks make loans to those from whom it accepts deposits.

A second theme that emerges from a historical inquiry is that despite all the regulation, commercial banking has witnessed periods of stability but also periods of great instability. Though not all scholars are in agreement on precise dates and definitions of instability, it may be said that each period of our banking history is scarred by episodes of crises or extreme fragility.[1] Antebellum banking saw numerous bank failures while the postbellum era experienced at least five serious bank panics. The early 1930s witnessed the failure of approximately 10,000 banks and a complete collapse in depositor confidence. After the Second World War, the banking sector enjoyed a period of stability, but by the mid-1960s it once again was plagued by a series of crises and failures. Bank performance, on the whole, did not recover until the early 1990s. Unfortunately, recovery was short lived. Weakness in the financial sector, including commercial banks, was exposed in 2007 with the mortgage-led financial crisis that resulted in 140 commercial bank failures in 2009 alone.

How can these two themes be reconciled in light of the common belief that a positive relationship exists between bank regulation and bank stability? Either bank instability is not related to regulation, i.e. public policy of regulating banks is not able to influence the stability of the industry, or regulation actually contributes to the instability. In either case, important implications for public policy exist. If regulation is unable to influence the performance of banking, much of the existing regulation is not necessary. If, on the other hand, regulation contributes to instability, it is time to re-think past policy decisions and move towards further deregulation. Philosopher George Santayana is famous for, among other things, his observation: "He who does not know history is fated to repeat it". Unless we understand the origins of contemporary problems in banking, public policy remedies are apt to be rather naïve.

Causes of bank instability

Many scholars have studied the consequences of bank crises and instability but fewer have researched the causes of these disturbances. Explanations offered by those who have analyzed the causes of bank crises and instability generally suggest one of three perspectives.[2] First, scholars such as Calomiris and Gorton (1991), and Carlson and Mitchner (2009) contend that the structure of U.S. commercial banking has historically made it vulnerable to instability. The structure of U.S. commercial banking has been determined, not by market forces, but by regulation and regulatory policy. Consequently, from this perspective, regulation may influence bank stability through regulation and regulatory policy.

A second perspective finds that bank failures and instability are caused by broader contractions in the real sector. For example, Temin (1976) finds that many bank failures during the Great Depression were the result of a contraction in consumer spending. Certainly it seems that the health of banking will be a function, to some extent, of the health of the real sector. More recently, a related set of literature considers the impact of bank stability on the aggregate output of the economy. The evidence in Ramirez (2009), for example, suggests bank instability can reduce economic growth.

A third perspective, for example Kindleberger and Aliber (2005), credits central bank policy with the necessary element to maintain bank stability. This perspective indicates that in the early history of U.S. commercial banking, a time in which a central bank did not exist, instability was caused by the absence of a central bank. Further, in later years, this perspective credits central banks for engendering stability.

While each of these three perspectives has merit, Grossman's (1994) analysis of all three finds evidence to support the first two but not the third. That is, Grossman does not find evidence that central bank policy contributed to bank stability.[3] The analysis in this book most closely aligns with the perspective that regulation alters the structure of banking and, in the process, contributes to bank instability more often than bank stability.[4]

Specifically, the perspective of this book is that regulation in commercial banking has largely been destabilizing in the long run. For example, many would argue that the creation of federal deposit insurance and interest rate ceilings imposed by the Banking Act of 1933 went a long way to stabilizing an extremely fragile banking system during the Great Depression. However, those very regulations later became an important source of bank instability as market conditions developed in such a manner that the regulation encouraged risk taking and led to severe disintermediation. The history of the U.S. banking system, from its inception, contains many illustrations of this relationship between regulation, the market, and ultimately the stability or instability of banking. An example from our early history is found in the regulation of state banknote production and distribution. State banks typically could print banknotes but this production was tied to the debt of state governments. Under some market conditions this regulation may not have been destabilizing. However, if states were not issuing bonds and banks wanted to expand their banknotes, the result was often a note shortage. This shortage made the banks unreliable in the eyes of their credit-seeking customers.

The author's view that banking regulation is often destabilizing stems, in part, from a particular perspective on markets and knowledge. The Austrian school of economic thought envisions the market as a process; instead of being at equilibrium, the market is seen as a dynamic course that forever changes and evolves as participants make new discoveries.[5] Being out of equilibrium creates proper incentives for new competition in search of profitable opportunities. At the same time, knowledge, in Austrian thought, is imperfect and dispersed. Indeed, if perfect knowledge existed, no further hidden or unknown profit opportunities would remain: the market would be in complete and final equilibrium. Rather, the market process provides the opportunity to mobilize knowledge and to open doors of discovery to new opportunities. That is, the market process creates knowledge.

If one looks at the world through the Austrian lens, regulation cannot be a harmless, stabilizing force. On the contrary, regulation interrupts the market process as well as the discovery, incentives, and competition of that process. At the same time, the state does not possess the knowledge necessary to make stabilizing and efficient regulation because such knowledge comes from the very process it is interrupting. However, even though government regulation drastically alters the market path, the entrepreneur still adjusts and continues to search for new and profitable opportunities. It is this continuous motion of the market, even while regulated, that makes regulation destabilizing because while regulation is static the market is not. This study of the evolution and dynamic nature of banking markets and regulation is an application of this vision.

Defining bank crises and financial stability

In order to analyze the role of regulation in promoting bank stability or instability, it is important to clarify two key terms. First is "bank crisis".[6] Scholars do not agree about how to define a bank crisis or when this term is appropriate for characterizing a period or event.[7] While there exists a rather extensive range of definitions, for purposes of this book, it is useful to create a working definition that may be used across all experiences in U.S. bank history. That is, each crisis is unique and contains elements not found in other crises. Yet, at the same time, there are certain elements found across all bank panics or crises. These shared elements form the definition of a bank crisis used here.[8]

Four elements are present in all bank crises in the United States. These four elements collectively form the definition of a crisis used throughout this book. First, an exogenous shock, to borrow from Kindleberger and Aliber (2005) terminology, sets the stage for profound optimism in both the real and financial sectors of the economy. This shock may take many different forms; the intense expansion of railways, fundamental shifts in production methods, rising real estate prices, etc. The important point of the shock is to form extremely favorable expectations for future profit and entrepreneurial opportunity.

The second element in all crises is the use and extension of credit as a response to the exogenous shock. As firms and entrepreneurs capitalize on expectations of future profits, they require credit to expand, create, and innovate. Banks are willing to accommodate because they too have high expectations for profits so loan extension is perceived as less risky. Taken together, the behavior of the firms, entrepreneurs, and banks lead to an extension of credit. As time passes, more and more debt is utilized as no one wants to miss the opportunity to participate in the profitable expansion. Minsky (1982) maintains that this increased reliance on debt makes the entire financial system more fragile largely because of the nature of the debt contracts are increasingly more risky. Debt taken out initially may be to cover new projects or to expand production facilities but as borrowers and lenders are swept away with optimism and more debt is accumulated, debt in the later stages may be, for example, to cover existing debt obligations. In this way, optimism gives way to a financial sector that is increasing susceptible to instability.

Since all good things must come to an end, the favorable conditions do not last. At some point, the optimism is replaced with caution and, ultimately, as loss in confidence. This may be because of a large business or bank failure, a sharp decline in the stock market, or a fall in real estate prices, among many other possibilities. The precise reason for the change in expectations is much less important than the changing expectations themselves. The loss in confidence regarding the future is the third element of all bank crises.

The fourth, and final, element of bank crises is that, as a response to the development that precipitated the change in expectations (loss in confidence), or that followed the change in expectations, banks fail in considerable numbers. That is, there is a systemic and significant rise in the number of bank failures. Borrowers realize that their indebtedness is too large and lenders recognize that their loans carry too much risk. The fragility of the credit expansion is made apparent and is exposed through a systemic spread of bank failures.

These four elements collectively form the definition of a bank crisis. An exogenous shock creates an environment of profound optimism about the economic future. Firms and entrepreneurs are increasingly interested in using credit to take advantage of the favorable expectations and banks are willing to lend because of shared expectations and also because they do not want to lose market share to competitors. The result is a considerable expansion of credit. Because the credit expansion necessarily adds to the fragility of the financial sector, at some point, the optimism is replaced with a loss in confidence and a re-evaluation of the credit outstanding as well as short-term credit moving forward. As the fragility of the system is exposed, banks fail systemically. The large number of bank failures marks the culminating affect of the other elements of a bank crisis.

This book asks if bank regulation has historically promoted financial stability. What is financial stability? Though this term is frequently used in the literature, it is often not defined. Here the term means that the primary financial institutions of an economy are functioning to engender a high level of confidence with their users and that external help to achieve the confidence is not required. Primary institutions in the financial sector include commercial banks, savings banks, bond markets, stock markets, mutual fund companies, and insurance companies. Many different developments may trigger a sudden and unanticipated loss in confidence. Political election outcomes, bankruptcies in the real sector, war or other political conflict, corporate or financial failures or fraud, are just a few conditions that may significantly hurt confidence in the institutions of the financial sector. Regardless of the cause, the key element to financial instability is a significant and unexpected loss in consumer confidence that prevents some or all financial institutions from functioning normally.

The relationship between a bank crisis and financial instability is as follows. If there is a bank crisis, there is necessarily financial instability since confidence has been eroded in at least one financial institution. However, it is possible to witness financial instability without a bank crisis. For example, large drops in equity prices could erode confidence without leading to a bank crisis. Indeed, it is easy to imagine a scenario in which individual investors sell stock and place the funds in a commercial bank account. In this case, there is an unexpected deposit inflow and so clearly not a bank crisis. Thus, a bank crisis necessarily results in financial instability, but financial instability does not require a bank crisis.

Book organization

The pages of this book contain numerous examples of bank crises and the response of regulators and policymakers throughout U.S. history. The details of each crisis are unique, but it is clear that these crises have shared elements that transcend time; certain elements that were true during the antebellum era remain true today. These shared elements shed light on the role regulation plays in bank performance.

Chapter 2 contains a discussion and critique of theories of general economic regulation and then narrows to a discussion of theories of commercial bank regulation. It begins by reviewing the neoclassical approach to regulation that essentially sees regulation as a means of either correcting market failures or as a means of bestowing rents on regulated parties, regulators and/or policymakers. A critique and introduction to the Austrian approach to understanding markets follows and sets the stage for analysis of regulation throughout the history of U.S. commercial banking.

Following the theoretical introduction to regulation, there are five interrelated chapters that serve as the foundation for understanding the evolution of U.S. commercial banking and its regulation. Chapter 3 focuses on the evolution of both private and public institutions in the early history of the U.S. commercial banking sector. This includes an analysis of the following: incorporated state banking, private banking, free banking, clearinghouses, and incorporated national banking. Most students of U.S. commercial banking are insufficiently exposed to these institutions and to the contributions these institutions have made on banking stability. This section carefully considers the regulation these institutions operated under and the resulting impact on bank stability.

The national banking era is investigated in Chapter 4. This period begins with the end of the Civil War and concludes with the 1913 creation of the Federal Reserve System. During this period, commercial banking underwent rather extensive change with the creation of nationally chartered banks and a central bank as well as the demise of free banks and Clearinghouse Associations. This was an important time in our commercial banking history because the institutions created during this era have had a tremendous impact on the structure and performance of commercial banking.

Chapter 5 covers perhaps the most famous historical period in commercial banking; the Great Depression. In response to thousands of commercial bank failures during this period, extensive regulation limited the activity of banks and increased the presence of federal governmental control. The regulatory response to the Great Depression bank crises would have far reaching implications on bank performance for many decades.

The post war years may be characterized as relatively stable and prosperous both from a general macroeconomic perspective and from the more narrow perspective of commercial banking. Chapter 6 provides an analysis of how the relative stability gave way to episodes of crises and instability in the mid to late 1960s. In the last half of this chapter, the analysis turns to the regulators' response to instability. Interestingly, whereas the response during the Great Depression and the national banking era was to *increase* regulation, beginning in early 1980, the response was to *decrease* regulation.

Chapter 7 highlights the first bank crisis of the twenty-first century by analyzing the role of regulation in the 2007–2009 financial crisis. This chapter begins with a discussion of how public policy, regulation and monetary policy contributed to the significant and unsustainable rise in house prices in the years prior to the crisis. It also analyzes the role of specific regulation in altering the supply of mortgage credit which, in the end, may help explain the cause of this most recent crisis. As history clearly illustrates, the outcome of this crisis is certain to include significant regulatory change to the financial sector and commercial banking. As with the Great Depression, the implications for such a response to the crisis will be critical for bank performance moving forward.

Finally, Chapter 8 reflects on the preceding chapters and asks what conclusions may be drawn about the relationship between regulation and stability throughout the history of U.S. commercial banking. It is here that the experiences and lessons learned from the evolution of banking and bank regulation come together to generate an overall understanding of regulation's role in the history of commercial banking in the United States.

2
Theories of Bank Regulation

Bank regulation in the United States has evolved since the first commercial bank was chartered in 1781. This evolution has largely been in response to bank crises. In other words, there has been no master plan for the regulation of commercial banks but, rather, a trial and error approach. In response to a crisis or instability, regulation has been established. If, down the road, the regulation is not working, it may be revised, replaced, or removed. Our commercial bank history, as this book demonstrates, is rife with examples of regulators responding to crisis with new or revised regulation. Figure 2.1 offers a timeline of the primary regulation and institutions in U.S. bank history and also highlights all of the bank crises throughout the history. From this illustration, it is easy to see the historical pattern of crisis followed by regulation. In order to properly evaluate the evolution of regulation, it is important to first understand the economic theory of regulation in general and then the theories of bank regulation more specifically. This chapter is designed to introduce the theoretical underpinnings of bank regulation so that we may critically analyze the evolution of commercial banking and commercial bank regulation in the chapters to follow.

General theories of economic regulation

Two general schools of thought attempt to explain why regulation, across all industries, is often utilized in a market system. These are the public-interest approach and the self-interest approach. Prior to 1970, prevalent economic thought followed the public-interest approach and in 1971 Stigler introduced a different way to consider the motivations behind regulation when he outlined the self-interest theory of regulation.[1]

Figure 2.1 The Evolution of U.S. Commercial Regulation, Institutions, and Crises: 1781–2010

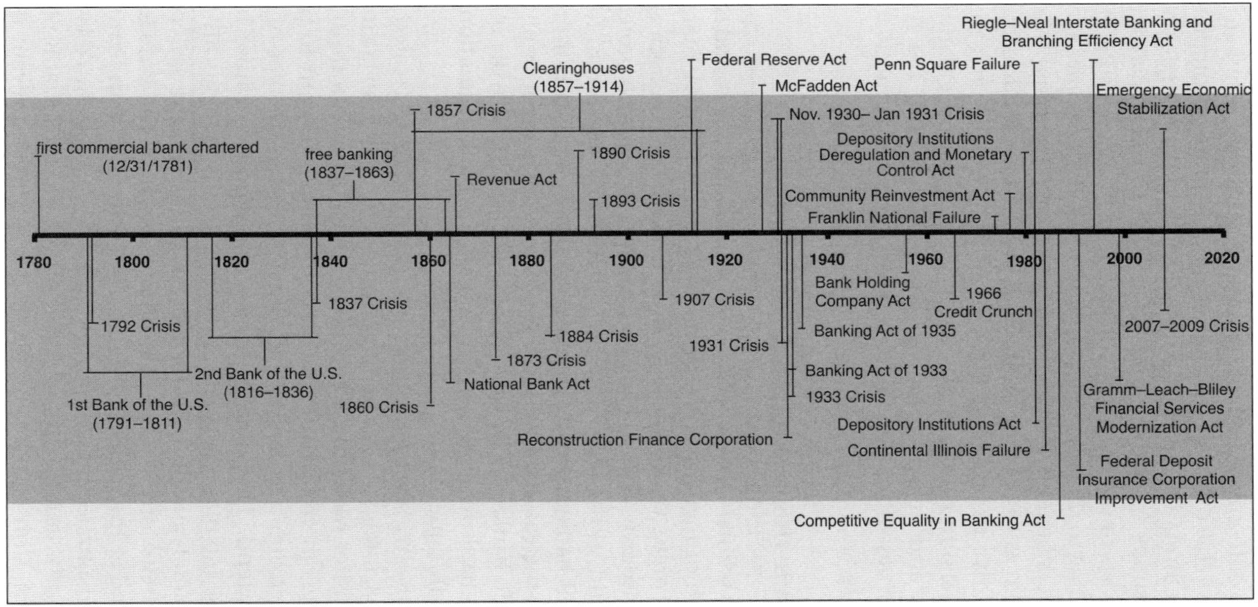

According to the public-interest approach, a market economy may produce outcomes which are undesirable to the consumer.[2] Examples of undesirable outcomes include monopoly rents, incomplete or asymmetric information, or externalities. Regulation, it is argued, can protect the consumer from these outcomes. From this perspective bank regulation exists to safeguard the consumer, be it the depositor or borrower.

According to the self-interest approach, regulation comes about because it produces benefits for the regulated group.[3] The group which stands to benefit, as well as the group which stands to be harmed, each have an incentive to influence the regulatory process so that the outcome is beneficial to them. As this theory of economic regulation evolved, scholars also began to include the politician and the regulator as other parties with incentive to influence regulation motivated by self-interest.[4]

Economic theories applied to banking

Banking scholars have applied both the public-interest and self-interest approach of regulation to the banking sector. Indeed, many banking scholars argue that bank regulation is motivated by both approaches simultaneously. That is, bank regulation serves to both protect the consumer and, at the same time, is influenced by subgroups, for example the small banker, within banking who may benefit from regulation. Perhaps the easiest way to see the two general theories of regulation applied to banking is by asking the question: what are the objectives or goals of bank regulation? A review of the bank regulation literature answers this question.[5]

Historically, bank regulation was supported and created to protect the public interest.[6] For example, during the antebellum era many feared the depositor was confused or misinformed because of the hundreds of banknotes in circulation. Regulation was called upon to protect the consumer. Similarly, banks were often limited in the type of loans they could extend. This was to protect the depositor whose funds were being used to make the loans. Perhaps the most obvious historic example of bank regulation meant to protect the depositor is deposit insurance. Discussions of deposit insurance began at the state level in the 1830s and at the national level in 1893 when William Jennings Bryan proposed a national deposit insurance bill to Congress. Today, national deposit insurance is still defended on the grounds that it protects the depositor. Contemporarily, regulation meant to prevent discrimination, such as the Community Reinvestment Act and predatory lending laws, also fall under the rubric of the public-interest approach to bank regulation.

Yet while the record of bank regulation clearly has elements of protecting the public interest, there exists many examples of bank regulation promoting the self-interest of bankers, subgroups within banking, and the legislators or regulators themselves.[7] American banking began with the creation of many small banks. Indeed, the very reason the banks were small was because of chartering restrictions that gave state regulators incentive to limit the number of banks by extracting rents from the banker. At the same time, the banker then had incentive to limit entry (i.e. limit competition) and paid off state regulators to minimize the number of charters granted. Another example of the self-interest theory of regulation at work is the prohibition on branching. From as early as the antebellum era banking experts recognized the benefits of branching.[8] Yet it was not until 1994 that interstate branching was allowed in the United States. Why did it take more than 200 years to eliminate branching restrictions? Because the politically powerful small banker did not want to have to compete with larger banks.[9] Another example of self-interest regulation comes from the national bank era. The passage of two important banks acts in 1863 and 1864 that created national banks was motivated, in large part, as a means of generating revenue for the federal government and had little to do with creating a healthy banking system.

Psychological attraction theory of financial regulation

Another theory, the psychological attraction theory of financial regulation, is also relevant to this study and is helpful in understanding why significant regulation follows bank crises. This theory argues that participants in the political process (voters, regulators, politicians, and the media) have psychological biases that are exploited by the regulatory process.[10] That is, psychological and social processes affect financial regulatory outcomes. While there are many such processes, here the focus is on introducing how some of these may help explain bank regulation.

One process, the response to vivid stimuli, is the tendency to respond to experiences and stories that are personal or deeply tap into our emotions. Extreme events, such as bank crises, influence the regulatory debate because of the strong psychological response to such events. Further, the media exploit these events with great zeal so that the process is exacerbated. One outcome is an increased demand for a regulatory response to the stimuli.

Another process, what psychologists call "negativity bias", sees people caring more about the financial loss of others than their financial gain. Of course, this is directly related to the vivid stimuli process since a story of financial loss often invokes the negativity bias. Not surprisingly, the media exacerbates this bias as well. In the most recent financial crisis, it was common to read about stories of home foreclosures and the hardship people were suffering as a result of not being able to pay their mortgages. Feeding off of the negativity bias can strengthen the desire voters have for regulation.

Scapegoating is another underlying process and refers to the desire to find blame in others when things go wrong. Scapegoating creates support for regulation generally with the promise that things will not go wrong again. Banking crises provide an excellent opportunity for scapegoating. Immediately following the 1929 stock market crash, the President organized a congressional commission to determine the cause of the crash. The results suggested that investors were to blame, despite evidence to the contrary. In the 2007–2009 crises, congressional hearings were harsh and accusatory towards the participants in the financial sector, even though there was no evidence of wrong doing. Indeed, lenders are often vilified in the scapegoating process which leads to demands for regulation. It is not intuitive to most that the intermediation process of banking is valuable so lenders are easy targets to blame.

Two additional processes influence banking regulation. First, is the human desire for equality. When one group is doing poorly people are eager to disdain those who are faring well. Since bankers are often characterized as doing well financially, this process reinforces the hostility toward the lender. Second, overconfidence is the psychological term for the belief that one's capacity is greater than it actually is. Overconfident regulators "know" that there is not a market solution to the banking problem and "know" that regulation can fix it. Because of the processes described above, voters demand the regulatory solution being offered by overconfident regulators or legislators.

The psychological attraction theory of financial regulation offers a way to understand why voters are increasingly eager for regulation and, at the same time, why regulators and politicians are eager to provide regulation, particularly financial regulation. This perspective also offers a way to understand why, throughout the history of commercial banking, the response to a bank crisis has always been to increase the regulation of banks.

The next five chapters of this book consider the evolution of banking and bank regulation. Each of these chapters contains numerous examples of bank regulation motivated by the public-interest, self-interest, or psychological attraction approach to regulation. Before moving onto a narration of that history and evolution, however, it is important to address two more issues surrounding the theory of bank regulation. First, as indicated at the beginning of this chapter, bank regulation has largely been a response to bank crises. This very statement implies that banking does not have a stable history. Since banking has always been a highly regulated industry, it is natural to ask how regulation affects bank stability. Second, this chapter outlines a perspective for understanding why regulation is often unable to successfully stabilize banks.

How regulation affects bank stability

Individual bank stability is impacted by regulation through five general channels.[11] First, regulation changes the risk-taking incentives of banks to either encourage or discourage risk taking. Consider, for example, capital requirements placed on banks mandating a certain level of capital be held. These restrictions should minimize the incentives for a bank to take on risk since the capital may be lost in the event of nonperforming investments or failure. At the same time, however, since capital acts as a cushion against problems, some bankers may actually take on *more* risk knowing the capital is there as a backup. Deposit insurance also serves to increase risk taking because the banker knows that, should the bank fail, the depositors will be protected. Asset restrictions that historically forbid banks from investing in certain equities or in making certain types of loans minimized the banker's ability to take on too much risk. These are just a few examples where bank regulation changes the risk incentives facing the banker and, in the process, affect the likelihood of bank problems or even failure.

Second, regulation constrains the opportunities a bank has to diversify. Historically banks have faced both asset and liability constraints that leave their balance sheets less diversified which, in turn, makes the bank more vulnerable to instability. For example, most national banks were prohibited from extending real estate loans for many years. At the same time the banks were also prohibited from investing in corporate equities. These restrictions narrow the opportunities to have a diversified asset base. Consider, for example, a small banker in a small town in the mountains of Tennessee during the 1890s. It is likely that the town was supported by one or a few companies, perhaps among them a coal mining firm. It is also likely that the bank extended loans to those few companies and had little else, other than perhaps government securities, in terms of assets. This means the fortunes of the bank are closely tied to the fortunes of the small community which, in many cases, could be a single firm. This lack of diversification certainly makes the bank position more fragile. Further, this entire scenario is exacerbated throughout our commercial bank history by the prohibition on interstate and intrastate branching.

Third, bank regulation changes the profit opportunities facing bankers by altering cost and revenue opportunities. After the Great Depression, regulators placed a limit on the interest rate that banks could pay to attract deposits. Certainly this minimized competition between bankers and also limited the cost of obtaining deposits. However, regulators also placed a ceiling on the interest rate the banker could charge on certain types of loans thereby limiting revenue opportunities. During both the antebellum and national banking eras some banks were required to purchase federal bonds in order to issue banknotes. This requirement meant that revenue was tied to the yield on government bonds and that these funds could not be used elsewhere to earn more or less revenue. After 1933 banks were prohibited from investing or underwriting corporate securities which also limited the revenues to other, permissible uses of their funds. These are examples of bank regulation that have historically changed the cost and revenue opportunities for the commercial banker. If the regulation increases costs or decreases revenue, or both, it compromises bank profitability and contributes to bank instability.

A fourth channel in which regulation impacts bank stability is by influencing the structure of commercial banking. That is, regulation influences the choices made by bankers which, in turn, determines the size and number of banks. Regulation in the United States has created a landscape of thousands of banks, most of whom are relatively small when measured by the dollar value of assets. The large number of banks is the product of chartering and asset restrictions as well as limits on branch banking. The small size of many of these banks also reflects limits on branching and regulation such as the tax on bank capital and deposit insurance. A landscape of many small banks is very different from a landscape of a few large banks. Canada is an example of a nation who historically has had less regulated bank markets and so ended up with a bank structure of a few large banks. Interestingly, the empirical evidence indicates that the Canadian structure is much more stable than the United States.[12]

Finally, regulation changes the nature of bank competition and, in the process, influences bank stability. How does competition in banking impact stability? It was long assumed that a trade-off existed between competition and stability: an increase in competition reduces the profits and/or increases the risk taking of existing banks and therefore makes banks more vulnerable to failure, particularly during crisis, and so increases instability. Indeed, much of the regulation placed on commercial banks stems from this belief as it has tended to reduce competition at the local level. Examples include the chartering process, the restrictions on assets and liabilities, the restrictions on the pricing of assets and liabilities, the prohibition on branch banking, and the prohibition on underwriting and distributing corporate securities.

However, there are two reasons to reconsider the assumption that competition in banking contributes to instability. First, it is possible that incumbent bankers will respond differently to new competitors than the scenario outlined above. For example, in a second possible scenario, increased competition causes existing firms to become more efficient, to cut costs, to alter their business plan. If efficiency is improved, this may improve profits and make banking more stable. Second, more recent scholarship has increasingly shown that there is a positive relationship between bank competition and stability and not necessarily a trade-off between the two.[13] For example, Carlson and Mitchener (2009) find that, during the Great Depression, banks that were exposed to new competition, due to branch entry, improved their efficiency and profits to remain viable. Further, their analysis indicates that banks that adjusted to higher levels of competition were more likely to survive the banking crisis of the early 1930s. The same authors, in earlier work, find empirical evidence that the greater competition caused by branch banking forced weaker banks to exit the market during the 1920s and 1930s.[14] Once the weaker banks were gone, the entire banking system was more stable. In this way, competition improved the stability of banking.

There is yet another possible scenario in the relationship between competition and bank stability. The issue of whether banks increase their risk taking in the face of competition is complicated by federal deposit insurance. That is, prior to 1933, the evidence suggests that competition forced all banks to be more efficient, to search for profits through the efficiency gains and, in the end, increase profits and stability. However, it is possible that, post deposit insurance, in the face of increased competition, the bankers would take on more risk and may be willing to do so knowing that deposit losses would be covered by insurance. Deposit insurance reduces the cost of risk taking and so may encourage excessive risk taking when the competitive environment is strengthened. Despite the destabilizing influences of deposit insurance, recent scholarship finds that when banking markets are opened to more free entry, portfolio risk declines, efficiency improves and loan losses decrease.[15] These findings suggest competition in banking is stabilizing despite deposit insurance.

In the end, there are five channels through which bank regulation affects the stability of banking. Under some conditions the regulation may contribute to stability and under other conditions it may contribute to bank instability. Unfortunately, the U.S. banking experience strongly suggests that the regulation tends to be more destabilizing than stabilizing. Why is it that regulation tends to have a negative impact on the performance of commercial banks? Is it something fundamentally wrong with the construction of bank regulation or is all regulation subject to the same shortcomings and criticism? The next section attempts to answer these questions and, in the process, sets the stage for viewing the evolution of banking and bank regulation from a particular perspective.

A critique of regulation: An Austrian perspective

Both the public-interest and self-interest theories of regulation outlined earlier come from a particular perspective of markets, namely the neoclassical perspective, that is pervasive in academia and with policymakers. From the neoclassical perspective, market equilibrium reflects supply and demand conditions where suppliers and demanders operate with complete information. A change in supply or demand, or both, leads to a new, static equilibrium. If the market equilibrium is not desirable, regulation is called upon to generate a more acceptable outcome. That is, government intervention in the market is seen as a mechanism that improves upon market outcomes. The public-interest approach to regulation is often defended on such grounds and the self-interest theory simply shows how regulators and bureaucrats can alter the market equilibrium for their own welfare. However in order for this framework to hold, many unrealistic assumptions about behavior, knowledge, and institutions must be in place. Relaxing these rigorous assumptions causes the neoclassical theories to crumble.

If, instead of viewing the world through the neoclassical lens, one views the world through a lens that does not demand impractical assumptions but rather embraces a more realistic approach to markets, the use of regulation as a panacea quickly becomes suspect at best. A perspective that the author finds much more realistic and convincing is that of the Austrian school.[16] An introduction to the Austrian perspective follows. From this introduction, it will become clear why regulation in general, and bank regulation more specifically, is not able to improve the performance of commercial banking.

Perhaps the most important departure the Austrian perspective makes from the neoclassical, as well as other, perspectives is in their understanding of markets as a process rather than a static equilibrium state. Mises (1949), Hayek (1937), Kirzner (1992, 1984), High (1991) and other Austrian scholars all stress the notion that markets are a dynamic, discovery process that continues to change and adjust to reflect new opportunities. As a continuous process, markets are never in equilibrium. Opportunities for new products, new production processes, new materials etc. keep the market moving and it is the entrepreneur searching for profitable new opportunities that provide the engine behind the dynamic market. The entrepreneur seeks to provide something new and unknown to the market in order to gain profits. Through this endeavor, markets are always in, and will always remain in, flux since the future is not known so future profitable opportunities are, at this time, unknowable. However, the future profitable opportunities will, at some time, be revealed through entrepreneurial effort.

A key to understanding the continuous nature of the market process lies within the distribution of knowledge. According to the neoclassical framework, knowledge is perfect so that all market participants know about all opportunities. In contrast, the Austrian perspective stresses the inescapable division of knowledge.[17] Each individual possesses a small amount of the total knowledge. We cannot know everything today nor can we know what the future will bring. In a true market economy, knowledge is revealed through the market process and the prices which result. This is a critical departure from the perfect knowledge assumed in the neoclassical framework. If knowledge is not perfect and if we accept the notion that the distribution of knowledge is wide and asymmetric as Hayek (1937) did, there are serious implications for regulatory policy. Perhaps this notion is best stated by Kirzner (1984: 631), a leading Austrian scholar:

> A realization that the market yields knowledge – the sort of knowledge that people do not at present even know they need – should engender among would-be social engineers who seek to replace or to modify the results of the free market a very definite sense of humility. To announce that one can improve on the performance of the market, one must also claim to know in advance what the market will reveal.

This is precisely why regulation often fails both in banking and in other industries. A regulated market interrupts the market process and changes the opportunities for entrepreneurial discovery and profit. It does not eliminate opportunities but because the path of the market is disturbed and must begin to move in another direction, the opportunities are not the same as they were before. Is the new regulated path better than the old market path? Probably not, because the regulated path was artificially created outside of the market process with incomplete knowledge so that discoveries and opportunities from the market process are stifled or lost. Regulation undermines the discovery process already in place and, in all likelihood, it is a process capable of self-correction. That is, if the market outcome is not desirable there exists an opportunity for gain by correcting the outcome. Alert entrepreneurs will take advantage of that opportunity and correct the market. It is certainly hard to envision a situation in which the government possesses better or more information than the entrepreneur to provide a market correction.

At the heart of the Austrian approach to understanding human economic action is the notion of a market process, the discovery process of entrepreneurship, and the asymmetric distribution of knowledge. Taken together, these concepts create a lens into our economic world that finds the entrepreneur a much more compelling solution to undesirable market outcomes than government intervention and regulation.

The next five chapters of this book tell the story of the evolution of commercial banking in the United States. It is largely a story of market outcomes that are not desirable (e.g. bank crises) and the government regulation called upon to correct the problem. As these chapters unfold it becomes clear that the regulatory responses contributed to additional bank problems and instability. This is not a surprising finding when viewing the world from the Austrian perspective outlined above.

3
Antebellum Banking: 1781–1863

The economy, as a whole, experienced healthy growth as well as substantial structural change between 1781 and the onset of the Civil War. In general terms, real gross national product (RGNP) grew at rather fecund levels throughout this period thereby continuing a trend started in the earliest colonial times (Figure A.1).[1] Foreign trade drove most of the growth prior to the early nineteenth century though the Embargo of 1807 ended, temporarily, most exporting. Between 1807 and 1837, production shifted away from home and small shops filled with skilled artisans in favor of the factory which certainly altered the nature of work and life for many Americans (Figure A.2). After 1837 and prior to the Civil War, the U.S. economy experienced even more robust RGNP growth and further structural change. Indeed, RGNP growth averaged approximately five percent during this period and per capital RGNP grew, on average, at a rate of 1.8 percent.[2] Industrial and commercial growth comprised much of this expanded production. As evidence, consider that in 1839, 37 percent of RGNP production was in industry, trade, or transportation but 20 years later 46 percent of all production fell under the industry classification.[3] Much of this economic growth may be traced to a time of intense entrepreneurial spirit. While most people worked the land, there was an increasing need and interest in improving the production process and its output. At the end of this era, entrepreneurs such as McCormick, in agriculture, and Vanderbilt, in transportation, seized existing opportunities and created new opportunities to advance the young economy. Faith in enterprise may be seen in the stability of the stock market (Figure A.3). However, the stock volatility in the latter half of this era corresponds with banking crises that characterize this historical period. Business failure rates were also low, in absolute numbers, during antebellum America (Figure A.4).

Population expansion could not match production expansion in antebellum America but was impressive nonetheless. For the 20 years bookended by 1840 and 1860 the rate of population growth translated to a doubling every 23 years (Figure A.5).[4] While much of this growth was among native-borns, it was also the period of highest immigration growth in our nation's history.[5] At the same time, the growing population was slowly shifting from the east to the open spaces of the West. For example, 1790 found Kent County, Maryland the geographic center of the nation but by 1860 the center lay just east of Chillicothe, Ohio.[6] Thus, in addition to significant population growth, great labor mobility characterized this period.

With the growing and enterprising population came expanded production and a real need for borrowed capital and financial intermediation. The stage had been set for banking not only to establish itself in America but to thrive and facilitate real economic prosperity. Only one obstacle, a rather formidable one, existed: many Americans distrusted the idea of banking. Indeed, seven states – Arkansas, California, Florida, Iowa, Oregon, Texas, and Wisconsin – actually prohibited banking altogether at some point during antebellum America. Ultimately, however, most Americans recognized the value of the banker and actually embraced several types of banking institutions before the antebellum era came to a close. These included state chartered banks, free banks, private banks, and two federal banks, thus making this perhaps the most diverse era in commercial banking history.

In considering this early episode in our banking history, several questions are posited. How did the different institutions develop? What was their relation to one another? How were they regulated? Did the regulation promote stability? What is the evidence? To answer these questions, this chapter details the institutions, regulation, and episodes of failure in American banking between 1781 and 1863. Many accounts of antebellum banking focus on the instability of this period. For example, much attention has focused on wildcat banking and unstable currency throughout the nation. This chapter re-examines this history and asks if the antebellum period was stable or unstable and, in turn, what exactly contributed to the stable or unstable bank performance.

General banking themes

Four general themes emerge from banking during the antebellum era. Throughout this chapter, all four of these themes are explored in detail. First is that economic integration in the United States was far from

Figure 3.1 Map of the United States of America in 1800

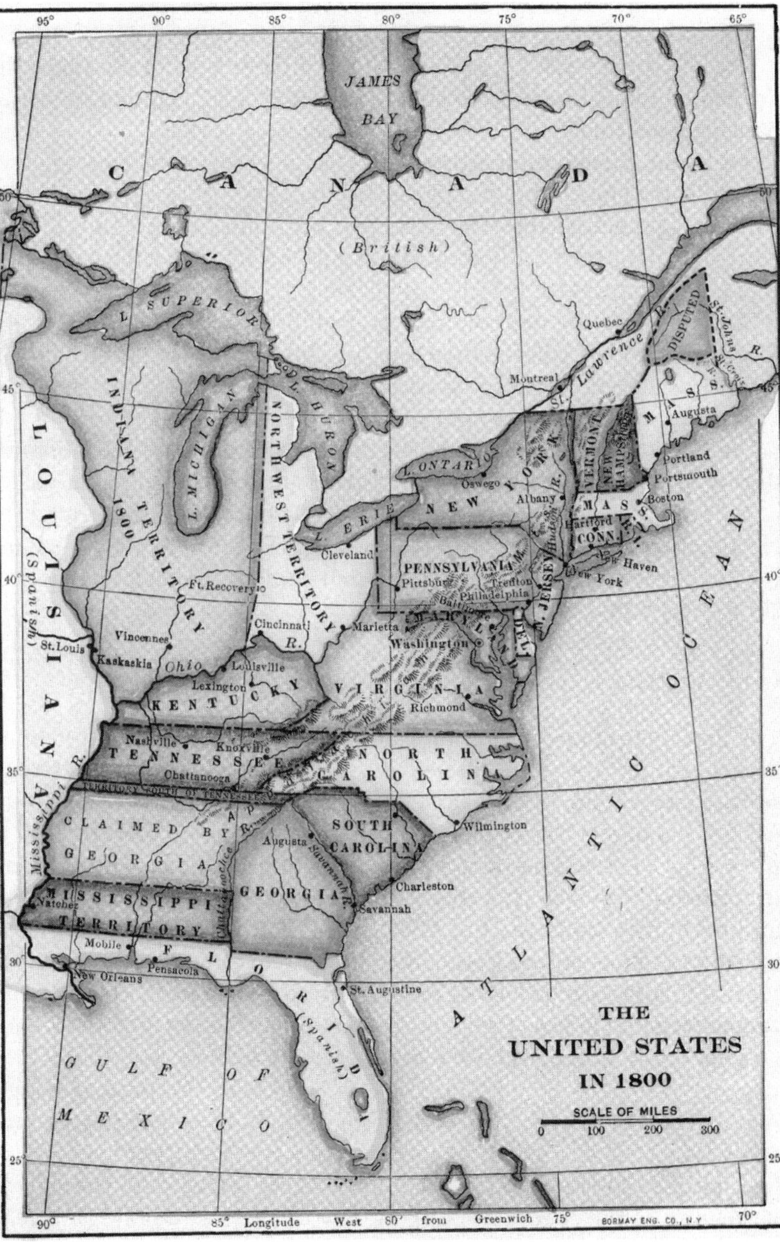

Source: http://www.earlyamerica.com/earlyamerica/maps/1800/.

complete. As illustrated in Figure 3.1, much of the nation was undeveloped and large territories marked much of the middle and western part of the nation. Within the East, the degree of progress was also highly diverse; the northeast tended to be more financially and economically developed than the southern states. This uneven integration impacted bank performance.

A second theme from this era is that regulation of banking was largely at the state level. Except for the chartering of two federal banks, banking was regulated by the states that distributed bank charters. This is in sharp contrast with the increasing degree of federal regulation that characterizes U.S. banking in all the eras which follow.

The final two themes concern the stability of antebellum banking. The fact that the earliest banking in U.S. history was the most stable is the third general theme. Few banks failed during the antebellum era and the panics were regional in nature. The regional nature of the panics is certainly a reflection of the diversity in economic development during this era. The fourth theme is that private, coordinated efforts contributed significantly to the stability of antebellum banking. In the North, these efforts took the form of Clearinghouse Associations and the Suffolk System. In the South, branch banking created a network of strong and stable banks.

Introduction to the antebellum banking era

The first incorporated bank in America was a state chartered bank in Pennsylvania. Operating alongside the state chartered banks were private banks. Though little attention has historically been paid to the private banker, scholars have more recently re-evaluated the role of private bankers finding them to be an important part of early financial intermediation.[7] Indeed, private bankers would never again play such an important role in the financial sector both in terms of their numbers and as a percentage of total banking assets.

Prior to 1837 and the birth of free banking, state bank charters were the product of legislative acts of incorporation. To obtain a bank charter, one would petition members of the state legislature. It does not take much imagination to anticipate the problems this process caused. Accusations of charter "selling" brought scandal to the process and those banks already in possession of a charter placed great pressure on legislatures to vote against new applicants. In response to these entry barriers arose the era of free banking. Essentially, free banking is a term to capture the notion that anyone meeting certain requirements was free to enter the business of banking. Free banking laws were born in 1838 in New York and quickly spread to other states. Traditional investigations into free banking have judged it to be a failure based on the number of such banks that failed and due to questionable note quality from some of these banks.

In addition to state chartered banks, private banks, and free banks, the antebellum banking era also saw two federal banks come and go. The U.S. constitution granted the federal government the right to coin silver and gold money and to determine the dollar value of the coins. Beyond this, the constitution did not grant any monetary authority to the federal government. Despite this, the federal government was able to charter two banks during antebellum America. The first bank had a 20-year charter from 1791 to 1811 and the second also survived 20 years from 1816 to 1836. Thus, antebellum banking was comprised of four different types of banking institutions; the state chartered commercial bank, the private bank, two federal banks, and free banks. At the close of the Civil War, only the state chartered and private bank would remain.

State chartered banking

Commercial banking in the United States began with the 1781 chartering of the Bank of North America in Philadelphia. It did not take long for commercial banking to spread throughout the country. By 1791, the four major cities, New York, Boston, Baltimore, and Philadelphia each had a bank with combined capital of $2.5 million. At the turn of the nineteenth century each state, except New Jersey, North Carolina, Vermont, and Georgia had chartered banks. Figure 3.1 illustrates the states and territories in America in 1800 and Figure 3.2 illustrates the rate of growth in banking in the early years of this era. Figure 3.2 indicates that after the first 15 years of commercial banking, the most robust growth occurred in 1803, 1812, 1818, and 1836. Two of these growth spurts coincide with the lapsed charters of the two federal banks during the antebellum period.[8] Growth in 1812 can be explained by the 1811 lapse of the charter of the First Bank of the United States which meant that a bank with $10 million in capital and eight branches closed its doors, thus paving the way for commercial bank expansion. Similarly, the Second Bank of the United States lost its charter in 1836 which was the catalyst for the explosion of banks during that period. The other growth spurts may be explained more generally. Our nation was in its infant stages of embracing paper currency, of expanding our economic possibilities, and advancing entrepreneurial ambitions. Indeed, a report

Figure 3.2 Number of State Chartered Banks in Antebellum and National Banking Era: 1782–1896

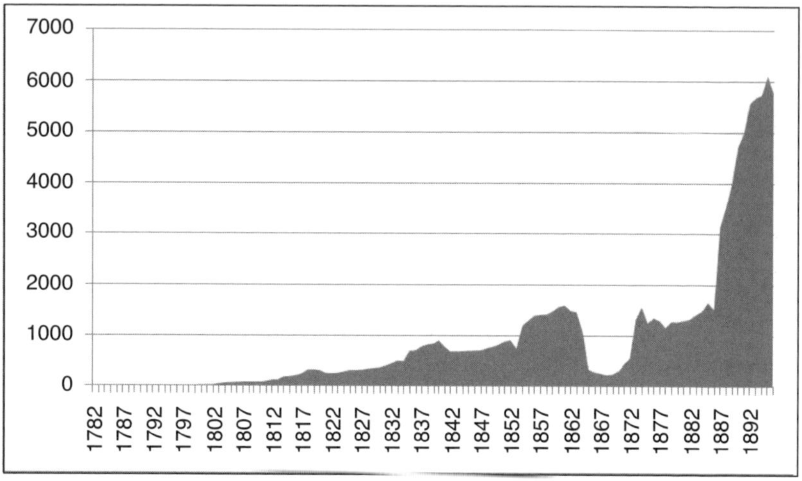

Source: Historical Statistics, Series Cj142, Cj149.

from Ohio in 1815 claimed that "a money mania like an epidemic seized the people."[9] Further, some of this growth was, in part, spurred by the War of 1812, which cost over $75 million; most of which was borrowed from the state banks. Figure 3.2 illustrates the significant growth in state banks near the end of this era. This may be explained, in part, by the rising population (Figure A.5) and significant economic growth (Figure A.1).

Banking operations in our early history were a far cry from the sophisticated banks in operation today. In terms of their assets, many banks were extending short-term credit to merchants and other commercial ventures (see Figure 3.3). Indeed, prior to the advent of banking, merchants simply lent to one another on a short-term basis. One merchant, for example, may have savings accumulated in anticipation of an upcoming shipment that he would lend to another for the short period prior to the shipment's arrival. Bodenhorn's (2000) analysis of bank lending activity reveals that banks tended to make loans to different commercial sectors in proportion to the sector's representation in the community. Merchants usually comprised the largest sector and so received the most loans. However, the manufacturing and services sectors also received loans in proportion to their size in the business community.[10] These loans, regardless of the receiving sector, were typi-

Figure 3.3 Hypothetical Commercial Bank Balance Sheet

ASSETS	LIABILITIES
Monetary Reserves	Banknotes
Loans	Demand and Time Deposits
Discounts	Interbank Deposits
Securities	Capital
Total Assets	Total Liabilities

cally short-term loans as often banks were reluctant to lend long term given the uncertainty and illiquidity of drawn out credit. However, lending policy quickly changed as borrowing needs progressed and banks soon began extending long-term credit to farmers and manufacturers, as well as merchants.

Antebellum banks also discounted domestic bills of exchange. Bills of exchange were used to facilitate domestic trade, particularly along the Mississippi and in southern states engaged in cotton and tobacco trade. The issuing bank typically would earn an interest rate of six to eight percent on the bill of exchange and an additional one to two percent for the actual discounting.[11] Another important bank asset, monetary reserves, consisted of specie (e.g. gold and silver coins), instruments which could quickly be converted to specie (e.g. banknotes of the First Bank of the United States), notes issued by other banks, and funds deposited at other banks. Finally, just as with contemporary banks, antebellum banks invested in accepted securities which, at the time, were usually limited to stock in certain industries (e.g. canal, turnpike, and railroad), bank stock, and state and federal government obligations.[12]

In terms of the bank's liabilities, these were largely banknotes in the early antebellum period and, increasingly, demand deposits as the antebellum period progressed. State banks printed and issued small denomination notes to borrowers and this currency was redeemable in specie.[13] The specie price of banknotes varied depending on location, as well as bank reputation and condition. For example, if a merchant from Chattanooga traveled to Nashville and wanted to spend his $5 note from the Bank of Chattanooga, he may have to exchange it for local notes or, more likely, for specie. To do so, he would find a private broker who would exchange the note for specie for a fee. How did the broker know the exchange rate of a $5 Bank of Chattanooga note? Typically, he would refer to the *Bank Note Reporters* which was a private publication listing all banks, the discount value of the note, and a description of any counterfeit notes. As is discussed below, more sophisticated banks began relying on deposit business rather than note issuance and early in our banking history, deposits exceeded banknotes. Table 3.1 and Figure 3.4 both indicate that the gap between banknotes and deposits began closing in early antebellum banking and by 1840, deposits exceeded banknotes. Early bank deposits usually paid interest and were quickly an important medium of exchange in antebellum America. As evidence, consider that the average bank's deposits were $66,998 in 1819 but exceeded $215,000 by 1836.[14]

The other important liability for the antebellum banker consisted of interbank deposits. Smaller, rural banks often found that their banknotes were being discounted at larger banks in commercial centers. As their notes moved from their rural origin to the urban centers for exchange, the notes would trade at a discount owing to the distance and uncertainty of redemption. To preserve par exchanges and to avoid redemption for specie, the rural banks began holding deposits at city

Table 3.1 Number and Balance Sheet Data on All Banks: Selected Years, 1840–1905

Year	Number of Banks	Capital	Banknotes*	Deposits	Loans
1840	901	358	107	120	463
1845	707	206	90	114	289
1850	824	217	131	146	364
1855	1307	332	187	236	576
1860	1562	422	207	310	692
1865	1643	452	180	689	518
1870	1937	648	336	775	864
1875	3336**	847	318	2009	1748
1880	3355	826	318	2222	1662
1885	4350	1040	269	3078	2272
1890	8201	1558	126	4576	3854
1895	9818	1780	179	5539	4269
1900	13,053	2075	265	8922	6093
1905	18,767	3066	445	13,772	9540

Source: *Historical Statistics of the United States Colonial Times to 1970*, Part 2 (1976: 1019).

Note: All banks include state banks, private banks, and national banks after 1863. Money figures in millions of dollars.

* includes notes of state and national banks.

** estimated number of nonnational banks.

Figure 3.4 Banknotes and Deposits in Early Antebellum America: 1819–1837

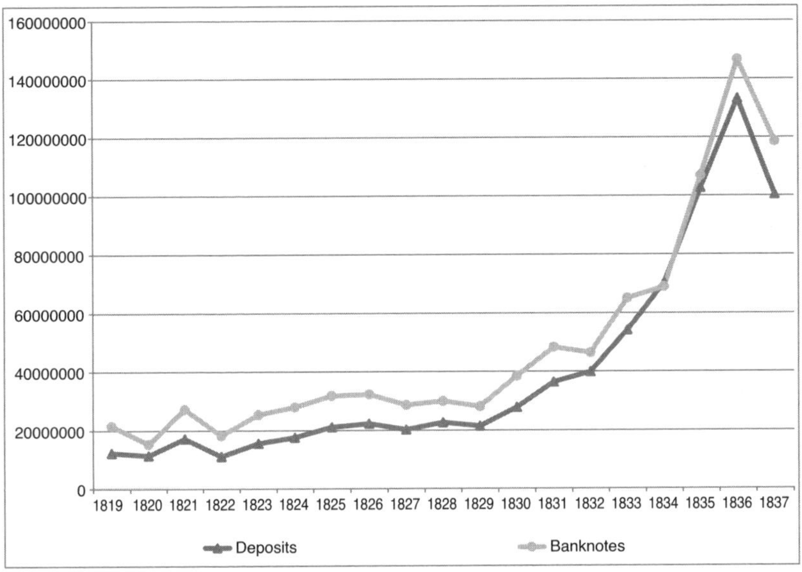

Source: Fenstermaker (1965: 670).

banks for note and demand deposit redemption. Though the Second Bank of the United States is often credited with creating currency uniformity, it also came, in large part, from the increased use of interbank deposits. Interbank deposits increased faster than the other bank liabilities increasing from $19,382 per average bank to $142,301 between 1819 and 1837.[15]

The final balance sheet item, capital, included paid-in capital, any surplus, undivided profits, unpaid dividends, discounts, interest, premiums, and exchange.[16] The amount paid by owners into the capital fund constituted the paid-in capital. Undivided profits were retained profits not paid out, and unpaid dividends were declared, but not yet paid, dividends of the bank. Discounts and interest represented interest earnings to the bank from bills of exchange, loans, and investments. Premiums were charges the bank made for some demand deposits and exchange captures the earnings from dealing in discounted banknotes.

Though the general activities of antebellum commercial bankers tended to be similar across the country, there were important differences in terms of the types of loans, the level of sophistication, the nature of the local economy, and the regulation the banks operated under. Because of this, the following section considers regional differences in antebellum state banking.

A. Regional bank survey

Just as the nation developed to different degrees in antebellum America, commercial banking also differed from region to region.[17] Table 3.2 contains a description of the states in different regions as well as the characteristics of banking in each region. The New England region contained many small commercial banks with a strong reliance on interbank deposits which, as mentioned above, contributed to the higher note quality. Another contributing factor to maintaining note quality was the presence of note redemption centers. In the early antebellum period, a note redemption center was located in Boston and in 1824,

Table 3.2 Regional Bank Characteristics in Antebellum America

Region	**States**	**Characteristics**
New England	Maine, New Hampshire, Vermont, Rhode Island, Massachusetts, Connecticut	• small banks • interbank deposits • note redemption centers • high note quality • unit banking • Suffolk system
Middle Atlantic	New York, Pennsylvania, Delaware, Maryland, New Jersey, DC	• important presence of the Second Bank of the U.S. • high note quality • unit banking • state intervention
Southeast	Virginia, South Carolina, North Carolina, Georgia, Florida territory	• important presence of the Second Bank of the U.S. • varied note quality • branch banking • state intervention
Southwest	Alabama, Tennessee, Louisiana, Mississippi, Arkansas	• important presence of the Second Bank of the U.S. • varied note quality • branch banking • state intervention
West	Ohio, Michigan, Kentucky, Indiana, Illinois	• important presence of the Second Bank of the U.S. • varied note quality • state intervention

Source: Compiled from Fenstermaker (1965) and Bodenhorn (2000: 31–44).

the Suffolk Bank took over this function. The banks in this region tended to be smaller than in other regions, in part, because of a tax placed on paid in capital. Smaller banks may also have been the product of the unit banking system prevalent in this region. Another explanation for the small nature of New England banks may rest in their lending policy.[18] Most of these banks tended to lend to those "inside" the bank including shareholders, directors, family members of these insiders, etc. Those who were outside then had trouble obtaining credit so they would turn around and open their own bank. This behavior then perpetuated the practice of lending to "insiders" and kept many of the banks relatively small. In terms of bank failures, only Maine experienced a significant number of failures during the early antebellum period, which confirms claims that this region of banking tended to be rather stable.[19]

Another important characteristic of New England banking, a characteristic that contributed to the quality of banknotes and general stability, was what became known as the Suffolk Banking System. The Suffolk Bank began as a private, state chartered bank in 1818 in Boston. In 1824 it joined six other state chartered banks to form a coalition and one year later the Suffolk Banking System was formed. The System was a clearinghouse accessible to all member banks. In its capacity as a clearinghouse, it would accept member banknotes at par and clear all notes. To become a member, a bank had to maintain a permanent, noninterest-bearing deposit with the Suffolk Bank or another member bank located in Boston. The dollar value of the permanent deposit was a function of the bank's capital; two percent of total capital must be kept on permanent deposit. In addition, another noninterest-bearing deposit sufficient to cover its notes received by the System was required for membership. Except for Rhode Island, all of the state banks in the New England region had the opportunity to join the System. In Vermont, all banks were actually required to join the system or pay a one percent tax on capital.[20] Financial historians have consistently given the Suffolk Banking System credit for the high quality of banknotes in this region and for enhancing the overall stability of New England banking during this period.[21]

Banknote quality in the Middle Atlantic region improved gradually throughout the period. Perhaps some of this may be attributed to the increased sophistication of bank operations and the reliance on interbank deposits. Since many of the large cities in this region were important port cities, it is not surprising that many of the bank loans in this region went to build infrastructure in order to expand interior trade. However, the banks in this region were vulnerable to the policies of the

Second Bank of the U.S. because this federal bank conducted a great deal of business in this region. When the Bank enacted contractionary policy, the banks in the Middle Atlantic region were forced to contract as well. While the New England states issued bank charters with no expectation of any quid pro quo, in the Middle Atlantic region, states often issued charters with the expectation of participating in and profiting from, the state banks.[22]

Whereas the Middle Atlantic bankers financed infrastructure and commercial improvements, the Southeastern banks were lending to tobacco and cotton farmers and also extending longer-term real estate loans.[23] Another distinguishing feature of the Southeastern banker during the early antebellum period was the network of branching that had been established. All of the states in the region allowed state banks to establish branch units within the state. In terms of note quality, this varied from state to state. Virginia banknotes traded near par and were hence of high quality but there were periods in North Carolina and Georgia in which banknote exchange occurred at a large discount. Like the Middle Atlantic region, the Second Bank's presence was hard to ignore. Indeed, the Bank's branch office in Fayatteville, NC devoted great time and energy to get the North Carolina and Georgia banks to redeem their banknotes for specie.[24] Again, the policies of the Second Bank were vital in the performance of the state banks of this region. In addition to the Second Bank, the states in this region also intervened heavily in the business of banking. For example, the state of Virginia required chartered banks to invest in state improvement programs while the state of South Carolina chartered a state owned bank whose purpose was to lend primarily to farmers.

The Southwest and Western regions of the country shared similar banking experiences during this era. The Southwest region also operated as a branching system thereby affording these institutions greater portfolio diversification. A similarity between these regions was the extensive state government intervention, particularly in Louisiana where government chartered several different types of banks intended to cater to different credit needs of the population.[25] In terms of note quality, this varied by state with Tennessee and Alabama having the greatest discount early in the period while Louisiana had the greatest quality. The Western region can by summed up in much the same way as the Southwest, though in this region it was Kentucky that struggled with note quality while the other states largely saw note exchange near par.

B. Clearinghouses: 1857–1914

During the later years of the antebellum period, banks began forming cooperative, voluntarily coordinated efforts to deal with unanticipated runs on their deposits and demands for specie.[26] Because banking is a fractional reserve system, banks are always vulnerable to runs and, during this period, when depositors and noteholders lost confidence in the banks, they would attempt to convert deposits and banknotes into specie.[27] However, banks often did not have enough specie on hand to meet demand during periods of crisis just as banks today could not convert all their deposits into cash. The private market response to this problem was the establishment of regional bank Clearinghouse Associations.

Clearinghouses provided liquidity to member banks during times of financial crisis using several tools. During crisis, a loan committee was formed which could authorize the creation and distribution of "clearinghouse loan certificates."[28] These certificates were large denomination, short-term maturity, backed by collateral, and were used between banks and not by the public. Further, member banks committed to assimilate any certificate losses as a group. Member banks could use these certificates to settle balances with one another rather than rely on cash which, then, freed up cash to be used to meet the demands of depositors. In addition, the Clearinghouses also issued certificates that circulated outside the banking system. These were also collateralized but were small denomination and essentially guaranteed by the Clearinghouse. Clearinghouses also pooled reserves which, in essence, was a redistribution of reserves among member banks to help those in need during crises. Finally, Clearinghouses would, at times, restrict the convertibility of deposits into currency (specie in the antebellum era). This was a method of rationing currency (specie) during times of crisis. However, banks usually continued to clear checks and so depositors were able to continue to make check payments, they simply could not exchange the check for specie or currency at par.

Thus, a Clearinghouse Association was a coordinated effort of interested banks to work together essentially providing lender of last resort functions to member banks. In exchange for the access to liquidity and coinsurance against failure, member banks voluntarily agreed to submit balance sheet information to the Clearinghouse. If the Clearinghouse was going to make sound decisions about which members to lend to, which members where solvent, etc. it needed information to assess the soundness and risk of the member bank. Further, since the members were lending to one another in times of crisis, they all had an incentive to know the financial condition of one another.

However, since the member bank knew that assistance would be provided by the other members of the Clearinghouse, a moral hazard problem surfaced. More specifically, a member bank would have incentive to take on additional risk knowing that, if the risk taking failed, it would be rescued through the membership. To avoid this moral hazard, member banks were subject to reserve requirements, capital requirements, interest rate restrictions, and frequent audits. Any bank not meeting these requirements could be dismissed from the Clearinghouse Association. The member banker was willing to subject itself to the regulation because of the public confidence garnered through membership.

C. Regulation

Today most students of banking know that this sector is one of the most heavily regulated industries in the United States. Indeed, the tradition of regulating banks is as old as banking itself. Consider that to even get *into* the business of banking, one had to obtain permission from the legislature and then had to comply with rules and regulations outlined by the state government. That is, the entry of banking has been regulated since its inception as have many bank operations and structures. Table 3.3 provides a brief description of state bank regulation and the impact of the regulation on stability during this period.

The first layer of bank regulation came from the process of chartering state banks. As was mentioned above, to obtain a banking charter the state legislature had, through a special legislative act, to grant the charter. In addition, most of the early bank charters required banks to make substantial loans or pay subsidies to the state from which the charter was obtained. This created a degree of monopoly privilege and, perhaps more importantly, created a group of bankers with incentive to maintain the unit bank system and a group of legislatures with an incentive to limit entry thereby extracting monopoly rents from existing banks.

In addition to the charter requirement, early antebellum banks faced regulation on the structure and organization of their institutions. Chapman and Westerfield (1942) and, more recently, Weber (2006) provide a thorough consideration of branching during the antebellum era and find that most states actually allowed for branching, either intrastate or intracounty. Table 3.4 contains a summary of the state branching laws during the antebellum period. The extent to which states participated in branching is found in Table 3.5. A quick comparison of the Tables illustrates that there were many states that did not establish branches, particularly those states north and east of the

Table 3.3 Summary of Regulation and Its Impact on State Chartered Banks in Antebellum America

Regulation	Description	Channel(s) Through Which Regulation Impacts Bank Stability	Conclusion from the Evidence
Legislative Charters	• Legislative act required to obtain a charter. • Resulted in barriers to entry. • Created a disincentive to states and existing banks to reduce barriers.	• Decrease competition. • Indirectly, discourage branching. • Indirectly, limits geographic diversification.	• Decreased stability to the extent that it discouraged branching and reduced competition (Table 3.5 and Table 3.9 show a reduction in bank failures in branching states).
Prohibit or Limit Branching	• Many states did not allow branching. • Resulted in many small banks with balance sheets that are tied to the local economy. • Resulted in barriers to entry.	• Decrease competition. • Limits geographic diversification.	• Decreased stability as branching increased stability through fewer failures and specie suspension (Table 3.5 and Table 3.9).
Restrictive Note Production	• Restrictions on note production to capital would keep over-issuance in check.	• Decrease risk.	• Ambiguous impact on stability; no evidence of over-issuance.
Usury Laws	• Limited the legal interest rate banks could charge on loans.	• Decrease competition. • Regulation not binding.	• Change cost and revenue structure.
Reserve Requirements	• Banks were required to hold reserves as a percentage of notes issued.	• Decrease risk. • Change cost and revenue structure.	• Ambiguous impact on stability; no evidence of over-issuance and in many states this was not completely binding since regulation was only on notes (Table 3.7).

Table 3.3 Summary of Regulation and Its Impact on State Chartered Banks in Antebellum America – *continued*

Regulation	Description	Channel(s) Through Which Regulation Impacts Bank Stability	Conclusion from the Evidence
Capital and Dividend Tax	• Banks paid a tax on capital and/or dividends. • Resulted in many small banks with smaller capital and reduced tax burden.	• Decrease competition. • Indirectly, discourage branching. • Indirectly, limits geographic diversification. • Change bank structure by limiting bank size.	• Decreased stability to the extent that it discouraged branching and reduced competition.
Social Overhead Lending Requirements	• Mandate certain lending to the banker. • Resulted in high risk lending.	• Change cost and revenue structure. • Increase risk.	• Decreased stability because of reduced profit and increased risk.
State Insurance Schemes	• Six states experimented with deposit insurance with mixed results.	• Decrease competition. • Decrease risk of runs. • Increase risk.	• Increased stability to the extent that bank runs were reduced. • Decrease stability by reducing competition for depositors and the accompanying moral hazard.

Notes: There are five identified channels through which regulation may impact stability; 1) change risk taking; 2) limit diversification; 3) change cost and revenue structure; 4) change the structure of the market; and 5) change the nature of competition.

Table 3.4 State Branch Banking Laws in Antebellum America

State	Branch Laws	State	Branch Laws
Alabama	B	Montana	
Alaska		Nebraska	
Arizona		Nevada	
Arkansas		New Hampshire	
California		New Jersey	
Colorado		New Mexico	
Connecticut	B	New York	B
Delaware	B	North Carolina	B
Florida		North Dakota	
Georgia	B	Ohio	B
Hawaii		Oklahoma	
Idaho		Oregon	
Illinois	B	Pennsylvania	B
Indiana	B	Rhode Island	U
Iowa	B	South Carolina	B
Kansas		South Dakota	
Kentucky	B	Tennessee	B
Louisiana	B	Texas	
Maine		Utah	
Maryland	B	Vermont	B
Massachusetts	B	Virginia	B
Michigan		Washington	
Minnesota		West Virginia	
Mississippi	B	Wisconsin	
Missouri	B	Wyoming	

Sources: Chapman (1934: 92–107) and Chapman and Westerfield (1942: 38–46).

Notes: No data give a complete picture of branch banking during the antebellum period. However, *Bankers Magazine* would periodically list branching activities and the antebellum data above is from that data as compiled in Chapman (1934). Chapman argues that the data presented presents a fairly accurate picture of branching during this period. U = Unit Branching, B = Branching.

Mason Dixon line. This difference may be explained by two developments. First, the northeastern states tended to be more economically developed and wealthier than the other regions and so individual bankers were able to set up independent banks across the states, particularly in more rural areas. In the southern and western states, it was often the case that smaller towns desired a bank but could not afford its creation. Consequently, the city banks would expand through branches to the smaller towns. A second reason that the northern and eastern banks preferred the unit system reflects the role of town governments and town attitude towards economic activity. These towns

Table 3.5 Extent of Branching in Antebellum America

State and Territories	1800–1810 Average Number of Branches Per Year	1811–1820 Average Number of Branches Per Year	1821–1830 Average Number of Branches Per Year	1831–1840 Average Number of Branches Per Year	1841–1850 Average Number of Branches Per Year	1851–1861 Average Number of Branches Per Year
Alabama	0	0	0	3.375	4	0
Arizona	0	0	0	3.33	7	0
Connecticut	0	1	1.6	2.8	2.4	1.1
Delaware	2	3.5	4.2	4	3	3
Florida	0	0	0	3.6	3.4	0
Georgia	0	5	5	10	8.2	4
Illinois	0	0	4	7	13	0
Indiana	0	3	3	9.83	11.8	16.44
Iowa	0	0	0	0	0	11
Kansas	0	0	0	0	0	0
Kentucky	2	7.2	12.2	8.6	10.9	25.2
Louisiana	0	0	0	0	0	1
Maine	0	0	0	0	0	0
Massachusetts	0	0	0	0	0	0
Maryland	2	2.3	3	3.2	3	1.6
Michigan	0	0	1	2.1	1.28	1
Minnesota	0	0	0	0	0	0
Mississippi	0	2	2	9.375	0	0
Missouri	0	0	0	1.33	2.53	11.4
Nebraska	0	0	0	0	0	0
New Hampshire	0	0	0	0	0	0
New Jersey	0	0	0	0	0	0

Table 3.5 Extent of Branching in Antebellum America – *continued*

State and Territories	1800–1810 Average Number of Branches Per Year	1811–1820 Average Number of Branches Per Year	1821–1830 Average Number of Branches Per Year	1831–1840 Average Number of Branches Per Year	1841–1850 Average Number of Branches Per Year	1851–1861 Average Number of Branches Per Year
New York	2	3.5	2.8	2	1.9	1
North Carolina	0	5	7	13.2	19.6	15.7
Ohio	0	0	0	0	27.6	42.3
Pennsylvania	3.57	6.1	2.3	2.3	1.5	1
Rhode Island	0	0	0	0	0	0
South Carolina	0	1.33	2.8	3	3	2.9
Tennessee	0	5	4	6.44	15.5	19.9
Vermont	4	4	0	0	0	0
Virginia	3	9	13	15.9	24.7	41.8
Wisconsin	0	0	0	0	0	0

Source: Weber (2006).

Notes: The average number of branches per year is calculated for those years in which there was at least one branch. For annual branch numbers for each state in the antebellum banking era, see Weber (2006: Table 1).

possessed more control over the economic development of the town than most Southern and Western states and did not want competition between towns. Consequently, a unit system created independent markets for unit banks and the local town leaders had more control or influence over the activities of the banker.

Regulation also took the form of limitations on bank activity including note production and usury laws. In terms of note production, it was not uncommon for states to prohibit the production of small denomination notes. For example, in 1799 Massachusetts passed a law

Table 3.6 Usury Laws in Antebellum America: 1840, 1850, 1860

State	Usury Rate 1840	Usury Rate 1850	Usury Rate 1860
Maine	6	6	6
New Hampshire	6	6	6
Vermont	6	6	6
Massachusetts	6	6	6
Rhode Island	6	6	6
Connecticut	6	6	6
New York	7	7	7
New Jersey	6	6	6
Pennsylvania	6	6	6
Delaware	6	6	6
Maryland	6	6	6
Virginia	6	6	6
North Carolina	6	6	6
South Carolina	7	7	7
Georgia	8	7	7
Alabama	8	8	8
Louisiana	10	8	8
Kentucky	6	8	8
Tennessee	6	6	6
Ohio	6	6	6
Indiana	10	6	6
Illinois	12	10	10
Michigan	10	10	10
Wisconsin	NA*	NA	10
Iowa	NA	NA	10
Missouri	10	6	10

Source: *Annual Report of the Comptroller of the Currency* (1876).

Notes: While most states had usury laws in antebellum America, often these laws were somewhat flexible. For example, in several states if both the borrower and lender agreed, the rate could exceed the interest rate limit by up to six percent (Bodenhorn (2000)).
*Not available.
All values are percentages.

prohibiting the creation of banknotes in denominations less than $5.[29] The belief at this time was that specie was superior, because of its inherent value, to paper banknotes. This law then encouraged people to use specie rather than banknotes since most transactions were for less than $5. Similarly, early legislative charters required banks to restrict note production given their capital. Another restriction took the form of usury laws. Most states placed a legal limit, a usury law, on the interest that banks could charge customers. Typically, the rate ranged from six to ten percent (see Table 3.6). What remains unclear is whether or not these rate limits were adhered to. Because the law required an injured party to file a written complaint, banks may have gotten away with charging above the limit since the customer may have been unwilling to complain for fear of injuring the banker-consumer relationship. Further, it is possible that the bank customer may have been unaware of the usury law and therefore unwittingly charged illegally. However, some states allowed banks to charge above the usury rate if both parties were in agreement. Indiana, Arkansas, Iowa, and Wisconsin are examples of such states.

While note production and usury laws placed limits on bank activity, other regulation demanded certain action on the part of the banker. Examples of this type of regulation include reserve requirements, capital tax and required social lending. Virginia was the first state to enact reserve requirements as we understand them today. In 1837, the state of Virginia required that banks maintain 20 percent of their notes in

Table 3.7 Reserve Requirements by State

State	Date Enacted	Required Cash Reserve	Base
Virginia	1837	20%	Notes
Georgia	1838	25%	Notes
Ohio	1839	33.33%	Notes
Mississippi	1840	33.33%	Notes
Louisiana	1842	33.33%	Notes and Deposits
Connecticut	1848	10%	Notes
Indiana	1853	12.5%	Notes
Missouri	1857	33.33%	Notes
Maine	1858	5%	Notes
Iowa	1858	25%	Notes and Deposits
Massachusetts	1858	8%	Notes and Deposits
Pennsylvania	1860	25%	Notes

Source: Hammond (1963: 11).

circulation as cash reserves. Table 3.7 shows the other states which followed. Notice that for the vast majority of the states in the antebellum period, the reserve requirement was only on notes and not on deposits. This is clear evidence that regulators misunderstood the importance of deposits as a source of funds to the banker. Finally, most state legislatures taxed either the capital or dividends of the state banks as a condition of the charter. This became an important source of revenue for the states. For example, in Pennsylvania in 1835, a gradual tax was placed on dividends with those in excess of 12 percent taxed at 50 percent.[30]

State governments took advantage of the demand for state bank charters during the early antebellum period to compel those receiving charters to finance programs aimed at long-term economic growth. More specifically, it was not uncommon for the state authorities to write provisions into the charters requiring banks to finance state transportation and education efforts or to make favorable commercial and agricultural loans.[31] Education provisions typically took one of two forms. Either the bank paid fixed sums into the state education fund or the bank paid a capital tax to generate funds for education (see Table 3.8). Similarly, compulsory contributions to a state's transportation development typically took one of two forms. State bank charters frequently obligated banks to either purchase stock in a transportation firm or to contribute to state transportation funds. Further, some states required, as a condition of the charter, banks to extend low interest loans to the states directly. Pennsylvania and

Table 3.8 Education Overhead Requirements Placed on State Banks in Selected States

State	**Education Requirements**
New York	Fixed Sum
Connecticut	Fixed Sum
Georgia	Fixed Sum
Louisiana	Fixed Sum
New Jersey	Fixed Sum
Maryland	Fixed Sum and Tax on Capital
New Hampshire	Tax on Capital
Maine	Tax on Capital
Vermont	Tax on Capital
Tennessee	Tax on Capital
Florida	Tax on Capital

Source: Compiled from Fenstermaker (1965).

Massachusetts serve as two examples. Additionally, many states, required banks to extend low interest agricultural, manufacturing, and industrial loans in return for the charter.[32]

While virtually all students of banking today recognize federal deposit insurance as a regulatory reality of the commercial banking sector, few students know that there were state level insurance systems in place during both the antebellum and national bank eras. Six states, New York, Vermont, Michigan, Indiana, Ohio, and Iowa all experimented with state level deposit insurance at some point in the nineteenth century. Though all of the insurance systems were aimed at protecting the depositor, they varied in terms of their funding mechanism, membership policy, and supervisory agency. New York, Vermont, and Michigan were all funded as safety funds while the remaining three states were funded as mutual guarantees.[33] The difference being that the safety fund required flat-rate insurance premiums by member banks while the mutual guarantee allowed for special assessments as necessary and uncovered liabilities at a failed bank were covered by member surviving banks. Each experience is discussed below.

In terms of the safety funds, New York's flat-rate premium of one-half of one percent of capital left the fund undercapitalized and compromised its integrity. Both Vermont and Michigan were similarly undercapitalized which meant the fund was not able to protect either depositors or their payments system. Membership in the safety funds also varied. In New York, for example, membership was required of all state banks but not of free banks. Further, after 1842, the safety fund of New York only insured notes and not deposits. This became a problem since banks were relying increasingly on deposits as a source of funds. The Vermont safety fund covered both notes and deposits but membership was voluntary. In Michigan, initial membership was mandatory so that the fund coverage was comprehensive. However, the Michigan fund was established in 1836, just prior to a bank crisis in 1837. During the crisis, healthy banks pressured the fund to drop the mandatory requirement thereby placing the Michigan fund in the same situation as both Vermont and New York. That is, in all three cases, not requiring comprehensive membership put the fund at risk to disintermediation, runs and failures.[34]

In these three instances, the safety fund structure of deposit insurance was flawed on several levels. Flat-rate premiums encouraged moral hazard problems of risk taking and reduced incentives for deposit monitoring. Further, these funds were greatly undercapitalized as bank liabilities far exceeded the resources of the safety funds. In addition, by failing to provide inclusive membership for both deposits and notes these funds could not provide protection to depositors or the payments system. For example, in New York, chartered banks that were in the insurance system had a failure rate of 11.1 percent.[35] In contrast, no chartered banks failed that were outside of the insurance system. Similarly, insured banks in Vermont failed at a greater rate than noninsured banks.

The other three states to experiment with antebellum deposit insurance, Indiana, Iowa, and Ohio, established a mutual guarantee system and were, on the whole, more successful than the safety funds. Through a mutual guarantee system, member banks could be subject to special assessments, as deemed necessary, and member banks covered uninsured liabilities of failed member banks. Both of these provisions served to reduce moral hazard problems on the part of the banker and, consequently, put less financial stress on the fund itself. Indeed, recent scholarship finds evidence that banks in the mutual guarantee systems were more likely to monitor one another for fear of financial losses to all member banks.[36]

In addition to the mutual guarantee provisions, the Indiana fund carefully created a supervisory network that worked to also reduce moral hazard. A supervisory board, comprised of individual member banks, had authority to examine member banks each six months, to set asset to capital requirements, and to close any member banks deemed unhealthy. Since the board was comprised of member bankers, there was great incentive to ensure that problem banks were promptly dealt with and to ensure that all member banks operated within an acceptable risk range. A Board of Control was given similar authority in Ohio though the Board also required a 30 percent reserve on notes and a deposit of an additional ten percent of notes with the Board itself. Further, in Ohio, the Board could mandate that member banks lend to one another during crisis. The supervisory system in Iowa was similar to the first two, though it required a 25 percent reserve of specie on notes and a 25 percent reserve on deposits.

It is worth noting that the mutual guarantee systems were successful in maintaining a functioning payments system (avoiding specie suspensions) and in avoiding failures. Both Indiana and Ohio avoided specie suspensions during the crisis of 1857, as no insured bank failed in either state. The Iowa fund, established in 1858, saw no failures under its watch.

D. Performance

As shown earlier, state chartered banking varied from region to region in terms of the types of loans, the quality of banknotes, whether the banks were unit or branch institutions, the extent of state involvement, the availability of cooperative assistance from other banks, and the nature of bank regulation. How did these banks fare during the antebellum period? The number and nature of failures and suspensions are considered, followed by discussions of the crises that plagued this period.[37]

Failures and specie suspensions

The origins of U.S. banking were a stable time as not a single bank failed during the first 27 years of commercial banking. The Farmers Exchange Bank of Glocester, Rhode Island was the first to fail in this country in 1809. A glimpse into the performance of antebellum banking may be gleaned from Table 3.9 which lists the number and date of each state bank failure. Three observations may be made regarding this failure data. First, many states and territories never witnessed a state chartered bank failure during the antebellum era; these are the states and territories not listed in Table 3.9. Second, in many of the states and territories there were very few failures. For example, five states (Indiana, Louisiana, Missouri, North Carolina, and Vermont) only had one failure the entire period. Many other states had less than five failures. Third, the vast majority of the failures were clustered in the few years following the most significant bank crisis, that in 1837, of this era. Indeed, outside of this crisis and the 13 failures in Kentucky in 1819, the antebellum era had very few state bank failures.

Several developments explain the unusual instability in Kentucky in 1819. First, Kentucky chartered 40 new banks between 1817 and 1818.[38] This is significant given that there were estimated to be only 500 banks in the entire country in 1818. Second, in the years leading up to 1818, speculation in real estate, using bank credit, was rising as were agriculture prices. Consequently, banks, many of them new banks in Kentucky, were lending on land speculation and to farmers in expectation of rising farm revenue. However, at the end of 1817 and beginning of 1818, agriculture and land prices began to fall and loan defaults mounted. The Kentucky experience reflected poor timing for the new banks; they entered when lending was profitable but were soon faced with drastically changed conditions and many new banks failed. Despite th is unique experience in Kentucky, these early banking years, when measured by failures, were truly stable (see Table 3.9).

Table 3.9 Number of Failures of Antebellum State Chartered Banks: 1812–1861

Year	AL	CT	FL	GA	IL	IN	KY	LA	MA	MD	ME	MI	MO	MS	NC	NE	NH	NJ	NY	OH	PA	RI	SC	TN	VA	VT	WI	Total
1812											1																	1
1813																												0
1814																												0
1815		1																										1
1816																												0
1817										1																		1
1818													1								4							5
1819							13			1										1								15
1820										3	2																	5
1821					1					3											2							6
1822																												0
1823					1																							1
1824						1													2									3
1825		1									3							1					1	1				7
1826																			4				1					5
1827	1																	1										2
1828										1		1																2
1829									1										1	1		1						4
1830																												0
1831							1															1						2
1832				1																								1
1833			1	1						1																		3
1834										1																		1
1835			1																			1						2
1836									2			1																3
1837									2		1										1							4
1838			1						3		1	4		6				1			1							17
1839			1									2		12			1			2							3	21

Table 3.9 Number of Failures of Antebellum State Chartered Banks: 1812–1861 – *continued*

Year	AL	CT	FL	GA	IL	IN	KY	LA	MA	MD	ME	MI	MO	MS	NC	NE	NH	NJ	NY	OH	PA	RI	SC	TN	VA	VT	WI	Total
1840				1					1	5				1			1		1	7	1						1	19
1841			1	4					1	2	5			1					5		1					1		21
1842	1		2	1	3					1									3		1							12
1843				2								1																3
1844			1																									1
1845										1		1																2
1846										1		1																2
1847																		1			2			1				4
1848																			1	2	1							4
1849																												0
1850				1						1																		2
1851										1								2		1								4
1852								1																				1
1853		1							1																			2
1854				1			2			2	2	4							1	1				1				14
1855				1																	1	1			1			4
1856										1	1								3	1	2	4		4				16
1857		1		2						1	3	1				2		1			1			3	1		1	17
1858		2								1						3					1						1	8
1859				1											1		1				1	3		1	2			10
1860																	1	1			1							3
1861																												0

Source: Compiled from Weber (2006).

Note: During this same time frame, Weber (2006) identifies 488 state chartered banks that closed and 134 free banks that failed. A closure is different from a failure in that with a closure there were no losses to depositors.

Specie suspensions, a temporary moratorium on the conversion of banknotes to specie, took place four times in the antebellum period. The first suspension occurred in 1814 when the British occupied Washington and it took several years for note convertibility to return to the entire nation. The other suspensions coincided with the later four bank crises discussed below.

1792 crisis

The first identified banking crisis in our history occurred in 1792, 11 years after the birth of commercial banking. Two factors contributed to this episode of financial fragility. First, speculator William Duer attempted to corner the U.S. debt securities market and the stock of the First Bank of the U.S. and the Bank of New York.[39] His attempt failed. Second, the policy of the First Bank of the United States also played a causal role. Specifically, the First Bank over injected notes and loans in January of 1792 only to severely restrict loans in February and March which caused borrowers to sell securities to pay off loans and caused the securities market crisis. Empirical evidence and more details on this crisis are found later in this chapter.

1837 crisis and the Suffolk System

Perhaps the most devastating crisis of antebellum banking occurred in 1837. Financial historians have not reached agreement on the cause of the crisis of 1837 though several explanations have been advanced. Some argue that the refusal of President Jackson to renew the charter of the Second Bank of the United States caused the financial instability.[40] Specifically, the government's loss of its regulatory control over the state banks, it was argued, led to an inflationary boom followed by crisis and citizens feared chaos would befall commercial banking. However, there is little empirical evidence to support this position.[41] Other historians point to tight monetary policy in England and falling cotton prices as the cause of the crisis.[42] Between December 1836 and May 1837, cotton prices fell 24.8 percent causing some to fear falling farm incomes would lead to loan and mortgage defaults thereby jeopardizing bank solvency.[43] Finally, some point out that the 1836 passage of the Specie Circular, which required specie as payment for all federal land, depleted the banks of specie and led to runs.[44]

The crisis manifested itself through bank suspensions and failures. By the end of May 1837, almost all banks in the United States had suspended payments on their banknotes. This suspension endured through the late fall of 1838 when the last of the banks, the southern banks, resumed payment. The failure data in Table 3.9 illustrates the severity of the crisis: for the five years following the crisis, the annual number of bank failures account for just over 36 percent of all antebellum state bank failures. The impact of the crisis spread outside the financial sector as it was followed by a five year recession in the economy.

Using balance sheet data from the Suffolk Bank, other large banks in the New England region, and large banks outside the region, scholars show that the Suffolk Bank operated much like a central bank during the crisis of 1837.[45] More specifically, the Suffolk Bank not only made loans to member banks during the crisis, it also was able to maintain its clearing function despite the nationwide suspension. Since specie was scarce, the only way a bank could increase its specie to note ratio was to reduce outstanding notes by calling in loans or not renewing them. Only through the Suffolk System was the bank sure that its own notes would make their way back to the bank.[46] Consequently, New England banks held fewer notes of other banks and reduced lending less than other regions of the country. Finally, a second specie suspension followed in 1839, and while not as widespread as the 1837 suspension, outside of Rhode Island, none of the New England states suspended note redemption. Their ability to avoid this second suspension is also empirically linked to the operations of the Suffolk Banking System.

Even in noncrisis times, the Suffolk System provided stability to banking in the Northeast. While the Suffolk System was fully operational, banks in the New England region had a much lower failure rate than banks in the East but outside of the system.[47] Because the Suffolk bank possessed the most information on the note issuing behavior of member banks, when it knew a bank issued excessively it would then redeem the notes for specie to discipline the bank. The Suffolk bank also was able to quickly return banknotes to the issuing bank which reduced the risk inherent in note exchange.[48] Further, the system increased the acceptability of rural bank banknotes outside of their immediate market because the public knew the notes were acceptable at par by the Suffolk Bank. Finally, some scholars argue that the system protected the public against unsound banks through its discipline.[49] The Suffolk Banking System brought about stability without the coercion of government. Rather, a voluntary cooperative agreement between bankers created a successful payments system.

Some argue that the demise of the Suffolk Banking System came at the hands of the rural banks that came to resent the powers of the system.[50] Specifically, they resented the constraints placed on their note issue and suspected the system enjoyed monopoly profit and power. Interestingly, contemporary evidence suggests that the New England banks issued more notes than banks in other regions, however evidence on profitability remains mixed.[51] Finally, the demise of the Suffolk System ultimately became inevitable with the passage of the 1865 Revenue Act which essentially put an end to state banknotes.

1857 crisis

Another bank crisis occurred during the antebellum era; this one in the final quarter of 1857. Financial historians have blamed the crisis on several developments though contemporary scholars seem to find evidence that the crisis began with falling land prices in the West (Kansas) which spread to banks in the East ultimately causing specie suspension in many states.[52] A real estate boom hit Kansas and with it came a huge influx of citizens and grand expectations for expanded infrastructure; primarily railways. Speculative brokers purchased railroad stock, usually with borrowed funds, in anticipation of large profits. Unfortunately, during the late summer months, land prices plummeted, security prices fell, and many speculators could not repay their loans. Many bankers refused to roll over the debt of the broker who, in turn, responded by selling their bond holdings at reduced prices. Through this process, eastern bankers became vulnerable because many of their loans were backed by these depressed bonds. In many states, runs ensued and banks were forced to suspend specie.

The extent to which the crisis manifested itself was a function of whether or not the states had a cooperative system in place to aid banks. States with cooperative systems such as Clearinghouses and branches fared better than unit states and states without coordination between banks.[53] For example, New York, a Clearinghouse state, did not witness any state bank failures during this crisis. Ohio had a network of cooperating insured banks and performed equally well. Banks in the South also fared well though their coordinating system was their branch network and not a formal group of banks. Branching in the South produced fewer banks able to coordinate amongst themselves easier and more cost effectively than in other regions. In Virginia, banks with branches saw their deposits rise during the crisis while nonbranching banks in the state saw a decline in deposits due to runs.[54] In Georgia, all of their bank failures were at unit banks. The banks that failed in Tennessee were either free banks or unit banks. This evidence suggests that banks that were members of some private coordination and cooperation with other banks fared better than those on their own.

1860 crisis

1860 began with great optimism and robust economic growth and trade. However, by the last quarter, the mood had soured and fear and pessimism replaced optimism. Ultimately, this reversal of expectations led to the fourth banking crisis prior to the Civil War. Initial sanguinity arose from an excellent farm harvest coupled with a poor European harvest. Banks extended loans on the expectation that trade and agriculture growth would continue. This persisted until the end of August when expectations about the outcome of the presidential election in November changed the mood of the nation, particularly of those farmers and entrepreneurs in the South.

By August most voters felt a presidential victory by Lincoln was a foregone conclusion. This greatly agitated many in the South as they were certain a Lincoln victory would mean a slavery war on the horizon. One scholar summarizes the cause of the 1860 crisis as follows:

> The fear and, at last, the certainty, of a bloody war caused the financial storm to break and spread ruin on every hand. Paper, which in normal times undoubtedly would have been liquidated by the future goods on which it was based, became worthless. Panic ensued.[55]

Banks across the nation severely cut back on loans, depositors demanded specie, banks from the South would not accept notes from northern banks, and all banks began demanding specie for notes. Interestingly, banks in the West (Illinois, Wisconsin) had, during the prosperous beginning of the year, issued loans to move the crops and also increased their note circulation. These notes were backed by state debt of many southern states including Virginia, Tennessee, and North Carolina. This state debt lost tremendous value the last quarter of the year when it became accepted that a war was inevitable. This, of course, made the banks of the West more vulnerable to crisis than other regions though no region was immune.

Indeed, specie suspensions occurred throughout the nation except in New York which found relief in the actions of the New York Clearinghouse Association.[56] During this crisis, the association allowed member banks to deposit acceptable securities with a committee of five members and, in return, receive clearinghouse certificates in denominations of five and ten thousand dollars. The member banks could then use the certificates to settle balances with one another. This meant that specie were free for the bank to use with the public and depositors. Hence, a suspension of specie never transpired in New York. During the crisis period, ten million in certificates were issued. Another aspect of the Clearinghouse policy was to equalize reserves across member banks. Member banks were required to submit a daily report of loans, deposits, specie, and loan certificates to the association. These reports allowed the association to determine which banks had extra specie reserves and to redistribute these among member banks with specie deficiencies. This policy also kept specie suspension at bay in New York. Thus, the coordinated efforts of the New York Clearinghouse allowed the banks in this region to successfully avoid an interruption in conversion and to minimize the impact of the 1860 crisis.

Private banking

Much less is known about the private banker than the state banker, particularly towards the end of the eighteenth century and the first few decades of the nineteenth century. Though financial scholars long believed the private banker to be a small and insignificant player in antebellum America, contemporary scholars have proven otherwise (see Table 3.10).[57] Today scholars largely agree on the importance and value of the private banker in the development of the antebellum economy and of their place within the financial sector.[58]

Private banks, also known as unincorporated banks, were comprised of individuals or groups of individuals using their own money as capital to conduct banking business. Private bankers were often family institutions with the Alexander Brown family, the Stephen Girard family, and the Jay Cooke family as prominent and often cited examples. Alex Brown & Sons was established in Baltimore in the early nineteenth century and ultimately established branches in the east as well as in London and Liverpool. Girard, a wealthy French immigrant, purchased the building in Philadelphia that housed the First Bank of the United States and began operation as a private bank in 1812. Jay Cooke & Co., established in Philadelphia in 1860, was instrumental in selling government loans to help finance the Civil War and later this private bank became heavily involved in financing the Northern Pacific Railroad. Though these three examples represent the most famous private bankers of antebellum banking, they had plenty of company because, as is shown next, private banking actually had at one point a larger presence than state chartered banking.

In keeping with the belief that the private banker played a rather insignificant role in antebellum financial markets, early research paints a different picture of the number and contribution of these bankers than does more recent work. For example, in his 1965 work, Fenstermaker

Table 3.10 Number of Private Banks by State: 1859 and 1860

State	**1859**	**1860**
Alabama	14	19
Arkansas	1	2
Connecticut	1	1
Delaware	2	2
Florida	7	9
Georgia	13	10
Illinois	124	136
Indiana	46	36
Iowa	100	76
Kentucky	33	31
Louisiana	14	10
Maine	3	3
Maryland	18	11
Massachusetts	18	15
Michigan	58	50
Minnesota	33	25
Mississippi	15	12
Missouri	31	32
New Hampshire	NA	NA
New Jersey	NA	NA
New York	35	33
North Carolina	6	5
Ohio	143	148
Pennsylvania	86	82
Rhode Island	7	4
South Carolina	2	3
Tennessee	18	9
Vermont	NA	NA
Virginia	20	18
Wisconsin	27	17
TOTAL	**875**	**799**

Source: Rockoff (1974: 162).

argues that the private banker was important prior to 1820 but that they essentially disappeared after that. More contemporary research, however, indicates otherwise and so does a comment made by Jay Cooke who observed the 1840s and 1850s as "a grand time for brokerage and private banking."[59] The number of private banks outnumbered state commercial banks between 1830 and 1844.[60] By 1860, the total number of private banks exceeded 1,000 or about 40 percent of the banks in America.[61] These numbers are larger than those contained in Table 3.10 which indicates the number of private banks, by state, for 1859 and 1860 from an alternative source. Regardless of the inconsistencies, the essential point remains; the private banker established a substantial presence in antebellum America. The catalyst for the growth in private banking occurred with the crisis of 1837 which destroyed many state chartered banks, thereby opening the door for private bank entry.[62] The rise in the number also corresponds to the repeal of some restraining acts and the advent of free banking.[63] Free banking laws certainly represented a more open attitude towards banking generally and the private banker took advantage of this opportunity.

Many private bankers performed similar functions as their state chartered counterparts. They accepted deposits, extended credit, discounted bills of trade, and exchanged securities. However, most private bankers were not able to issue notes as did the state banks. As explained below, regulation often prohibited note issuance by unincorporated banks. Thus, absent issuing notes, the private banks largely functioned much like commercial banks. However, there is evidence to suggest that the private banker may have catered to a segment of borrowers neglected by commercial banks. Bodenhorn (1997) provides a detailed and data rich account of a small private banker from Virginia; Thomas Branch & Sons. He finds that Branch & Sons tended to lend to younger entrepreneurs who were just embarking on their commercial careers and generally these borrowers had fewer accumulated assets than commercial bank borrowers. Thus, if the Branch & Sons operation is characteristic of antebellum private banking in general, it is clear that private bankers were crucial in the intermediation process, particularly for younger entrepreneurs.

Early private bankers relied on note issuance as a source of funds but also on deposits. As state governments began regulating against the private banker, he had to rely increasingly on deposits in order to survive. Some argue that the private banker as well as the state chartered banker relied on deposits much earlier than they are given credit for.[64] Balance sheet data for state chartered banks indicates that banks held much more in deposits than in specie so that many of the deposits had to be created. As Table 3.1 illustrates, deposits exceeded banknotes as early as 1840.

Most of the state regulation of private banking came in the form of restraining acts which, at one extreme, prohibited private banking and, at the other, forbid the institutions from issuing notes.[65] By 1820, 19 of the 24 Union states passed restraining acts. It appears as though the impetus behind these acts was, in part, state bankers lobbying to keep competition at bay. The state banker was able to take advantage of the nation's distrust of bankers in order to have regulatory barriers erected that either kept the private banker out of the state or limited the ability of the banker by prohibiting note issuance.

The regulatory attempts to thwart the private banker were not met passively. Rather, the enterprising banker simply found ways around the restraints. For example, some private bankers continued to issue notes, they simply called the notes something else. Between the late 1830s and early 1850s, George Smith of Chicago issued "engraved issues of deposit" and "checks" rather than notes. Similarly, the E. W. Clark banks issued "drafts". In both instances, these instruments were printed on banknote paper, issued in small denominations, and were redeemable for specie on demand. Since these instruments functioned as notes, they were *de facto* notes and evidence suggests that these private bankers were quite successful in this enterprise. Smith's notes outstanding peaked at approximately $1.5 million in 1852 and, at the same time, the Clark's issuance reached approximately $2 million.[66]

Experiments in federal banking: 1791 and 1816

The First Bank of the United States received a 20-year charter in 1791 but the charter did not come without controversy. There were essentially two camps in the debate with the Secretary of the Treasury Alexander Hamilton advocating the creation of a federal bank and the Jeffersonian party opposing it. Hamilton argued that the bank would be useful to the government and to the banking industry as it would regulate coinage, collect and facilitate the payment of taxes, borrow money and distribute funds. The Jeffersonian's responded that a national bank with the backing of the federal government would be more dangerous to the needs of the small borrower, that it would charge usurious rates and, most importantly, it was unconstitutional. Despite the criticism and the concerns of constitutionality, Congress voted in favor of the national bank by a margin just shy of two to one.

The First Bank, and the Second Bank that followed, operated as both a public and a private institution. Headquartered in Philadelphia, the bank had eight branches extending its influence from Boston to New Orleans. The Bank's initial capital subscription totaled $10 million which represented an enormous sum in the 1790s. Indeed, the five state banks existing at the time of the charter only had $3 million in combined capital.[67] In its capacity as a public institution it attempted to maintain the safety of banking by keeping banks from overissuing banknotes. Being the largest bank and the fiscal agent of the federal government, it was in a position to accept state banknotes on a regular basis.

The Bank would accumulate the banknotes and then redeem them for specie to discipline the state banks. In its capacity as a private institution, the First Bank operated similarly to state chartered banks. It accepted deposits, issued banknotes, made loans and other investments.

Given the size of the bank, it is hard to overestimate the influence it had on the banking sector in general. However, not all of its functions were deemed a success. On the contrary, the First Bank actually played a causal role in the crisis of 1792. This crisis manifested itself as a dramatic drop, over 20 percent, in security prices between February and May of 1792. Most historical accounts of this crisis blamed speculator William Duer who attempted to corner the market for U.S. debt securities and the stock of large banking interests, including the First Bank. His plan failed because as stock prices started falling Duer was unable to fulfill contracts to purchase additional securities. While Duer's failed financial scheme may have contributed to the 1792 crisis, new evidence suggests that the bulk of the blame belongs to the First Bank itself.[68]

Careful analysis of the Bank's balance sheets indicate that during its first two months of operation, December 1791 and January 1792, the Bank issued notes in excess of $886,000 and made loans of $2,675,441.[69] As it turns out, many of these were very short-term loans (30 days) often made to market speculators, including Duer.[70] This path of rapid money expansion was abruptly abandoned in early February as Bank officials worried about the quality of their notes and the extent of market speculation. In February and early March close to $625,000 in loans were called in or not renewed. Evidence suggests that to pay for these loans most borrowers were forced into selling their securities. This liquidation, in turn, led to falling stock prices and the crisis of 1792. Thus, the First Bank's erratic policy of injecting liquidity followed by an abrupt reversal of policy led to the stock market sell-off and ensuing crisis.

While the First Bank was in operation, those critical of the Bank's constitutionality fought hard to block the renewal of its charter. The debate in the House of Representatives reveals that the anti-bank camp protested the renewal, much like the creation of the Bank, on several grounds. First, and most importantly, protesters fiercely objected that the Bank was unconstitutional. The U.S. government was not granted any authority to incorporate by the constitution and so the Jeffersonians fought loudly against the Bank. Second, protesters argued the Bank would favor the rich at the expense of the poor which really was an extension of the anti-bank antagonism prevalent in antebellum America. The third characterization of the debate was a question of state's rights and state sovereignty. Indeed, late in the debate, many state legislatures adopted resolutions against the renewal because it was feared the Bank would compromise state sovereignty. Perhaps the most passionate and characteristic summary of the anti-bank position is found in the words of Representative Desha of Kentucky who asked:

> Whether we will foster a viper in the bosom of our country that will spread its deadly venom over the land, and finally affect the vitals of your republic institutions; or whether we will, as it is our duty, apply the proper antidote by a refusal to renew the charter, thereby checking the cankering poison, the importation and dissemination of foreign influence, that has already brought our government to the brink of ruins.[71]

Ultimately, the anti-bank constituency was successful in their campaign and the Bank closed its doors in 1811 after its charter renewal application was denied.

As was mentioned earlier, the state banks financed most of the War of 1812. After the war, there was concern over the quantity and quality of banknotes in circulation. Prominent politicians believed that the only way to reduce the number of outstanding banknotes was by creating a central bank. As discussion of a federal bank started to spread, its opponents once again protested on the grounds that such a bank was unconstitutional. Nonetheless, in April of 1816 a 20-year charter was granted to the Second Bank of the United States which had initial capital of $35 million.[72] Opponents continued to press the constitution issue and in 1819 it went before the Supreme Court. In a landmark ruling that forever changed the nature of banking and also of constitutional law, Chief Justice Marshall ruled that the bank was constitutional under the "necessary and proper" clause. This clause essentially provided Congress with the ability take a wider interpretation of the constitution; rather than be limited by what the constitution specifically allowed. Congress had the authority to extend its powers in ways not prohibited by the constitution. According to the ruling of Chief Justice Marshall, since the constitution did not prohibit the creation of a federal bank, the formation of such a bank was ruled constitutionally acceptable.

Functionally, the Second Bank was very similar to the First Bank as it served as the fiscal agent to the federal government. However, the Second Bank took more seriously its central bank like opportunity to control the money supply by redeeming state banknotes for specie. Nearly all existing literature on the First and Second Banks of the United States credit them with successfully restraining state banks from over issuing notes. By collecting, and then redeeming state banknotes for specie, it is argued that both Banks effectively kept note issue in check.[73] If this is true, then certainly the number or growth in banknotes would be expected to decline under the watch of both Banks. Financial historian empirically tested whether either bank caused a reduction in the money supply or its rate of growth in New England and find that neither bank had an impact in restraining the state banks.[74] Admittedly, the empirical study is limited to the New England states so the Banks may have been more effective outside this region. Nonetheless, these findings do give pause to the subjective assertion that the Banks successfully controlled the money supply during their tenure.

Free banking: 1837–1863

In 1836 the charter of the Second Bank was allowed to lapse without renewal. Opposition to the Second Bank was rooted in the belief that government could not, and should not, be in the business of banking generally and, more importantly, monopoly banking specifically. Opponents were also concerned that the existing method of obtaining a charter, through state legislative acts, also created monopolies to those with charters and created incentives for the legislature not to grant further charters thereby perpetuating monopoly banking. The lapse of the Second Bank charter left a large hole in the business of banking as the Second Bank had opened 25 branches throughout the country by the time of its closing.

With the federal government out of the business of banking and with the process of obtaining a state charter time consuming, monopolistic, and political, states began reexamining their chartering systems. The states wanted a banking system that was stable and that would allow for the quick expansion of banking. To achieve this, many states began considering free banking laws.[75] At the onset of the Civil War, more than half of the states had adopted free banking laws (see Table 3.11). While the crux of these laws was to provide less restrictive entry into the business of banking, entry was still not free as states imposed minimum capital requirements. Nonetheless, entry was easier in states with free banking laws than obtaining a charter through state legislative acts.

While precise laws varied from state to state, typical free banking requirements shared several characteristics. First, anyone meeting the capital requirements could set up a bank. Second, there was a bond collateral requirement applied to the issue of banknotes. That is, all free banknotes must be secured with the purchase of state or federal debt or, in some states, private debt such as railroad bonds or mortgages.

Table 3.11 Free Banking Laws by State: 1860

State	Banking Law	Year Passed
Alabama	Free banking	1849
Arkansas	No free banking	NA
California	No free banking	NA
Connecticut	Free banking	1852
Delaware	No free banking	NA
Florida	Free banking	1853
Georgia	Free banking	1838
Illinois	Free banking	1851
Indiana	Free banking	1852
Iowa	Free banking	1858
Kentucky	No free banking; bond collateral note issue	1850
Louisiana	Free banking	1853
Maine	No free banking	NA
Maryland	No free banking	NA
Massachusetts	Free banking	1851
Michigan	Free banking	1837*
Minnesota	Free banking	1858
Mississippi	No free banking	NA
Missouri	No free banking; bond collateral note issue	1858
New Hampshire	No free banking	NA
New Jersey	Free banking	1850
New York	Free banking	1838
North Carolina	No free banking	NA
Ohio	Free banking	1851**
Oregon	No free banking	NA
Pennsylvania	Free banking	1860
Rhode Island	No free banking	NA
South Carolina	No free banking	NA
Tennessee	Free banking	1852
Texas	No free banking	NA
Vermont	Free banking	1851
Virginia	No free banking; bond collateral note issue	1851
Wisconsin	Free banking	1852

Source: Rockoff (1975: 3).

Notes: *This law was revoked in 1840 in Michigan but another passed in 1875. **Six years earlier Ohio also passed a law allowing "Independent Banks" with bond collateral note issue.

The purpose of the bond collateral requirement was that the bonds were to be sold off if the free bank failed and the proceeds of the sale went to meet the claims of noteholders.[76] Further, banks would receive the interest on the bonds so long as they redeemed notes for specie on demand. Third, free banknotes were redeemable on demand and noteholders had the first claim in the event that the bank failed. Like state banks, free banks were fractional-reserve institutions because they held specie that were only a fraction of their total outstanding notes. Fourth, bank shareholders were subject to limited liability. Fifth, in many states there were restrictions against investments in real property and restrictions against branch banking. Sixth, most states placed a maximum on the ratio of notes issued to bank capital. Finally, many free banks were subject to usury laws.

Though free banks did not emerge in the United States until after the first two experiments with federal government banking, they did operate along side state chartered banks and private banks between 1837 and 1863. From a regulatory perspective, free banks and state banks shared constraints such as usury laws, branching restrictions, and capital requirements. However, the regulation of free banks and state chartered banks differed on two fronts. On the one hand, free banks had easier access to the banking markets because they did not require legislative charters. On the other hand, free banks were constrained by the bond collateral requirement when issuing notes; a constraint that state chartered banks were not subjected to. As is shown below, this regulatory contrast made all the difference in terms of the survival of free banking in the United States.

The free banking laws did achieve the objective of encouraging growth in banking.[77] For example, the number of banks more than doubled during the first three years of free banking in New York.[78] During the first year of free banking, 40 new banks were established in Michigan, 30 new banks in Indiana, 18 new banks in Wisconsin, and 16 new banks in Minnesota. Despite this growth, free banking may not have produced the stability that states were looking for when they enacted the free banking laws during the middle nineteenth century. Table 3.12 shows the number of free bank closings and failures in four selected states. A closure is defined as a bank that has shut its doors to business and a failure is a bank that closed *and* redeemed its notes at less than par.[79] Thus a failure means that the noteholders suffered a loss while a closure does not. The data in Table 3.12 seems to validate the notion that free banking was a period of great instability as 48 percent of all free banks closed. However, notice that only 15 percent of free

Table 3.12 Free Bank Closings and Failures in Selected States

State	Free Bank Closures (% total free banks)	Free Bank Failures (% free banks with redemption information)
New York	160 (36)	34 (8)
Wisconsin	79 (56)	37 (26)
Indiana	89 (86)	24 (31)
Minnesota	11 (69)	9 (56)
Total	339 (48)	104 (15)

Source: Rolnick and Weber (1983: 183).

banks failed. Thus, the failure rate was not terribly high during the free banking era.

Is the distinction between a closure and a failure purely academic or are there important implications for the distinction? Free banking laws allowed for less restrictive entry into the banking industry but this freedom certainly did not guarantee success and profits to all who entered. A closure rate of 48 percent may be interpreted to mean that there was more entry than the market could sustain so that, after a period of time, some banks closed their doors because it was not profitable to remain in business. This happens across industries and was a part of the learning process in a market economy both in the nineteenth century, as well as the twenty-first century. Failures, however, are a different bird altogether. As defined above, a failure created losses for the public, so failures, unlike closures, necessarily were undesirable. The important implication of the distinction then between closures and failures is that a much less severe picture of instability during the antebellum banking era emerges. Perhaps the free banking era in America's history was more successful than previous scholars gave it credit for.

How did free banking come to an end? Though a plethora of scholarly work has analyzed the stability of the free banking era, little is said about how or why free banking concluded. According to several scholars, free banking ended in 1865 after the passage of the Revenue Act placed a ten percent tax on all banknotes.[80] Existing literature and data sources make no mention or indication that free banks survived the two banking acts implemented during the Civil War. Indeed, with the passage of the ten percent note tax, the free banking laws became moot because they were originally designed to regulate note-issuing institutions. Recall that these laws allowed individuals, subject to a bond collateral requirement, to establish a note-issuing bank without special legislative action. Thus, the tax essentially killed those banks chartered under the free banking laws.[81] State banks, however, did survive the Civil War, the creation of national banks, and the ten percent tax on their notes. Thus, banks chartered under free banking laws fared differently than state banks in the transition to a national banking regime.

Assessment of regulation and stability

A reflection on regulation during the antebellum banking period reveals that there was only one small window in which banking, throughout its entire history, was not subject to federal regulation. This window is the 27 years after the demise of the Second Bank of the United States and before the 1864 National Bank Act. In this period, regulation was left entirely to the states, many of whom responded by setting up free banking laws and systems. During the remaining years, banks were regulated by both state and federal authorities.

Whether antebellum banking was an era of stability or instability lacks consensus in existing literature. For example, some see this period as one that was largely stable though certain regions of the country were subject to more instability than others.[82] Others make the case that banks were more stable in the years prior to federal deposit insurance.[83] In contrast, some scholars characterize antebellum banking as chaotic and unstable.[84] Finally, others argue that any instability in antebellum banking was the product of excessive state regulation.[85] The next section of this chapter attempts to establish a clearer picture of banking during the antebellum period by considering all four types of institutions during this period and the role that regulation played in their stability. The findings are summarized in Table 3.3.

Assessment of state chartered banking

To assess the relationship between bank regulation and bank stability, previous discussions of regulation and performance must be tied together. Theoretically, it has been argued that the process of issuing charters through special legislative acts has two important consequences.[86] First, it creates incentives for legislatures to withhold charters thereby creating a monopoly privilege that allows them to extract higher rents. It also discourages the creation of a branch system since the branch units are not "valuable" to the legislatures. Second, the antebellum chartering process creates a powerful group of unit bankers with great incentive to limit new entry and hence limit competition by maintaining a unit rather than a branch system.

Does the evidence from the antebellum era support this hypothesis? Data in Weber (2006) indicate the number of banks in each state which, in turn, indicates the extent to which legislatures were willing to extend or withhold charters. In both the New England and Middle Atlantic regions there were many small banks in part because of the tax placed on bank capital. While the large number of banks created small bank monopolies in the towns throughout this region, it does not appear as though the chartering process limited entry in a significant way. At the same time, however, neither of these regions embraced branch banking during this period. This supports the theoretical claim that chartering through legislative acts created a group of unit banks with great incentive to maintain the status quo and limit competition through branching. Both the Southeast and Southwest regions had far fewer chartered banks. However, it is not clear if this was the result of limited entry or if there were fewer individuals with the requisite capital to establish a bank. Historical evidence indicates that the latter was more of a factor in these regions. Unlike the northern part of the country, the South, particularly the southeast region established and maintained a rather extensive branching system until the Civil War (see Table 3.5). Finally, in the western region, there were even fewer charters than the two southern regions but little in the way of branching. Thus the evidence does not clearly support or refute the theoretical hypothesis of the impact of legislative chartering.

In terms of the regulatory restrictions on branching, scholars often argue that such restrictions harm banks by limiting their ability to diversify. A unit bank is forced to extend loans and make investments in its immediate community which is frequently not too diverse. This means that an adverse development to the community could wipe out most of the bank's loans since its loan portfolio is the homogenous reflection of the community. This same argument was leveled against branching restrictions until their repeal in 1994 but the homogeneity of community life was certainly no truer than in antebellum America. Branching restrictions also make a bank vulnerable on the liability side of its balance sheet. Like the assets, the liabilities of a unit bank cannot be too diversified which, in turn, magnifies the possibility of runs and gives banks a more narrow base from which to draw deposits.

Interestingly, the antebellum era was actually one in which most states allowed for branching (see Table 3.4). However, as illustrated in Table 3.5 many of the New England and Middle Atlantic regions did not actually participate in branching, though it may have been legally recognized. The Southeast and, to a lesser extent, Southwest, regions embraced branching and the evidence from those branching experiences is clear: there were fewer failures and specie suspensions in those states with established branch systems. Consider that only four banks failed in Virginia during the antebellum era and Virginia had one of the most extensive branching systems in the country. Similarly, there were no bank failures after the crisis of 1837 in South Carolina, another extensive branch banking state.[87] Comparing the data in Table 3.5 with that in Table 3.9 the heavy branching states of the Southeast also had few failures and no or less trouble with specie suspensions even during crises. North Carolina embraced branching and only one state chartered bank failed during this era. Similarly, Tennessee was an active branching state and outside of the 1857 crisis, witnessed only three state bank failures. The data also indicate that states such as Kentucky and Ohio established branch systems but also experienced failures in the antebellum years. This apparent contradiction may be explained by the fact that in Ohio a branch system was not established until 1845 and after that time not a single bank failed.[88] Kentucky established a branch system earlier than Ohio but it was not until 1841 that a full network of branches was established and functioned "with great success for the twenty years before the Civil War."[89] At the same time, predominately unit bank states, such as New York and Maine, experienced many more failures.

As discussed earlier, there were a number of reasons that the northern states chose to establish a unit rather than branch system. It seems probable that the northern states' reluctance to embrace branch banking is precisely why that part of the country was the most in need for Clearinghouses and the Suffolk System. Indeed, many scholars have argued that the branch system in the southern half of the country functioned to perform the same note redemption and lender of last resort functions as the Suffolk System and Clearinghouses of the North. Existing evidence on antebellum branching and performance strongly suggests that those states that utilized a network of branches were highly successful and stable in terms of limiting the number of failures and incidence of specie suspension. Indeed, the instability of the unit system required private and coordinated initiatives such as the Clearinghouses to bring about the stability garnered through branching.

Banks were also regulated in terms of their note production and on the interest rate they could charge borrowers. As discussed earlier, the limits placed on small denomination note production was meant to encourage the use of specie. There is no evidence that such restrictions improved the stability of banking or that it engendered any instability. Usury laws, found in Table 3.6, were established to limit competition between bankers and these rate ceilings tended to be rather stable throughout the antebellum period. However, given the nature of the enforcement and flexibility afforded to the banker, this type of regulation was largely not binding during the antebellum era. Consequently, the illusory nature of the usury laws limits their utility in understanding how these laws impacted stability.

The rationale for requiring reserves during this period was essentially to keep banks from over issuing notes thereby creating inflationary conditions. Reserve requirements were not put into place until 1837 when Virginia imposed a 25 percent requirement on all banknotes issued. Interestingly, there is no evidence that over issuing or inflation were a problem prior to the Virginia development. Further, as Table 3.7 indicates, most of the states that mandated reserve requirements did so on notes only. This is clear evidence that the state regulators did not understand the growing reliance the banks were developing on deposits as a source of funds and, at the same time, calls into question the effectiveness of the reserve requirement itself. Ultimately, there is no clear evidence that this form of regulation promoted stability in antebellum banking.

Bank regulation also took the form of taxation on either bank dividends or the more prevalent tax on bank capital. An important consequence of the capital tax was to encourage the proliferation of smaller banks with lower capital levels. At the same time, it discouraged the creation of a branch system since these structures would require more capital and hence greater capital taxation. Because the capital tax worked to encourage small banks over large or branch systems, it may be argued that the tax was destabilizing to the extent that unit systems are more unstable than branch systems.

Regulated social overhead lending also had a destabilizing impact on antebellum banking. State governments used their monopoly chartering position to force banks into lending situations that often were high risk and which also drained bank profitability. Banks, today and since their birth in antebellum America, are profit maximizing institutions. They extend loans which have a high probability of generating revenue to the bank. If regulation is required to mandate certain lending, it is highly unlikely that the banks would make the loans without the regulation. The destabilizing impact of required lending in the antebellum era is summarized as:

> Banks were forced to make large quantities of illiquid loans to states which at times refused to honor their debts, to farmers who often had difficulty in repaying loans in good times, and to invest in transportation networks which were located in basically undeveloped areas. If we add to these risky assets the liabilities of bonuses and taxes, the most surprising element of this period is not that so many banks failed but that so many survived the financial stresses or were able to liquidate in an orderly fashion.[90]

Finally, antebellum banking saw our nation's first experiment with deposit insurance. Today, scholars continue to discuss the costs and benefits of deposit insurance and while today's discussion focuses on federal deposit insurance, the same arguments may be extended to state level systems of insurance. On the one hand, deposit insurance may stabilize a banking system by keeping crises and runs to a minimum. Further, it may contribute an element of confidence in banking to depositors. However, it is well known that deposit insurance also encourages risk taking on the part of the banker and it keeps depositors from monitoring bank activity. The cost of deposit insurance, in addition to bank and depositor moral hazard, is the poor agency behavior by regulators in granting excessive forbearance: with deposit insurance there is no run or disintermediation so there is no incentive for the regulators to act. Given these benefits and costs, it is difficult to know which impact is greater. In antebellum America, the evidence suggests that deposit insurance was destabilizing in some cases (for example, New York) but stabilizing in others (for example, Indiana).

Assessment of private banking

Contemporary scholars no longer debate the value and economic importance of the private banker in antebellum America. The evidence is clear that these institutions were instrumental in the growth of the economy and in supporting young entrepreneurs in the growth process. It is equally clear that these institutions operated under arguably the most oppressive regulation of all bank types in the nineteenth century. Recall that most states passed restraining acts which, in some cases, prohibited note issuance and, in more extreme cases, prohibited private banking all together. From this competitive disadvantage, it is somewhat surprising to learn that these banks were successful and many managed to survive the antebellum period. In those states in which private banking was allowed but note issuance prohibited, the private banker largely relied on deposits as a source of funds. Perhaps because of this restriction, they realized earlier than their state bank counterparts the value of the deposit over the note. At the same time, however, the private banker was necessarily hurt by the inability to issue notes because this was an important source of profit for early American banks. Indeed, the state prohibition on private banking clearly hurt their ability to compete with the state chartered, and even free, banks. Given these regulatory constraints, it is not surprising that the zenith of the private banker took place in antebellum America. Regulatory constraints simply did not allow them to grow and evolve with the state banker after the war.

Assessment of federal banking

Almost all accounts of the two experiments with federal banking during antebellum America tend to credit these institutions with restricting the state banks from over issuing their notes. In this function, the two Banks acted as central banks in controlling the money supply. However, there is little, if any, empirical evidence to support the claim that the Banks were successful in this function and the one empirical study which tested this claim actually found that neither Bank had an impact on note restraint in the New England states.[91] Though it is inappropriate to extend the findings outside of New England, the results do suggest that one must be careful to accept, without evidence, the claim that the two federal banks of antebellum America played an important role in restraining note issues. Even to the extent that the Banks were able to restrain note issues, this may have interfered with the market process of bank expansion. If the First and Second Banks were able to redeem large amounts of banknotes for specie, this action diminished state banks' ability to expand.[92] To extend the analysis further, an inability to expand means that loan demand may have gone unmet because of the constraints imposed by the two Banks.

State and private bank growth may also have been hindered by the interstate branching advantage permitted to both the First and Second Banks of the United States. That is, while state and private banks were prohibited from interstate branching, both federal banks established networks of branches across the states thereby affording them all the advantages of branching; including perhaps most importantly, portfolio diversification. At the same time, the sheer size of both federal banks far exceeded their private sector counter parts, thus providing them another advantage.

As established above, it is also clear that these two institutions contributed to financial market instability. The quick expansion followed by a quick contraction of money from the First Bank led to the stock market crisis of 1792. Deflationary policies of the Second Bank led to the failure of hundreds of commercial banks during its early years of operation. Following the War of 1812, the nation was flooded with state banknotes issued to help finance the war effort. After the war, the federal government felt that only through the creation of a central bank could this inflation and heterogeneous money supply be brought under control. Hence, the creation of the Second Bank. The Bank's policy in 1819 was to sharply curtail lending and to redeem the state banknotes for specie. A famous financial writer at the time, William Gouge, commented that through the deflationary policy, "the Bank was saved and the people ruined."[93]

Assessment of free banking

The discussion of free banking above indicates that this period in our banking history achieved great growth in the number of banking institutions but that it was also a period of instability in the form of failures and closures. What explains this instability? Was it excessive fraudulent banking as told by many financial historians? Was it too much freedom and not enough regulation over free banks? Or did regulation compromise the banks' ability to operate profitably? As with the history of commercial banking generally, there are two types of evidence with which to analyze the free banking era. Historical analysis that is based on economic theory and observation, and statistical analysis based on econometric modeling. Much of the existing literature on this period in our history attempts to use statistical methods to determine the cause of instability and failures. Most of this statistical evidence indicates that the instability may be attributed to the bond collateral requirement placed on free banks. In addition, there is some statistical evidence to indicate that contagious bank runs were a part of the landscape of free banking. These runs were typically caused by some shock exogenous to the banking sector and noteholders were unable to determine whether or not the shock would adversely impact their institution. However, the evidence also indicates that these runs did not lead to the permanent closure of the free banks. Further, statistical evidence does not bear out the long held belief that fraudulent, or wildcat, banking dominated the free banking era. Thus, the statistical evidence indicates that regulation, in the form of bond collateral requirements, contributed to most free bank failures.

The historical and theoretical evidence corroborates the statistical evidence with a few additional observations. As expected, more economically and financially developed states witnessed greater stability than frontier states. Further, states with more liberal branching laws also had more success with free banking. And while the statistical evidence indicates that fraudulent banking explained only a small fraction of the bank failures it may be argued theoretically that the cases of wildcat banking may actually have been made possible by the bond collateral requirement. That is, individuals may have been willing to accept unknown banknotes *because* of the bond collateral behind the notes. Thus, historical evidence also indicates that it was regulation, namely branching restrictions and the collateral requirements, which largely explains the instability of the free banking era. In the discussion that follows, both the statistical and historical evidence is presented.

Conventional wisdom blames the instability on the lack of regulatory control over entry and the resulting wildcat banking that emerged. Wildcat banking is a term used to describe unscrupulous bankers whose intent was to establish a free bank with the sole purpose of defrauding note holders by never redeeming the notes for specie.[94] The term wildcat banking ostensibly comes from the notion that these individuals would perpetrate their fraud by setting up redemption offices off in the woods and forests where only wildcats roam. Wildcatting occurred when states allowed free banks to secure bonds as collateral when the price of the bond was less than par (face) value. Consider a scenario in which a suspect individual with $100,000 in capital could use the capital to purchase bonds that had depreciated by 50 percent. The $100,000 capital will purchase $200,000 in bonds, and consequently, $200,000 in banknotes. Once the notes are in circulation, the wildcat banker could close its doors and walk away with a profit of $100,000: there would be noteholders with $200,000 in claims but only $100,000 in collateralized bonds (see Figure 3.5). This fraudulent behavior caused depositors to refer to these banknotes as shinplasters, shingles, stump tails or red dogs.[95] Early scholars of this period focused their criticism of the free banking era on the widespread outbreak of wildcat banking.[96] However, a closer examination of this period in our history indicates that wildcat banking was not as widespread as originally believed.

Figure 3.5 Hypothetical Wildcat Bank Balance Sheet

ASSETS	LIABILITIES
Bonds $100,000	Banknotes $200,000
Loans $200,000	Capital $100,000
Total $300,000	Total $300,000

Using state auditor data for each free bank failure in Minnesota, Indiana, Wisconsin, and New York, scholars tested the wildcat banking hypothesis.[97] They found that the Minnesota failures appear to be related to wildcat banking because the bonds were selling at less than par and seven of the nine failures were in business for less than one year. However, the data indicate that the free bank failures in the other three states were not consistent with the wildcat hypotheses. Specifically, in Indiana, the bonds were not selling substantially below par and all but one of the failed banks was in business for more than one year. The empirical evidence for Wisconsin and New York strongly rejects the wildcat hypothesis. In Wisconsin, 35 of the 37 failures were in business for more than one year and the bonds, because of state law, were not purchased at less than par. Finally, only five of the 34 failed banks in New York were in business for less than one year and the bonds were selling at less than par. Based on this empirical evidence, the authors are compelled to reject the wildcat hypothesis as an explanation for the incidence of failures during the free banking period.[98] Thus, there must be some other explanation for the instability of free banking as the evidence suggests that wildcat banking was a small part of the free banking era.

The second line of thought on free bank failures argues that they may be explained by the falling price of state debt. Since the free banks were required to hold as assets at minimum, the value of bonds equivalent to their note issue, the banks were vulnerable to falling bond prices. The nominal value of the banks' liabilities was fixed, thus a fall in the price of the bonds would greatly compromise the net worth of the bank and, consequently, lead to failure. There is both theoretical and empirical evidence to suggest that this regulation played an important role in explaining the incidence of bank failures during the free banking era.

Theoretically, L. White (1986) finds that the collateral requirement promoted bank failures during the free banking period in three different ways. First, the requirements may have contributed to fraudulent behavior in those cases in which the collateralized bond value exceeded market value (as in the example above). What made this possible was the public's willingness to accept unfamiliar notes and this willingness, in turn, may have contributed, in part, to the bond collateral requirement behind the notes. Second, White theorizes that the bond collateral requirement exposed banks to the risk of declining bond prices. If the value of the state bonds fell, it wiped out the banks' net worth. Third, the bond collateral requirement may have contributed to the number of free bank failures by forcing banks to meet currency demands using reserve currency. Consider a scenario in which, for whatever reason, depositors want to convert deposits to currency. The banks could not meet those deposit withdraws by immediately issuing additional notes so, instead, they are forced to use reserve currency. A decline in bank reserves may lead to failure by requiring banks to quickly sell assets at reduced prices to replenish reserves.[99] From this theoretical perspective, it was not the lack of regulation that contributed to instability in the free banking era but, rather, the bond collateral requirements placed on note issuance.

The empirical evidence supports the theory advanced by L. White (1986). Rather than blame wildcat banking for the instability of the free banking era, some contend that it was the drop in state debt prices that reduced the banks' net worth and led to the large number of failures.[100] Looking at the correlation between periods of falling debt prices and the incidence of failures, the scholars find a high correlation. Indeed, they find that approximately 80 percent of all bank closings during the free banking era occurred during periods of substantial declining bond prices. Further, the declining bond prices were linked to the fiscal condition of the issuing state. For example, the fall in the price of Indiana bonds in the early 1840s was tied to fears that the state was going to default on the bond issue.[101] Thus, it was the debt collateral requirement that led to bank failures during the free banking era and not the lack of entry restrictions or excessive wildcat banking. These scholars use bank specific data to empirically determine that free banking not only led to fewer failures than typically attributed to this period but they also found that losses to noteholders were also much less than previously thought.

In addition to arguing that the bond collateral system may have made free banks more susceptible to failure, scholars argue that the regulation restricting branching also contributed to the failures of that period.[102] By restricting branching, banks are severely limited in their ability to diversify their portfolios both from the asset and liability perspective.

Observation of limited empirical data supports the position that states with more liberal branching rights tended to have more success with free banking. Table 3.11 indicates those states that had free banking laws while Tables 3.4 and 3.5 indicate the branching laws for states during Antebellum America. Notice that the states with the most instability with free banking, Michigan and Minnesota, did not allow branching while states with the most free banking success, notably New York, did allow branching.

Finally, the experience with free entry tended, *ceteris paribus*, to be more successful in those regions of the country that were more developed economically and financially. The developed states such as New York and Pennsylvania had much more success than frontier states such as Michigan. If we are going try and extrapolate insight from the free bank era, it is more relevant to consider the developed rather than the frontier state experience.[103]

Concluding remarks

A defining characteristic of both the antebellum economy and of antebellum banking was its diversity. The eastern region of the nation was more advanced in terms of its institutions of production, financial sophistication, population density, and technology and innovation. The West was still somewhat wild as many states were large territories much of which was unexplored, manufacturing and finance were likewise in the infant stages of development, and climate and crop production differed greatly from that in the East. One's experiences economically were extremely varied depending on physical location prior to the Civil War.

Just as economic development was diverse, antebellum banking was similarly diverse. Four bank institutions were born in antebellum America beginning with state chartered and private banks followed by two experiments with federal banking and ending with the free banking era. In the end, only state chartered and private banks remained to operate in postbellum America.

While these different institutions shared many similar regulatory constraints, there was also a diversity of state law that cannot be ignored, particularly in terms of state and free banks. For example, legislative regimes ranged from unit banking states to free branching states and from states which prohibited banking to free banking states. Ultimately, the diversity of economic development, banking institutions, and state banking laws and regulation combined to create diverse banking experiences across the states.

Despite this heterogeneity in antebellum banking, there were, at the same time, some consistent outcomes from this period. The empirical evidence presented in this chapter make clear that old stereotypes of the performance of antebellum banking are simply that; stereotypes without basis in evidence. States with stable governments saw fewer bank failures and states that were more liberal in their branching allowances also witnessed fewer failures. Ultimately, branch banking, which had taken hold in the South during the middle nineteenth century, largely ended with the devastation of the southern region during the Civil War. It would not be until late in the twentieth century that branching once again characterized American banking. By many accounts, this development explains much of the instability that characterizes the evolution and further regulation of banking in the United States.

Earlier it was mentioned that existing literature does not reach a consensus on whether the antebellum era of banking was stable or unstable. Most of this literature focuses on one particular aspect of the entire banking experience. In contrast, this chapter attempts to consider all institutions, experiences, regulation, and outcomes. From this perspective, it appears that antebellum banking was actually rather stable despite the clearly destabilizing affects of regulation. Indeed, it seems that the relative stability stemmed from the private, coordinated efforts of the North combined with branching in the South. These are two defining characteristics of the antebellum era that would soon be rendered history because the Civil War essentially wiped out the South and, with it, branch banking. Further, the 1913 passage of the Federal Reserve Act effectively eliminated private solutions to bank instability such as the Clearinghouses.

4
National Banking Era: 1864–1912

Financial historians refer to the national banking era as the period between the creation of nationally chartered banks and the creation of the Federal Reserve. The opportunity to obtain national bank charters came with the passage of the 1863 National Currency Act and its subsequent revision as the National Bank Act of 1864. The Federal Reserve Act was codified in December of 1913. Thus, the national bank era refers to a period of approximately 51 years in American banking history. As this chapter details, it was a period of much greater federal regulation and instability than the antebellum era that preceded it.

This chapter carefully considers the national bank era, focusing on the regulation and performance of commercial banks during this period. In the previous chapter, we found that the regulation of antebellum bank institutions increased the fragility of banking. Yet, we also concluded that it was, largely, a period of stability despite the destabilizing influences of regulation. The postbellum period, like the antebellum period, was one in which regulation, increasingly, added to bank instability. However, unlike the antebellum era, this chapter shows that the national bank era was increasingly unstable. In other words, the structural conditions of banking had changed after the Civil War to the extent that bankers could not maintain stability in the face of increasing regulation.

Introduction to the national banking era

Postbellum America is best described as a period of significant growth and change throughout all aspects of life; from demographics, production, and the role of banking and finance, to the role of government in the economy. So significant was the change that by the end of the half decade following the Civil War, antebellum life was almost unrecognizable. Life moved from the farm to the city for millions of Americans (Figure A.5), special-purpose machinery was used in production to improve efficiency, and automobiles became the preferred mode of transportation (Figure A.6). Growth in real gross domestic product (RGDP) reflects the significant economic changes and general prosperity of this era (Figure A.7). Despite a general trend of growth, it is worth noting that there were three recessions between 1890 and 1898 and, at its peak in 1894, unemployment exceeded 18 percent.[1]

An important aspect of this era is the significant growth in the U.S. population. Figure A.5 illustrates the population increase; between 1860 and 1910 the rate of increase was 193 percent. This growth was fueled, in part, by the millions of immigrants who entered the country to make America home. Like the antebellum era that preceded it, the American populace during the national bank era may be characterized as one of intense entrepreneurial spirit. Consider that between 1870 and 1900, over 4000 patents were granted by the U.S. Patent Office; this marked an increase of ten percent over the previous 80 years.[2] Immigrants and nonimmigrants alike created opportunities for profitable enterprise. Examples include Scottish born steelmaker Andrew Carnegie, banker J. P. Morgan, and John D. Rockefeller, Standard Oil Company founder. Some of these entrepreneurial gains are reflected in the general growing trend in the industrial stock index during this period (Figure A.8). However, not all entrepreneurial activity was successful. While the absolute number of business failures was low (Figure A.4), the number of failures per 10,000 businesses was historically high (Figure A.9).

Despite the general economic growth illustrated in the RGDP data, not all regions of the economy enjoyed prosperity. While overall RGDP growth was impressive, the South was devastated by the Civil War. As one historian summarized:

> By 1865, the Union forces had ... destroyed two-thirds of the assessed value of Southern wealth, two-fifths of the South's livestock, and one quarter of her white men between the ages of 20 and 40. More than half the farm machinery was ruined, and the damages to railroads and industries were incalculable ... Southern wealth decreased by 60 percent.[3]

Southern banking and the branch system established in the antebellum era was also destroyed. Figure 3.2 illustrates a sharp decline in the number of state banks during and following the Civil War; many of those lost banks were in the South.

Outside the South, a growing population with robust entrepreneurial talent created strong economic growth with an increasing need for banking and financial services. The same figure that shows the decline in state banking during and immediately following the war (Figure 3.2) shows the astonishing growth in the number of state chartered banks during the national bank era. In addition to state banks, by 1910, there were over 7000 nationally chartered banks operating in the United States.[4] Thus, the national banking era witnessed an enormous expansion in the commercial banking sector in the United States.

General banking themes

The experience of the national banking era may be captured by four general themes. First, while the regulation of this era drew, to some extent, from the free banking regulation established in the antebellum era, the national banking era is clearly defined by an increased federal presence in U.S. commercial banking. This is evidenced by the creation of nationally chartered banks under the supervision of the Comptroller of the Currency at the beginning of the national banking era and by the creation of the Federal Reserve System at its close. Federal banking legislation in 1864 was meant, in part, to improve the health of commercial banking but was not particularly successful as this period was marked by crises that became increasingly more frequent. In response, policymakers extended the role of the federal government in banking by creating a central bank in December of 1913.

Second, the increased federal presence manifested itself as increased restrictions, primarily on the newly formed nationally chartered banks. These restrictions included barriers to entry, limits on bank's use of funds, note collateral requirements and restrictions, and capital and reserve requirements much more onerous than those contained under state chartered law.

A third theme that emerges is that the national bank era was one marked by greater instability than the antebellum era in terms of the fluctuations in the number of institutions and, perhaps more importantly, the number and severity of bank crises. While some of the crises during this period were limited in scale and scope, others were systemic and resulted in a significant number of suspensions and failures.

Finally, until the end of the national bank era and the creation of the Federal Reserve System, the instability and panics were largely resolved through private, coordinated banking efforts. This chapter provides evidence of the success of the Clearinghouse Associations in quelling the damage of banking crises during this period in U.S. history. However, as the national banking era came to a close, the U.S. commercial banking system had moved even further from private market outcomes and more toward government determined outcomes.

Provisions of the National Bank Act of 1864[5]

According to one of the sponsors of the acts, Senator John Sherman, there were both short-term and long-term objectives to establishing a national banking system.[6] Short term, the federal government needed help funding the war effort. Indeed, at the end of the Civil War, federal debt stood at $3 billion while the Treasury had less than $100 million in cash.[7] Long term, the objectives were to replace the heterogeneous collection of state banknotes with a unified, national banknote and to eliminate the state bank. Thus, legislators wanted to replace the antebellum system of state and private banks with a system of exclusively national banks.

To meet the short-term goal of war finance, all national banks were required to purchase U.S. government bonds in order to issue notes. Specifically, national banks were required to purchase $100 par value in government bonds for every $90 in banknotes they wanted to circulate. This provision, taken from the free banking provisions of the antebellum period, created an instant demand for federal debt and, in the process, allowed the federal government to rapidly reduce the $3 billion war debt. As evidence, consider that by 1893, the federal debt was less than $600 million.[8]

A second provision limited the total amount of national banknotes to be issued at $300 million, though this restriction was repealed in 1875. The distribution of these limited notes was on a first-come first-serve basis which ultimately resulted in the vast majority of these notes finding homes in banks in the New England, Middle Atlantic, and West regions of the country. Table 4.1 illustrates this disparate distribution of banknotes as most notes were in the Northeast and what we today consider the Midwest (the West during the national banking era).

Third, all national banks were required to hold minimum capital reserves, depending on their location. More specifically, a minimum of $50,000 was required in cities with less than 6000 in population, $100,000 in cities with populations between 6000 and 50,000 and a capital requirement of $200,000 for any city with more than 50,000 residents. Thus, bankers wishing to establish a nationally chartered bank in a larger city had to hold more capital than those in smaller communities.

Table 4.1 National Banknotes Outstanding by State: 1870–1910

State (by region)	1870	1880	1890	1900	1910
Maine	$7,901,056	$8,744,432	$5,241,584	$6,516,725	$6,343,682
New Hampshire	$4,540,535	$5,248,325	$3,528,580	$4,501,169	$5,602,865
Vermont	$6,269,900	$7,360,780	$2,954,939	$4,204,392	$4,916,479
Massachusetts	$62,528,720	$71,248,677	$27,449,074	$31,675,073	$32,963,022
Rhode Island	$13,442,430	$14,105,558	$5,292,242	$6,887,244	$4,996,619
Connecticut	$18,849,100	$18,466,293	$7,883,323	$10,390,354	$14,114,560
New York	$79,051,860	$54,257,746	$26,396,689	$56,777,725	$99,094,660
New Jersey	$10,193,065	$11,214,926	$5,671,269	$8,107,217	$16,173,806
Pennsylvania	$42,202,030	$45,618,325	$21,264,689	$44,586,052	$90,775,762
Delaware	$1,298,025	$1,589,700	$1,132,808	$877,012	$1,367,762
Maryland	$9,865,050	$8,373,007	$3,647,595	$7,487,228	$14,061,998
DC	$1,379,000	$995,082	$743,914	$1,471,705	$6,479,738
Virginia	$2,288,880	$2,596,282	$1,314,038	$3,895,540	$12,532,815
West Virginia	$2,131,200	$1,636,434	$891,809	$2,448,507	$8,480,401
North Carolina	$539,900	$1,964,490	$822,839	$1,650,889	$6,534,491
South Carolina	$333,000	$1,362,701	$455,094	$1,505,149	$3,884,320
Georgia	$1,249,600	$2,037,837	$1,102,826	$2,727,097	$9,340,060
Florida	NA	$70,800	$289,183	$642,467	$4,429,442
Alabama	$369,200	$1,443,895	$1,274,967	$1,968,665	$7,885,052
Mississippi	$66,000	$346	$281,997	$921,787	$3,017,706
Louisiana	$1,272,020	$2,099,831	$1,642,549	$2,220,289	$6,434,139
Texas	$492,245	$778,440	$4,138,233	$8,190,621	$29,560,159
Arkansas	$183,500	$239,670	$349,991	$330,427	$2,169,023
Kentucky	$2,573,560	$9,161,001	$4,214,248	$9,035,286	$16,470,228
Tennessee	$1,589,270	$2,685,795	$1,492,426	$3,379,830	$9,775,191
Ohio	$19,851,715	$22,214,858	$12,388,609	$25,150,526	$47,902,701
Indiana	$11,816,855	$11,944,692	$5,405,924	$7,252,680	$23,159,736
Illinois	$10,839,080	$10,189,649	$6,010,127	$16,664,766	$47,042,096
Michigan	$4,230,755	$7,072,035	$3,438,603	$5,741,378	$11,169,626
Wisconsin	$2,745,050	$2,641,060	$1,867,638	$4,708,717	$13,204,203
Minnesota	$1,687,950	$2,744,274	$1,861,550	$4,151,961	$15,490,101
Iowa	$3,831,135	$4,697,314	$3,232,048	$7,922,604	$17,723,057
Missouri	$4,765,479	$2,367,037	$2,455,8'7	$12,821,374	$28,542,060
North Dakota	NA	NA	$465,953	$573,153	$3,382,298
South Dakota	NA	NA	$619,053	$661,235	$2,971,203
Nebraska	$177,100	$721,960	$2,442,955	$4,220,784	$11,010,250
Kansas	$428,800	$911,200	$3,204,797	$4,572,802	$10,579,186
Montana	$36,000	$286,497	$685,758	$1,038,483	$2,799,428
Wyoming	NA	$57,600	$229,145	$379,215	$1,387,493
Colorado	$264,300	$936,384	$1,308,391	$3,337,050	$8,355,286
New Mexico	NA	$355,670	$239,228	$493,191	$1,494,723
Oklahoma	NA	NA	$44,990	$473,425	$7,955,882
Washington	NA	$164,600	$1,263,090	$1,340,250	$7,150,745
Oregon	$88,500	$225,600	$722,344	$1,070,434	$4,746,607
California	NA	$700,500	$1,429,405	$4,619,975	$38,858,090
Idaho	$65,200	$81,901	$110,892	$218,976	$1,783,109
Utah	$171,500	$192,544	$446,354	$1,026,509	$2,499,749
Nevada	$131,700	$38,643	$49,977	$16,782	$1,684,411
Arizona	NA	NA	$42,130	$213,077	$684,235
Alaska	NA	NA	NA	$12,500	$53,180
Hawaii	NA	NA	NA	$50,000	$162,398

Source: Compiled from the *Annual Report of the Comptroller of the Currency* (1870: 16), (1880: LXXXV), (1890: 116), (1900: 254), (1910: 83).

Note: * not available.

Table 4.2 Number of National Banks in National Banking Era: 1870–1910

State (by region)	1870	1880	1890	1900	1910
Maine	61	69	78	82	72
New Hampshire	41	47	51	55	58
Vermont	42	47	51	48	51
Massachusetts	206	242	260	247	192
Rhode Island	62	61	59	45	22
Connecticut	81	84	84	84	79
New York	292	296	319	336	449
New Jersey	54	66	94	115	194
Pennsylvania	196	240	349	469	819
Delaware	11	14	18	19	28
Maryland	31	35	59	72	108
DC	3	6	12	12	12
Virginia	17	17	32	43	125
West Virginia	14	17	21	40	103
North Carolina	6	15	21	31	75
South Carolina	3	12	16	17	39
Georgia	8	13	30	27	113
Florida	NA*	2	15	16	43
Alabama	2	9	30	28	79
Mississippi	0	0	12	12	32
Louisiana	2	7	15	21	31
Texas	4	13	189	223	519
Arkansas	2	2	9	7	45
Kentucky	17	49	76	81	148
Tennessee	13	23	51	50	102
Ohio	130	170	233	276	380
Indiana	69	92	100	123	262
Illinois	81	136	192	240	432
Michigan	41	79	110	83	101
Wisconsin	32	35	68	88	129
Minnesota	17	30	60	83	270
Iowa	43	75	139	196	326
Missouri	18	21	79	67	129
North Dakota	NA	NA	29	27	149
South Dakota	NA	NA	39	28	99
Nebraska	4	10	135	110	238
Kansas	5	12	159	110	208
Montana	1	3	25	21	54
Wyoming	NA	2	11	14	29
Colorado	3	14	49	39	122
New Mexico	NA	4	9	9	41
Oklahoma	NA	NA	3	24	225
Washington	NA	1	51	31	79
Oregon	1	1	37	27	75
California	NA	10	37	38	187
Idaho	1	1	7	9	47
Utah	1	1	10	10	21
Nevada	0	1	2	1	12
Arizona	NA	NA	2	5	13
Alaska	NA	NA	NA	1	2
Hawaii	NA	NA	NA	NA	4
TOTAL	**1615**	**2084**	**3537**	**3840**	**7172**

Source: Compiled from the *Annual Report of the Comptroller of the Currency* (1910: 371–401).
Note: * not available.

Fourth, many national banks could not extend mortgage loans.[9] This particular provision greatly discouraged bankers from opening nationally chartered banks in agricultural and rural areas where most of the borrowing needs were for real estate. As indicated in Table 4.2, most national banks were located in populous and economically developed states such as New York, Pennsylvania and Illinois. At the same time, more rural and less developed states such as those in the South and those in the West had few, if any, nationally chartered banks for the first 30 years following the National Bank Act. Banning national banks from extending mortgage loans stemmed from the theoretical beliefs about banking at the time. Banking practices during the national banking era were established according to the real-bills perspective, which theorized that bank loans should only be made on a short-term basis to finance the production of real goods. This way, once production was complete, the loan was immediately paid in full. This minimized the riskiness of the loan and assured the banker a match of short-term liabilities (demand deposits) with short-term assets. A mortgage loan was long term and hence not compatible with the real bills doctrine.

A fifth provision of the National Bank Act required national banks to maintain reserve requirements. The act created three classes of national banks which, in turn, established the reserve system. Initially, New York was established as the central reserve city, 18 other cities were named reserve cities, and the remaining banks were designated as nonreserve city banks. New York national banks were required to hold 25 percent of their deposits and notes in reserve.[10] Banks in a reserve city also faced 25 percent reserve requirements and the reserve city banks themselves maintained 25 percent reserves, though half could be on deposit with New York banks. All national banks outside of New York and the reserve cities maintained 15 percent reserves, nine percent of which could be deposited at a reserve bank. Thus, most nationally chartered banks could meet reserve requirements through deposits at other banks. As is shown later in this chapter, this caused problems because most of the reserves were concentrated either in New York or the reserve city banks. Thus, when depositing banks called for their reserves, immense pressure was placed on the holding banks to produce the reserve money.

Further, the National Bank Act was interpreted to prohibit the branching of national banks. That is, the act did not specifically prohibit branching, but the act required that all business take place at the location designated on the certificate of operation. The second Comptroller of the Currency, Freeman Clark, interpreted this to mean that national banks could not open branches.[11]

Thus there were essentially six important provisions to the National Bank Act of 1864. These restrictions on national banks discouraged state banks from converting their state charters as was the long-term goal of policymakers. For example, the minimum capital requirement on a national bank was set at $50,000 in small communities while most state banks had capital requirements of less than $10,000.[12] Another example can be found in the reserve requirements. Most states placed reserve requirements only on notes (see Table 3.7) while the national banks were required to hold reserves on both notes and deposits.

Sensing that their long-term goals would not be met with the current regulatory regime in place, legislatures and regulators needed to facilitate a conversion and attempted to do so through the 1865 Revenue Act. This act placed a ten percent tax on all state and free banknotes effective July 1, 1866. As shown in Table 4.3, the Revenue Act was successful in so far as it vastly reduced the number of state chartered banks in the years immediately following the act (see also Figure 3.2). However, this was only a temporary set back for the state banks and, ultimately, the National Bank Act of 1864 failed in its long-term objective to eliminate the state banker from the U.S. banking landscape. The reality, as shown in Table 4.4, was quite the contrary. In 1880 there were 841 state banks and by 1910 that number grew to 12,482 a 1384 percent rate of growth during the national banking era.

The evidence above indicates that the National Bank Act was not successful in meeting its long-term objective of creating a more homogenous currency because state banks did not convert their charters. Additional legislation, namely the 1865 Revenue Act, was required to achieve a more homogenous currency. Indeed, consider that in 1864, fully 85 percent of all banknotes in circulation were issued from state chartered institutions and by the middle of 1866 these state notes had essentially disappeared.[13]

Episodes of crises and the Clearinghouses

Most financial historians identify five banking crises or panics during the national banking era.[14] These occurred in 1873, 1884, 1890, 1893, and 1907. Figure 4.1 illustrates the number of bank failures during this period, including these crises episodes. It is difficult to find precise bank data for these crises since the Comptroller of the Currency collected data on a quarterly or, more commonly, annual basis. However, Wicker (2000) examined the crises of the national bank era and using data from a private source as well as from local newspapers and financial

Table 4.3 Number of State and Free Banks Before and After the Revenue Act of 1865

State (by region)	**Number of State and Free Banks before or on 1865 (Year)**	**Number of State and Free Banks Closed or Converted (Year)**	**Percent of Banks Closed or Converted**
Maine	69 (1863)	68 (1878)	98.5%
New Hampshire	52 (1863)	49 (1870)	94.2%
Vermont	38 (1864)	33 (1875)	86.8%
Massachusetts	183 (1862)	NA[a]	NA
Rhode Island	88 (1863)	68 (1868)	77.2%
Connecticut	61 (1864)	54 (1869)	88.5%
New York	308 (1863)	256 (1869)	83.1%
New Jersey	12 (1863)	10 (1892)	83.3%
Pennsylvania	94 (1863)	82 (1868)	87.2%
Delaware	8[b] (1863)	3 (1866)	37.5%
Maryland	32 (1863)	24 (1868)	75.0%
Virginia	66 (1861)	64 (1867)	96.9%
North Carolina	31 (1861)	28 (1871)	90.3%
South Carolina	20 (1861)	12 (1871)	60.0%
Georgia	18 (1861)	17 (1869)	94.4%
Florida	2 (1861)	1 (1885)	50.0%
Alabama	8 (1861)	6 (1869)	75.0%
Mississippi	2 (1858)	0 (1868)	0.0%

Table 4.3 Number of State and Free Banks Before and After the Revenue Act of 1865 – *continued*

State (by region)	**Number of State and Free Banks before or on 1865 (Year)**	**Number of State and Free Banks Closed or Converted (Year)**	**Percent of Banks Closed or Converted**
Louisiana	13 (1860)	3 (1865)	23.0%
Arkansas	10 (1845)	1 (1875)	10.0%
Kentucky	45 (1860)	7 (1865)	15.5%
Tennessee	39 (1859)	34 (1864)	87.2%
Ohio	55 (1863)	51 (1868)	92.7%
Indiana	37 (1860)	19 (1865)	51.3%
Illinois	94 (1861)	88 (1867)	93.6%
Michigan	4 (1862)	3 (1868)	75.0%
Wisconsin	69 (1863)	53 (1873)	76.8%
Minnesota	NA[c]	NA	NA
Iowa	NA	NA	NA
Missouri	42 (1863)	34 (1868)	80.9%
Nebraska	1 (1861)	NA	NA

Source: Knox (1903, various pages).

Notes: Column two, the number of state banks, indicates that number for the year closest to 1865. Column three indicates the number of banks closed or converted to national charters soon after the 1865 act as data is available. NA indicates the data is not available. [a] In Massachusetts, there was one national bank in 1863 and 207 by 1868 as an indication of the growth in national banks following the 1863 act. [b] Incomplete data. [c] In Minnesota, the first state bank was not chartered until 1858.

Table 4.4 Number of State Banks in National Banking Era: 1880–1910

State (by region)	1880[a]	1890	1900	1910
Maine	1	NA*	NA	NA
New Hampshire	1	1	13	9
Vermont	5	NA	2	NA
Massachusetts	3	NA	6	NA
Rhode Island	15	9	4	3
Connecticut	2	8	11	7
New York	49	164	244	202
New Jersey	11	21	25	18
Pennsylvania	85	82	198	164
Delaware	5	1	4	4
Maryland	4	8	29	88**
DC	NA	NA	6	NA
Virginia	54	76	110	216
West Virginia	17	17	81	166
North Carolina	9	NA	63	306
South Carolina	4	18	91	223
Georgia	27	42	171	441
Florida	NA	6	31	111
Alabama	6	12	62	180
Mississippi	17	47	106	329
Louisiana	3	6	58	187
Texas	18	4	112	533
Arkansas	2	15	104	219
Kentucky	49	123	202	424
Tennessee	23	52	136	317
Ohio	31	49	424	422
Indiana	27	45	302	269
Illinois	25	26	514	445
Michigan	31	37	301	360
Wisconsin	28	80	256	477
Minnesota	22	76	410	632
Iowa	60	105	926	281
Missouri	95	301	564	1038
North Dakota	NA	13	133	519
South Dakota	NA	67	178	501***
Nebraska	12	336	432	648
Kansas	31	224	386	827
Montana	NA	2	25	73
Wyoming	NA	NA	8	45
Colorado	7	24	81	112
New Mexico	NA	NA	10	28
Oklahoma	NA	NA	96	680
Washington	NA	24	64	206
Oregon	NA	8	41	126

Table 4.4 Number of State Banks in National Banking Era: 1880–1910 – *continued*

State (by region)	1880[a]	1890	1900	1910
California	58	131	237	364
Idaho	NA	NA	22	139
Utah	NA	2	20	68
Nevada	4	NA	9	17
Arizona	NA	6	17	36
Alaska	NA	NA	2	12
Hawaii	NA	NA	NA	10***
TOTAL	**841**	**2268**	**7444**	**12,482**

Source: Compiled from the *Annual Report of the Comptroller of the Currency* (1880: LXXXVII), (1890: 208), (1900: 298), (1910: 733–5).

Notes: * not available. ** includes stock savings banks. *** includes private banks. [a] 1880 data includes trust companies.

Figure 4.1 State and National Bank Failures During the National Bank Era

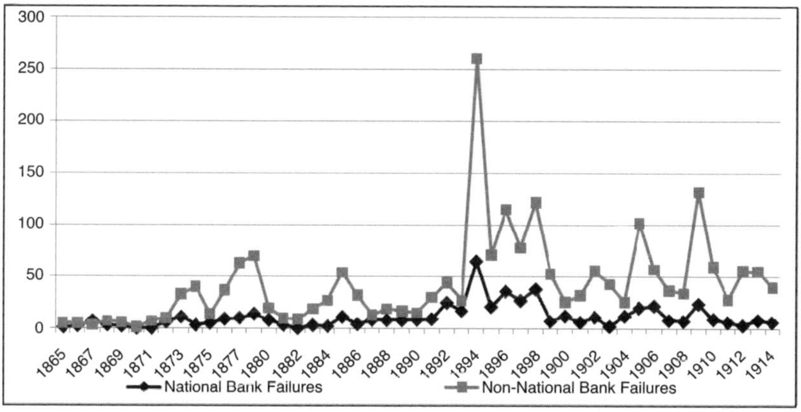

Source: *Annual Report of the Comptroller of the Currency* (1931: 6–8).

journals, he was able to estimate some critical data for analyzing these events. While the data in Figure 4.1 and in Tables 4.5, 4.6, and 4.7 paint a broad picture of bank stability during this period, the data found in Tables 4.8 and 4.9 are borrowed from Wicker and provide a more focused glimpse into bank performance at the time of the crises.

The postbellum crises shared many features of those crises in the antebellum era typically including an unexpected shock, a loss in depositor confidence, bank runs, suspensions and failures, and potentially a suspension in cash payments. Further, most of the national banking era

Table 4.5 Number of National Bank Failures by State: 1865–1910

State (by region)	1865–1870	1871–1880	1881–1890	1891–1900	1901–1910
New Hampshire	0	0	0	2	2
Vermont	0	0	2	2	3
Rhode Island	0	0	0	0	0
Massachusetts	0	0	0	5	11
Connecticut	0	0	2	0	2
New York	2	12	11	10	11
New Jersey	0	1	2	1	4
Pennsylvania	1	10	3	8	17
Maryland	0	0	0	1	0
DC	1	2	0	0	0
Virginia	0	3	1	1	0
West Virginia	0	0	0	0	1
North Carolina	0	0	1	3	1
South Carolina	0	0	1	5	1
Georgia	0	0	0	5	1
Florida	0	0	1	7	2
Alabama	1	0	1	4	3
Mississippi	1	0	0	1	0
Louisiana	1	2	0	2	0
Texas	0	1	1	21	10
Arkansas	0	1	2	1	0
Kentucky	0	0	0	3	3
Tennessee	1	0	1	5	0
Ohio	0	3	4	7	13
Indiana	0	5	2	5	4
Illinois	1	8	3	6	4
Michigan	0	0	1	12	3
Wisconsin	0	1	0	2	3
Minnesota	0	2	2	3	1
Iowa	1	2	1	7	5
Missouri	0	5	1	4	2
North Dakota	0	0	2	10	2
South Dakota	0	0	2	7	2
Nebraska	0	0	1	19	0
Kansas	0	3	8	24	2
Montana	0	2	1	11	1
Wyoming	0	0	0	2	0
Colorado	0	2	2	7	1
New Mexico	0	0	0	4	0
Oklahoma	0	0	0	1	7
Washington	0	0	0	23	2
Oregon	0	0	0	6	1
California	0	0	1	5	2
Idaho	0	0	0	1	0
Nevada	1	0	0	0	1
Utah	0	1	0	0	0
Arizona	0	0	0	0	1
TOTAL	**11**	**66**	**60**	**253**	**129**

Source: Compiled from the *Annual Report of the Comptroller of the Currency* (1910: 212–33).

Notes: The data of the failure represents the date the bank was placed in receivership. The Comptroller of the Currency defines failure as those banks placed in the hands of a receiver. Following Grossman (1994: 300) this is perhaps the best measure of failure because banks had the option of suspension and those that did end up in receivership were probably in a more dire financial position.

Table 4.6 Number of State Bank Failures by State: 1892–1909

State (by region)	1892	1893	1894	1895	1896	1897	1898	1899	1900
Maine	0	0	0	0	0	1	0	0	0
New Hampshire	0	0	0	0	0	1	0	0	0
Vermont	0	0	1	0	0	0	0	0	0
Massachusetts	0	0	0	0	0	0	0	0	0
Rhode Island	0	1	0	0	0	0	0	0	0
Connecticut	0	0	0	0	0	0	0	0	0
New York	1	6	2	1	0	2	0	0	0
New Jersey	0	1	0	0	0	0	0	0	0
Pennsylvania	0	2	1	0	0	0	0	0	0
Delaware	0	0	0	0	0	0	0	0	0
Maryland	0	0	0	0	0	0	0	0	0
Virginia	0	5	0	0	0	0	0	0	0
West Virginia	0	1	0	0	0	0	0	0	0
North Carolina	0	2	0	0	0	0	0	0	0
South Carolina	0	1	0	0	0	0	0	0	1
Georgia	0	3	0	0	0	2	0	0	0
Florida	0	2	2	0	0	1	0	0	0
Alabama	0	1	0	0	0	1	0	1	0
Mississippi	1	0	0	0	0	0	0	0	1
Louisiana	1	1	0	0	2	1	0	0	1
Texas	1	0	0	0	0	1	1	0	0
Arkansas	0	2	0	0	2	1	0	0	0
Kentucky	1	2	3	1	0	0	0	0	1
Tennessee	3	5	2	1	0	0	0	0	0
Ohio	0	3	0	1	0	0	0	0	0
Indiana	0	12	0	0	1	0	0	0	0
Illinois	0	0	0	0	1	1	0	1	1
Michigan	1	1	0	0	0	2	0	0	0
Wisconsin	1	13	0	1	0	3	3	1	0
Minnesota	0	15	0	1	5	4	0	0	1
Iowa	0	4	0	0	4	0	1	0	0
Missouri	1	8	2	10	9	8	0	0	0
North Dakota	0	0	0	0	0	0	0	0	0
South Dakota	0	0	0	0	0	0	0	0	1
Nebraska	4	10	2	18	17	6	0	0	0
Kansas	6	25	6	2	7	4	6	0	1
Montana	0	3	0	0	0	0	0	0	0
Wyoming	0	1	0	1	0	0	0	0	0
Colorado	0	9	0	0	0	1	0	0	0
New Mexico	0	0	0	0	0	0	0	0	0
Oklahoma	0	0	2	0	0	3	1	0	0
Washington	0	4	2	4	5	1	2	0	0
Oregon	0	4	1	0	0	0	0	0	1
California	0	19	0	0	1	0	0	2	0
Idaho	0	3	0	2	0	0	0	0	0
Utah	0	1	1	0	0	0	0	0	0
Nevada	0	0	0	0	0	0	0	0	0
Arizona	0	1	0	0	0	0	0	0	0
TOTAL	**21**	**171**	**27**	**44**	**54**	**44**	**14**	**5**	**9**

Source: Barnett (1911: 186–90).

Notes: * not available.

Table 4.6 Number of State Bank Failures by State: 1892–1909 – *continued*

State (by region)	1901	1902	1903	1904	1905	1906	1907	1908	1909
Maine	0	0	0	0	0	0	0	0	0
New Hampshire	0	0	0	0	0	0	0	0	0
Vermont	0	0	0	0	0	0	0	0	0
Massachusetts	0	0	0	0	0	0	0	0	0
Rhode Island	0	0	0	0	0	0	0	0	0
Connecticut	0	0	0	0	0	0	0	0	0
New York	0	1	0	2	2	0	0	7	0
New Jersey	0	0	0	0	0	0	0	0	0
Pennsylvania	0	0	0	2	0	0	0	2	2
Delaware	0	0	0	0	0	0	0	0	0
Maryland	1	1	0	1	0	0	0	0	0
Virginia	0	0	0	1	0	0	0	0	0
West Virginia	0	0	0	1	0	0	1	1	0
North Carolina	0	0	0	3	2	1	0	0	0
South Carolina	0	0	0	1	0	0	0	0	1
Georgia	0	2	1	0	1	0	0	2	0
Florida	0	0	1	0	0	0	0	0	0
Alabama	0	1	1	0	0	0	0	0	0
Mississippi	0	0	0	0	1	2	1	2	0
Louisiana	0	0	0	0	0	0	0	0	0
Texas	0	0	0	0	0	2	0	1	0
Arkansas	1	0	2	3	0	2	1	6	2
Kentucky	0	0	0	0	0	1	0	1	0
Tennessee	0	1	0	2	1	1	0	3	0
Ohio	0	1	0	4	2	1	0	2	2
Indiana	0	0	0	0	0	0	0	1	0
Illinois	0	0	0	1	0	0	1	0	1
Michigan	0	0	0	0	2	0	0	0	3
Wisconsin	0	0	0	2	1	0	0	0	0
Minnesota	0	0	0	1	0	0	0	0	1
Iowa	0	0	0	1	0	2	0	0	0
Missouri	0	0	0	0	1	1	0	1	0
North Dakota	0	1	0	0	0	1	0	0	1
South Dakota	1	0	0	3	0	0	1	0	0
Nebraska	1	2	1	0	0	0	1	0	0
Kansas	3	0	0	1	0	0	0	3	1
Montana	0	0	0	0	0	0	0	0	0
Wyoming	0	0	0	1	0	0	0	0	0
Colorado	0	1	0	1	0	0	0	0	0
New Mexico	0	0	0	0	0	0	0	0	0
Oklahoma	0	0	0	3	1	0	0	0	0
Washington	1	1	0	0	1	1	2	2	4
Oregon	0	0	0	0	0	0	0	1	1
California	0	1	0	0	0	0	0	3	0
Idaho	0	0	0	0	0	0	0	2	0
Utah	0	0	0	0	0	0	0	0	0
Nevada	0	0	0	0	0	0	0	2	0
Arizona	0	0	0	1	1	0	0	0	0
TOTAL	8	12	6	37	16	15	10	42	19

Source: Barnett (1911: 186–90).
Note: * not available.

Table 4.7 Aggregate Number and Assets of National and State Bank Failures: 1865–1910

Year	Number of National Bank Failures	Assets of National Bank Failures	Number of State Bank Failures	Assets of State Bank Failures
1865	1	0.1	5	0.2
1866	2	1.8	5	1.2
1867	7	4.9	3	0.2
1868	3	0.5	7	0.2
1869	2	0.7	6	0.1
1870	0	0	1	0.0
1871	0	0	7	2.3
1872	6	5.2	10	2.1
1873	11	8.8	33	4.6
1874	3	0.6	40	4.1
1875	5	3.2	14	9.2
1876	9	2.2	37	7.3
1877	10	7.3	63	13.1
1878	14	6.9	70	26.0
1979	8	2.6	20	5.1
1880	3	1.0	10	1.6
1881	0	0	9	0.6
1882	3	6.0	19	2.8
1883	2	0.9	27	2.8
1884	11	7.9	54	12.9
1885	4	4.7	32	3.0
1886	8	1.6	13	1.3
1887	8	6.9	19	2.9
1888	8	6.9	17	2.8
1889	2	0.8	15	1.3
1890	9	2.0	30	10.7
1891	25	9.0	44	7.2
1892	17	15.1	27	2.7
1893	65	27.6	261	54.8
1894	21	7.4	71	8.0
1895	36	12.1	115	11.3
1896	27	12.0	78	10.2
1897	38	29.1	122	17.9
1898	7	4.6	53	4.5
1899	12	2.3	26	7.8
1900	6	11.6	32	7.7
1901	11	8.1	56	6.4
1902	2	0.5	43	7.3
1903	12	6.8	26	2.2
1904	20	7.7	102	24.3
1905	22	13.7	57	7.0
1906	8	2.2	37	6.6
1907	7	5.4	34	13.0
1908	24	30.8	132	177.1
1909	9	3.4	60	15.8
1910	6	2.6	28	14.5

Source: *Annual Report of the Comptroller of the Currency* (1931: 6–8).
Note: Assets are in millions of dollars.

Table 4.8 Total Number of Bank Suspensions During National Banking Era Crises According to Institution

Crises Date	National Bank	State Bank	Savings Bank	Private Bank	Trust Company	Unclassified	Total
1873 (September)	16	11	7	59	4	4	101
1884 (May)	5	7	4	26	0	0	42
1890 (November)	1	3	1	13	0	o	18
1893 (May–August)	142	149	41	157	14	0	503
1907 (October–December)	11	33	4	10	15	0	73

Source: Wicker (2000: 4).

Table 4.9 Number of Bank Suspensions in New York City During National Banking Era Crises According to Institution

Crises Date	National Bank	State Bank	Savings Bank	Private Bank	Trust Company	Total
1873 (September)	0	1	0	34	2	37
1884 (May)	1	3	1	10	0	15
1890 (November)	0	1	0	9	0	10
1893 (May–August)	0	2	0	0	1	3
1907 (October–December)	0	6	1	2	4	13

Source: Wicker (2000: 5).

crises were associated with stock market declines.[15] The national banking era crises are chronicled next.

1873 crisis

After the Civil War, railroad expansion westward became a priority for large railroad companies and entrepreneurs alike. This desire to expand West was driven, in part, by the Pacific Railway Act which financed some of the expansion and by technological change that standardized rail production and made it more efficient.[16] Though some westward expansion was financed with federal funds, most was financed privately though financial intermediaries. Specifically, private banks financed the majority of railway expansion though commercial banks and trust companies also lent for railroad construction and expansion. The railroads ultimately had trouble financing this debt resulting in the lenders experiencing losses.[17] Since many of the lenders were private bankers, it is not surprising that they suffered the most suspensions (see Table 4.8). Indeed, as Table 4.8 indicates, only 27 national and state commercial banks had serious trouble during this crisis. Nonetheless, as word of the railroad financial problems spread, bank runs began in New York and quickly spread across the nation. Investors became nervous and market selling caused the stock market to close for ten days at the end of September.[18] This marked the first closing of the exchange since its inception.

In response to the crisis, the New York Clearinghouse used three tools to try and put an end to the panic and uncertainty. First, it issued Clearinghouse certificates. Second, it redistributed reserves to solvent banks experiencing runs and cash shortages. Third, because reserves were so low, on September 24, 1873 the Clearinghouse suspended conversion in New York and by the 27th this suspension spread nationwide. By the beginning of November the panic had subsided and the suspension of cash payments was lifted.

1884 crisis

The 1884 crisis was not as serious as the 1873 crisis from the perspective that far fewer suspensions took place (Tables 4.8 and 4.9). It also appears that depositor confidence was not shaken in any general way. Rather, deposit withdraws took place specifically at institutions with financial troubles primarily in New York and Pennsylvania. Thus, the 1884 crisis was also more concentrated than the 1873 event.

The surprise event, or shock, in May of 1884 was the announcement of a rather large bank failure in New York and the subsequent failure of a large brokerage house in the same city. The source of these failures appears to have been speculative and illegal activities by top management at these firms.[19] Soon after, the market reacted to these developments as nervous investors began selling. As additional private and commercial banks closed due to speculative dealings, market participants panicked with even more market selling.

With the stock market in crisis and an important large bank involved in these speculative dealings, the New York Clearinghouse took action so as to avoid any contagion of the panic. Specifically, they authorized loan certificates to the troubled bank and to other member banks in need of liquidity. Scholars have credited the swift and appropriate action of the Clearinghouse as crucial to averting a wide spread banking panic.[20]

1890 crisis

The third crisis of the national banking era was also largely contained to the New York area and, when measured by bank suspensions, was much less disruptive than the first crisis (see Tables 4.8 and 4.9). Like the 1884 event, the 1890 crisis was the result of speculative behavior that led to a significant decline in the stock market as investors responded to negative news.

The surprise event in 1890 came in November when a large brokerage house in New York failed without public warning. It became financially vulnerable when a vast portion of its security holdings lost value. In addition to selling in the stock market, the brokerage firm's banker then became susceptible to problems triggered by the collapse of the brokerage house. At this point, the New York Clearinghouse stepped in and issued loan certificates to the troubled bank as well as other member banks. The action of the Clearinghouse again averted a serious bank panic though the stock market lost significant value from the failures and speculation. Thus, the 1890 crisis was similar to the 1884 crisis in that both were really more stock market crises rather than banking crises due, in part, to the actions of the Clearinghouses. Further, in both instances, speculation played an important role in establishing panic conditions.

1893 crisis

Three years later, the U.S. banking sector experienced a much more serious crisis.[21] This time, over 500 bank suspensions developed (see Table 4.8) and more than 15,000 nonfinancial firms filed for bankruptcy making it perhaps the most devastating crisis of the national banking era.[22] Railroads were particularly hard hit with over 70 failures.[23] However, whereas the first three crises of this period originated in New York City, this time the crisis was outside of New York, in the interior of the country, and spread throughout the nation (Tables 4.5 and 4.6). As Table 4.8 indicates, there were 503 suspensions between May and August of 1893 and only three of these were in New York City (Table 4.9). Wicker (2000) compiled interesting bank suspension data by region during this particular crisis which is reproduced in Table 4.10. From this data, it is clear that the Western and Northwestern (what we know today as the Midwest) regions of the nation were hardest hit with bank suspensions both in terms of the number and liabilities of the banks involved.

Table 4.10 Banking Crisis of 1893: Suspensions and Liabilities by Region

Region	Number of Bank Suspensions	Percent of Total	Liabilities of Suspended Banks (in millions)	Percent of Total
New England	12	2	$10	7
Middle	22	4	7	5
Western	188	37	45	30
Northwestern	137	27	42	28
Southern	67	13	17	11
Pacific	68	14	27	18
Territories	9	2	1	1
Totals	503		149	

Source: Wicker (2000: 55).

Notes: The regional classification comes from *Bradstreet's* in which the Western region includes Ohio, Indiana, Illinois, Kentucky, Michigan, Missouri, Kansas, and West Virginia. The Northwestern region includes Minnesota, Iowa, Wisconsin, Nebraska, and North and South Dakota. The Pacific region was comprised of Washington, Idaho, Oregon, and California.

Whereas the previous national banking era crises tended to include many private bank suspensions, during this crisis national, state, and private bank suspensions each comprised just under one third of the total number of suspensions.[24] From this perspective, this crisis affected these different types of institutions more evenly, though the national and state chartered banks suspended in 1893 were much larger than were the private banks.

A defining characteristic of the 1893 crisis is that there was no single shock or surprise event that precipitated the nationwide run on both solvent and insolvent banks. In May of that year the stock market crashed in response to low gold reserves at the Treasury which made investors nervous about the Treasury's financial position.[25] The federal government was running a surplus so that government securities were in short supply. This generated a liquidity problem for banks since they could not issue additional banknotes. During these summer months, bank runs ensued throughout the nation in cities such as Kansas City, Omaha, Chicago, Spokane, Detroit, Louisville, Milwaukee, and Portland, Oregon to name a few. Banks cut back on loans as business conditions deteriorated, and in the case of loans that were made, banks typically required more collateral and usually lent to existing customers. Between January 1, 1893 and October 31, 1893, there were 584 total suspensions in the United States.[26] Of those, 171 had resumed operation by the last day in October while 413 had still not resumed operation.

However, most of the suspended banks reopened within the next few months. Further, total liabilities of the 584 suspensions equaled $169,185,791 while the assets amounted to $183,283,514.[27] This data indicates that many of the runs were at banks that were solvent. This, in turn, implies a loss in depositor confidence as another characteristic of this crisis.

In response, the New York Clearinghouse issued loan certificates in June of 1893 to add liquidity to the system. At least 12 other Clearinghouses followed with additional certificate issues. The Clearinghouses were also shipping reserves to interior banks to help them meet withdraws. In addition, there was a partial suspension of cash payments.

1907 crisis

Much like the first three national banking era crises, the 1907 crisis began in New York City with the collapse of two prominent brokerage houses followed quickly by runs on large trust companies in the city. However, the bank suspensions spread to the interior and most of these suspensions were state chartered banks (Table 4.8). Though in total there were only 73 suspensions resulting from the 1907 crisis versus over 500 during the 1893 episode, in the later crisis the total liabilities at suspended institutions exceeded the liabilities in the earlier crisis by over 20 percent.[28] Thus, though there were fewer suspensions in 1907, the size of the average suspension was much larger than in 1893. Another factor which distinguishes this crisis from others in this era is that it is the only panic that began in an intermediary outside the Clearinghouse system. In 1907 the bank crises began with the trust companies of New York, none of whom were members of the Clearinghouse at the time of the crisis. As is shown below, this had important implications for the nature of the crisis and for the reform debates that began in 1908.

The first banking crisis of the twentieth century began when an attempt to corner the stock of the United Copper Company failed, bringing down two important brokerage houses connected with the stock trades. When word spread that several bank officers were connected with the scam, bank runs ensued on those particular institutions. The New York Clearinghouse, fearing that the runs would spread, authorized loan certificates to those banks involved but found to be solvent. Nonetheless, a few days later additional runs took place on several large trust companies in New York City.[29] These runs followed investigations into the financial condition of the trusts and when it was announced that they were not solvent, depositors panicked. Trust companies were state

Table 4.11 Total Assets at National Banks and Trust Companies in New York City: 1896 and 1907

Date	National Banks in New York City	Trust Companies in New York City
1896	$577,924,838	$396,700,000*
1907	$1,364,729,602	$1,205,019,000

Source: Moen and Tallman (1999: 11).
Note: * indicates total assets for Trust Companies in the state of New York.

institutions and so were regulated by state level authorities. Typically, they operated under much less regulation than did state or national commercial banks. For example, they were allowed to invest directly in equities and to underwrite and distribute securities, they often did not have required reserves, and could invest, to some extent in real estate.[30] Thus, while the trust was competing against commercial bank business, they also had opportunities not afforded commercial bankers.

Trust companies, at least in New York, were not members of the Clearinghouse at this time. Because of this, trusts were perceived to have taken on greater risk and because they were nonmembers, the Clearinghouse decided against lending to the trusts.[31] Runs spread from trust companies in New York City to commercial banks, private banks, and trust companies in the interior during the final quarter of 1907. Clearinghouses across the country responded by issuing loan certificates as well as small denomination loan certificates to the public. Payments were also suspended for a time.

Crises summary

The five banking crises of the national banking era were different in terms of the number and size of actual failures or suspensions. Certainly, the 1893 crisis had the greatest impact from a shear numbers perspective though the suspensions of 1907 hit larger banking institutions more than the earlier crisis. National and state commercial bank suspensions were relatively insignificant in the first three crises. Despite these differences, these crises all shared an important characteristic. Like the 1860 crisis during the antebellum era, the Clearinghouses played an important role in minimizing the damage of each national banking era crisis.[32] Indeed, though there was a suspension of cash payments, the regular transaction functions of the payments system continued. This was due, in part, to the actions of the Clearinghouses as banks were able to provide cash substitutes such as Clearinghouse certificates and checks.

Regulatory response to crises

The series of panics during the national banking era led, not surprisingly, to many discussions of reform. How could the banking system be made more stable? Rather than attempt to alter existing legislative defects in the banking system, reform preserved the small bank structure of U.S. banking.[33] At the national level, reform took the form of creating a central bank. At the state level, the focus was on creating deposit insurance rather than fixing the instability of the existing structure.[34]

State deposit insurance

Empirical evidence indicates that those states that implemented a deposit insurance system were states predominately comprised of many small country banks and states opposed to branching.[35] The small, country bankers felt deposit insurance would protect them from uncertain market fluctuations and the associated danger of panics. Though branch banking offered an alternative method of stability to the country banker, it was opposed because small bankers feared the competition that would come with branching and their belief that larger banks with little concern for the local community would emerge.[36] Consequently, during this period in U.S. banking history, states embraced deposit insurance as a way to bring about stability.

Following the panic of 1907, five states established state deposit insurance and three more states established deposit insurance after the creation of the Federal Reserve System.[37] All five of the national banking era insurance programs suffered from asymmetric information problems, similar to those unsuccessful insurance programs of the antebellum era. For example, all five programs were safety funds that did not allow for special assessments, so the funds were undercapitalized and risk taking did not match with assessment. Further, membership was not compulsory for all banking institutions which resulted in serious adverse selection problems.[38] By 1931, all of the deposit insurance schemes had failed or ceased operation due to mounting bank failures and insufficient funds.

The Federal Reserve System

As mentioned earlier, the series of crises during the national banking period generated interest in banking reform. After the 1907 crisis, at the state level, deposit insurance was embraced as a means of creating stability. At the national level, interest and support grew for creating a central bank. Numerous scholars have studied the creation of the

Federal Reserve System. Many focus on the political economy of this important legislative development while others have focused on the performance and structure of banking and the Clearinghouses as a blueprint for the central bank.[39] This chapter considers whether the existing regulatory regime contributed to the creation of the central bank and, like the work of others, it also inquires as to the timing of the central bank's creation.

Contemporary legislators and economists alike agreed that the Clearinghouse system had been effective in quelling panics during the national banking era. At the same time, however, it was recognized that the Clearinghouse certificates issued during these crises were illegal. Consequently, discussions of reform often embraced the Clearinghouse structure coupled with a "legal" emergency currency. Emergency currency was made legal by placing its administration under the Secretary of the Treasury.[40] Thus, those involved in monetary reform recognized, on the one hand, the effectiveness of the Clearinghouse structure but, on the other hand, insisted that the federal government control currency to provide elasticity. As the Federal Reserve Act was debated in Congress it was clear that legislators insisted that the federal government control currency in the United States, despite the fact that the private market effectively issued emergency currency throughout the national banking era. As pointed out by Timberlake (1984: 292–3) this marked a crucial turning point in U.S. commercial banking because it substituted political influence for market discipline in the monetary arena.

During the antebellum era of banking, the federal government tried to establish a leadership role in commercial banking but was ultimately unsuccessful. Then the federal government attempted to reestablish itself through the creation of national banks and the Comptroller of the Currency. In terms of the number of national banks created, this was also an unsuccessful development as the number of state banks far exceeded national banks (see Tables 4.2 and 4.4). The end of the national banking era is marked by the creation of the Federal Reserve which, as shown above, was another attempt by the federal government to establish control over money and banking issues in the United States. Because the private Clearinghouses were used as a blueprint in creating the Federal Reserve, existing structures influenced the creation of the central bank. Further, existing regulation, such as the bond collateral requirement, destabilized banking which, in turn, was a rational for creating a central bank.[41] Thus, existing regulation did contribute to the creation of the Federal Reserve System.

As this chapter has established, the 1907 crisis was not the largest of the national banking era nor did it have the greatest impact on the macroeconomy.[42] So, why was it that a central bank emerged after the 1907 crisis and not before? Was there something unique about the 1907 crisis that made reform possible that was not feasible or desirable earlier? Recall that one unique feature of the 1907 crisis was that it began with the trust companies. That is, it began outside of the commercial banking sector with institutions that were not members of the Clearinghouse Associations. Since the trusts were not members, the Clearinghouses could not properly evaluate the riskiness of the trusts and, hence, did not lend to them when the crisis was still contained within the trusts companies themselves. The different experiences of the member and nonmember institutions during the 1907 crisis were striking.[43] Specifically, institutions that were members of a Clearinghouse system suffered substantially fewer demand deposit withdrawals than nonmember institutions.[44] This experience provided political support for the creation of a central bank. That is, if one believed that belonging to an organization with the authority to oversee the activities of its members and to assist members in times of need meant fewer runs and fewer failures, a central bank created in the image of the Clearinghouse made sense and garnered political support. Scholars have also argued that meaningful bank reform could not have transpired without the support of the New York banker.[45] The New York banker, prior to 1907 was not interested in a central bank since with all national banking era crises, their actions were able to stem runs and panic. However, with the 1907 crisis bankers became vulnerable to instability and crisis through nonmember institutions. Thus, because of the unique nature of the 1907 crisis, both political and banker support were in place for serious reform.

Assessment of regulation and stability

Both the creation of nationally chartered banks in 1864 and the creation of the Federal Reserve System in 1913 mark an increased presence of the federal government in commercial banking in the United States. Both of these developments were intended to increase the stability of banking. At the state level, several attempts to bring about stability resulted in the creation of deposit insurance schemes. At the same time, Clearinghouses became increasingly prominent as they attempted to bring about stability through their actions during times of crisis. In this chapter, we evaluate how successful each of these institutions were during the national banking era. Table 4.12 contains a summary of the

Table 4.12 Summary of Regulation and Its Impact on National and State Chartered Banks in the National Banking Era

Regulation	Description	Channel(s) Through Which Regulation Impacts Bank Stability	Conclusion from the Evidence
Bond Collateral Requirement	• Provision in the National Bank Act. • National banks required to purchase $100 in government debt for every $90 banknotes issued. • Resulted in inelastic currency.	• Decrease competition. • Change cost and revenue structure.	• Decrease stability to the extent that competition is desirable (Carlson and Mitchener (2005, 2009), Mengle (1990), Jayarathne and Strahan (1998)). • Inelastic currency creates instability when bond prices are volatile (Figure A.10).
$300 million restriction on national banknote issuance	• Provision in the National Bank Act. • Limited aggregate circulation of national banknotes to $300 million. • Resulted in a concentration of banks in the northeast region and an inelastic currency.	• Decrease competition.	• Decrease stability to the extent that competition is desirable (Table 4.13 and Table 4.14). • Nonbinding.
Capital requirements	• Provision in the National Bank Act. • Capital requirements varied by location. • Resulted in a barrier to entry because the requirements were greater for national banks so fewer banks opened.	• Decrease competition. • Decrease risk. • Change cost and revenue structure.	• Decrease stability to the extent that competition is desirable (Carlson and Mitchener (2005, 2009), Mengle (1990), Jayarathne and Strahan (1998)).

Table 4.12 Summary of Regulation and Its Impact on National and State Chartered Banks in the National Banking Era – *continued*

Regulation	**Description**	**Channel(s) Through Which Regulation Impacts Bank Stability**	**Conclusion from the Evidence**
Prohibited Mortgage Loans	• Provision in the National Bank Act. • Central city national banks prohibited from originating mortgage loans.	• Decrease competition.	• Decrease stability to the extent that competition is desirable (Carlson and Mitchener (2005, 2009), Mengle (1990), Jayarathne and Strahan (1998)).
Reserve Requirements	• Provision in the National Bank Act. • Reserve requirements varied by location. • Resulted in reserve pyramiding.	• Decrease risk. • Increase risk through pyramiding. • Change cost and revenue structure.	• Increase stability when reserves are available. • Decrease stability when banker could not meet reserve demand (Calomiris and Gorton (1991)). • Increase costs.
Prohibit or limit branching	• Creates many small banks with balance sheets that are tied to the local economy. • Resulted in barriers to entry.	• Decrease competition. • Limits geographic diversification.	• Branching for state banks increased stability through fewer failures and specie suspension (Tables 4.6 and 4.15).

Table 4.12 Summary of Regulation and Its Impact on National and State Chartered Banks in the National Banking Era – *continued*

Regulation	Description	Channel(s) Through Which Regulation Impacts Bank Stability	Conclusion from the Evidence
10 percent tax on state banknotes	• Provision in the 1865 Revenue Act. • Placed a 10 percent tax on all state banknotes. • Resulted in banks increasing their reliance on deposits to avoid the tax.	• Change cost and revenue structure.	• Decrease stability if tax compromises revenue and viability of bank. • Nonbinding.
State Deposit Insurance Schemes	• Five states adopted insurance in response to the 1907 crisis. • Resulted in the failure of all systems.	• Decrease competition. • Decrease risk of runs. • Increase risk taking.	• Increased stability to the extent that bank runs were reduced. • Decrease stability by reducing competition for depositors and the accompanying moral hazard.

Notes: There are five identified channels through which regulation may impact stability; 1) change risk taking; 2) limit diversification; 3) change cost and revenue structure; 4) change the structure of the market; and 5) change the nature of competition. See Chapter 2 for a discussion of each.

regulation of this era, its impact on stability, and the evidence used to substantiate the findings. The narrative that follows explains Table 4.12 in detail and adds an assessment of the performance of the Clearinghouses as well.

Assessment of the National Bank Act

As discussed earlier in this chapter, there were essentially six provisions in the 1864 National Bank Act that formed the regulatory structure of nationally chartered banks. First, the bond collateral requirement was a provision borrowed from free banking laws of the antebellum period. Just as this provision was destabilizing for free banks, it was equally destabilizing for national banks. The problem was that banks could not extend currency unless the federal government was selling bonds which leads to inelastic currency unable to respond to the needs of borrowers. At the same time, banks were more vulnerable to the health of the government since if the price of the bonds fell, the net worth of the bank fell as well. Figure A.10 contains the average yield to maturity on U.S. government debt and from this we can see that during most of the early national bank era, yields were falling so bond prices were generally rising. Finally, requiring bankers to purchase government bonds meant those funds were not available for profitable uses which may also compromise the stability of the bank. Indeed, by 1910 approximately $750 million was devoted to the purchase of U.S. bonds to secure circulation.[46] Interestingly, in 1893 the American Bankers' Association (ABA) called for the deregulation of the bond collateral requirement and the creation of interstate branching to engender bank stability. However, the unit banker reacted powerfully against the branch banking allowance fearing that they would be unable to compete so the ABA resolution died.

The second provision of the 1864 act restricted national banknote issue to $300 million. This provision, like the bond collateral requirement, contributed to the inelasticity of currency since there was a ceiling on the amount of circulating notes. In addition, since the notes were distributed on a first come first serve basis, this provision lead to an increased concentration of national banks in the northeast region of the country and created barriers to entry elsewhere. Table 4.2 indicates that national banks were initially clustered in the Northeast from Maine south to Maryland and Delaware. Growth of national banks was slow in the South and West regions of the country, in part because of this regulatory provision. Table 4.1 indicates the dollar value of outstanding banknotes by state and again it is clear that most of the notes

Table 4.13 Deposits at National Banks in National Banking Era: 1870–1910

State (by region)	1870	1880	1890	1900	1910
Maine	$4,855	$8,184	$13,364	$21,834	$37,307
New Hampshire	$2,318	$3,944	$7,779	$12,285	$18,469
Vermont	$2,664	$5,038	$7,708	$10,857	$17,092
Massachusetts	$64,133	$110,042	$167,167	$213,179	$282,423
Rhode Island	$5,941	$8,909	$16,673	$17,405	$27,739
Connecticut	$11,982	$21,147	$29,534	$42,912	$56,318
New York	$214,715	$307,495	$357,020	$560,820	$1,024,953
New Jersey	$14,727	$24,525	$46,978	$73,462	$162,996
Pennsylvania	$68,553	$119,561	$211,716	$380,756	$675,173
Delaware	$1,326	$3,057	$4,420	$6,253	$10,510
Maryland	$12,878	$21,432	$30,956	$42,941	$77,191
DC	$1,362	$2,155	$10,626	$18,211	$23,126
Virginia	$3,593	$6,690	$14,309	$20,473	$69,821
West Virginia	$2,069	$2,040	$5,262	$15,549	$42,731
North Carolina	$1,562	$2,883	$4,673	$7,477	$23,081
South Carolina	$961	$2,586	$3,511	$5,172	$15,492
Georgia	$1,682	$2,012	$6,335	$10,865	$37,739
Florida	NA*	$157	$3,364	$6,435	$25,837
Alabama	$536	$1,319	$7,025	$10,938	$28,129
Mississippi	$0	$0	$1,806	$3,879	$10,535
Louisiana	$1,446	$8,478	$14,784	$20,308	$30,138
Texas	$1,006	$2,081	$30,450	$49,749	$145,249
Arkansas	$104	$265	$2,235	$3,102	$12,526
Kentucky	$1,859	$8,510	$17,189	$27,755	$52,631
Tennessee	$2,831	$6,586	$15,121	$22,083	$49,948
Ohio	$21,046	$46,773	$88,220	$158,018	$284,212
Indiana	$7,965	$19,871	$30,906	$57,728	$131,113
Illinois	$21,608	$49,392	$102,696	$181,866	$374,082
Michigan	$6,282	$18,295	$38,659	$54,065	$107,399
Wisconsin	$3,865	$9,759	$23,648	$62,733	$118,479
Minnesota	$2,985	$8,918	$31,000	$45,805	$153,123
Iowa	$5,248	$11,608	$26,800	$49,041	$107,462
Missouri	$5,826	$8,391	$45,011	$64,449	$139,093
North Dakota	NA	NA	$3,810	$5,016	$29,005
South Dakota	NA	NA	$4,075	$6,081	$28,416
Nebraska	$1,192	$3,724	$26,152	$32,917	$87,663
Kansas	$748	$2,548	$20,685	$29,195	$67,846
Montana	$118	$1,102	$12,807	$13,360	$31,563
Wyoming	NA	$535	$2,694	$3,948	$12,461
Colorado	$1,553	$8,288	$26,326	$51,214	$85,323
New Mexico	NA	$591	$2,301	$3,558	$11,831
Oklahoma	NA	NA	$169	$2,956	$38,817
Washington	NA	$292	$14,341	$20,934	$82,957
Oregon	$266	$984	$9,843	$11,782	$46,680
California	NA	$3,873	$18,236	$35,195	$202,533
Idaho	$69	$128	$1,398	$3,799	$16,700
Utah	$148	$944	$4,442	$5,072	$14,966
Nevada	$0	$65	$245	$433	$5,727
Arizona	NA	NA	$293	$2,076	$6,225
Alaska	NA	NA	NA	$118	$1,094
Hawaii	NA	NA	NA	NA	$1,305

Source: Compiled from the *Annual Report of the Comptroller of the Currency* (1910: 371–401).

Notes: * not available.

Table 4.14 Deposits at State Banks in National Banking Era: 1880–1910

State (by region)	1880[a]	1890	1900	1910
Maine	$2,340	NA*	NA	NA
New Hampshire	$36,003	$24,717	$989,536	$5,871,262
Vermont	$1,607,553	NA	NA	NA
Massachusetts	$1,323,634	NA	NA	NA
Rhode Island	$3,611,242	$1,229,596	$720,580	$2,188,926
Connecticut	$3,767,165	$4,036,279	$7,145,744	$9,006,797
New York	$19,581,388	$183,139,592	$251,059,315	$431,219,848
New Jersey	$2,973,119	$5,667,583	$8,144,031	$13,694,751
Pennsylvania	$10,072,689	$39,467,922	$73,345,813	$153,757,559
Delaware	$917,742	$987,265	$1,685,302	$2,110,791
Maryland	$441,056	$2,954,287	$7,106,607	$34,325,522
DC	NA	NA	NA	NA
Virginia	$5,137,229	$13,767,424	$22,451,581	$40,128,783
West Virginia	$3,189,199	$3,638,021	$18,999,142	$50,102,693
North Carolina	$1,447,416	$2,552,817	$6,345,312	$27,013,823
South Carolina	$611,067	$1,507,985	$3,263,144	$24,567,442
Georgia	$4,341,983	$11,090,547	$22,009,164	$35,536,158
Florida	NA	$559,749	$3,489,436	$18,672,967
Alabama	$1,012,426	$1,237,574	$4,588,607	$19,547,928
Mississippi	$1,441,669	$4,321,263	$12,547,103	$30,273,472
Louisiana	$4,632,122	$7,486,897	$12,683,333	$54,216,850
Texas	$2,280,131	$760,292	NA	$27,573,308
Arkansas	$412,310	$1,107,743	$4,464,013	$18,939,951
Kentucky	$5,902,969	$27,004,077	$32,295,874	$48,757,767
Tennessee	$3,050,686	$7,437,181	$7,303,710	$30,879,863
Ohio	$3,132,931	$15,988,908	$85,157,634	$149,651,510
Indiana	$2,169,517	$4,913,915	$16,798,432	$57,416,064
Illinois	$3,228,683	$10,076,217	$169,203,991	$151,761,388
Michigan	$3,378,821	$3,905,718	$102,448,609	$197,045,246
Wisconsin	$2,654,682	$30,648,161	$45,929,285	$115,898,260
Minnesota	$1,911,978	$18,975,459	$28,130,738	$91,002,851
Iowa	$6,100,367	$9,437,205	$32,938,940	$76,818,707
Missouri	$10,360,654	$60,932,254	$80,563,205	$173,534,260
North Dakota	NA	$439,195	$5,741,792	$37,951,307
South Dakota	NA	$1,634,634	$5,322,384	$50,851,230
Nebraska	$480,354	$13,494,436	$25,256,035	$72,472,623
Kansas	$1,810,416	$10,807,780	$28,491,889	$86,473,514
Montana	NA	$300,244	$6,066,057	$12,541,753
Wyoming	NA	NA	$627,381	$4,555,843
Colorado	$545,512	$4,046,355	$8,136,722	$10,249,416
New Mexico	NA	NA	$1,688,896	$4,036,995
Oklahoma	NA	NA	$3,542,224	$44,963,206
Washington	NA	$4,149,483	$7,308,687	$51,142,835
Oregon	NA	$551,492	$3,301,580	$36,888,818
California	$11,269,822	$50,714,988	$85,881,584	$127,142,589
Idaho	NA	NA	$537,902	$17,414,104
Utah	NA	$354,824	$17,434,051	$23,274,088
Nevada	$98,560	NA	$1,474,337	$6,804,227
Arizona	NA	$322,167	$2,296,908	$10,643,075
Alaska	NA	NA	NA	$1,321,010
Hawaii	NA	NA	$1,818,672	$12,789,742

Source: Compiled from the *Annual Report of the Comptroller of the Currency* (1880: LXXXVII), (1890: 211), (1900: 545), (1910: 736–7).

Notes: * not available. [a] 1880 data includes trust companies.

were in the Northeast banks. Further, the provision limited competition outside of the Northwest. Lower competition means lower interest on deposits so that we would expect to find fewer deposits outside the Northeast. Table 4.13 shows that deposits at national banks were much lower in the South and in the West. At the same time, however, deposits at state banks (Table 4.14) in the South and Midwest were comparable or greater than those at state banks in the Northeast with the exception of New York and Pennsylvania. This data suggests that the note restriction provision added to bank instability to the extent that competition in banking is desirable. However, this provision and its impact on stability was relatively short lived because of its 1875 repeal.[47]

The third provision of the 1864 Act, minimum capital requirements, had an impact on stability similar to that of restricted banknotes. The higher capital requirements of nationally chartered banks created reluctance on the part of existing state chartered bankers to convert their charters.[48] Further, high capital requirements made national banking more expensive thus erecting a barrier to entry that lead to less bank competition in rural areas as bankers were reluctant to open a more expensive institution along side a state bank. There is data to indicate that the rural banks charged higher interest rates than other banks because there was less competition due to, in part, the high capital requirements.[49]

The National Bank Act of 1864 also prohibited or limited most national banks from extending mortgage and other real estate loans. State banks were not similarly regulated so, like the previous two provisions, this restriction limited interest in national banks and limited competition in rural regions of the country. The evidence is similar to the capital requirement and restriction on banknotes (see Table 4.12).

A primary consequence of the fourth provision of the National Bank Act, required reserves, was reserve pyramiding. Many nationally chartered banks would deposit their reserves at either a reserve city bank or in central reserve cities because these deposits earned interest. Thus, it was more profitable for the country bank to make an interbank deposit than to hold vault reserves. Central reserve and reserve city banks would then use these deposits to extend call loans which were short-term loans, payable on demand, made to those buying securities on margin. Thus, from the reserve banks' perspective, they would pay one interest rate for the reserve funds and turn around and lend it out at a higher interest rate to those engaged in equity trading. The problem with this pyramid of reserves came when country bankers demanded their reserves in cash and the reserve city banks could not meet those demands unless they called in their call loans which, in turn, hurt equity values. Indeed, according to one financial historian: "The inverted pyramid...and its intimate connection to the call loan market are widely regarded as key elements in financial crises that punctuated the era."[50] Evidence of the fragility caused by the required reserve practices of this period can be seen in the declining stock values that preceded and followed all of the bank crises in the national banking era.[51]

Finally, nationally chartered banks were not allowed to establish branches either within a state or between states. At the same time, many states prohibited branching for state banks and even in those states that afforded branching opportunities, few banks actually participated. Table 4.15 indicates the state branching laws for selected dates and shows that, in 1896, of the 48 states, 15 prohibited branching and 11 did not legally specify which typically meant banks could not branch. Thus, approximately 54 percent of the states did not allow for intrastate branching. Figure 4.2 illustrates the extent to which banks participated in branching during the national banking era. From this, it is seen that throughout the entire national banking era, there were fewer than 500 branches in the entire country.

There is no agreement in the literature about why states that allowed branching witnessed so little branching in the immediate postbellum era. In the years preceding, and immediately following, the passage of the National Bank Act, there was little serious discussion about branching in the United States.[52] However, with the series of crises that marked this period, discussion of bank and monetary reform often surfaced. Interestingly, it was not until 1894 that a proposal was put before Congress which embraced branching as a solution to the failures and runs. Before the turn of the century, several other proposals also surfaced but they were always tied to other reform issues. This created confusion for the public and led government officials who were in favor of branching to oppose the bills because of the other provisions. Thus, for a brief period, policymakers and bankers were interested in allowing national bank branching but nothing came from the discussions. Then with the turn of the century came a change in policy attitude. The new Comptroller of the Currency and the Secretary of the Treasury both opposed branching and, at the same time, the nation, fearing industrial concentration, was embracing antitrust laws. Both of these developments hurt any further progress on the branching front. Further, the small, unit banker possessed most of the political banking power during this era and this banker, not surprisingly, opposed branching fearing the competition that would inevitably result.[53]

This discussion has established that there was little in the way of branching during the national banking era because of the political

Table 4.15 State Law Regarding Branching for Selected Years

State	1896	1910	1924
Maine	Branching Permitted*	Branching Permitted*	Branching Permitted*
New Hampshire	Branching Prohibited	No Law Specified	No Law Specified
Vermont	Branching Permitted	No Law Specified	No Law Specified
Massachusetts	Branching Prohibited	Branching Prohibited*	Branching Permitted*
Rhode Island	Branching Prohibited	Branching Permitted	NA
Connecticut	Branching Prohibited	Branching Prohibited	NA
New York	Branching Prohibited	Branching Permitted*	Branching Permitted*
New Jersey	Branching Permitted*	No Law Specified	No Law Specified
Pennsylvania	Branching Prohibited	Branching Prohibited*	Branching Prohibited*
Delaware	Branching Permitted	Branching Permitted*	Branching Permitted
Maryland	No Law Specified	No Law Specified	Branching Permitted
Virginia	Branching Permitted	No Law Specified	Branching Permitted
West Virginia	Branching Prohibited	No Law Specified	Branching Permitted
North Carolina	Branching Permitted	No Law Specified	Branching Permitted
South Carolina	Branching Permitted*	No Law Specified	Branching Permitted
Georgia	NA**	Branching Permitted	NA
Florida	Branching Permitted	Branching Permitted	Branching Prohibited
Alabama	NA	No Law Specified	Branching Prohibited
Mississippi	Branching Permitted	Branching Prohibited	Branching Permitted*
Louisiana	Branching Permitted	Branching Permitted*	Branching Permitted*
Texas	NA	Branching Prohibited	Branching Prohibited
Arkansas	Branching Permitted*	No Law Specified	Branching Prohibited
Kentucky	No Law Specified	No Law Specified	No Law Specified*
Tennessee	Branching Permitted	Branching Permitted*	Branching Permitted
Ohio	Branching Permitted	No Law Specified	Branching Permitted*
Indiana	Branching Prohibited	No Law Specified	Branching Permitted*
Illinois	Branching Prohibited	No Law Specified	Branching Prohibited
Michigan	Branching Permitted*	No Law Specified	NA
Wisconsin	Branching Permitted	Branching Prohibited	Branching Prohibited
Minnesota	Branching Prohibited	No Law Specified	Branching Prohibited
Iowa	Branching Prohibited	No Law Specified	No Law Specified
Missouri	Branching Prohibited	Branching Prohibited	Branching Prohibited
North Dakota	No Law Specified	No Law Specified	No Law Specified
South Dakota	Branching Permitted*	No Law Specified	No Law Specified
Nebraska	Branching Prohibited	No Law Specified	No Law Specified
Kansas	No Law Specified	No Law Specified	No Law Specified
Montana	No Law Specified	No Law Specified	No Law Specified
Wyoming	Branching Prohibited	No Law Specified	Branching Permitted*
Colorado	Branching Prohibited	Branching Prohibited	Branching Prohibited
New Mexico	No Law Specified	No Law Specified	Branching Prohibited
Oklahoma	No Law Specified	No Law Specified	No Law Specified
Washington	No Law Specified	Branching Permitted*	Branching Prohibited
Oregon	No Law Specified	Branching Permitted*	NA
California	Branching Permitted	Branching Permitted*	Branching Permitted
Idaho	No Law Specified	No Law Specified	Branching Prohibited
Nevada	Branching Permitted	Branching Prohibited	Branching Prohibited
Arizona	No Law Specified	Branching Permitted*	Branching Permitted
Utah	Branching Permitted	No Law Specified	Branching Prohibited

Source: Dhawan (1996).

Notes: * restrictions apply. ** not available. Also note that according to Barnett (1911: 136) if the state did not specify branching rules it was meant to mean that branching was unlawful. Also note that according to Barnett (1911: 136) even if the state allowed for branching, in most states additional capital was required for the branch and branch openings required permission of state authorities. This explains in part, according to Barnett, why there was little branching in the immediate postbellum era.

Figure 4.2 Number of Operating Branches Between 1895 and 1926

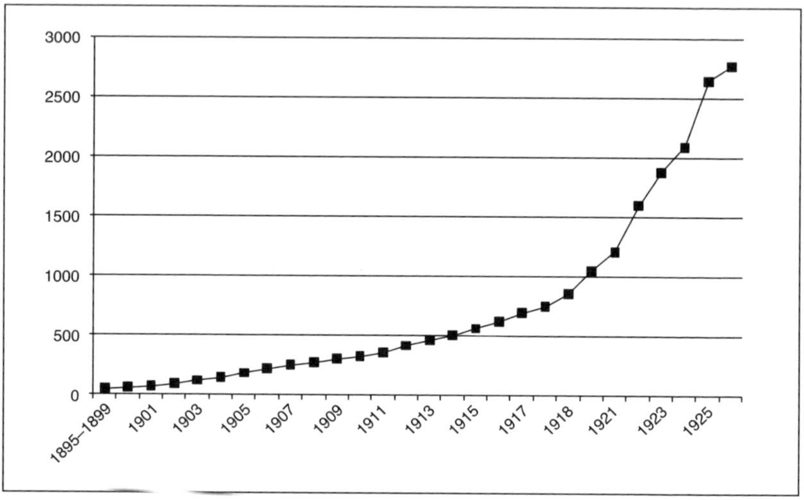

Source: *Federal Reserve Bulletin*, various years.

environment and because of the opposition from the unit banker. This despite the fact that most contemporary economists and political leaders recognized the stabilizing benefits of branching. Theoretically, the ban on branching creates more small banks with undiversified portfolios since their borrowers and lenders come from the immediate community. This means the banks' fortune is directly tied to the fortune of the local economy in both good times and bad times. How can we know if branching is indeed destabilizing? Based on the argument above, states without branching, *ceteris paribus*, should witness more failures than branching states. Data on branching laws and failures for state banks may provide important evidence (Table 4.6 and 4.15). If, for present purposes, we define a state banking situation to be unstable if ten or more banks fail in one year, Table 4.6 indicates that seven states were unstable during the early years of the national banking era. Of these seven, five states prohibited branching and another, Wisconsin, prohibited branching sometime between 1897 and 1910. Only California may be characterized as unstable and with branching. However, in California, prior to 1900, there was only one bank with branches and by 1908, there were only eight branches in San Francisco and 11 more outside the city.[54] Further, statewide branching laws were not passed in California until 1909 so while there was instability in the state, there was virtually no branching during the national bank era. Thus the evidence supports the theory that prohibitions on branching may increase instability in banking by limiting competition and forcing banks to hold undiversified assets.[55]

The above analysis focuses on state bank failures and branching. We cannot do the same analysis for national banks since they were prohibited from branching in all states. However, if one compares the performance of national banks in the United States, who were prohibited from branching, with the performance of similar banks in Canada who were allowed to branch, again the conclusion must be that branching stabilizes banking. As evidence, consider that between 1870 and 1909, the failure rate for national banks in the U.S. was 0.36 percent while the failure rate for Canadian banks was less than 0.1 percent.[56]

The evidence presented above suggests that the provisions of the National Bank Act tended to destabilize commercial banking. Given that this era saw more crises with more failures than the antebellum era it seems clear that the 1864 legislation meant to engender stability was not terribly successful. A general theme that transcends each individual regulatory provision of the National Bank Act is that collectively these provisions encouraged the growth of the small, unit banker which added to general instability. With inadequate portfolio diversity, these small banks could not take advantage of any scale economies and were vulnerable to any local economic downturn which, because the economy was still highly agrarian, was frequent.

Assessment of the 1865 Revenue Act

As was mentioned earlier, the 1865 Revenue Act placed a ten percent tax on all state banknotes (notes issued by both free banks and by state banks). Thus state chartered and free banks either had to pay the tax, rely less on banknotes as a source of funds, convert from state charters to national charters, or close their doors. As Table 4.3 indicates, the regulation was successful in reducing the importance of the state banker as most banks either closed or converted to national charters immediately following the 1865 act. However, a different picture is painted if one considers the period between the 1863 creation of national banks and the 1865 tax on state banknotes. During this small window, only 169 state banks converted to a national charter versus the 731 that converted between November of 1864 and December of 1865.[57] In other words, state banks were reluctant to convert to a national charter prior to the tax on their banknotes.

It is interesting to consider the number of state and free banks in operation prior to the 1865 tax and compare that with the years immediately following the act. Table 4.3 indicates the number of state chartered and free banks in operation just prior to or in 1865, the number of closures and conversions for the earliest date after the Revenue Act, and the percentage of banks that converted or closed. Several observations may be made. First, it is clear that the act did go a long way, at least temporarily, to reducing the number and influence of both the state and free banks. Unfortunately, the data combines the state chartered and free banks so it is not possible to determine how many, if any, of the remaining banks were free banks and how many were state banks.[58] Nonetheless, the reduction in number was substantial throughout the nation. Second, four states did much better than the others in terms of maintaining state banks after the tax. Mississippi, Louisiana, Arkansas, and Kentucky had substantially fewer conversions or closures than did the other states. Thus, this cluster of southern states managed to more successfully avoid closure or conversion.

At the same time, it is interesting to note that the number of state banks increased sharply following the clear decline immediately following the passage of the Revenue Act (see Figure 3.2). Why did the number of state banks decline rapidly after 1863 only to reappear in great numbers in the years to follow? According to several scholars, it is because the use of deposits and checks gained popularity and acceptance so that banks had a source of funds without issuing expensive notes.[59] Prior to 1865, the use of deposits was extremely limited, particularly in the countryside so that banks relied heavily on note issuance as a source of funds.

State bankers were unwilling to convert their charters as legislators had hoped. According to the Comptroller of the Currency at that time, Hugh McCulloch, state banks were fearful that the national system would be more unstable and more prone to wildcat banking than the state system. Further, many state bankers had established reputations and established clientele that they feared losing through a national charter. Scholars have also argued that state banks were reluctant to convert to a national charter because of the additional regulation associated with such a change.

The conventional financial historical analysis of this tax argues that it was necessary to improve the quality of banknotes. Proponents of this view believed that the quality of state banknotes varied too extensively causing confusion and loss amongst its users. It has also been argued rather extensively that another reason for the tax was to boost demand for federal debt because nationally chartered banks were required to purchase federal government bonds. However, a more critical consideration of the act and the circumstances of American banking in 1865 calls into question the merits of conventional historical analysis.

The charge against the state banknotes system was that the quality of notes was too variable. One measure of quality is the rate of discount on state banknotes. Analysis of the discount status of state banknotes across the country finds that discounts were rather small though regional differences were apparent.[60] Though state notes were often discounted, particularly if the note was used in exchange a far distance from its issue, the extent of the discount was small, particularly compared to discounting early in the history of American banking. The discount represented a known risk to the note holder: the loss in currency value in distance or interstate exchange. This is not unlike the currency risk facing international travelers today with fluctuations in foreign exchange rates. Thus, the evidence indicates that quality was not an important issue in the taxation of the state banknote. Indeed, it has been pointed out that during the congressional debates surrounding the tax, little was actually said about quality issues.[61]

If the issue was not note quality, there must have been some other rationale for the tax. Selgin (2000) makes a compelling case that actually there were too many applications for new national bank charters so that the demand for federal debt was never lacking. Because there was a $300 million quota on national banknotes, the Treasury knew it would have to limit the number of national charters it granted. A large demand for new national bank charters, rather than conversions, meant that there would be the $300 million in national notes *in addition to* the circulating state notes. The Treasury wanted the state banks to convert to national charters thereby *replacing* state notes with national notes. When the state banks showed little interest in the conversion, the Treasury knew immediately that inflation posed a serious threat. It was this inflationary threat that prompted legislatures into taxing the state banknote.[62] Getting rid of the state bank would eliminate the state banknote and, in turn, reduce the danger of inflation. In this way, the state banks were used as scapegoats because the Treasury needed someone to blame for inflationary pressures and for the wartime financial policy of issuing greenbacks and selling bonds to national banks.[63]

The 1865 Revenue Act was perhaps temporarily stabilizing since it reduced the number of small and free banks. Indeed, 1571 state banks converted to national banks between 1863 and 1910.[64] One may argue that eliminating these small institutions would add stability to banking but the reduction in numbers was only temporary. Table 4.4 indicates that between 1880 and 1910 the number of state banks grew 1384 percent.

Onerous regulation on national banks and an increased reliance on deposits rather than banknotes kept the state banker a vital member of commercial banking. The folly of the 1865 Revenue Act is that the federal government, at that time, clearly misunderstood the functioning of commercial banks. Because the banks were relying heavily on deposits rather than banknotes as a source of funds, the Act was ultimately ineffective.

Assessment of state deposit insurance

As discussed in the previous chapter, deposit insurance may be both stabilizing and destabilizing. Deposit insurance often engenders confidence amongst depositors and in the process allays the concerns that lead to runs on banks during times of uncertainty. At the same time, however, there are well known information asymmetries associated with deposit insurance that encourage bank risk taking and minimize depositor monitoring. In the case of state deposit insurance during the national banking era the five insurance schemes were all ultimately undercapitalized. This means that the potential stabilizing impact of deposit insurance fails. At the same time, the structure of the insurance programs led to moral hazard and adverse selection problems discussed earlier. As one scholar remarked on deposit insurance during this era: "State deposit insurance schemes all ended in dismal failure. They had contributed to the rapid growth of many small and vulnerable unit banks in the least economically diversified areas of the country."[65]

In the five states that created deposit insurance during this era, all were no branching states except for South Dakota which initially had limited insurance and then no insurance sometime between 1897 and 1910. Further, the data in Tables 4.5 and 4.6 indicate that three of the five deposit insurance states, Texas, Kansas, and Nebraska had substantially more failures than the average.[66] It is not clear if these failures are the result of branching prohibitions, other regulatory constraints, or because of increased risk taking due to the insurance. Nonetheless, one cannot discount the insurance as a contributor to the instability.

Assessment of Clearinghouse Associations

Clearinghouse Associations were able to effectively solve several important problems in commercial banking during the national bank era. First, they were able to minimize some asymmetric information problems.[67] Since member banks were subject to periodic audits and restrictions to limit moral hazard, the public was able to learn something about the health of member banks. Second, by issuing certificates and pooling reserves, the Clearinghouses were able to provide some relief to the inelastic currency problems discussed earlier. By minimizing these two problems, asymmetric information and inelastic currency, the Clearinghouse promoted confidence amongst the public in member banks.

As a consequence of this confidence, member banks performed much better than nonmember banks. For example, member banks experienced far fewer runs than nonmember banks during crisis.[68] This is because depositors knew more about the health of a member bank than a nonmember bank because of the Clearinghouse Association. Other research uses balance sheet data for both member and nonmember institutions from New York and Chicago to determine if membership explained changes in demand deposits during the 1907 crisis.[69] The empirical analysis reveals that the contraction of demand deposits was significantly smaller at member institutions than nonmember institutions. This suggests that the public was aware of the benefits of Clearinghouse membership and knew that member banks were either more solvent or had the potential to be more solvent given the support of the Association.

In terms of the inelasticity of currency, during the 1893 and 1907 crises Clearinghouses issued certificates not only to member banks but also directly to the public.[70] This smaller denomination paper essentially functioned as regular currency even though the Clearinghouse had no legal ground for issuing paper money.[71] However, given the crises, the federal government ignored the legality issue as these certificates played an important role in maintaining liquidity and recapturing confidence in the banking system. Finally, as discussed earlier in this chapter, the Clearinghouses redistributed reserves during several of the bank crises which also contributed to depositor confidence and added elasticity to the currency problem.

Thus, while the behavior of the Clearinghouse Associations had a stabilizing impact on banks both during crisis and noncrisis times, they could have been even *more* effective had certain legal restrictions not been in place. Specifically, had their ability to issue emergency currency been legal, they may have been able to provide more liquidity to the system during crises.[72] In addition, branch restrictions reduced the Clearinghouses effectiveness by keeping them from branching and reaching economies of scale.[73] Further, the branch restrictions made member banks inherently more fragile which, in turn, made it harder for the Clearinghouses to provide stability.

Concluding remarks

Commercial banking in the United States during the postbellum era was, in some ways, similar to the antebellum era. Both epochs witnessed several crises in banking and both witnessed the federal government take action to become more involved in the business of banking. However, the presence of the federal government was relatively fleeting in the antebellum era whereas the postbellum era saw the federal government successfully establish a permanent role for itself. Further, this role became larger as the national banking era progressed because the number of nationally chartered banks increased and because of the creation of the Federal Reserve System at the end of the era.

The increased federal presence manifested itself, in part, as an increase in regulatory restrictions, particularly on national banks. However, it is equally clear that the regulatory constraints on national banks could have been greater had the state bank been phased out. That is, once the state banks survived and flourished following the 1865 Revenue Act, the Comptroller recognized that to remain competitive with the state banks, regulation may have to become more relaxed. Indeed, between the state regulators and the Comptroller there developed a "competition in laxity" in terms of regulation with each group interested in maintaining their place in the market.[74] National banks could not afford to be burdened with too much regulation or they would be unable to compete with the state banker. In this way, while the national bank era had more regulation than the antebellum era, the growth in regulation remained relatively contained.

Nonetheless, the state charter was often preferred to the national charter and thus, the era witnessed a tremendous growth in the number of small, state banks. At the same time, because of limits on branching, many of these state banks were not properly diversified which made them more fragile and vulnerable to economic downturns. Thus, as established above, the regulatory restrictions tended to have a destabilizing impact on commercial banks during the national banking era, despite the intentions of legislation to improve stability.

Unfortunately, rather than try to create a more stable environment by removing the regulatory restrictions that were causing the instability, policymakers and regulators moved toward more government in the form of a central bank. Thus, the end of the national banking era was an important turning point in commercial banking because public institutions replaced private institutions as the Federal Reserve essentially supplanted Clearinghouse Associations. As the next chapter demonstrates, the new central bank would fail its first real test to stabilize commercial banking when the largest banking crisis in U.S. history occurred in the early 1930s.

5
Era of Instability and Change: 1913–1944

Introduction to the era of instability and change

As demonstrated in Chapters 3 and 4, the national banking era was an extension of the antebellum banking era in terms of the increasing instability in banking and the growth in federal regulation. This era marks another extension of the historical trend in commercial banking to become both more regulated and more unstable. As this chapter demonstrates, between 1913 and 1944, commercial banking in the United States witnessed an increase in the severity of bank crises, a tremendous number of bank failures and, in response, a significant increase in the federal regulation of commercial banks.

The macroeconomic backdrop to the banking industry in the 1920s and 1930s is a famous tale of two extremely different experiences. The 1920s enjoyed tremendous productive, entrepreneurial, and socio-economic gains for the people of America. As the name implies, the Roaring Twenties saw a surge in manufacturing and innovation; RGDP expanded at an impressive rate (Figure A.11), while unemployment was consistently under five percent with the exception of the sharp recession in 1920–1921 (Figure A.12). Americans were driving cars in record numbers (Figure A.6), General Motors passed Ford in total auto production, complementary enterprises such as glassworks, tire manufacturing, etc. grew, and road construction paved the way for far more professional and personal freedom.[1] Productivity gains came from many areas but the increased reliance on electric power was striking. By the end of the 1920s, electric power accounted for over 80 percent of installed horsepower and estimates suggested that this could increase productivity by two thirds.[2] New technologies such as the radio and motion pictures contributed not only to the economic prosperity but also to the quality of leisure time. Further, more people were able to enjoy these activities as personal earnings rose significantly (Figure A.13).

Much has been made about the stock market expansion during this time frame. The impressive expansion, shown in Figure A.14, was the result of the private market prosperity described above. As the real sector grew, manufacturing turned to the financial sector to finance expansion. Commercial banks, investment banks and brokerage firms were consolidating and growing alongside the real sector in an effort to keep pace. Some of the stock market gains were a reflection of the real gains in the wider economy. At the same time, monetary policy at the central bank also contributed to the stock market run up.[3] There were considerable gold outflows in the late 1920s. An appropriate response would have been tighter monetary policy to increase the price of gold domestically. However, the central bank, instead, injected more money into the economy which led to real estate and stock speculation. Financial historians, including Friedman and Schwartz (1963), contend that central bank policy caused the stock market crash as well as the bank crises which followed.

While much of the economy enjoyed prosperity during the 1920s, the agriculture sector never recovered from World War I. Throughout the decade, farm prices declined (Figure A.15) as a result, in part, of productivity gains from mechanical farm equipment invented by entrepreneurs such as John Deere and Cyrus McCormick. The increased production outpaced the increased demand so prices fell. Farm income fell significantly during the beginning of this decade but rebounded and stabilized at the end (Figure A.16). The latter performance reflects a slight rebound in agricultural commodity prices (Figure A.15). Further, as illustrated in Figure A.17, many farming operations failed in the final two years of the decade.

October 1929 marked an end of both the stock market and real gross domestic product expansion. Why did the economy collapse? To this day, this question remains unresolved. What we do know is that the agriculture sector was under significant stress. Further, the money supply leveled off towards the end of the decade and between August of 1929 and March 1933, the money stock fell by over one third.[4] Some have argued that the Federal Reserve was trying to keep banks from using deposits to buy equities.[5] With money hard to come by, the manufacturing sector slowed as bank credit became scarce. Further, the 1930 Smoot-Hawley Tariffs have been blamed for some of the 40 percent reduction in U.S. exports in the two years following the tariffs and a significant decline in global trade as other nations retaliated.[6] Clearly, a reduction in exports of this magnitude will contribute to a slowing economy. Another avenue through which these tariffs may have contributed to the economic decline is that business perceptions changed immediately. Businesses knew that the price of all imported inputs would rise substantially so they responded by reducing production and laying off employees.[7] Indeed, today scholars believe this response by domestic producers had a larger impact than the reduced sale of U.S. exports due to retaliation. In the end, the contraction was so significant that economic life in America was altered forever.

The 1930s macroeconomy witnessed the most severe economic downturn in the history of the United States. 1932 and 1933 saw unemployment rates of 24 and 25 percent respectively (Figure A.12) and real total output fell by close to 30 percent between 1929 and 1932 (Figure A.11). As mentioned above, prices fell in the early 1930s and struggled to return to pre 1930 levels and, in the case of most agricultural commodities, prices remained extremely low throughout the 1930s. The cumulative effect of the depressed economy put tremendous pressure on many small bankers who held the deposits of the local community and had loan portfolios comprised primarily of agricultural loans to the local farmer. However, before turning the focus to the banking sector, it is important to first understand the earliest developments of this era.

Federal Reserve System

The era of instability and change opened in 1914 with a new central bank. Codified on December 23, 1913 the Federal Reserve Act created a network of reserve banks that were established to provide the elastic currency previously provided through Clearinghouses. The 1913 act empowered an organizational committee with the authority to set up between eight and 12 regional districts and banks. Membership into the Federal Reserve was compulsory for all nationally chartered banks and optional for state chartered banks. Member banks were subject to reserve requirements and were required to purchase stock in the regional Federal Reserve Bank to which it belonged. Stock dividends were capped at six percent. The regional Federal Reserve banks were established as the banker's bank. This meant that the member banks could borrow from, hold deposits with, and process their deposits through their regional Federal Reserve Bank.

Two additional provisions of the 1913 act note mentioning. First, Federal Reserve notes replaced national banknotes and were backed by gold at the U.S. Treasury. Second, a Federal Reserve Board was created and empowered largely to supervise and examine the regional Federal Reserve Banks and member banks.

Prior to the creation of the Federal Reserve, the U.S. commercial banking industry had two types of institutions; state chartered and nationally chartered banks. After 1914, the industry structure became a bit more complex. Nationally chartered banks all became member banks, some state banks also became member banks, while most state banks remained nonmember banks. By the middle of 1917, only 53 of the some 8500 state banks, or approximately 0.06 percent, joined the system.[8] State bankers opted not to join for several reasons. From the beginning most bankers (and the public) were skeptical of the Federal Reserve and skeptical that membership would offer much in the way of benefits. This was particularly true for state banks that were members of a Clearinghouse as the Clearinghouse already had a proven track record and reputation for offering similar services. Further, membership was costly both in terms of higher reserve requirements and the stock provision. These factors combined to keep state bankers outside the Federal Reserve System.

Growth and consolidation in banking: 1920s

In the history of U.S. commercial banking, the 1920s are often overlooked because it was a decade that produced no crises or panics. It was, nonetheless, an important decade in shaping commercial banking as it was a period of tremendous growth in the number of commercial banks (Figures 5.1 and 5.2) and, paradoxically, a period of consolidation as the number of mergers increased throughout the decade.

In terms of the number of commercial banks, in 1920 there were over 22,000 state banks and over 8000 national banks (Tables 5.1 and 5.2). At the end of the decade, there were 7530 nationally chartered and 17,440 state chartered banks. While the absolute number of commercial banks fell by the end of the decade, as shown in Figures 5.1 and 5.2 the first few years witnessed growth in the absolute number of banks across the United States. Where, more specifically, were the banks located? State level data on the number of national and state banks are found in Tables 5.1 and 5.2. These data indicate that nationally chartered banks were most popular in the Northeast and Midwest. New York, New Jersey, Pennsylvania, Delaware, and Maryland collectively accounted for 1665 national banks or 20.78 percent of the total in 1920. Five years later that same region contained 1767 national banks or 21.94 percent of the total. Similarly, the eight Midwest states housed 27.36 percent of all nationally

Figure 5.1 Number of State Chartered Banks: 1896–1940

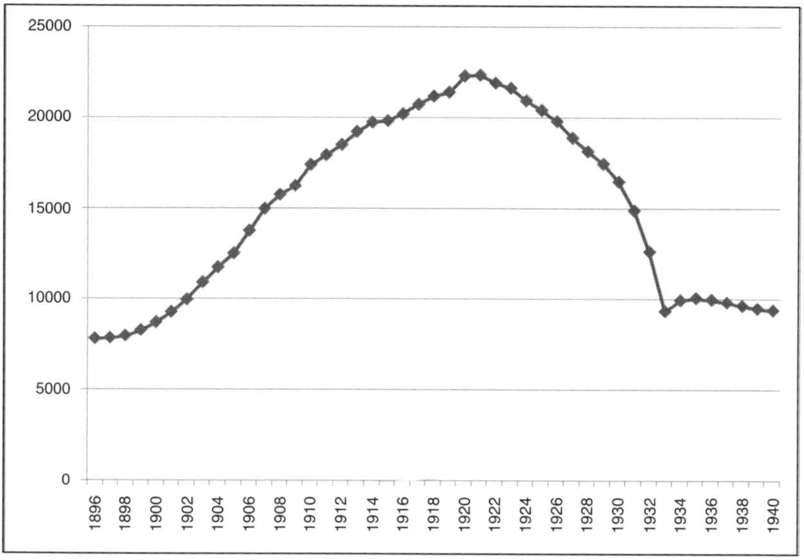

Source: Historical Statistics, Series Cj158.

Figure 5.2 Number of National Chartered Banks: 1896–1940

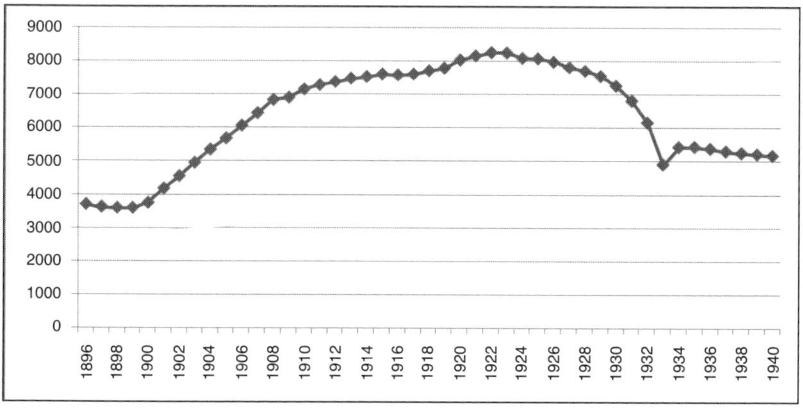

Source: Historical Statistics, Series Cj212.

charted banks in 1920 and just slightly more than 27 percent in 1925.[9] Outside of these two regions, the data in Table 5.1 indicates that both Oklahoma and Texas were home to a significant number of nationally chartered banks in the 1920s. The growth in state commercial banks

Table 5.1 Number of National Commercial Banks: 1915–1935

State (by region)	1915	1920	1925	1930	1935
Maine	70	63	58	52	40
New Hampshire	56	55	54	56	52
Vermont	48	49	46	45	43
Massachusetts	170	159	156	152	129
Rhode Island	18	17	17	10	12
Connecticut	74	66	62	62	54
New York	478	491	533	556	459
New Jersey	201	212	265	297	237
Pennsylvania	833	851	867	845	709
Delaware	24	19	18	16	16
Maryland	100	92	84	77	63
Virginia	136	165	181	157	132
West Virginia	117	122	124	111	79
North Carolina	80	87	83	64	44
South Carolina	71	82	75	35	19
Georgia	113	93	89	75	58
Florida	56	53	57	55	50
Alabama	92	101	102	101	69
Mississippi	35	30	36	35	25
Louisiana	30	38	33	31	30
Texas	537	556	642	593	457
Arkansas	58	83	86	67	51
Kentucky	141	134	139	133	100
Tennessee	116	98	105	99	73
Ohio	378	370	356	308	252
Indiana	258	254	246	210	125
Illinois	468	480	501	462	295
Michigan	104	112	126	126	85
Wisconsin	136	151	157	155	106
Minnesota	277	331	320	263	206
Iowa	348	358	340	241	121
Missouri	131	136	131	125	87
North Dakota	153	181	160	112	67
South Dakota	111	136	111	95	58
Nebraska	212	188	172	171	137
Kansas	215	249	258	245	191
Montana	64	145	85	63	46
Wyoming	33	47	32	25	26
Colorado	122	141	137	120	81
New Mexico	38	47	31	26	23
Oklahoma	351	348	393	278	215
Washington	78	87	112	105	67
Oregon	86	90	99	93	52
California	265	303	268	205	125
Idaho	56	81	57	41	24
Utah	23	28	21	18	13
Nevada	10	10	10	10	6
Arizona	13	20	18	14	7
TOTAL	**7584**	**8009**	**8053**	**7235**	**5416**

Source: Compiled from *All-Bank Statistics: U.S. 1896–1955* (1959).

Table 5.2 Number of State Commercial Banks: 1915–1935

State (by region)	1915	1920	1925	1930	1935
Maine	46	56	55	48	32
New Hampshire	24	26	27	26	24
Vermont	37	39	40	39	34
Massachusetts	115	171	111	107	76
Rhode Island	16	16	14	14	12
Connecticut	68	91	107	116	71
New York	439	493	488	435	335
New Jersey	139	164	217	238	167
Pennsylvania	533	621	754	700	416
Delaware	17	20	27	30	31
Maryland	129	151	150	139	126
Virginia	275	331	341	307	196
West Virginia	193	217	221	177	101
North Carolina	396	491	466	372	202
South Carolina	313	379	298	138	121
Georgia	660	686	549	339	284
Florida	200	210	261	150	98
Alabama	261	251	252	220	148
Mississippi	257	302	301	258	184
Louisiana	209	229	214	191	120
Texas	997	1125	943	762	481
Arkansas	395	404	396	329	191
Kentucky	453	450	468	415	344
Tennessee	390	450	447	382	258
Ohio	738	772	740	678	459
Indiana	723	798	846	700	422
Illinois	1430	1489	1403	1226	594
Michigan	703	739	765	701	415
Wisconsin	686	819	826	775	514
Minnesota	927	1177	1043	746	477
Iowa	1444	1564	1371	1070	550
Missouri	1368	1516	1427	1110	627
North Dakota	630	718	499	255	137
South Dakota	490	543	415	279	148
Nebraska	803	1037	939	625	305
Kansas	944	1100	1019	806	537
Montana	231	286	150	122	72
Wyoming	76	113	64	59	33
Colorado	206	262	199	152	84
New Mexico	47	76	35	27	18
Oklahoma	558	612	381	322	193
Washington	279	306	249	224	134
Oregon	174	187	180	135	52
California	468	414	385	222	140
Idaho	125	141	104	96	37
Utah	90	105	94	84	46
Nevada	21	23	24	25	4
Arizona	46	67	40	33	10
TOTAL	**19,769**	**22,237**	**20,345**	**16,404**	**10,060**

Source: Compiled from *All-Bank Statistics: U.S. 1896–1955* (1959).

appears to be more widespread than the national banks during the 1920s. The data in Table 5.2 indicate that state commercial banks were popular in the South, Midwest, and Central Western regions of the country.[10] At the beginning of this decade, the South housed 24.85 percent of all state banks, while the Midwest housed 39.9 percent and the Central West had 21.34 percent of all state banks. Five years later, the Midwest and South regions had an even greater percentage of the total (41.39 percent and 25.34 percent respectively) while the Central West was down to 18.19 percent. Outside of these three regions, Pennsylvania and New York both had large numbers of state banks in the 1920s.

When comparing the data in Table 5.1 and 5.2 it is clear that the number of state bank institutions began to fall off prior to the decline in national banks. That is, the number of national banks increases from 1915 to 1925 before declining between 1925 and 1930. In contrast, the number of state banks fell between 1920 and 1925. The discussion that follows regarding bank mergers and consolidation explains this different experience for national and state banks.

Branch banking

Between 1929 and 1936, there was a significant shift in the landscape of branch banking. In 1920, only nine states allowed for statewide branching and another 13 limited branching to specific areas, for example, cities with a certain threshold population (see Table 5.3). By 1936, 17 states embraced statewide branching and another 17 allowed for limited branching (see Table 5.4). Figures 5.3 and 5.4 illustrate the extent to which national and state banks were establishing branches and also the location of the branches. Both charter types had approximately 20 percent of their aggregated branches within the headquartered city in 1900 which means that the majority of branching, at the turn of the century, was outside the home city of the bank. In contrast, both state and national banks increasingly opened branches within the headquartered city so that quickly the branching emphasis shifted away from rural areas. For example, by 1915, 57 percent of national bank branches were within the headquarter city while 55 percent of state bank branches were within the city. However, as pointed out in a 1932 report by a committee established to study branching at the Federal Reserve, in the East and the South, branching remained primarily rural.[11] Thus, the trend throughout the United States was towards more branching within large cities and the West and Midwest regions focused on branching in urban areas while the East and South regions expanded branching rurally.

What was the impetus behind such a major shift in bank management? There is empirical evidence to suggest that the high rate of bank failures

Table 5.3 Summary of State Branch Banking Laws: 1929

States Permitting Statewide Branching	**States Permitting Branch Banking Within Limited Areas**	**States Prohibiting Branch Banking**	**States With No Legislation Regarding Branch Banking**
Arizona	Georgia	Alabama	New Hampshire
California	Kentucky	Arkansas	North Dakota
Delaware	Louisiana	Colorado	Oklahoma
Maryland	Maine	Connecticut	South Dakota
North Carolina	Massachusetts	Florida	Wyoming
Rhode Island	Michigan	Idaho	
South Carolina	Mississippi	Illinois	
Vermont	New Jersey	Indiana	
	New York	Iowa	
	Ohio	Kansas	
	Pennsylvania	Minnesota	
	Tennessee	Missouri	
		Montana	
		Nebraska	
		Nevada	
		New Mexico	
		Oregon	
		Texas	
		Utah	
		Washington	
		West Virginia	
		Wisconsin	

Source: *Federal Reserve Bulletin*, April 1930: 151.

increased political pressure in many of these states to allow for branching.[12] That is, small, unit bankers who opposed the expansion of branch banking lost some of their political weight as small banks failed. Further, the pro branching sentiment was bolstered by the stability of branching states relative to nonbranching states. However, as the number of bank failures declined, the incentive to move towards more branching was significantly reduced.[13] Similarly, with the creation of federal deposit insurance in 1933, many believed that the stability derived from branching could be achieved through deposit insurance. Indeed, there is evidence to suggest that one reason federal deposit insurance was a popular idea with small bankers was because it was seen as a mechanism for keeping the encroachment of branching at bay.[14] Taken together, the reduction in the number of bank failures and the adoption of federal deposit insurance, the trend towards freer branching laws came to an end.

Table 5.4 Summary of State Branch Banking Laws: 1936

States Permitting Statewide Branching	States Permitting Branch Banking Within Limited Areas	States Prohibiting Branch Banking	States With No Legislation Regarding Branch Banking
Arizona	Alabama	Colorado	Kentucky
California	Arkansas	Florida	New Hampshire
Connecticut	Delaware	Illinois	North Dakota
Idaho	Georgia	Kansas	Oklahoma
Maine	Indiana	Minnesota	Wyoming
Maryland	Iowa	Missouri	
Michigan	Louisiana	Nebraska	
Nevada	Massachusetts	Texas	
North Carolina	Mississippi		
Oregon	Montana		
Rhode Island	New Jersey		
South Carolina	New Mexico		
South Dakota	New York		
Utah	Ohio		
Vermont	Pennsylvania		
Virginia	Tennessee		
Washington	Wisconsin		

Source: *Federal Reserve Bulletin*, November 1936: 858.

Figure 5.3 Number of State Banks Operating Branches and Number of State Bank Failures: Selected Years, 1900–1941

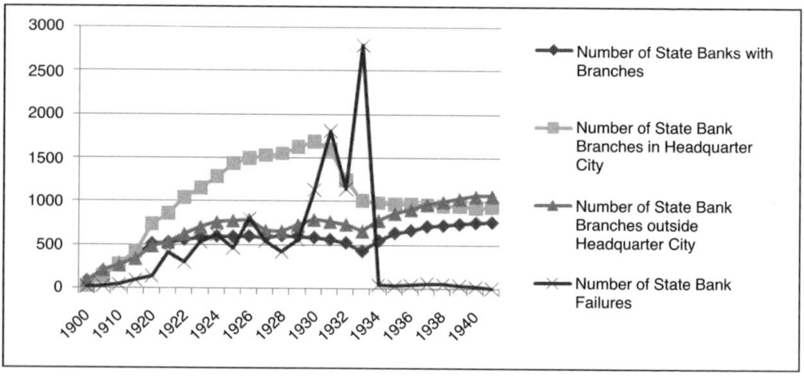

Source: Board of Governors, *Banking and Monetary Statistics, 1914–1941*.

Merger movement

While the absolute number of banks grew, another trend was working to reduce the number of banks. White (1985) has constructed the most comprehensive data on bank mergers during the 1920s and early

Figure 5.4 Number of National Banks Operating Branches and Number of National Bank Failures: Selected Years, 1900–1941

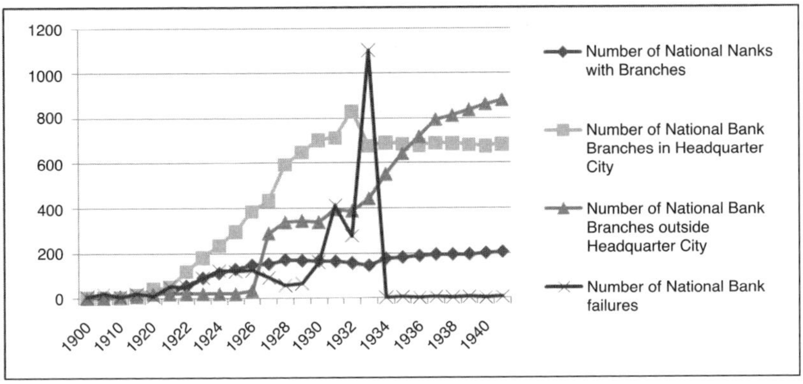

Source: Board of Governors, *Banking and Monetary Statistics, 1914–1941*.

Figure 5.5 Annual Number of Bank Mergers: 1919–1933

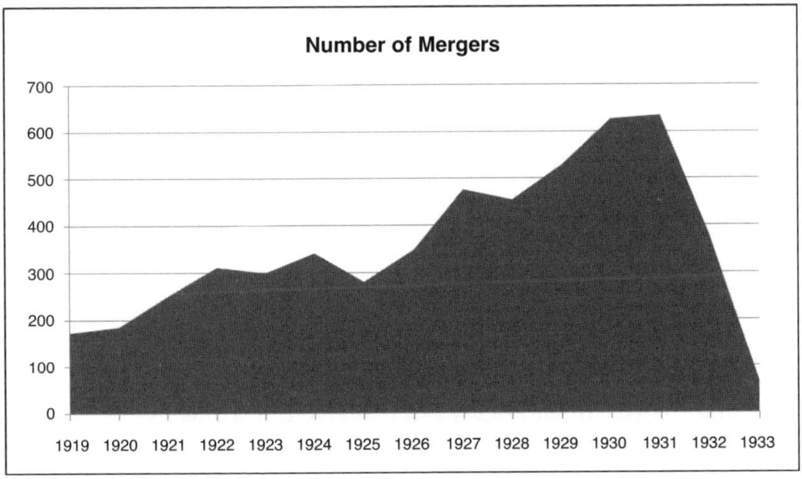

Source: White (1985: 286).

1930s. As shown in Figure 5.5, the number of merged banks, which includes member and nonmember commercial banks, increased dramatically during the 1920s before falling off during the bank crises of the early 1930s. There are several possible explanations for this merger movement in banking.[15] First, the Act of November 7, 1918 provided a mechanism for national bank mergers. Prior to this act, national banks intending to merge were compelled to have one of the merging institutions liquidate and the other purchase its assets and liabilities. However, the act did not allow for the easy merging of national banks with other banking institutions. Indeed, if a national bank wanted to merge with a state bank it had to first convert to a state charter, merge, and then be a merged state bank. Nonetheless, after the 1918 act, it was marginally easier for the national banks to merge and often the national banks would use the merging process to establish branch units.

Consolidation in banking was also the result of restrictive regulation placed on both national and state chartered banks and developments in the stock market. Banks were not allowed to extend loans in excess of ten percent of capital to any one borrower. This meant that many banks were not able to accommodate the needs of their large business clients. Scholars argue that one reason for consolidation in the 1920s was to create bigger banks in order to service large corporate borrowers.[16] This banking consolidation wave may also be understood in terms of the 1920s growth of the stock market (Figure A.14). Many small bankers saw merging with larger banks as a means to participate in the stock market boom given that larger bank shares were more widely traded.

During the 1920s banks were also looking for new revenue sources due to rather weak commercial loan demand. Investment banking and trust business offered an important revenue source to commercial banks and also an avenue for remaining competitive with nonbanks. Banks merged, or created affiliates, with investment and trust businesses in order to acquire the expertise and skills for these new services. By 1929, large commercial banks were underwriting $11.6 billion in new issues; more than twice the level of the early 1920s.[17] As further evidence of the growth of investment bank activity at commercial banks, consider that in 1922, national banks had ten security affiliates but, by 1931, there were 114 affiliates offering investment bank activity through national bank affiliates.[18]

Finally, banks in the 1920s often merged as a means of avoiding failure.[19] Since many banks were prohibited from branching, they were often small and had limited diversification. Merging would allow the bankers to grow in size, enjoy economies of scale, and to diversify both their assets and liabilities. Because of this, it has been argued that the 1920s process of consolidation probably went a long way toward strengthening the banking sector prior to the economic downturn that became the Great Depression.[20] Quite likely, had it not been for the wave of mergers and consolidations between 1919 and 1929, the banking crises of the early 1930s would have been much worse because we would have entered the 1930s with more smaller and weaker banks.

McFadden Act of 1927

In addition to the growth and consolidation during the 1920s, there was an important regulatory development during this decade. In 1927 Congress passed the McFadden Act, in part due to concern over the number of conversions from national to state banks and the growing number of bank branches. Increasingly, the Federal Reserve worried that it was losing members because many state banks were allowed to branch which prompted many national banks to convert their charters in order to enjoy branching privileges. At the same time, the Comptroller of the Currency was concerned that state chartered banks had an advantage over national chartered banks in those states in which branching was allowed. The McFadden Act of 1927 was a response to the market developments of increased branching and a decline in the number of national bank charters. The act allowed national banks to branch within the cities in which they were located, if state law permitted, and provided that the city had a population of at least 25,000.[21] However, the McFadden Act effectively prohibited intrastate branching because a national bank or a state member bank could not open branches throughout the state. State charted nonmember banks did not face this constraint. In 1927, and for many years thereafter, states prohibited interstate branching for state chartered banks and the 1927 McFadden Act extended that prohibition to nationally chartered banks. Thus, the bank regulation of the 1920s, on the one hand, allowed for consolidation while, on the other hand, confined banks geographically by prohibiting intrastate and interstate branching for national banks.

Outside of the branching provisions, the McFadden Act addressed several other banking issues. First, it allowed national banks to merge with a state bank and also allowed the bank to retain any branches it absorbed through the merger.[22] Clearly, the intention of this provision was to arrest the decline in the number of national bank charters. The 1927 Act also addressed the growing trend of commercial bankers to engage in securities activity. The Act codified the practice of national banks of buying and selling investment securities; national banks were legally allowed to trade investment grade securities up to 25 percent of their capital.[23]

Bank crises and the regulatory response

As indicated earlier in this chapter, the 1920s ended with a severe crash in the stock market, a loss of confidence in the economy in general, and the banking industry in particular, and set the stage for the Great

Table 5.5 Number of National Bank Failures by State: 1925–1933

State (by region)	1925	1926	1927	1928	1929	1930	1931	1932	1933
Maine	0	0	0	0	0	0	0	0	17
New Hampshire	0	0	0	0	0	0	1	0	5
Vermont	0	0	0	0	0	1	0	0	14
Massachusetts	0	0	0	0	0	0	5	1	14
Rhode Island	0	0	0	1	0	0	0	0	0
Connecticut	0	0	0	0	0	0	0	1	0
New York	0	0	0	0	0	1	24	8	84
New Jersey	0	0	0	0	0	1	16	5	53
Pennsylvania	3	1	6	0	1	6	42	20	145
Delaware	0	0	0	1	0	0	0	1	1
Maryland	0	0	0	0	0	0	3	1	24
Virginia	0	1	0	0	1	2	6	2	17
West Virginia	1	0	1	1	1	5	18	2	21
North Carolina	4	0	2	3	1	10	14	5	10
South Carolina	5	3	2	5	4	4	5	3	6
Georgia	7	0	0	3	3	3	4	8	9
Florida	1	1	2	1	11	4	3	2	4
Alabama	1	2	0	0	2	7	8	6	11
Mississippi	0	1	0	0	1	3	8	1	3
Louisiana	0	0	0	0	0	1	0	1	8
Texas	6	7	6	4	2	14	30	10	32
Arkansas	0	3	2	0	1	13	8	1	8
Kentucky	0	0	0	0	0	3	4	10	20
Tennessee	0	1	0	0	0	3	4	3	14

Table 5.5 Number of National Bank Failures by State: 1925–1933 – *continued*

State (by region)	1925	1926	1927	1928	1929	1930	1931	1932	1933
Ohio	0	2	2	2	2	3	19	2	58
Indiana	0	2	3	3	1	4	8	12	44
Illinois	1	4	2	4	4	20	37	46	107
Michigan	0	0	1	0	1	2	14	5	54
Wisconsin	1	1	1	1	0	1	7	4	38
Minnesota	15	14	12	3	1	1	13	9	27
Iowa	16	31	21	6	8	13	21	24	67
Missouri	1	2	1	1	1	6	12	8	13
North Dakota	7	11	4	5	8	8	13	3	10
South Dakota	12	12	2	2	0	3	13	6	7
Nebraska	1	3	3	3	3	4	8	3	25
Kansas	0	1	1	4	1	3	4	9	21
Montana	9	2	1	0	1	2	3	3	5
Wyoming	0	0	0	0	0	0	0	0	0
Colorado	7	4	0	0	1	1	7	6	26
New Mexico	2	0	0	0	0	0	1	0	3
Oklahoma	9	8	8	2	1	6	2	9	15
Washington	2	2	0	0	1	1	6	5	18
Oregon	1	0	2	1	0	0	4	8	11
California	2	3	4	0	1	2	8	14	22
Idaho	4	1	2	1	1	0	4	6	3
Utah	0	0	0	0	0	0	1	0	1
Nevada	0	0	0	0	0	0	0	2	1
Arizona	0	0	0	0	0	0	1	1	1
TOTAL	**118**	**123**	**91**	**57**	**64**	**161**	**409**	**276**	**1097**

Source: *Federal Reserve Bulletin* (1937: 869).

Table 5.6 Number of State Member Bank Failures by State: 1925–1933

State (by region)	1925	1926	1927	1928	1929	1930	1931	1932	1933
Maine	0	0	0	0	0	0	0	0	1
New Hampshire	0	0	0	0	0	0	0	0	0
Vermont	0	0	0	0	0	0	0	0	0
Massachusetts	0	0	0	0	0	0	1	1	3
Rhode Island	0	0	0	0	0	0	0	0	1
Connecticut	0	0	0	0	0	0	0	0	1
New York	0	0	0	0	0	1	8	0	2
New Jersey	0	0	0	0	0	1	4	1	5
Pennsylvania	0	0	0	0	0	0	6	1	6
Delaware	0	0	0	0	0	0	0	0	0
Maryland	0	0	0	0	0	0	0	0	2
Virginia	0	0	0	0	0	0	1	0	2
West Virginia	0	0	0	0	0	0	4	0	2
North Carolina	0	0	0	0	1	0	0	0	1
South Carolina	1	0	4	1	0	1	2	0	0
Georgia	4	7	1	1	4	3	4	2	2
Florida	0	0	1	2	2	1	0	0	1
Alabama	1	0	1	0	1	1	1	3	1
Mississippi	0	1	0	0	0	3	0	0	1
Louisiana	0	1	0	0	0	0	0	1	3
Texas	4	3	1	1	1	1	9	3	6
Arkansas	0	2	1	0	0	3	6	1	6
Kentucky	0	0	0	0	0	1	0	1	0
Tennessee	0	0	1	0	0	0	1	0	1
Ohio	0	0	3	2	0	1	15	0	12
Indiana	2	0	1	0	0	1	2	0	5

Table 5.6 Number of State Member Bank Failures by State: 1925–1933 – *continued*

State (by region)	**1925**	**1926**	**1927**	**1928**	**1929**	**1930**	**1931**	**1932**	**1933**
Illinois	0	0	2	1	0	3	5	11	6
Michigan	0	1	0	0	2	0	23	11	50
Wisconsin	0	0	0	0	1	0	0	0	2
Minnesota	0	1	0	0	2	0	1	0	7
Iowa	6	15	5	7	2	2	3	3	6
Missouri	1	2	1	0	0	1	1	1	18
North Dakota	0	0	0	0	0	0	0	0	0
South Dakota	1	0	0	0	0	1	0	0	0
Nebraska	0	0	0	0	0	0	0	2	1
Kansas	0	0	1	0	0	0	0	0	0
Montana	4	0	1	0	0	0	0	0	4
Wyoming	0	0	0	0	0	0	0	0	0
Colorado	0	0	0	0	0	0	0	0	0
New Mexico	0	0	0	0	0	0	0	0	0
Oklahoma	1	0	0	0	0	0	0	0	1
Washington	0	0	0	0	1	1	2	5	9
Oregon	1	2	3	0	0	0	3	4	7
California	0	0	0	0	0	0	1	0	2
Idaho	2	0	3	1	0	0	2	2	1
Utah	0	0	1	0	0	1	2	2	1
Nevada	0	0	0	0	0	0	0	0	0
Arizona	0	0	0	0	0	0	0	0	0
TOTAL	**28**	**35**	**31**	**16**	**17**	**27**	**107**	**55**	**174**

Source: *Federal Reserve Bulletin* (1937: 870).

Table 5.7 Number of State Nonmember Bank Failures by State: 1925–1933

State (by region)	1925	1926	1927	1928	1929	1930	1931	1932	1933
Maine	0	0	1	0	0	0	2	0	15
New Hampshire	1	0	0	0	0	0	1	0	1
Vermont	0	0	0	0	0	1	0	0	4
Massachusetts	2	0	0	0	0	2	13	1	3
Rhode Island	1	0	0	0	0	0	0	0	0
Connecticut	0	0	0	0	0	4	8	5	4
New York	0	0	0	0	2	3	20	2	18
New Jersey	0	0	0	0	1	1	18	2	12
Pennsylvania	3	1	1	1	4	9	80	21	65
Delaware	0	0	0	0	1	0	0	0	2
Maryland	0	0	0	0	1	1	15	3	44
Virginia	2	3	4	7	8	18	30	7	24
West Virginia	3	2	4	4	13	5	35	4	26
North Carolina	12	12	12	5	16	83	49	26	57
South Carolina	35	42	18	16	13	22	27	15	25
Georgia	20	98	17	22	13	25	27	15	7
Florida	0	42	28	32	52	34	14	9	25
Alabama	3	2	1	1	11	26	27	9	25
Mississippi	4	5	6	5	7	53	48	11	28
Louisiana	4	9	4	3	0	9	7	12	48
Texas	19	23	24	15	6	16	37	18	31
Arkansas	7	11	13	14	11	118	42	11	65
Kentucky	6	7	8	7	1	26	23	27	19
Tennessee	7	12	16	4	12	26	26	25	28
Ohio	1	5	9	7	8	19	71	21	113
Indiana	5	4	20	19	19	73	81	47	130

Table 5.7 Number of State Nonmember Bank Failures by State: 1925–1933 – *continued*

State (by region)	**1925**	**1926**	**1927**	**1928**	**1929**	**1930**	**1931**	**1932**	**1933**
Illinois	6	15	25	13	26	102	196	152	132
Michigan	2	0	3	0	1	4	62	61	184
Wisconsin	10	10	14	5	10	23	41	63	326
Minnesota	35	78	53	43	28	21	87	52	94
Iowa	47	74	32	32	21	55	160	111	320
Missouri	42	54	44	31	22	96	109	71	224
North Dakota	25	48	33	33	29	51	53	11	34
South Dakota	50	101	25	4	13	51	60	16	20
Nebraska	20	22	22	49	149	42	101	46	177
Kansas	19	45	34	20	11	40	34	60	56
Montana	3	6	0	1	0	9	8	4	12
Wyoming	3	3	1	0	1	0	3	2	3
Colorado	8	10	4	3	4	4	14	18	33
New Mexico	8	0	1	0	1	0	0	1	4
Oklahoma	10	13	20	3	20	16	22	23	68
Washington	4	0	4	2	5	1	14	18	35
Oregon	1	3	7	2	1	2	7	14	20
California	1	2	2	0	3	5	9	19	25
Idaho	2	3	2	0	2	1	4	16	12
Utah	1	0	1	2	1	2	6	12	4
Nevada	0	0	0	1	1	0	2	14	1
Arizona	3	1	1	0	0	5	4	6	3
TOTAL	**433**	**766**	**514**	**406**	**547**	**1104**	**1697**	**1085**	**2616**

Source: *Federal Reserve Bulletin* (1937: 871).

Figure 5.6 Number of Commercial Bank Failures by Bank Type: 1925–1933

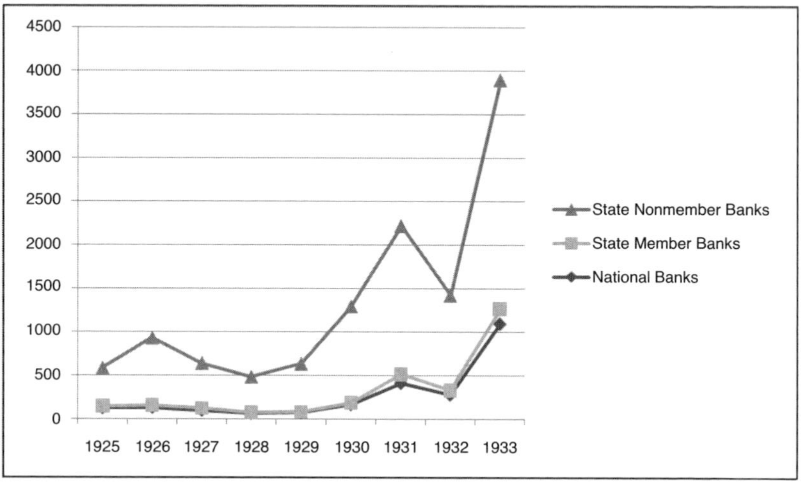

Source: *Federal Reserve Bulletin* (1937: 869–71).

Depression at the beginning of the 1930s. While the late 1920s witnessed a fair number of bank failures (see Tables 5.5 through 5.7), these tended to be isolated in rural areas, did not impact depositor confidence, and did not have broader, national implications.[24] Hence, there was no banking crisis in the 1920s, despite the number of failures. 1930 began without alarm as the number of failures did not depart much from the 1920s. However, by the end of 1930, a banking crisis was at hand with two more to come by the middle of 1933. Figure 5.6 illustrates the number of failures, by bank type for this period.

November 1930–January 1931 crisis

There is disagreement amongst scholars of U.S. banking history regarding the situation in late 1930 and early 1931. The crisis was not a national event but, rather, was a regional disruption. Because of this, some scholars do not characterize this episode as a crisis. However, the regional disturbances fit the definition of crisis outlined in Chapter 1 and the hangover from this regional crisis had serious implications for the crisis later in 1931.

The aggregate bank failure data in Tables 5.5 through 5.7 provide some indication of a crisis in 1930. Between 1929 and 1930, the number of national banks failures increased by 149 percent (Table 5.5), the number of state member bank failures increased approximately 59 percent

Table 5.8 Percent of Bank Failures by State: Crises Years

State (by region)	*Crisis of 1930*		*Crises of 1931*		*Crisis of 1933*	
	Percent of National Banks that Failed in 1930	Percent of State Banks that Failed in 1930	Percent of National Banks that Failed in 1931	Percent of State Banks that Failed in 1931	Percent of National Banks that Failed in 1933	Percent of State Banks that Failed in 1933
Maine	0.0	0.0	0.0	4.5	68.0	64.0
New Hampshire	0.0	0.0	1.8	3.8	10.4	4.0
Vermont	2.0	2.5	0.0	0.0	42.4	12.1
Massachusetts	0.0	1.8	3.3	13.7	11.0	7.5
Rhode Island	0.0	0.0	0.0	0.0	0.0	8.3
Connecticut	0.0	3.4	0.0	7.7	0.0	6.4
New York	0.17	0.92	4.4	7.1	20.2	6.2
New Jersey	0.33	0.84	5.4	9.7	24.7	10.7
Pennsylvania	0.71	1.2	5.2	13.3	24.1	17.2
Delaware	0.0	0.0	0.0	0.0	6.6	6.6
Maryland	0.0	0.71	4.1	11.1	53.3	56.7
Virginia	1.3	5.8	3.4	11.1	13.9	12.7
West Virginia	4.5	2.8	17.3	24.6	33.8	26.4
North Carolina	15.6	22.3	25.4	15.8	28.5	31.6
South Carolina	11.4	16.6	16.1	26.4	40.0	25.5
Georgia	4.0	8.2	5.8	10.2	19.9	3.2
Florida	7.2	23.3	5.8	10.1	8.8	27.3
Alabama	6.9	12.3	8.7	14.4	16.6	18.9
Mississippi	8.6	21.7	28.6	21.9	13.0	15.3
Louisiana	3.2	4.7	0.0	3.9	36.3	43.6
Texas	2.3	2.2	5.6	6.5	7.1	6.8
Arkansas	19.4	36.7	14.3	18.1	17.7	47.0
Kentucky	2.2	6.5	3.3	5.9	22.9	5.7
Tennessee	3.0	6.8	4.3	7.9	20.9	10.9
Ohio	0.97	2.9	7.9	13.7	27.6	30.7

Table 5.8 Percent of Bank Failures by State: Crises Years – *continued*

State (by region)	*Crisis of 1930*		*Crises of 1931*		*Crisis of 1933*	
	Percent of National Banks that Failed in 1930	**Percent of State Banks that Failed in 1930**	**Percent of National Banks that Failed in 1931**	**Percent of State Banks that Failed in 1931**	**Percent of National Banks that Failed in 1933**	**Percent of State Banks that Failed in 1933**
Indiana	1.9	10.6	4.3	13.4	42.3	35.2
Illinois	4.3	8.6	8.8	19.1	44.7	22.5
Michigan	1.6	0.57	11.8	13.5	98.8	94.7
Wisconsin	0.64	2.9	4.7	5.4	45.2	97.7
Minnesota	0.38	2.8	5.3	12.8	13.2	21.9
Iowa	5.3	5.3	9.8	16.8	72.0	89.5
Missouri	4.8	8.7	10.2	11.2	15.6	43.0
North Dakota	7.1	20.0	13.2	25.8	14.9	26.7
South Dakota	3.2	18.6	14.1	26.3	11.1	13.4
Nebraska	2.3	6.7	4.8	17.3	19.4	63.4
Kansas	1.2	4.9	1.7	4.6	10.6	9.6
Montana	3.2	7.3	5.2	7.4	10.8	20.5
Wyoming	0.0	0.0	0.0	5.2	0.0	7.7
Colorado	0.83	2.6	6.2	10.1	35.6	42.3
New Mexico	0.0	0.0	3.8	0.0	13.0	21.0
Oklahoma	2.2	4.9	0.76	7.5	5.7	36.3
Washington	0.95	0.89	6.0	7.5	28.6	37.6
Oregon	0.0	1.5	4.4	8.0	19.6	52.9
California	0.97	2.2	4.2	4.7	16.3	18.0
Idaho	0.0	1.0	10.3	6.5	12.5	20.9
Utah	0.0	3.6	5.8	10.1	7.1	9.0
Nevada	0.0	0.0	0.0	8.7	16.6	20.0
Arizona	0.0	15.1	8.3	14.8	7.7	23.1

Source: Compiled from *All-Bank Statistics: U.S. 1896–1955* (1959).

(Table 5.6), and the number of state nonmember failures increased by over 100 percent (Table 5.7). While absolute number of failures provide some information about the severity of crisis, it may also be helpful to consider the number of failures as a percentage of the total number of banks. Table 5.8 contains the calculations for the percentage of bank failures for each state during each crisis year. If we assume that a failure rate in excess of ten percent is significant, three states, North Carolina, South Carolina, and Arkansas, experienced significant national bank failure rates and ten states, primarily in the South and including the three aforementioned, experienced significant state bank failure rates in 1930.[25] Thus, the crisis was regional in nature.

Currency in circulation, in addition to the number of failures, is another important indicator of crisis because it signals the extent to which depositor confidence is lost.[26] When depositors become less certain about the viability of their bank, the first response is to convert deposits into currency. Hence, increases in the amount of currency in circulation may indicate a bank crisis. Figure 5.7 shows the monthly currency in circulation for the years 1929 through 1933. The data show a sharp increase in the amount of currency being held in the final months of 1930 and the beginning of 1931 which corresponds with the first identified banking crisis in this era.

What caused the failures and loss in depositor confidence? Several large bank failures, one in November and several in December, set off a

Figure 5.7 Currency in Circulation (in Millions of Dollars): December 1928–December 1933

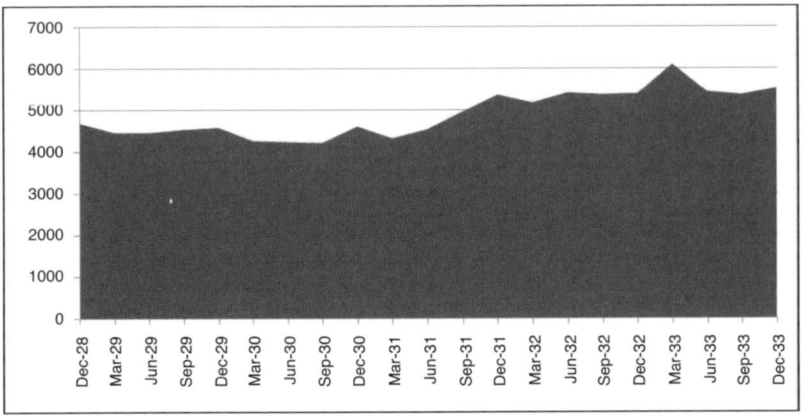

Source: Board of Governors, *Banking and Monetary Statistics, 1914–1941.*
Note: In millions of dollars.

wave of panics and failures at affiliated institutions in the surrounding regions.[27] In addition, drought conditions in the middle of the country led to agricultural loan defaults and, consequently, bank failures, particularly at small and nondiversified banks. Perhaps the most important implication of this regional crisis was that depositor confidence, measured by currency in circulation, rebounded slightly after January of 1931 but never returned to pre-crisis levels. That is, the amount of currency in circulation fell after January of 1931 but did not fall to 1930 levels. This suggests that while the number of bank failures abated, depositors were still concerned about bank viability.

1931 crisis

The second banking crises of this era took place in 1931. However, like the first crisis, there is scholarly debate about the appropriateness of characterizing this event as a "crisis". There is also debate about the cause of the crisis, and some scholars argue that there were actually two distinct crises in 1931. Using monthly data, Wicker (1996) identifies two crises in 1931: the first began in April and ended in August and the second began in August and ended in October. Since the majority of the analysis in the book is at the annual state level, the two waves of failures in 1931 are treated as a single crisis.

Tables 5.5 through 5.7 provide annual bank failure numbers according to bank type. From this, it is clear that most failures were nonmember state banks, though, over 400 national banks also failed in 1931. The data also suggest another regional bank crisis as most of the failures were in the Midwest and Southern regions of the country. If, instead of considering absolute numbers, one considers the percent of banks that failed, 25 states experienced an annual state bank failure rate in excess of ten percent (Table 5.8). All of the Midwest states, except Wisconsin, saw more than ten percent of their state banks fail in 1931 and nine of the 13 Southern states also witnessed a greater than ten percent failure rate. Ten states had a greater than ten percent failure rate for national banks. From this perspective, the 1931 banking crisis was more severe than the crisis at the end of 1930.

Scholars offer varying explanations as to the cause of this second crisis. One perspective argues that the bank failures were set off by falling security prices which compromised a significant portion of the bank's assets.[28] Table 5.9 contains the performance of common stock during these crises years and tends to support the notion that a bank with significant security holdings may have been hurt by market performance. As evidence, consider that in 1932 there was a 48.5 percent

Table 5.9 Monthly Stock Prices: 1929–1934

Year and Month	Common Stock Index (1935–1939 = 100)	Year and Month	Common Stock Index (1935–1939 = 100)
1929		***1932***	
January	195.6	January	61.3
February	196.9	February	59.6
March	199.7	March	60.0
April	197.0	April	46.3
May	198.3	May	42.0
June	201.4	June	35.9
July	218.9	July	37.9
August	230.3	August	56.3
September	237.8	September	61.5
October	213.0	October	52.7
November	159.6	November	50.2
December	162.4	December	50.1
1930		***1933***	
January	165.0	January	51.8
February	174.8	February	47.5
March	182.0	March	45.6
April	191.1	April	50.2
May	180.0	May	66.4
June	161.4	June	79.1
July	157.7	July	85.0
August	155.9	August	79.3
September	157.1	September	79.0
October	134.7	October	73.3
November	123.2	November	73.0
December	115.5	December	74.3
1931		***1934***	
January	118.5	January	79.9
February	126.5	February	85.0
March	128.4	March	81.3
April	115.3	April	84.1
May	103.5	May	75.8
June	100.4	June	77.6
July	103.7	July	75.4
August	100.8	August	71.6
September	86.3	September	70.7
October	73.7	October	71.1
November	75.7	November	73.3
December	61.0	December	73.1

Source: Board of Governors, *Banking and Monetary Statistics, 1914–1941* (1943: 481).

decline in the common stock index throughout the year (Table 5.9). Another perspective finds the increase in the number of bank failures corresponds to the announcement that the British pound would no longer be tied to gold.

Regardless of the cause of the crisis, there seems to be some scholarly agreement on why the crisis came to an end. In October of 1931, the National Credit Corporation (NCC) was created under the guidance of President Hoover. The President and other leaders at the time felt the Federal Reserve was an inadequate liquidity source for both member and nonmember banks and so they approached commercial bankers hoping that a private solution could be found. The bankers were asked to form a voluntary association that would lend to other association banks in difficulty. Ultimately, the President promised the bankers that, should their private association fail to stabilize the situation, he would ask Congress to intervene. The bankers agreed and pooled $500 million under the National Credit Corporation. While the NCC ultimately did not extend much of the $500 million, the mere creation of the pool of funds went a long way to restoring, temporarily, confidence in the banking system.

Evidence that depositor trust returned, at least temporarily, may be found in Figure 5.7 as currency in circulation leveled off in the final months of 1931. This may be interpreted to mean that some deposits returned to the banking system and the level of currency hoarded was constant or, at the very least, not growing. However, what is equally clear from Figure 5.7 is that the restoration of confidence in the banking system at the end of 1931 was temporary at best. Early in 1932, currency in circulation reached historical high levels suggesting that depositor trust in the banking system was fragile and increasingly weak. The fragility of depositor confidence combined with the large number of failures in 1931 set the stage for the worst crisis in U.S. banking history two years later.

1932 Reconstruction Finance Corporation

As mentioned above, the National Credit Corporation was a voluntary group of bankers brought together to lend to other bankers in need. However, the group was formed with little enthusiasm and the promise of the President to create a government agency, if needed, created the wrong incentives for the NCC to succeed. Indeed, the NCC leaders procrastinated and delayed lending knowing that the government would step in and take over responsibility. Realizing that the private initiative had failed, President Hoover made good on his promise and the

Reconstruction Finance Corporation (RFC) was signed into law in January of 1932.

The RFC was created to make low-interest loans to commercial banks, savings and loan associations, insurance and mortgage companies, and railroads. The administration believed that this injection of funds would end bank suspensions, prevent the collapse of the railroads which were struggling to meet even fixed costs, relieve liquidity fears, and restore credit.[29] The central mission of loan extension stemmed from Hoover's belief that the economic problem of the day was too little credit. For Hoover, the problem was a loanable funds problem because he assumed that businesses were demanding credit but were unable to obtain it as banks were holding onto reserves in anticipation of bank runs. Further, there is evidence that the Federal Reserve was reluctant to take action so another mechanism was sought to help banks and some nonfinancial firms.[30]

Created as a temporary agency with an initial charter of ten years, all RFC loans were limited to a one year period though the President had authority to extend loan maturity to three years. Initial capital of $500 million was subscribed by the federal government and the RFC was empowered to issue bonds and notes to obtain an additional $1.5 billion. In addition, the RFC was required to publish quarterly reports indicating the volume of loans provided in specific classes of borrowers. Not surprisingly, this provision often made potential borrowers hesitant to exercise their borrowing privileges as it was feared that the use of RFC loans would ruin public confidence in the debtor.

Though 1932 was without a bank crisis it was not without instability. Indeed, 276 national banks, 55 state member banks, and 1085 state nonmember banks failed that year. While these numbers were large, they were less than the failure numbers in 1931. Further, there does not seem to be any evidence of significant loss in depositor confidence. Indeed, currency in circulation actually fell through the beginning of 1932 and tended to level off indicating that consumer confidence improved throughout the year (Figure 5.7). While the RFC ultimately was not successful in restoring confidence and prosperity to banking and the economy, in the very short run it provided temporary relief to bankers and railroads.

1933 crisis

The first month of 1933 began without much fanfare. Depositor confidence held steady despite banks failing in greater numbers than historically acceptable. This tenuous situation of many failures coupled with steady, but not strong, consumer confidence changed in the middle of February when the Governor of the state of Michigan declared a statewide banking holiday in which all banks were temporarily closed. As word of this statewide holiday spread to nearby states, fragile depositor confidence crumbled causing bank runs and panics. Unfortunately, panic and loss of confidence proved contagious and spread to commercial banks throughout the United States. It culminated in a national bank holiday as declared by President Roosevelt two and a half weeks after the Michigan declaration.

The initial problem in Michigan was that a large bank in Detroit with over thirty affiliates throughout the state was in serious financial jeopardy and headed towards failure.[31] The RFC and bank leaders held extensive negotiations in an attempt to get funds extended to the failing bank. Given the network of affiliates throughout the state, officials were concerned that the failure of the bank would compromise the stability of banking in Michigan generally. Negotiations failed and the bank holiday was declared. In the weeks following, a resolution for dealing with closed and troubled Michigan banks could not be reached. As a consequence, panic and bank runs spread to other Midwestern states and eventually throughout the country. In the two and a half weeks following the Michigan declaration, 18 states had declared bank holidays and 12 additional states had deposit restrictions in place.

The contagious panics, consequent increase in bank failures and runs, and large number of state holidays prompted drastic federal government intervention. On March 6, 1933, President Roosevelt invoked the Trading with the Enemy Act thereby allowing him to proclaim a nationwide bank holiday. All banks were officially closed through March 9, 1933. The Emergency Bank Act of 1933 became law on March 9 which, among other things, gave the President complete power to control banks by opening those which were determined to be sound, requiring bank reorganization if deemed necessary, and controlling foreign exchange transactions as well as all bank transactions. In addition, the Emergency Bank Act empowered the President to extend the bank holiday indefinitely. The first reopening began on March 13 with the Federal Reserve Banks and sound commercial banks within cities which housed Federal Reserve Banks. By March 15, one half of the commercial banks were reopened and by the middle of April, 817 commercial banks were found to be sound and reopened. When the dust settled at the end of 1933, 3887 commercial banks had failed.[32]

Unlike the earlier regional crises of this era, the 1933 crisis was nationwide. Using the ten percent rule as significant, Table 5.5 indicates the national scope of this crisis. Thirty-nine states witnessed a national bank failures rate in excess of ten percent and 36 states had a state bank failure rate in excess of ten percent throughout 1933. This means that very few states escaped without serious bank instability. Consumer confidence, as measured by currency holdings, plummeted particularly during the crisis months of February, March, and April (Figure 5.7).

Like the bank crises of earlier eras, the response to this crisis was additional regulation of the commercial banking industry. Indeed, the two primary legislative developments, the Banking Act of 1933 and Banking Act of 1935 worked to limit competition amongst and between commercial bankers and, at the same time, created a federal safety net under the commercial bank industry. These two landmark regulations significantly changed the face of commercial banking.

Banking Act of 1933

Three months after President Roosevelt declared the nationwide banking holiday in March of 1933, the Banking Act of 1933 was codified. While the act had a direct impact on the functioning of all the predominant financial intermediaries, its impact was overwhelmingly felt within the commercial banking sector. In the broadest of terms, the purpose of the act was to restore confidence, to protect depositors from loss, and to stabilize commercial banking. In the end, four primary provisions emerged which significantly altered the structure of commercial banking.

Perhaps the most famous provision of the Banking Act of 1933 was the creation of federal deposit insurance and the Federal Deposit Insurance Corporation (FDIC). Not surprisingly, a proposal to create federal deposit insurance generated intense debate, particularly in light of the failed state deposit insurance schemes of both the antebellum and national banking eras. Many doubted the wisdom of borrowing a failed state concept and applying it to the nation. However, given the severity of conditions in the economy as a whole, and the banking sector in particular, conditions were optimal for selling the concept of federal deposit insurance to skeptical bankers, regulators, and depositors.

Federal deposit insurance was established under both a temporary plan, to begin six months after the June 16, 1933 act was signed, and a permanent plan. The permanent deposit insurance fund was scheduled to begin on July 1, 1935. Under the 1933 act, premiums for insurance coverage were proportional to total deposits though no limit was placed on the total amount each bank could be assessed. Uncertainty regarding premium obligations was erased with the passage of the Banking Act

Table 5.10 Maximum Deposit Coverage per Depositor of the Federal Deposit Insurance Corporation

Year	Coverage Limit
1933	$ 2,500
1934	$ 5,000
1950	$ 10,000
1966	$ 15,000
1969	$ 20,000
1974	$ 40,000
1980	$100,000
2008	$250,000

Source: FDIC.gov.

of 1935. The 1935 act established that banks would pay one-half of one percent of their deposits. The temporary plan afforded 100 percent deposit coverage up to $2500 but the limit was adjusted to $5000 late in 1934 (see Table 5.10 for historical changes in coverage). Finally, according to the Banking Act of 1933, to be eligible for deposit insurance, membership into the Federal Reserve System was required. However, this provision was amended by the Banking Act of 1935 when the timeframe for banks to join the Federal Reserve System was extended from 1937 to 1942. The time extension for membership was repeatedly extended in the years following 1935 and ended with the provision's legal elimination in 1939.

A second provision of the 1933 act placed further limits on branch banking. The distressed financial situation of the 1930s brought branch banking issues to the forefront of debate as the liberation of branch banking, to some, was the answer to the instability in commercial banking. Branch banking was possible in many regions of the country during the antebellum era. However, increasingly throughout the national banking era states passed anti-branching legislation. As a consequence of the limits placed on branching, the landscape of banking witnessed a proliferation of more and smaller banks. Many experts and scholars argued during the 1930s that the best way to stabilize banking was to allow for branch banking which would create fewer, larger banks with more diversified portfolios.[33] These scholars argued that many of the failures during the 1930s were small and often rural banks that were not a part of a branch network. The data in Tables 5.11 and 5.12 overwhelmingly confirm this as most bank failures, regardless of bank classification, were small banks in small towns.

Table 5.11 Capital Stock of Failed Banks: 1930–1934

	1930	1931	1932	1933	1934
National Banks					
Small	137	316	205	869	1
Medium	15	75	57	177	0
Large	9	18	14	55	0
State Member Banks					
Small	20	58	40	104	0
Medium	3	24	7	39	0
Large	4	25	8	34	0
State Nonmember Banks					
Small	1023	1486	990	2393	36
Medium	71	173	77	181	5
Large	10	38	18	42	2

Source: *Federal Reserve Bulletin* (1937: 897–8).

Note: A small bank had capital stock of $100,000 or less, a medium bank had capital stock of between $100,001 and $499,999 and a large bank had capital stock of $500,000 or more.

Table 5.12 Number of Failed Banks by Population of Towns and Cities: 1930–1934

Population (number of inhabitants)	1930	1931	1932	1933	1934
0–2499	976	1492	980	2701	42
2500–24,999	244	487	324	888	7
25,000 and over	130	314	149	411	8

Source: Federal Reserve Bulletin (1937: 901).

Despite interest in expanding branch banking as a solution to the instability in commercial banking, reform ultimately took the form of reinforcing prohibitions on branch banking. Indeed, the Banking Act of 1933 liberalized the McFadden branch banking rights of the national banks by extending to them the same intrastate branching rights enjoyed by state banks. However, interstate branch banking rights were still restricted as established by the 1927 McFadden Act.

The regulation of deposit interest rates marked the third significant provision of this Banking Act. This provision was the product of the belief that excessive interest rate competition contributed to financial instability. As early as 1918, officials voiced concern over rising deposit interest rates arguing that the higher the rate paid on deposits, the higher the cost of doing business to the banker and, consequently, the lower bank profitability. In the early 1930s, the argument shifted somewhat to one that stressed the relationship between rising deposit interest rates and bank risk. The argument was that as banks were forced to pay higher deposit interest rates, because of competition from other bankers, the bank would feel compelled to make high risk loans and investments in an attempt to recoup the higher interest rate cost.[34] Though empirical evidence suggests that interest rate competition in the 1920s and 1930s did not contribute to financial instability, Congress was convinced otherwise as evidenced by this regulation of interest rates.[35]

The regulation of deposit interest rates became known as Regulation Q. Section 11(b) of the Banking Act of 1933 prohibited all member banks from paying interest on demand deposits. The same section empowered the Federal Reserve Board with the authority to set the interest rate which could be paid by member banks on time and savings deposits. Regulation Q went into effect on November 1, 1933 at which time the Federal Reserve Board set a maximum rate of three percent on time and savings deposits.

After its activation in January of 1934, the Federal Deposit Insurance Corporation extended the interest rate ceiling to all insured commercial banks that were not members of the Federal Reserve System. However, early in 1935, when the Federal Reserve and the Federal Deposit Insurance Corporation moved to reduce the interest rate ceiling to two and one half percent, the statutory authority of the Federal Deposit Insurance Corporation to regulate interest rates was called into question. The Federal Deposit Insurance Corporation's regulation was consequently suspended until the Banking Act of 1935. Hence, it was not until the passage of the 1935 act that nonmember banks were subject to the rate controls of Regulation Q.[36]

The fourth significant provision separated commercial from investment banking. The impetus for this development came from two different arenas. First was the belief that bankers and brokers, through their dishonest and discreditable dealings, had contributed to the 1929 stock market crash and subsequent series of bank crises.[37] Though historians now believe that any unscrupulous behavior contributed insignificantly to the instability, bankers and brokers shouldered much of the blame at the time.[38] A second reason for this provision was the belief that there exists an inherent conflict of interest between commercial bankers' involvement in the securities market and their clients. More specifically, because commercial banks have access to a large number of depositors, they may push upon the depositor securities that may help the bank but not the depositor.[39] Legislative changes reflected both the concern that banks contributed to the stock market crash and that they were defrauding the public through what has been termed the "Glass–Steagall Act". This refers to those sections of the Banking Act of 1933 that deal specifically with the relationship between investment and commercial banking.

Four sections of the 1933 act were designed to separate investment from commercial bank activity. Sections 16 and 20 prohibited state member and national banks from underwriting corporate securities. Further, national banks, state member banks and their affiliates were banned from securities dealings. At the same time, however, the affiliates of state nonmember banks retained authority to engage in securities activity.[40] Section 21 prohibited any financial institution that accepted deposits from underwriting almost all types of securities. Several types of securities, including the issues of the U.S. federal government and the states, were exempt from section 21 prohibition. Finally, section 32 made it illegal for member bank officers to engage in the purchase or sale of securities.

The significance of the Banking Act of 1933 to the U.S. commercial banking sector cannot be overstated. The four significant provisions of the act changed the structure of banking as no other legislative development before. The provisions collectively preserved the dual banking system, limited competition between banks and between banks and other financial intermediaries and, at the same time, created a federal safety net under the commercial banking sector. Though in recent years some of these provisions have been repealed either entirely or partially, other provisions remain intact and continue to influence the performance of commercial banking in the twenty-first century.

In addition to restructuring commercial banking, the Banking Act of 1933 made substantial changes to the structure of the Federal Reserve System. When the Federal Reserve System was created in December of 1913 great measures were taken to avoid creating a central banking system. Instead, the system was structured to diffuse responsibility throughout a regional banking system. For example, the regional banks controlled open market operations. By the early 1930s, blame for the stock market crash of 1929 and the prolonged depression was largely placed on the financial community and often on the Federal Reserve.

In response, the Federal Reserve was restructured initially by the 1933 act and then again two years later with the passage of the Banking Act of 1935. In 1933, the control over open market operations was shifted away from the regional banks to the Board of Governors. After

1933 no regional bank was allowed to engage in open market operations except in accordance with the regulations set by the Board. The 1933 act also created the Federal Open Market Committee (FOMC) which was empowered to handle all purchases and sales on the open market. However, the regional banks had the authority to refuse to participate in the policies adopted by the FOMC. Thus while individual regional banks could no longer initiate open market operations they could abstain from participating in the process.

The 1933 act also empowered the Board of Governors with the authority to suspend regional and member banks from the use of the credit facilities of the system if the Board judged that prior credit policies were unsafe or did not accommodate the needs of commerce and industry. This control was a marked departure from the original Federal Reserve structure in which the reserve banks were free to extend credit to their members at their own discretion.

Finally, the 1933 act restructured the Federal Reserve by providing the Board the power to limit loans extended by the regional banks. This provision was to prevent the excessive use of bank loans for speculative purposes, as it was believed that the Federal Reserve System was too liberal in its loan extensions and thereby contributed to the stock market growth of the 1920s. The provisions of the 1933 act centralized the Board of Governor's powers within the Federal Reserve. However, less than two years later additional legislation was passed that would further centralize power and authority in the Federal Reserve, thereby leaving no doubt that it was truly a central bank.

Banking Act of 1935

The Governor of the Federal Reserve Board, Marriner Eccles, drafted the legislative proposal which became the Banking Act of 1935. In essence, this act restructured the Federal Reserve by empowering the Board with greater responsibilities and control over monetary policy.[41] First, the Board was given authority to approve or disapprove the appointment of president (previously governor) and vice president of each regional bank. Second, all Board members were placed on the Federal Open Market Committee. Third, regional banks were no longer allowed to engage in or decline to engage in open market operations. These two provisions not only gave the Board the majority voice on the Open Market Committee, it also eliminated what remained of the regional banks' discretion in open market decisions. At its core, this restructuring gave the Board almost complete control over monetary policy.

Assessment of regulation and stability

Much like the earlier history of U.S. commercial banking the response to the episodes of instability and crises in this era was increased regulation. Indeed, in the eight year span between 1927 and 1935 there were five significant bank legislative developments. However, this regulatory response differs from earlier responses because it was largely national in scope. In contrast, during the antebellum era regulation was largely at the state level and during the national banking era much of the regulation was still at the state level. Thus, this era of regulation completes a gradual shift of bank regulation from the state level to the national level.

Did this regulation contribute to bank stability? The short answer is that some of it did, some of it did but only temporarily, and some of it did not. Table 5.13 captures a summary of the impact this regulation had on bank stability. Since the focus of this work is on the relationship between commercial bank stability and regulation, the assessment presented here is only on the regulation that was primarily aimed at the commercial bank sector. Consequently, the Federal Reserve Act and the Banking Act of 1935 which both focused on the central bank and monetary policy are not included in this assessment. The discussion which follows elaborates on the assessment of the relationship between regulation and bank stability for the remaining three significant regulatory developments.

Assessment of 1927 McFadden Act

The 1927 McFadden Act made it easier for national and state banks to merge. This development created conditions of greater stability because the larger, merged bank enjoyed economies of scale and a more diversified balance sheet.[42] The data in Table 5.11 confirm this by showing, for example, that of all the banks that failed in 1933, 86.4 percent of them were small banks. Thus, the merger provision of the McFadden Act enhanced bank stability to the point where one wonders how much worse the crises of the 1930s would have been without it.

One provision of the McFadden Act liberalized branching by allowing national banks to branch in cities with a population over 25,000, if state law allowed. Table 5.12 indicates that bank failures were relatively less in cities with a population in excess of 25,000. These are the same cities that national banks were allowed to branch in with the passage of the McFadden Act. From this perspective, the extension of branching rights was stabilizing.

Table 5.13 Summary of Regulation and Its Impact on National and State Chartered Banks in the Era of Instability and Change

Regulation	Description	Channel(s) Through Which Regulation Impacts Bank Stability	Conclusion from the Evidence
McFadden Act of 1927			
1. Merging of national and state banks	• Reduced cost for national and state bank mergers. • Resulted in more diversified banks.	• Change bank structure by increasing bank size. • Decrease risk by increasing geographic diversification.	• Increased stability through substantially lower failures rates for larger banks (Table 5.11, Table 5.13 and Figure 5.8).
2. National banks may branch in headquarter city, provided state law allows	• National banks could establish branches in cities with populations above 25,000, provided state law allowed.	• Increase competition.	• Increased stability by increasing competition as evidenced by a reduction in the number of bank failures in those markets in which the banks were allowed to branch (Table 5.12).
3. Prohibited intrastate branching for national banks	• National banks prohibited from intrastate branching. • Created barriers to entry and protected the unit banker.	• Decrease competition. • Change bank structure by limiting bank size. • Increase risk by limiting geographic diversification.	• Decreased stability as eight states allowed for branch banking (Table 5.3) and there were very few banks failures in almost all of these states for the 1925–1933 period (Tables 5.5–5.7). Further evidence in Table 5.13 which indicates that small banks were more likely to fail. • Decreased stability by limiting balance sheet diversification (Carlson and Mitchener (2005)).

Table 5.13 Summary of Regulation and Its Impact on National and State Chartered Banks in the Era of Instability and Change – *continued*

Regulation	Description	Channel(s) Through Which Regulation Impacts Bank Stability	Conclusion from the Evidence
4. Prohibited interstate branching for banks	• National and state banks prohibited from interstate branching. • Created barriers to entry and protected the unit banker.	• Decrease competition. • Change bank structure by limiting bank size. • Increase risk by limiting geographic diversification.	• Decreased stability as eight states allowed for branch banking (Table 5.3) and there were very few banks failures in almost all of these states for the 1925–1933 period (Tables 5.5–5.7). Further evidence in Table 5.13 which indicates that small banks were more likely to fail. • Decreased stability by limiting balance sheet diversification (Carlson and Mitchener (2005)).
5. Made legal national bank security activity	• National banks could buy and sell investment grade securities up to 25 percent of capital.	• No change.	• No impact on stability as this provision did not change the market since banks were already engaged in the activity. This was a legal recognition of market activity.

Table 5.13 Summary of Regulation and Its Impact on National and State Chartered Banks in the Era of Instability and Change – *continued*

Regulation	Description	Channel(s) Through Which Regulation Impacts Bank Stability	Conclusion from the Evidence
Reconstruction Finance Corp.			
1. Lending to commercial banks	• Commercial banks could borrow from the RFC.	• No change.	• Ambiguous impact on stability because (1) currency in circulation (Figure 5.7) fell in 1932 but increased in 1933; (2) bank loans continued to fall so credit was not restored ; (3) The number of bank failures in 1932 declined from 1931 but relief was temporary (Tables 5.5–5.7).
Banking Act of 1933			
1. Creation of federal deposit insurance	• Provided federal deposit insurance for all commercial banks that purchased it.	• Increase risk. • Decrease competition.	• Increased stability because (1) currency in circulation indicates the degree to which confidence is restored (Figure 5.7); and (2) significant reduction in the number of bank failures (Figures 5.3 and 5.4). • Decrease stability by reducing competition for depositors and the accompanying moral hazard.

Table 5.13 Summary of Regulation and Its Impact on National and State Chartered Banks in the Era of Instability and Change – *continued*

Regulation	Description	Channel(s) Through Which Regulation Impacts Bank Stability	Conclusion from the Evidence
2. National banks to branch statewide, provided state law allows	• National banks could establish branches throughout the state, provided state law allowed.	• Increase competition. • Decrease risk by increasing geographic diversification. • Change bank structure by increasing bank size.	• Increased stability by improving efficiency and profits (Carlson and Mitchener (2009)). • Increased stability by diversifying balance sheet risk (Carlson and Mitchener (2005)). • Increased stability because smaller banks were more likely to fail (Table 5.11, 5.12, Figure 5.8).
3. Prohibited interstate branching	• National and state banks prohibited from interstate branching.	• Decrease competition. • Increase risk by limiting geographic diversification. • Change bank structure by limiting bank size.	• Decreased stability because the outcome is the opposite of (2) above.
4. Ceiling interest rate on time and savings deposits	• Placed a ceiling on time and savings deposits.	• Decrease competition.	• No impact on stability while the regulated rate was not binding.[a] • Decrease stability to the extent that competition is stabilizing.

Table 5.13 Summary of Regulation and Its Impact on National and State Chartered Banks in the Era of Instability and Change – *continued*

Regulation	Description	Channel(s) Through Which Regulation Impacts Bank Stability	Conclusion from the Evidence
5. Prohibit interest payments on demand deposits	• Prohibited interest rate payments on demand deposits.	• Decrease competition. • Decrease cost of demand deposits.	• Decrease stability to the extent that competition is stabilizing. • Increased stability by reducing a cost to obtaining deposits.[a]
6. Separate commercial and investment banking	• Prohibit the underwriting or dealing of securities by commercial banks.	• Decrease competition. • Increase risk by limiting geographic diversification.	• Decreased stability by reducing competition (Hayes et al. (1983)). • Decreased stability by limiting branching though affiliates (E. White (1986)).

Notes: There are five identified channels through which regulation may impact stability; 1) change risk taking; 2) limit diversification; 3) change cost and revenue structure; 4) change the structure of the market; and 5) change the nature of competition. See Chapter 2 for a discussion of each.
[a]See Chapter 6 for an analysis of Regulation Q once the regulated rate became binding.

However, the other key provisions of the 1927 Act, the prohibition on intrastate and interstate branching, contributed to bank instability rather than stability. Table 5.3 indicates that there were eight states that permitted statewide branching during this period. In all of these states, there were very few banks failures during the 1925 through 1933 period (Tables 5.5 through 5.7) with the exception of state nonmember failures in North Carolina and South Carolina. During this period, North Carolina averaged 30.2 failures per year and South Carolina averaged 23.6 state nonmember failures each year. In contrast, the states that performed poorly in terms of the number of failures were Arkansas, Minnesota, Iowa, Illinois, South Dakota, Nebraska, and Kansas which either prohibited branch banking or, in the case of South Dakota, had no branch laws.

Taken together, the McFadden Act enhanced stability through the merger provision and the extension of intra-city branch rights to national banks. However, the provisions to prohibit intrastate and interstate branching were destabilizing as it preserved a system of small, undiversified, unit banks.

Assessment of 1932 Reconstruction Finance Corporation

The primary function of the RFC was to extend loans to banks in the hopes that they would turn around and extend credit to nonfinancial firms. Recall that President Hoover was convinced that the central problem in banking was too little credit. Bankers, at that time, insisted that credit demand was weak.[43] Regardless, it is clear that the RFC did not reverse the trend as loans fell at commercial banks between 1929 and 1936.[44] From this perspective, the RFC, was not successful in its immediate goal of increasing credit. While banks did borrow from the RFC, they did not use the funds to extend credit. As evidence, consider that between March 1929 and the end of 1932, loans extended by commercial banks fell 64 percent.[45] Indeed, most bankers quickly repaid their RFC loans and some of the incentive for repayment surely was the result of the decision to make public quarterly reports on the RFC's lending activity. Bankers were quick to repay loans and hesitant to take out future loans because they thought the public would interpret such borrowing as a sign of weakness.[46] Thus, while those bankers who did borrow failed to lend, other bankers were unwilling to even borrow from the RFC. Both instances complicated the Corporation's quest to alleviate the perceived credit deficit.

In the end, the RFC had an ambiguous impact on bank stability. Credit may be given to the RFC for the 1932 decline in currency holdings. This may reflect an improvement in consumer confidence; depositors may have reacted positively to the creation of the RFC by holding less currency. This would certainly be a stabilizing element. However, because the RFC did not improve credit availability nor did it keep bank failures at bay, this regulation did not contribute significantly to stabilizing the banking sector. Further, the lower currency holdings were temporary; currency holdings increased substantially in 1933 so any stabilizing element of the RFC was temporary and short lived.

Assessment of the Banking Act of 1933

The impact of the four primary provisions of the Banking Act of 1933 on the stability of banking is discussed below (see Table 5.13). This is followed by a brief discussion of the four provisions collectively and the general impact of this legislative act on bank stability.

A. Federal Deposit Insurance

As explained in Chapters 3 and 4, several states during the antebellum and national banking era experimented with deposit insurance. These were generally perceived to be failures because they increased risk taking and failed to keep bank runs and failures at bay. Deposit insurance comes with a price; depositors have no incentive to monitor and discipline banks and bankers have an incentive to take on excessive risk because any loss to depositors will be covered by insurance. This is the moral hazard of deposit insurance. In the nineteenth and early twentieth century's, the moral hazard cost of deposit insurance was well known and understood. For example, in 1908 the Bankers' Association of Illinois studied the possibility of a federal deposit insurance scheme and concluded that, because of moral hazard risks, the idea was not desirable. In 1933, President Roosevelt, the Federal Reserve, the Treasury Secretary, and the American Bankers' Association were opposed to the idea of federal deposit insurance because of moral hazard concerns.[47] Indeed, in the 57 years prior to the 1933 establishment of federal deposit insurance, there were at least 149 previous proposals that all failed.[48] Nonetheless, the extreme number of bank failures in the early 1930s created the conditions necessary for certain lawmakers to push through federal deposit insurance.[49]

Just as in earlier eras, deposit insurance was both stabilizing and destabilizing. To the extent that deposit insurance restored confidence and eliminated bank runs, it was certainly stabilizing to the commercial bank sector. In 1933, there were 4000 commercial bank failures and only 57 failures the following year.[50] This is strong evidence that, in the immediate time frame, deposit insurance stabilized commercial banking. However, deposit insurance was also destabilizing from the perspective that it increased the moral hazard problems outlined above. Further, deposit insurance reduces competition in the banking sector more generally. Depositors no longer have an incentive to monitor their bank or to be thoughtful in even choosing a bank. From the perspective of the depositor, banks become homogeneous; deposits are insured to the same extent at all insured commercial banks. Consequently, rather than choose a bank because of its record of prudent management and risk taking, depositors rationally ignore that information and make choices based on location and convenience. The element of depositor discipline is removed with deposit insurance and this may certainly contribute to instability in banking.

B. Branch banking

The Banking Act of 1933 liberated branching rights through the provision that allowed national banks to branch statewide, if state law allowed. *The Federal Reserve Committee on Branch, Group, and Chain Banking* (1932) describe the position of the Federal Reserve and of the Comptroller regarding branches. Both were highly in favor of creating a branch system because they were sure it would prevent bank failures and would place national banks on equal competitive ground as state chartered banks. Indeed, the Comptroller of the Currency authorized national banks to open additional offices in the early 1920s despite the interpretation of the National Bank Act to the contrary. However, the Comptroller stressed that these additional offices must be in compliance with state law. Thus, the provision in the Banking Act of 1933 that afforded national banks interstate branching rights was, to a certain extent, a legislative recognition of market developments during the 1920s and early 1930s. That is, markets and regulators had moved beyond the constraints set by Congress and the provision in the 1933 Act codified these developments. Nonetheless, this provision enhanced bank stability through two channels: by increasing competition and by expanding geographic diversity which reduces bank risk.

Existing literature on the relationship between increased competition through branching and bank stability overwhelmingly indicates that competition enhances stability.[51] This relationship holds both historically and contemporarily but a significant amount of research has investigated this relationship during the 1920s and 1930s. For example, Carlson and Mitchener (2009) find evidence that incumbent banks, when exposed to increased competition because of branch banking, reacted by improving their efficiency, cutting costs, and increasing profits. Further, these scholars find that the banks that responded this way were more likely to survive the crises of the early 1930s. This is important evidence of the stabilizing influence of branch banking and competition.

Further, during this era, urban banking environments tended to be extremely competitive, even in those states that did not allow for branching. In contrast, in many of the smaller towns where one bank was common, there was little to no competition. These were the banks that failed in significant numbers (see Table 5.12). It is difficult not to correlate the stability of more competitive markets and the instability of less competitive markets.

Branch banking is also said to increase stability through geographic diversification. When banks are not allowed to branch, their financial health is determined by a narrow set of liabilities and assets. The banker accepts deposits from individuals near the bank and extends loans to clients near the bank. Since these clients all share the same microeconomic environment, a downturn or adverse shock to the community can quickly make the bank vulnerable to failure because its balance sheet is not diversified. Branching, it is argued, can allow the banker to diversify the balance sheet and make it stronger when there is a local or industry specific economic downturn.

During the 1920s and 1930s, banks with branch offices were recognized typically to be larger and more diversified that the smaller unit

Figure 5.8 Average Size of Failed Banks by Bank Type: 1921–1941

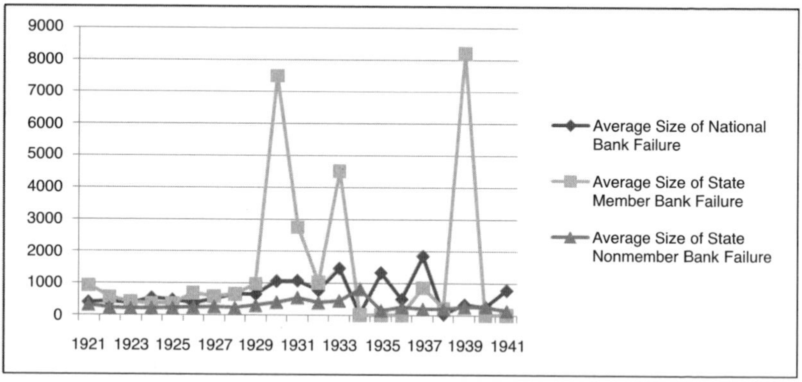

Source: Board of Governors, *Banking and Monetary Statistics, 1914–1941*.

Note: Amount in thousands of dollars; calculated as the ratio of deposits at failed banks to the number of failures. Deposit data for failed banks is not available prior to 1921.

banks.[52] Table 5.11 indicates that, for all bank types, the larger banks were less likely to fail than smaller banks. If larger banks were those with branches, perhaps some of their stability in terms of survivorship comes from their ability to diversify their portfolios. A comparison of failure data in Tables 5.5 through 5.7 indicate that state nonmember banks were the most likely to fail during this period. Further, Figure 5.8 indicates the average sized failure at state nonmember banks was much smaller than failures at national and state member banks. Taken together this data clearly indicates that smaller banks were more likely to fail during the 1920s and 1930s. Further, as indicated in the earlier discussion regarding bank mergers, in those states with branching, weaker banks could merge with stronger banks rather than fail.[53] Merging was a mechanism for obtaining the diversification that was prohibited through restrictions on branching.

While most scholars have tested the competition and stability relationship through the two channels of competition and diversity separately, Carlson and Mitchener (2005) test which channel is most profound. They find that during the 1920s and 1930s, increased competition from branching caused weaker banks to exit the industry leaving behind a stronger and more stable collection of banks. They find that both the competition and geographical diversification channels improve stability but their results indicate that the competition effects were more important in stabilizing banking.

While the provision that allowed for intrastate banking certainly enhanced bank stability, the Banking Act of 1933 contained another provision that banned interstate banking. Banning interstate banking is tantamount to keeping all of the stabilizing benefits of intrastate banking within the state. Consequently, to the extent that intrastate banking improved stability through increased competition and geographic diversification, the prohibition on interstate branching makes the banking system more fragile by decreasing competition and geographical diversification.

The impact on stability of the two branching provisions is probably not offsetting. The prohibition on interstate banking applied to all banks in all states. The extension of intrastate branching applied only to national banks only in those states that allowed for such branching. In 1936, 17 states allowed for intrastate branching (see Table 5.4) so the stabilizing benefits from the intrastate provision were less than the destabilizing costs from the interstate branching ban. In the end, the two provisions that concern branch banking had an opposite impact on bank stability but, on the whole, were more destabilizing.

C. Regulation Q

Like the other provisions of the Banking Act of 1933, Regulation Q limited bank competition. Since banks could no longer pay interest on demand deposits and the interest on time and savings deposits was controlled, banks could no longer price compete for deposits. This, of course, was the intention of the provision. In terms of its impact on stability, the immediate impact of Regulation Q, on its own, was to reduce the cost of demand deposits. In this way, it may have enhanced stability by reducing bank costs. Yet, even this is not a forgone conclusion because whether profits increase depends on the elasticity of demand and supply for demand deposits; with a zero interest rate regulation in place, the number of demand deposits that bankers are able to attract will fall.[54] Indeed, scholars find that Regulation Q did not improve bank profitability.[55] Further, since the market interest rate on time and savings deposits were below the ceiling set by the Federal Reserve of three percent in 1933 and 2.5 percent in 1935, this provision had no impact on costs in the first 30 or so years of its implementation (see Figure 5.9).[56] Consequently, the impact of Regulation Q on bank stability, in the short run, appears to have been negligible. Bank profitability did not improve and the cost of obtaining time and savings deposits were determined by the market since the ceiling rate was not binding. As will be shown in the next chapter, however, Regu-

Figure 5.9 Average Interest Rate Paid on Time Deposits at Member Banks: 1930–1968

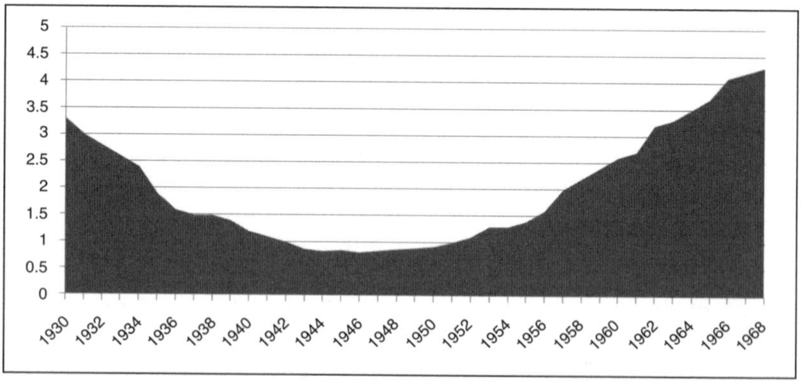

Source: Board of Governors, *Banking and Monetary Statistics, 1914–1941*, and *Banking and Monetary Statistics, 1941–1970.*

Note: This is the ratio of interest paid on time deposits to total time deposits.

lation Q became a significant source of instability in the 1960s when market interest rates rose above the regulated rates and banks faced nonprice competition and disintermediation.

D. Glass–Steagall

The Glass–Steagall provision of the Banking Act of 1933 separated commercial and investment banking because conventional wisdom believed that bankers had recklessly speculated in the stock market and, in doing so, caused the 1920 stock market crash and subsequent bank crises. Despite this common belief, there is little or no evidence that during the 1920s, bank behavior contributed to the stock market crash of 1929. An empirical analysis finds that the securities operation at national banks did not increase the probability of bank failure, that bank earnings did not coincide with the earnings at the investment affiliates, and that the presence of an investment affiliate did not negatively impact bank capital.[57] Rather, the banks that engaged in securities activity had the opportunity to diversify and enjoy economies of scale that made the institutions more stable, not less, which was the contention during the crises of the 1930s.[58] Further, scholars have found that commercial banks that were engaged in securities activity were underwriting securities of higher quality than investment bankers.[59]

If bank securities activity was not excessively risky and if it did not compromise bank profits, what impact did the separation of commercial and investment banking have on the stability of commercial banking? To the extent that the security affiliates were profitable, the separation would hurt bank profits and hence compromise stability. As evidence of the stability of banks operating security affiliates, consider that between 1930 and 1933, 26.3 percent of all national banks failed but only 6.5 percent of those with security affiliates failed during that same time frame.[60] Further, investment affiliates allowed banks to circumvent geographical restrictions on their activities so that to prohibit this was to limit or reduce the benefits of diversification and dispersed risk.[61] That is, prior to this 1933 regulation, national banks were able to circumvent, to some extent, limits on branching by opening these affiliates.

The separation also reduced competition between both bankers themselves and between commercial bankers and investment bankers. As indicated earlier, there is a plethora of evidence that indicates that competition in banking is stabilizing.[62] Consequently, to the degree that competition improves stability, the separation of commercial and investment banking reduces competition and contributes to bank instability.

E. Provisions collectively

All of the major provisions of the Banking Act of 1933 share one common element: they all reduced competition. Consequently, when evaluating the Banking Act of 1933 as a single legislative development, to understand its impact on stability is to understand the relationship between competition and stability. As introduced in Chapter 2, the relationship between competition and stability in banking is complex. It was long assumed that, in banking, an increase in competition would increase instability and fragility. The assumption was that bankers would respond to competition by taking greater risks. As a result, legislation in the earlier two eras, as well as this one, focused on reducing competition in banking. Unfortunately, as indicated in the analysis of the individual provisions, the decrease in bank competition had the opposite affect; it made banking more fragile and unstable in the long run.

In addition, the major provisions of the Banking Act of 1933 were not adopted independent of one another. When the provisions of the Banking Act of 1933 were under debate, bankers were vehemently opposed to deposit insurance for reasons mentioned earlier. One reason for opposition was the cost that deposit insurance would impose on the banks. Some members of Congress favored the Regulation Q provision as a means of lowering bank cost to offset the cost of deposit insurance. Indeed, Regulation Q was seen as a concession to the banker to get deposit insurance passed.[63] Similarly, the separation of commercial and investment banking was seen as necessary once deposit insurance was agreed upon. That is, regulators and lawmakers did not want banks to be utilizing insured deposits to invest in securities or to be used in the underwriting process.

Concluding remarks

The Banking Act of 1933 is often credited for saving the banking system and for restoring bank stability. In the years following the bank crises of the 1930s, it appeared as though the regulation to constrain bank competition had worked; bank failures were significantly reduced, over time confidence in banking was restored, and perhaps most importantly, there were no bank crises. Certainly, deposit insurance was an important measure in getting depositors to return to banks and to ending bank runs. In the short run, it appears as though the deposit insurance provision was stabilizing. Unfortunately, the long run impact of deposit insurance and its application significantly increased moral hazard and bank fragility. Further, there is no evidence to indicate that the other provisions stabilized commercial banking in either the short or long run. Indeed, as will be shown in Chapter 6, some of the provisions from the Banking Act of 1933 that were thought to have brought about stability were the source of bank instability in later years.

Regulation can be stabilizing at one point in time and destabilizing later because of the dynamic nature of markets. Recall from Chapter 2 that markets are constantly in flux as entrepreneurs search for profitable opportunities revealed through the market itself. The process of seeking profits reveals information about the market that cannot be known in advance. Thus, the dynamic market process produces important economic information that the market participants rely on. As markets are dynamic and regulation is static, and because regulatory decisions are based on incomplete information, the regulation necessarily will affect bank stability differently over time. In the case of deposit insurance, the market conditions in 1933 were such that deposit insurance enhanced stability. However, over time, the market process evolved revealing a different set of opportunities and conditions that resulted in risk taking and other moral hazard problems. The remaining chapters of this book will explore more thoroughly the evolution of markets and how the provisions of the Banking Act of 1933 increasingly became a source of fragility for the banking sector.

Reflecting on the previous two chapters, from the inception of commercial banking in the United States through the Great Depression, the regulatory framework in banking grew considerably. Regulation that had largely been the domain of states became, with the Banking Act of 1864, the domain of the federal government. The regulation of the 1920s and 1930s continued the trend of increasing federal banking regulation. At the same time, the banking sector became increasingly fragile as measured by the number and severity of both bank crises and failures. The immediate postwar period is a stable time in U.S. commercial banking but the stability does not last as the constraints of the regulatory structure become destabilizing in the face of a dynamic market.

6
Postwar Banking Era and Regulatory Response: 1945–1999

Introduction to the postwar banking experience

The immediate postwar years were rather quiet and stable for the national economy generally and for commercial banking specifically. However, that all changed by the middle of the 1960s and calm was replaced with volatility and uncertainty. Consequently, it may be helpful to think of this era as one in which the first 20 or so years were stable and generally uneventful followed by a rather long period characterized by volatility in real and financial markets and an unprecedented series of banking legislation. Indeed, this era in commercial banking is unlike the three previous. In the earlier banking eras, a pattern developed in which either a series of bank crises was followed with regulation or a few significant crises resulted in a regulatory response. The period between the middle of the 1960s and the end of the twentieth century did not have a defining bank crisis or singular regulatory response. Rather, moving forward from the mid-1960s, this era is one characterized by several developments: significant change in the competitive environment in banking; considerable change in the balance sheet and management of commercial banks in response to the increased competition; a landscape dotted with both large and small bank failures; a substantial crises in the savings and loan industry; and the passage of eight important federal bank regulations.[1] While this era may have lacked a single, defining bank crisis, understanding it is an important part of understanding the overall relationship between bank regulation and stability in the United States. This is because the era witnessed a protracted wave of bank failures interspersed with a few large failures and a series of regulatory responses. This period is also important because, as will be shown in Chapter 7, there are some who blame the first financial crisis of the twenty-first century on regulatory developments during this era.

Macroeconomic backdrop

Despite relatively favorable growth in real gross domestic product, the national macroeconomic conditions during the postwar banking era may be characterized as relatively volatile after the mid-1960s. Inflation was climbing by the end of the 1960s, and then was volatile and at times extremely high at the end of the 1970s and beginning of the 1980s (Figure A.18). During the 1970s, major foreign currencies were allowed to float and exchange rate volatility followed (Figure A.19). In response to inflation, inflation expectations, and monetary policy, interest rates were also rising and highly unstable (Figure A.20). Taken together, this volatility, particularly in interest rates, interjected a destabilizing element to commercial banking on the national level.

At the same time, there were regional recessions that hurt commercial banking in some sections of the country more than others. Four regional recessions have been identified during this period.[2] First was the rapid and significant decline in agricultural prices in the middle of the 1980s. The decline in prices reduced farm income which led to many farm loan defaults. The second regional recession was in Texas, Oklahoma, and other energy-producing state in the Southwest. Both in 1981 and 1985, oil prices unexpectedly dropped. Banks that had a high concentration of energy loans failed when these loans went into default. Further, in the Southwest, the post 1981 period was one of boom and bust in the commercial real estate market which hurt banks in the region. The third regional decline occurred in the Northeast in 1980 and 1981 when gross state product in many of these states declined. The fourth and final recession was in California in 1991 and 1992 when gross state product turned negative. As discussed later in this chapter, these regional recessions, particularly the first two, were highly correlated with bank failures in the region.

Trends and challenges in commercial banking

The macroeconomic conditions of this era may be described as unsettled. Concurrent with the variable macroeconomy, the banking sector was undergoing significant changes of its own. Two trends describe commercial banking between the middle of the 1960s and the end of the twentieth century. First is an increasingly competitive environment.

Commercial bankers faced increased competition for both their assets and liabilities. Specifically, bankers had a difficult time retaining depositors as mutual fund companies offered products that paid higher interest rates. Further, bankers faced increased competition as nonfinancial firms moved away from traditional bank loans to issue their own commercial paper and securities.[3] Banks were also under competitive pressure from finance companies who increasingly offered business loans. At the same time, foreign banks expanded significantly into the U.S. commercial banking markets which also increased competitive pressure on bankers. The second trend was the changing nature of bank management in response to the increased competition. Banks, while constrained by regulation, responded to the highly competitive environment by finding new revenue sources, offering new products to both depositors and borrowers, and by consolidating with other banks and financial institutions. Both trends are discussed below.

Increased competition

Innovations in communications and computer technology combined to make entry into the traditional banking market more readily accessible. By reducing the cost of obtaining information, carrying out financial transactions and monitoring credit risk, commercial bankers lost their advantage in the traditional functions of gathering deposits and extending credit. In addition, regulatory constraints limited banks leaving them unable to respond to market changes which then opened the door for new competition. Further, the new competitors operated with a significant cost advantage since they were not subject to the regulation that burdened commercial banks (e.g. capital and reserve requirements, loans limits, regulation Q, lending mandates in the Community Reinvestment Act, etc.).[4]

A. Commercial paper and finance companies

Nonfinancial firms typically borrow from commercial banks or they issue debt to investors. Historically, these firms relied on commercial bank loans because they were often less expensive than debt. However, as is explained later in this chapter, banks had trouble meeting nonfinancial loan demands during the credit crunch of 1966 leaving nonfinancial firms unable to obtain the credit that they desired.[5] Part of the reason banks could not meet loan demand was because market interest rates rose above the regulation Q rate. In response, depositors pulled their time deposits out of commercial banks leaving the banks with fewer loanable funds. In 1969, like 1966, interest rates rose above the regulated rate and banks faced disintermediation.[6] This time, however, they tapped two new sources of funds in an attempt to continue lending. First, U.S. banks increasingly borrowed funds from their overseas branches who were able to borrow in the Eurodollar market.[7] Second, many bank holding companies were able to sell commercial paper and transfer the proceeds to their banks by purchasing loans originated at the bank. At the same time, nonfinancial firms were increasingly issuing commercial paper as an alternative to issuing debt or borrowing from commercial banks. The nonfinancial sector did not want to be vulnerable to a credit crunch like that in 1966 by over relying on bank loans. The commercial paper market provided these firms with an alternative funding source. Figure A.21 illustrates the extent to which commercial paper grew in importance at nonfinancial firms. Clearly, after 1966, nonfinancial firms increasingly relied on commercial paper for some of their short-term borrowing.

Another source of competition for the banker came from finance companies.[8] Finance companies, like commercial bankers, make business (and consumer) loans. However, while bank loans are typically not backed by assets, finance company loans do require inventories, accounts receivable, or equipment as collateral. Generally, finance companies issue commercial paper to raise funds for lending and most of the lending is short term. Like the commercial paper market, finance companies increased their share of the business credit market (see Figure A.22) as they increasingly devoted more of their assets to short-term lending. The increased lending commitment by finance companies was particularly strong during the 1970s and 1980s. Indeed, some have argued that finance companies offer one of the greatest sources of competition to the banker because they offer the same functions but without the regulatory costs.[9]

B. Foreign banks

While the growth in foreign-owned banks operating in the United States was most pronounced in the 1990s, the growth began in earnest in the 1970s. Consider that in 1973, foreign-owned banks had 7.6 percent of the total market in business lending in the United States and their assets comprised 3.8 percent of the bank market.[10] By 1980, foreign-owned banks increased their share of the business lending market to 19.2 percent and their assets comprised 11.9 percent of bank assets. In terms of their share of bank deposits, over this same time frame, foreign-owned deposit shares increased from 1.7 percent to 6.6 percent. By 1990, the assets of foreign-owned banks were 21.4 percent of the total; they had 18 percent of the total lending market, and 14.5 percent of the bank deposits in the United States.

The growth in foreign-owned banks represented new competition for U.S. commercial banks and often put the U.S. banks at a competitive disadvantage. Until regulatory changes in the 1980s, foreign-owned banks were not subject to domestic regulation, including the provisions from the 1930s. Commercial bankers became increasingly concerned that the Glass–Steagall provisions limited their ability to compete not only with nonbanks but also with competition from foreign banks.[11] Bankers were right to worry as the increased lending from foreign banks has been found to be the largest source of competition for commercial bankers since the middle of the 1980s.[12]

C. Mutual funds

Mutual funds have a long history, largely outside of the United States.[13] Their appeal historically, and today, is that they provide the investor a low cost means of diversification and liquidity. In the United States, mutual funds have their origins in the Northeast region during the 1920s. At that time, most funds were closed-ended.[14] Indeed, in 1929, there were nearly 700 closed-ended funds and only 19 open-ended funds.[15] By the beginning of the 1950s, there were over 100 open-ended funds and more than 100 additional funds were established during the 1960s. The 1970s gave rise to no-load funds which were extremely popular and facilitated growth in the industry.[16] Another measure of the growth in this industry is the number of shareholder accounts as this indicates participation by investors.[17] In 1970, there were 10,690 thousand accounts and by 1980 it increased to 12,088 thousand accounts. By the end of this banking era, in 1999, there were 226,212 thousand mutual fund accounts which is an increase of 2016 percent from 1970 (see also Figure A.23).

Mutual funds and money market mutual funds were an important source of new competition for commercial bankers. Mutual funds were not subject to regulation Q or any of the other banking regulation discussed thus far. Consequently, when interest rates rose above the regulated price ceiling on time deposits, depositors left commercial banks and placed many of those funds in money market mutual funds to earn the market interest rate. Initially, banks were at an impasse; they could not offer the same interest rate and were thus faced with disintermediation.

At the same time that mutual and money market mutual funds are competition for banks' liabilities, they also facilitate the competition from finance companies. Mutual funds purchase a significant portion of the commercial paper that is sold by finance companies. These purchases, in turn, are liabilities to finance companies so that they can compete in lending markets with commercial bankers. Further, the symbiotic growth of finance companies and mutual funds has fueled the commercial paper market. Thus, in the end, the growth in the nonfinancial firm's use of commercial paper and the growth in competition from finance companies and mutual fund companies were reinforcing the competitive disadvantage facing the commercial banker.

Bankers' response to competition

Commercial bankers were feeling competitive pressure from all sides. As described above, there were many new entrants in the traditional commercial bank market and often the commercial bankers were unable to counter because of regulatory constraints. In response, bankers began to innovate and find ways to circumvent the regulation enabling them to regain their competitive position and respond, albeit slowly, to changing market conditions. Bankers were innovative in finding new sources of income, of creating new ways to retain or attract deposits, and finding ways to diversify and expand, despite ceilings on time deposits and other regulatory constraints. The process by which bankers responded to the increased competition is described below.

A. Bank off-balance sheet activity

Banks earn income from the loans and securities on their balance sheet but they also earn income from off-balance sheet activities. These are income generating activities that are not on the balance sheet because they do not affect the assets or liabilities at the bank. Three of the most important off-balance sheet activities are introduced.[18] First, banks often make loan commitments which provide an individual or a firm the right to borrow a certain amount of money in the future. Banks charge a fee for this commitment which means that it will generate income, even if the potential borrower fails to actually use the commitment. Second, banks issue letters of credit which are guarantees that the bank will cover a payment if the firm does not. A firm pays a fee for the letter of credit which often gives the firm more credibility when engaged in business with foreign firms. Another variety is called a standby letter of credit in which the bank promises payment on a security. When a nonfinancial firm issues commercial paper, for example, it will also purchase a standby letter of credit which informs the buyer that the bank is standing ready to pay for the paper if the firm cannot. The standby letter of credit is also helpful to the firm issuing the paper because it will improve the rating on the commercial paper and, as a result, lower the interest rate the firm will pay to borrow. A third type of off-balance sheet activity is derivatives, such as futures and options.[19] Many large banks trade derivatives in bonds, stocks, and foreign currency. Since these are agreements about future transactions, they do not appear on the bank balance sheet.

While off-balance sheet activities are not new, during the late 1960s and early 1970s, they grew in importance. The lack of capital requirements on off-balance sheet activity is a factor in explaining their growth.[20] Further, as indicated above, as firms increasingly issued commercial paper, this certainly increased the demand for standby letters of credit. By definition, off-balance sheet activities generate income for the bank that is not interest earnings on loans and securities. Consequently, one measure of the extent to which banks are engaged in off-balance sheet activity is to consider noninterest income data.[21] Figure 6.1 illustrates the extent to which banks rely on noninterest income to improve profitability. Noticeably, the late 1970s and early

Figure 6.1 Noninterest Income at U.S. Commercial Banks: 1966–1999

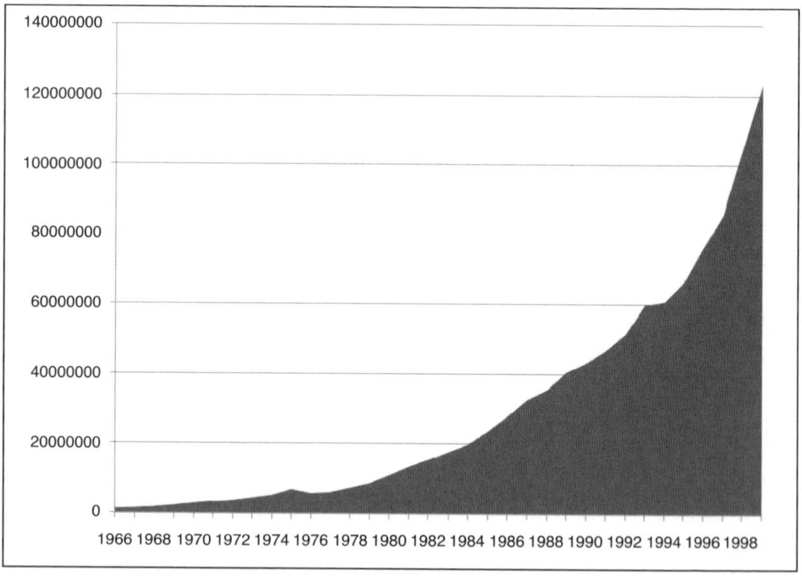

Source: http://www2.fdic.gov/hsob/hsobRpt.asp.

Note: Amount in thousands.

1980s mark a significant increase in noninterest income at commercial banks, a trend which has continued to this day.

B. State level branching regulation

In addition to the growth in off-balance sheet activities, bankers successfully pushed beyond geographical constraints to expand and diversify. As shown in Chapters 3 through 5, intrastate branching was prohibited from the earliest commercial bank experiences in the United States. Over time, national banks were afforded equal branch opportunities with state chartered banks. At the same time, interstate branching and banking had been legislatively banned. In terms of intrastate branching, state legislators increasingly relaxed limits on branching within state boundaries. Much of the movement towards freer intrastate branching came about in the 1980s and 1990s. As seen in Table 6.1, all but 14 states allowed for limited branching either before or during the 1960s and, by 1994, all but 13 states allowed for intrastate branching. At the same time, another trend developed that allowed some banks to avoid the interstate banking ban. States started forming regional pacts in which bank holding companies (BHCs) were allowed to bank, either completely or with restrictions, in other states that agreed to the pact.[22] Indeed, as Table 6.1 illustrates, all states, except Hawaii had regional interstate banking agreements in place by 1994. Most of these agreements were made in the mid-1980s and this certainly marked a departure from all of U.S. commercial banking experience to date as it was the first movement into the interstate banking arena.[23] Further, as will be shown below, in 1994, legislative action allowed for interstate banking across the country and also opened the possibility of interstate branching.

C. Consolidation

Entering this era in banking, all the provisions from the Banking Act of 1933 were in place; indeed between 1935 and 1977, there was only one significant legislative development in commercial banking. In 1956, congress passed the Bank Holding Company Act (BHCA). This regulation, and subsequent amendments to it, prohibits the interstate ownership of banks by bank holding companies owning more than one bank, unless the state of the bank to be purchased allows. It also gives the Federal Reserve the authority to determine all activities at bank holding companies. Further, the Federal Reserve has authority to allow a bank holding company to own any company whose activities are closely related to banking. The 1956 act was important because it opened the door for bank holding companies to expand both across state lines and into other lines

Table 6.1 Evolution of Branch Banking Laws by State

State	Limited Branching	Intrastate Branching	Interstate Regional Pacts
Alabama	Before 1960	June 1990	July 1987
Alaska	Before 1960	Before 1960	July 1982
Arizona	Before 1960	Before 1960	October 1986
Arkansas	April 1973	Forbidden	January 1989
California	Before 1960	Before 1960	July 1987
Colorado	August 1991	Forbidden	July 1988
Connecticut	Before 1960	October 1988	June 1983
Delaware	Before 1960	Before 1960	January 1988
Florida	January 1977	December 1988	July 1985
Georgia	Before 1960	Forbidden	July 1985
Hawaii	Before 1960	January 1986	Forbidden
Idaho	Before 1960	Before 1960	July 1985
Illinois	September 1988	June 1993	July 1986
Indiana	Before 1960	May 1991	January 1986
Iowa	July 1972	Forbidden	January 1991
Kansas	May 1987	February 1990	July 1992
Kentucky	Before 1960	Forbidden	July 1984
Louisiana	Before 1960	July 1988	July 1987
Maine	Before 1960	October 1975	January 1978
Maryland	Before 1960	Before 1960	July 1985
Massachusetts	September 1961	October 1984	July 1983
Michigan	September 1969	August 1988	January 1986
Minnesota	April 1980	Forbidden	July 1986
Mississippi	Before 1960	Forbidden	July 1988
Missouri	December 1990	December 1990	August 1986
Montana	January 1990	Forbidden	October 1993
Nebraska	September 1983	Forbidden	January 1990
Nevada	Before 1960	Before 1960	July 1985
New Hampshire	October 1963	July 1987	September 1987
New Jersey	Before 1960	February 1983	September 1986
New Mexico	Before 1960	July 1991	June 1989
New York	Before 1960	Forbidden	July 1982
North Carolina	Before 1960	Before 1960	January 1985
North Dakota	July 1987	Forbidden	June 1991
Ohio	Before 1960	January 1989	October 1985
Oklahoma	October 1983	Forbidden	July 1987
Oregon	Before 1960	March 1985	July 1986
Pennsylvania	Before 1960	March 1990	September 1986
Rhode Island	Before 1960	Before 1960	July 1984
South Carolina	Before 1960	Before 1960	January 1986
South Dakota	Before 1960	Before 1960	February 1988
Tennessee	Before 1960	March 1990	July 1985
Texas	January 1987	November 1988	January 1987
Utah	Before 1960	July 1981	May 1984
Vermont	Before 1960	January 1970	January 1988
Virginia	January 1962	January 1987	July 1985
Washington	Before 1960	July 1985	July 1987
West Virginia	July 1982	January 1987	January 1988
Wisconsin	January 1967	August 1989	January 1987
Wyoming	Before 1960	Forbidden	June 1987

Source: Berger et al. (1995: 188–9).

Note: These reflect existing laws through 1994.

of financial services. In this way, the BHCA was a small step towards the erosion of both the ban on interstate banking and the separation of commercial and investment banking as established in the 1930s.

Conventional wisdom holds that, despite the commercial bankers' response to competition described above, they continued to lose market share. Indeed, the number of banks fell throughout this entire era as illustrated in Figure 6.2. However, while the number of banks was declining, the number of branches and offices was increasing (Figure 6.2). Thus, the industry experienced consolidation in terms of the total number of banking institutions while individual institutions expanded their market presence. The conventional wisdom that commercial banking was in a state of decline is based on data that shows that commercial banks have lost market share since the middle of the 1960s when the market is defined as total assets at financial firms (commercial banks, insurance companies, savings and loans, finance companies, etc.). However, scholars have pointed out that to consider only balance sheet activity is to miss the changes in bank behavior described above. Most importantly, a salient feature of banking during this era was the growth in off-balance sheet activity. Consequently, failure to consider this activity when measuring bank market share is a significant oversight. Indeed,

Figure 6.2 Changing Commercial Bank Structure: 1966–2008

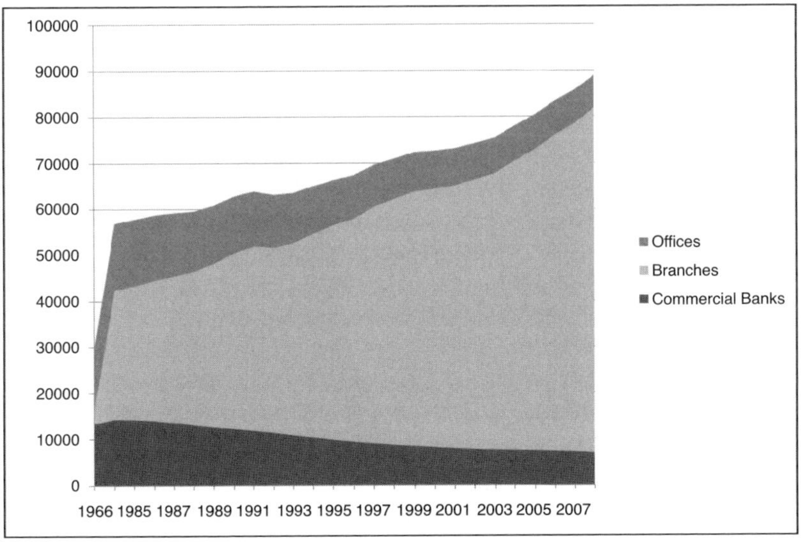

Source: Federal Reserve Flow of Funds, http://www.federalreserve.gov/releases/z1/current/data.htm.

as shown in Figure 6.1, noninterest income at commercial banks has risen dramatically. Since the middle of the 1970s through the early years in the 1990s, noninterest income went from about 20 percent of total bank income to over one third of total income.[24] When the conventional measure of market share is adjusted to include off-balance sheet activity, it becomes clear that during this era commercial banking was not in decline but was able, through its competitive efforts, to generally maintain its position in the financial sector.

Episodes of instability and regulatory response

That commercial banks were able to maintain their market share is remarkable given the increased competition as well as the extreme instability of this era. Scholars have characterized the 1980s and early 1990s as the most turbulent period in commercial banking since the bank crises of the 1930s.[25] This section of the chapter provides a chronological account of

Figure 6.3 Number of Commercial Bank Failures: 1966–1999

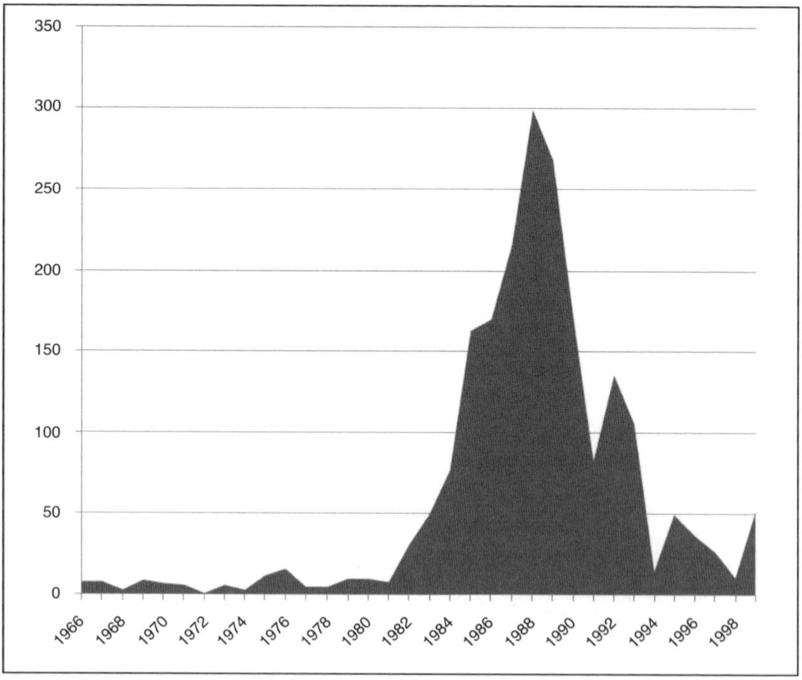

Source: www2.fdic.gov.

the cycle of bank failures and regulatory responses that characterize this era. This narrative includes an explanation of the larger bank failures against the backdrop of an ongoing wave of smaller failures. A majority of the commercial bank failures during this era were related to the regional recessions described earlier. The general pattern in banks failures can be found in Figure 6.3 which illustrates the total number of commercial bank failures between 1966 and 1999. From this, it is apparent that most of the failures occurred in the 1980s and the early 1990s. To get a clearer idea of where the failures were and how they were related to the regional recessions, state level bank failure data is found in Table 6.2 for the years 1980 through 1994, which captures the period of greatest failures. In absolute numbers, four states had over 100 bank failures each during this period; Texas, California, Oklahoma, and Colorado. Further, these four states experienced much greater bank instability than any of the other states. A closer look at the regional recessions may explain some of the concentrated failure rates.

Bank level failure data illustrates the concentration of failures a few states or regions. Throughout the agricultural downturn in the mid-1980s, 34.7 percent of all bank failures were in the top five agricultural producing states.[26] Clearly, as farm prices fell and farm loans became nonperforming, banks in the region had difficulty staying in business. During the collapse of energy and real estate prices in the Southwest, banking was equally hard hit. Between 1981 and 1987, there were 627 bank failures or banks requiring assistance from the FDIC and 35.8 percent of these were in the Southwest region of the country. The regional recession in the Northeast in the early 1980s account for just over five percent of all bank failures during that period and 14.45 percent of all bank failures were in California during their recession of the early 1990s. From this data, it seems clear that the agriculture recession and the energy and real estate collapse were regional events that had a significant influence on bank stability. Further, this firm level data is consistent with the state level data found in Table 6.2 as the vast majority of bank failures were in states involved in these regional disturbances.

The response to the instability in the thrift and commercial banking sectors was significant regulatory change.[27] However, the regulation was not guided by a single policy. Rather, the regulatory change may best be thought of as three waves of regulation. In the first, policymakers and regulators recognized that market conditions were changing so significantly that the regulation from the 1930s was contributing to bank difficulties. Consequently, the initial regulatory response was actually deregulation seeking to enable banks to respond to market conditions.

Table 6.2 Commercial Bank Failures by State: 1980–1994

State	Number of Bank FailuresBank	State	Number of Failures
Alabama	9	Montana	9
Alaska	8	Nebraska	34
Arizona	20	Nevada	1
Arkansas	12	New Hampshire	16
California	138	New Jersey	15
Colorado	121	New Mexico	11
Connecticut	23	New York	27
Delaware	7	North Carolina	7
Florida	66	North Dakota	9
Georgia	5	Ohio	12
Hawaii	3	Oklahoma	130
Idaho	2	Oregon	15
Illinois	28	Pennsylvania	10
Indiana	16	Rhode Island	7
Iowa	39	South Carolina	2
Kansas	66	South Dakota	8
Kentucky	7	Tennessee	37
Louisiana	69	Texas	627
Maine	2	Utah	24
Maryland	3	Vermont	2
Massachusetts	21	Virginia	8
Michigan	3	Washington	4
Minnesota	31	West Virginia	6
Mississippi	3	Wisconsin	3
Missouri	42	Wyoming	20

Source: http://www2.fdic.gov/hsob/hsobRpt.asp.

Note: The number of failed banks is the sum of the three categories (mergers, paid off, other) that the FDIC refers to as failures.

However, this deregulation was too little too late as both banks and thrifts continued to struggle to catch up with the rest of the financial sector and meet the needs of the nonfinancial sector. As thrifts and banks continued to fail, regulators and policymakers shifted their focus away from deregulation and towards stabilizing the financial sector. Thus, the second wave of regulation was meant to provide stability to banking. By 1994, the crisis of failures was over and the emphasis once again shifted towards deregulation as it was clear that both market and nonmarket conditions had eroded much of the existing bank regulation of the 1930s. Further the destabilizing influence of that regulation was increasingly difficult to ignore, thus the final legislative developments

Table 6.3 Three Waves of Regulation in the Postwar Banking Era: 1980–1999

Wave	Nature of the Regulation	Regulation Title and Date
1	Deregulation	Depository Institutions Deregulation and Monetary Control Act: 1980
1	Deregulation	Depository Institutions Act: 1982
1	Deregulation	Competitive Equality in Banking Act: 1987
2	Regulation	Financial Institutions Reform and Recovery Act: 1991
3	Deregulation	Riegle–Neal Interstate Banking and Branching Efficiency Act: 1994
3	Deregulation	Gramm–Leach–Bliley Act: 1999

in this era were a return to deregulation. Table 6.3 offers a summary of these three waves in regulation.

Credit crunch: 1966

The first signs of financial fragility in the postwar period surfaced in 1966.[28] Investment spending was strong when the year began, but inflation and interest rates were rising. With rising interest rates and falling profits, the nonfinancial firms had trouble meeting debt obligations internally. Consequently, they turned to external funds including issuing debt and borrowing from commercial banks. By the third quarter of 1966, nonfinancial firms were cut off from the commercial loan market. It was largely monetary policy that kept banks from extending further credit to the corporate sector.[29] Specifically, the Federal Reserve tightened monetary policy at the end of 1965 and increased the discount rate from four percent to 4.5 percent. In response, banks increasingly relied on time deposits as a source of funds because they had a lower reserve requirement than demand deposits. This allowed the commercial banks to accommodate loan demand. However, in June, the Federal Reserve increased the reserve requirement on time deposits making it more expensive for banks to raise funds through the time deposit market. Perhaps part of the motivation for the Federal Reserve was that the President had indicated he was counting on the Federal Reserve to keep credit in check to avoid inflation.[30] At the same time, the Federal Reserve refused to raise the regulation Q ceiling on large time deposits and, in the summer, the market interest rate rose above the regulated rate for both long- and short-term certificates of deposit (CDs). These policies of the Federal Reserve made it difficult for banks to continue to lend which is why the corporate sector was shut out of the credit market towards the end of 1966.

While this certainly is not a bank crisis in line with the definition from Chapter 2, it is an important development in the history of commercial banking because it sets the stage for later developments. In addition, it is an important illustration of the role of monetary policy in bank instability. Further, the credit crunch of 1966 exposed weaknesses in the regulatory regime; specifically in the constraints caused by binding price ceilings. Perhaps most importantly, the 1966 experience was the impetus behind a significant shift in the financial sector generally. Nonfinancial firms started looking for alternative sources of funding, depositors began seeking better returns that were not subject to regulation Q, and bankers recognized that their business model was going to have to change in important ways if they were to remain viable.

Franklin National bank failure: 1974

In 1974, Franklin National, the twentieth largest bank in the U.S. failed.[31] This is an important failure in the history of commercial banking not only because of its size but also because of the expansion of lender of last resort function of the Federal Reserve that accompanied the bank's resolution. Franklin National was expanding its loans and did so by borrowing heavily in the Eurodollar interbank market. Unfortunately, many of the loans that were made became nonperforming and the bank responded by speculating in the foreign exchange markets to recoup loan losses. The speculation failed and once word spread of its difficulties, financial market participants lost confidence, particularly in the Eurodollar and foreign exchange markets. Rather than let Franklin National fail, the Federal Reserve extended 1.7 billion in discount loans to the troubled bank. Much of this was used to replace lost deposits in London. Further, the Federal Reserve arranged for the New York Federal Reserve bank to acquire over $700 million of foreign exchange liabilities at Franklin National. Both of these Federal Reserve interventions allowed Franklin National to remain solvent until the FDIC could find a purchaser a few months later. This use of the Federal Reserve to assume foreign exchange liabilities and to support foreign deposits was unprecedented at the time. It marked a significant expansion of the lender of last resort function of the Federal Reserve to stabilize foreign financial markets.

Community Reinvestment Act: 1977

A few years after the Franklin National failure, significant commercial bank legislation was passed that was not related to reducing regulatory constraints nor was it an attempt to add stability to banking. Rather, the Community Reinvestment Act (CRA) was a response to charges that commercial banks were engaged in discriminatory lending practices. As such, the act was intended to encourage depository institutions to help meet the credit needs of the communities in which they operated, including low-income neighborhoods, consistent with safe and sound banking operations. The CRA required that each insured bank's record in helping meet the credit needs of its entire community be evaluated periodically. That record is taken into account in considering an institution's application for mergers, branch openings, and acquisitions. The act was not significant in terms of impacting bank stability in the twentieth century largely because the act, as passed in 1977, did little to change bank behavior. That is, the CRA was not well understood or enforced for the first 20 or so years of its existence. However, as is shown in Chapter 7, the CRA was given more teeth when it was revised in 1995 and many contend that the CRA was a contributing factor in the 2007–2009 financial crisis.

Capital regulation

Capital requirements are used to minimize risk taking at commercial banks. A bank holding more capital is less likely to engage in excessive risk taking because it has more to lose in the case of failure. Until 1981, capital regulation in commercial banking was rather ad hoc.[32] At that time, capital requirements were based on the leverage ratio (ratio of total capital to total assets) at the bank. A well capitalized bank has a leverage ratio over five percent. Lower leverage ratios trigger increases in regulatory oversight. However, as off-balance sheet activity increased, regulators realized that capital to asset ratios, which reflect on balance sheet activity, were no longer an adequate measure of risk. Consequently, a new type of capital requirement was established in 1988 that attempted to closely tie requirements with risk-weighted assets by placing assets into different risk-adjusted categories. For example, mortgage loans are considered less risky than commercial loans so they are in a lower risk-weighted category. In addition, off-balance sheet activities were also assigned a risk-weighted category. This relatively newer type of capital requirement is called Basel requirements after the Committee on Banking Supervision who developed the standards in Basel, Switzerland.[33]

Depository Institutions Deregulation and Monetary Control Act: 1980

Commercial banks continued to struggle with retaining liabilities and problems of disintermediation. For most years subsequent to the 1933 implementation of regulation Q, commercial bankers did not worry about liability management. However, when market interest rates rose above the regulated rate, banks started losing deposits to other depository institutions as well as nonbanks, such as money market mutual funds. Bankers responded, in part, by creating accounts that could legally pay market interest rates. Two important developments were the negotiable order of withdraw (NOW) accounts and automatic transfer system (ATS) accounts. The NOW account was essentially a checking account that paid market interest rates and with an ATS account, each evening the balances in the account were moved into an interest-bearing overnight account and redeposited each morning.

The Depository Institutions Deregulation and Monetary Control Act (DIDMCA) of 1980 made it legal for commercial banks to offer both the NOW and ATS accounts across the country, so it represented a legal recognition of market developments. At the same time, the act phased out regulation Q over six years ending March 31, 1986 in an attempt to limit the disintermediation problems banks were facing. Further, the act increased deposit insurance from $40,000 to $100,000 per account.

Prior to the passage of the DIDMCA, state nonmember banks had a different set of reserve requirements than did member banks. More specifically, the member bank reserve requirement was set by the Federal Reserve and interest was not paid on the reserves. In contrast, for nonmember banks, the state regulators set reserve requirements and often allowed banks to count interest bearing assets as reserves. This difference made it more costly to be a member bank. The DIDMCA corrected for this inequality by subjecting all banks to the reserve requirement of the Federal Reserve.

The DIDMCA may be characterized as the first in the deregulation wave of bank legislation in this era (see Table 6.3). Certainly, the most important provision was the phaseout of regulation Q. Commercial banks faced significant disintermediation and needed to be free to pay market interest rates on deposits in order to attract funds. However, as is shown below, this deregulation of price ceilings was too little and too late as disintermediation continued even after the 1980 legislative act.

Penn Square bank failure: 1982

In the middle of 1982, a small bank, Penn Square, failed with large implications.[34] Penn Square had rapidly expanded its energy loans, largely in Oklahoma, as energy prices rose in the late 1970s and early 1980s. In addition to extending energy loans, the bank also sold loan participations in those same loans. With a loan participation, Penn Square would initiate the energy loan and then invite other banks to enter the transaction. By 1982, 43 other banks, both large and small, had loan participations with Penn Square. These loan participations are important because they correlate the health of many banks to that of Penn Square. Consequently, when energy prices declined in late 1981 and early 1982, many of the energy loans became nonperforming and this severely impacted Penn Square as well as many other banks.

The Penn Square failure is also important because of how the bank obtained many of the funds used to finance the energy loans. Seeking to attract deposits, Penn Square offered higher interest rates on large CDs than many other banks across the country. They were able to do this in light of regulation Q because some categories of large time deposits (denomination greater than $100,000) were exempt from the ceiling rates as of June 24, 1970.[35] Brokers would seek out banks paying the highest rates for their customers and buy CDs at those banks. These are known as brokered deposits and they were a quick way for Penn Square to obtain the funds it required to extend the energy loans. However, when it was learned that the energy loans were nonperforming and Penn Square failed, many investors departed the CD market. Combined with regulation Q, this failure made it increasingly difficult for banks to maintain and attract deposits.

Depository Institutions Act: 1982

The gradual phaseout of regulation Q from the DIDMCA in 1980 was ineffective in reducing disintermediation.[36] Banks continued to lose depositors. As shown in Figure 6.4, the sharpest declines in time and savings deposits were in the late 1970s and throughout the 1980s. As a result, the Depository Institutions Act (DIA) of 1982 was passed. This act, also known as the Garn-St Germain Act, addressed the disintermediation problem by authorizing commercial banks to offer money market deposit accounts (MMDA). The MMDAs were exempt from regulation Q price ceilings and also had no required reserves so they were a close substitute to money market mutual funds.

The DIA also addressed the ongoing instability both in commercial banking and the thrift industries. In terms of addressing the commercial

Figure 6.4 Time, Savings, and Demand Deposits per Commercial Bank: 1966–2009

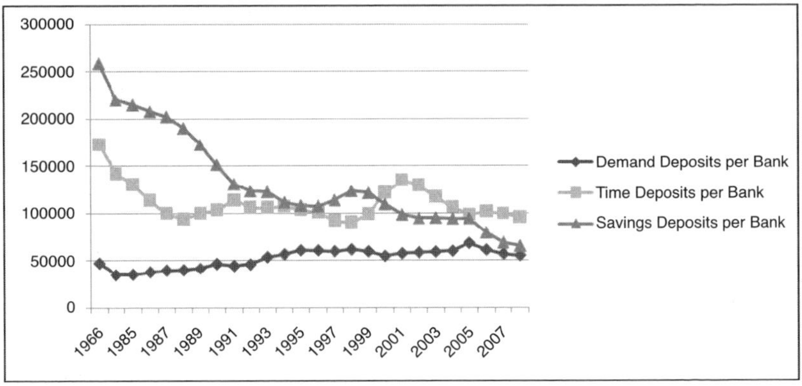

Source: www2.fdic.gov.

Note: Amount in thousands.

banking sector, the act expanded FDIC powers to assist troubled banks. For the first time, the FDIC allowed a healthy bank to go across state lines to acquire a failing bank with assets greater than $500 million. This was important to the FDIC since it needed more resources for stabilizing banking. At the same time, it was an important step in breaking down the interstate banking barriers that were erected at the beginning of banking in the late eighteenth century. The asset size restriction was included in the law to placate those who believed that the provision was an erosion of the McFadden Act and limits on interstate banking.[37]

Another provision of the DIA in 1982 was an expansion of lending and borrowing rights to national banks.[38] The Comptroller was worried that national banks were at a competitive disadvantage to state banks in terms of the national banker's ability to extend large loans. Prior to 1982, national banks were prohibited from extending a loan whose value exceeded ten percent of the bank's capital. State banks had more liberal laws when it came to large loans. Consequently, the DIA increased the limit at national banks to 15 percent of bank capital.

Continental Illinois failure: 1984

Continental Illinois, the eleventh largest bank holding company in the country, failed in 1984, largely as a result of its loan participations with Penn Square.[39] Much like Penn Square, Continental Illinois was using brokered deposits to obtain funding for their rapid expansion into the energy loan market. Continental Illinois also bought more energy loans from Penn Square than any other bank; over $1.1 billion in 1982, and suffered significantly when Penn Square failed. Continental Illinois was able to stay open a few more years, in part, because it turned to the Eurodollar market for additional funds. This new borrowing simply delayed the inevitable and the bank was in extreme distress by 1984. What sets the 1984 failure apart from the 1982 Penn Square failure was its size. Regulators could not find another bank holding company willing and able to purchase Continental Illinois. Consequently, the regulators established an assistance program that, among other things, covered all deposits at the bank and the FDIC purchased nonvoting stock in the bank. It was a significant development that all depositors at the bank were covered for this marked the beginning of what has been termed the "too-big-to-fail" failure resolution policy at the FDIC. As will be shown later in this and the following chapters, "too-big-to-fail" has serious ramifications in the relationship between regulation and stability.

Competitive Equality in Banking Act: 1987

Large bank failures, like Continental Illinois, were not as common as smaller bank failures. Indeed, Figure 6.3 indicates that even after the 1984 failure of Continental Illinois, the number of smaller bank failures continued to mount. This put great pressure on the insurance fund and so Congress took further action. While the Competitive Equality in Banking Act of 1987 (CEBA) was largely aimed at recapitalizing the insurance fund for the thrift industry, there was an important provision in this act that is germane to commercial bank stability. Specifically, this act expanded the DIA provision that allowed banks to purchase failing institutions across state lines. The CEBA provision allowed for healthy banks to purchase not only failing institutions across state lines but also banks that were in danger of failing. In the era of significant instability, this increased greatly the population of banks that could be purchased across state lines and provided some relief to the insurance fund at the FDIC.

Federal Deposit Insurance Corporation Improvement Act: 1991

Despite the regulation of the 1980s, banks continued to fail. Some regulators and policymakers recognized that the ongoing bank problems were, in part, a result of the regulatory constraints from the 1930s that kept banks from adapting to and participating in, the realities of the market place. In the late 1980s and early 1990s there were several legislative attempts to remove the Glass–Steagall provisions and allow bankers broader powers in insurance, real estate, and securities.[40] However, the legislation that ultimately passed did not remove any of the restrictions from the 1930s. The Federal Deposit Insurance Corporation Improvement Act of 1991 (FDICIA), which began as an attempt to remove the separation between investment and commercial banking, may be thought of as regulation in the second wave described earlier: it was aimed at stabilizing the banking sector.

The FDICIA greatly increased the powers and authority of the FDIC. Major provisions recapitalized the insurance fund and allowed the FDIC to strengthen the fund by borrowing from the Treasury. Because many policymakers believed that the number of bank failures could have been reduced through stronger on-site examinations, the FDICIA also mandated annual safety and soundness evaluations at each bank. Further, the act mandated a least-cost resolution method and prompt resolution approach to problem and failing banks. This was an attempt to address the growing "too-big-to-fail" policy of the FDIC and the moral hazard problems associated with it.[41] The FDICIA also ordered the creation of a risk-based deposit insurance assessment scheme.

The law also required that bank regulators develop categories of capital classification. At one end of the classification spectrum, a "well capitalized" bank was operating safely while at the other, a "critically undercapitalized" bank was most vulnerable and least likely to withstand any negative shock. These classifications were used to signal to regulators when additional supervision and action was necessary and also for establishing permissible activities, such as brokered deposits as mentioned below.

The FDICIA also limited bank activity in two areas.[42] First, brokered deposits, a problem that surfaced with the Penn Square failure, and the solicitation of deposits were restricted for banks that were not well-capitalized. More specifically, undercapitalized banks could not accept brokered deposits and deposits that the bank solicited were subject to interest rate ceilings. Adequately capitalized banks could accept brokered deposits, provided the FDIC approved, and they were also subject to interest rate ceilings. Well capitalized banks, however, were not subject to the interest rate ceiling and could accept brokered deposits. The second way in which the FDICIA limited bank activity was to prohibit state chartered banks from engaging in activities not permitted to national banks unless the bank met capital requirements and had the approval of the FDIC.

Riegle–Neal Interstate Banking and Branching Efficiency Act: 1994

As shown in Figure 6.3, the bank failure problem was significantly diminished by the early 1990s. Consequently, regulators shifted away from crisis mode to focus on the wider sources of instability in banking. The final two legislative developments in the era are in the third wave of regulation because both the 1994 and 1999 acts primarily deregulated banking by removing major constraints on commercial banking (see Table 6.3). The first, in 1994, addresses the ban on interstate banking and branching and the second, in 1999, essentially repeals Glass–Steagall.

The Riegle–Neal Interstate Banking and Branching Efficiency Act (IBBEA) of 1994 may be understood broadly in terms of two types of provisions: those which pertained to interstate banking and those pertaining to interstate branching. As described earlier in this chapter, by 1994 all but one state (Hawaii) participated, through regional pacts, in some form of interstate banking. Consequently though the IBBEA, permitted adequately capitalized and managed bank holding companies to bank (via merger, acquisition, or establishing a new bank) in any state one year after enactment, most banks were already participants. States' participation in interstate banking was made compulsory by the IBBEA.

In contrast, very few states, in 1994, were engaged in interstate branching and states were given, in the IBBEA, an opportunity to customize the extent to which they would participate in the interstate branching provisions. In 1994, only eight states (Alaska, Massachusetts, New York, Oregon, Rhode Island, Nevada, North Carolina, and Utah) allowed for some form of interstate branching.[43] Consequently, the real importance of the IBBEA was in terms of interstate branching rights. Between the passage of the IBBEA (September 1994) and June 1997, states were granted a window in which they could customize the extent to which they would allow for interstate branching. More specifically, there were four provisions that related to interstate branching and each state could opt-in or opt-out of the provisions to make interstate branching more or less free in their state. All states opted for some restrictions to interstate branching.

The 1994 IBBEA marked an important legislative development in commercial banking as it repealed the industry ban on interstate banking that existed from the inception of American commercial banking. At the same time however, states were given the right to determine the extent to which interstate branching would be viable.

Gramm–Leach–Bliley Financial Services Modernization Act: 1999

The final significant legislative change during this era was also deregulatory in nature. The Gramm–Leach–Bliley Financial Services Modernization Act (GLBA) of 1999 repeals the last vestiges of the Glass–Steagall provisions from the Banking Act of 1933. The law created a new financial holding company authorized to engage in underwriting and selling insurance and securities, investing in and developing real estate and other complementary banking activities. Further, the GLBA amends the CRA to require that financial holding companies not be formed before their insured depository institutions receive and maintain a satisfactory CRA rating.

The 1999 repeal of Glass–Steagall, in the end, was the culmination of many years of erosion in the separation of commercial and investment banking. [44] Over the years, court and regulator decisions slowly chipped away at the wall between these two financial institutions so that by 1999 the legislative development was more a formalization of what was largely a market place reality. For example, in 1986, the Office of the Comptroller of the Currency announced that nationally chartered banks were eligible to sell insurance nationwide.[45] The following year, the Federal Reserve Board authorized subsidiaries of BHCs to earn up to five percent of total revenue from underwriting certain securities. In 1988, the Supreme Court declined to hear a case from a lower court in which the court ruled banks could underwrite securities through an affiliate. In 1996, the revenue maximum established by the Federal Reserve Board was increased to 25 percent from securities underwriting. Developments in the market reflected these decisions as commercial banks moved into these once prohibited areas and as large BHCs merged and acquired nonbanks.

In addition to changes made by courts and regulators, state banking authorities were also permitting state chartered banks to engage in securities activity. By the end of 1987, eight states allowed for securities underwriting, 22 states permitted some degree of real estate development by banks, and five states had extended insurance activities to state banks.[46] Thus, by the time the 1999 act was passed, many bankers had already moved beyond the restrictions imposed by the 1933 Glass–Steagall provisions either because of court or federal regulator decisions or because of changes in state laws.

In the end, there were six important legislative changes to commercial banking laws between 1980 and 1999. Table 6.3 provides a summary of where each legislative development falls in terms of the waves of regulation described earlier in this chapter. Specifically, the first wave of deregulation includes the legislation from 1980, 1982, and 1987. The second wave, more regulation in banking, contains the 1991 FDICIA and the third wave of deregulation includes the two legislative developments that further repeal provisions from the Banking Act of 1933; these are the IBBEA in 1994 and the GLBA in 1999. The final task of this chapter is to analyze the impact of these regulatory developments on the stability of commercial banking.

Assessment of regulation and stability

Entering the postwar banking era, all of the regulation from previous eras was in place. As mentioned in Chapter 5, market conditions were such that these provisions often had a negligible impact on bank stability. For example, in an environment of low and stable interest rates, regulation Q is not binding. However, once market conditions changed, the destabilizing impact of the regulation was revealed. The analysis of the impact of regulation on bank stability is summarized in Table 6.4 and explained in what follows.

Existing regulation

Regulation Q

Problems arose for commercial bankers once regulation Q became binding in the mid-1960s. The primary problem was that of disintermediation. Bankers could not keep deposits when they were legally constrained to pay less than market interest rates. Depositors took their money elsewhere (see Figure 6.4).[47] This, in turn, gave rise to the growth of mutual funds and money market mutual funds which were able to pay market rates and offer depositors more sophisticated savings tools that were not available at commercial banks because of the Glass–Steagall provisions. Regulation Q kept banks from responding to market conditions and, in the process, forced banks to lose ground to competitors.

There is also evidence that regulation Q contributed to the instability of banking by increasing costs. Scholars have found evidence that banks were forced to rely on nonprice methods of competing for regulation Q deposits and that this increased the noninterest expense at banks.[48] Higher noninterest expenses, in turn, offset any savings the banks may have enjoyed from the regulation itself. Indeed, separate empirical analysis finds that the disintermediation from regulation Q and the resulting decline in profits resulted in the large number of bank failures.[49] Thus there is evidence connecting regulation Q with the incidence of bank failures during this era.

Table 6.4 Summary of Regulation and Its Impact on Commercial Bank Stability in the Postwar Banking Era

Regulation	Description	Channel(s) Through Which Regulation Impacts Bank Stability	Conclusion from the Evidence
Existing			
1. Ceiling interest rate on time and savings deposits	• Placed a ceiling on time and savings deposits.	• Decrease competition. • Increase costs. • Change the nature of competition.	• Decreased stability by creating disintermediation problems (Figure 6.4, Cook (1978)). • Decreased stability by contributing to lower profitability (Kilcollin and Hanweck (1981)) and increased number of bank failures (Cebula and Saltz (1994)). • Decreased stability by not allowing banks to respond to a new competitive environment.
2. Glass–Steagall	• Prohibit the underwriting or dealing of securities by commercial banks.	• Decrease competition. • Increase risk by limiting geographic diversification.	• Decreased stability by reducing competition. • Decreased stability by limiting branching through security affiliates.
3. Deposit Insurance	• Federal deposit insurance.	• Increase risk.	• Increased stability by maintaining confidence in light of the large number of failures. • Decreased stability by reducing depositor-monitoring and increasing moral hazard (Brumbaugh (1993)).

Table 6.4 Summary of Regulation and Its Impact on Commercial Bank Stability in the Postwar Banking Era – *continued*

Regulation	Description	Channel(s) Through Which Regulation Impacts Bank Stability	Conclusion from the Evidence
4. Prohibit interstate branching	• Commercial banks prohibited from interstate branching.	• Decrease competition. • Increase risk by limiting geographic diversification. • Change bank structure by limiting bank size.	• Decrease stability by limiting geographic diversification (Mengle (1990)). • Decrease stability by reducing competition (Carlson and Mitchener (2005, 2009), Jayarathne and Strahan (1998), Mengle (1990) for example). • Decrease stability because smaller banks are more likely to fail (www2.fdic.gov).
Capital Regulation			
1. Risk-weighted standards	• Created risk-weighted capital standards for balance sheet and off-balance sheet activity.	• Reduce risk.	• Potential to increase stability by reducing risk taking. • In practice, decreased stability be providing incentives for bankers to take on more risk (Mishkin (2010), Norberg (2009)).
CRA			
1. Meet Credit Needs of Community	• Required banks make loans to all members of the community with emphasis on low-income borrowers.	• Increase risk by extending higher risk loans. • Increase regulatory compliance cost.	• No impact on stability while the regulation was largely not effectively implemented prior to its revision.

Table 6.4 Summary of Regulation and Its Impact on Commercial Bank Stability in the Postwar Banking Era – *continued*

Regulation	Description	Channel(s) Through Which Regulation Impacts Bank Stability	Conclusion from the Evidence
DIDMCA			
1. Phaseout deposit ceilings	• Six year phaseout of interest rate ceiling on time and savings deposits.	• Partially increase competition. • Change the nature of competition.	• Decrease stability by ongoing disintermediation. • Decrease stability by increasing noninterest expenses (Kilcollin and Hanweck (1981)). • Decreased stability by contributing to bank failures rate (Ostrosky (1997)). • Decrease stability by not allowing banks to respond to a new competitive environment.
2. Extend reserve requirements	• Extended reserve requirements of the Federal Reserve to nonmember banks.	• Reduce cost whenever requirements are reduced.	• Increase stability when required reserves are decreased (Feinman (1993)).
DIA			
1. Authorize money market deposit accounts	• Authorize banks to offer money market deposit accounts not subject to interest rate ceilings.	• Increase competition.	• Increase stability by increasing banks' ability to compete for deposits (Figure 6.5).

Table 6.4 Summary of Regulation and Its Impact on Commercial Bank Stability in the Postwar Banking Era – *continued*

Regulation	Description	Channel(s) Through Which Regulation Impacts Bank Stability	Conclusion from the Evidence
2. Acquire failing banks	• Authorize healthy banks to cross state lines to purchase a failing bank.	• Decreased risk by expanding geographic diversification. • Increase competition. • Change bank structure by expanding bank size.	• Potential to increase stability by creating larger banks with increased geographic diversification. However, the laws applied only to the population of failing banks with assets in excess of $500 million in assets. • In practice, little impact on stability since so few failing banks were eligible during the postwar era.
CEBA			
1. Acquire weak banks	• Authorize healthy banks to cross state line to purchase a weak bank.	• Decreased risk by expanding geographic diversification. • Increase competition. • Change bank structure by expanding bank size.	• Potential to increase stability by creating larger banks with increased geographic diversification. However, the laws applied only to the population of failing banks with assets in excess of $500 million in assets. • In practice, little impact on stability since so few failing banks were eligible during the postwar era.

TTable 6.4 Summary of Regulation and Its Impact on Commercial Bank Stability in the Postwar Banking Era – *continued*

Regulation	Description	Channel(s) Through Which Regulation Impacts Bank Stability	Conclusion from the Evidence
FDICIA			
1. Least cost resolution	• Encouraged the FDIC to use the least cost failure resolution method.	• Reduce risk.	• Potential to increase stability by reducing moral hazard of the purchase and assumption method. • In practice, decreased stability by actually increasing moral hazard through more intensive use of purchase and assumption method (www2.fdic.gov, Stern and Feldman (2004)).
2. Risk-based deposit insurance	• Authorize the creation of deposit insurance that is risk-based.	• Reduce risk.	• Increase stability by reducing moral hazard to the extent that regulators correctly identify risk.
3. Bank activity and capital requirements	• Ties accepted bank activities to capital levels.	• Reduce risk.	• Increase stability by reducing risk associated with certain activities since more is at stake.

Table 6.4 Summary of Regulation and Its Impact on Commercial Bank Stability in the Postwar Banking Era – *continued*

Regulation	Description	Channel(s) Through Which Regulation Impacts Bank Stability	Conclusion from the Evidence
IBBEA			
1. Allow interstate banking	• Lift ban on interstate banking.	• Increase competition. • Decrease risk by expanding geographic diversity. • Change bank structure by increasing bank size. • Decrease costs associated with interstate banking.	• Increase stability by increasing competition (Carlson and Mitchener (2005, 2009), Jayarathne and Strahan (1998), for example) and geographic diversity. • Increase stability because larger banks are less likely to fail (www2.fdic.gov). • Increase stability by reducing costs (Mengle (1990)).
2. States to determine interstate branching	• Each state determines the extent to which there will be interstate branching across its border.	• Increase competition. • Decrease risk by expanding geographic diversity. • Change bank structure by increasing bank size. • Decrease costs associated with interstate branching.	• Potential to increase stability by increasing competition (Carlson and Mitchener (2005, 2009), Jayarathne and Strahan (1998), for example) and geographic diversity. • In practice, decrease stability since states that created barriers to branching performed worse than states with freer branch opportunities. • Potential to increase stability because larger banks are less likely to fail (www2.fdic.gov). • Potential to increase stability by reducing costs (Mengle (1990)).

Table 6.4 Summary of Regulation and Its Impact on Commercial Bank Stability in the Postwar Banking Era – *continued*

Regulation	**Description**	**Channel(s) Through Which Regulation Impacts Bank Stability**	**Conclusion from the Evidence**
GLBA			
1. Remove Glass–Steagall	• Authorize commercial bankers to underwrite and sell insurance and securities.	• Increase competition. • Decrease risk by expanding geographic diversification.	• Increase stability by increasing competition (Flannery (1984)) and geographic diversity (White (1982, 1986)). • Increase stability by decreasing risk (Macey et al. (1991)).

Notes: There are five identified channels through which regulation may impact stability; 1) change risk taking; 2) limit diversification; 3) change cost and revenue structure; 4) change the structure of the market; and 5) change the nature of competition. See Chapter 2 for a discussion of each.

Glass–Steagall

The separation of commercial and investment banking is destabilizing to the extent that it decreases competition between bankers and between commercial and investment bankers. As indicated in previous chapters, most existing scholarship on the relationship between bank competition and stability indicates that there is a positive relationship; increased competition enhances stability.[50] Further, as indicated earlier in this chapter, during this era, the competitive position of commercial bankers was further compromised by Glass–Steagall as foreign banks entered the U.S. market without these same regulatory constraints. At the same time, the Glass–Steagall provisions made it increasingly difficult for bankers to compete with money market mutual funds who were offering depositors and savers access to securities that banks could not match. Further, the separation of commercial and investment banking kept banks from meeting the changing needs of their corporate clients who increasingly wanted to extend debt.[51] Thus, this regulation may have contributed to more instability as it further compromised banks' ability to compete and respond to new competition in the market.

The rationale behind the Glass–Steagall provisions was that it would reduce risk at commercial banks because securities activity was assumed to be of higher risk. In their empirical analysis of banking between January 1980 and December, 1984, Macey et al. (1991) test if the addition of investment services to commercial bank increases their riskiness. They find that it does not add risk; rather, they find a reduction in risk from combining stock from two industries that are not perfectly correlated with each other.[52] The corollary to this finding is that the separation of commercial and investment banking may increase bank risk particularly for those banks not afforded the new securities opportunities through the courts, states, or regulatory decisions.

Deposit insurance

The relationship between deposit insurance and bank stability is complex. As was shown in the previous banking eras, there are elements of deposit insurance that are stabilizing and other elements that are destabilizing. That is, there is a trade-off between stability and moral hazard with deposit insurance. Depending on the circumstances, the balance of this trade-off may be tipped in favor of deposit insurance or toward moral hazard. As was shown in Chapter 5, the balance favored stability in the immediate aftermath of the banking crises in the early 1930s. Empirical work during the postwar banking era, however, finds that conditions changed sufficiently so that risk was increased. More specifically, prior to the 1980s, the incentive for risk taking created by deposit insurance was offset by bank's desire to protect and maintain their valuable bank charters. However, as the banking sector became increasingly competitive with foreign banks and nonbank financial firms, scholars find that the commercial bank charter value fell making bankers more willing to engage in riskier behavior associated with deposit insurance.[53] Other scholars have also stressed that changing conditions alter the incentive towards risk taking. Deposit insurance, as constructed in 1933, was a flat rate insurance so all banks paid the same for the same insurance; it was not risk based.[54] When banks are not allowed to compete in the market place because of regulatory constraints the deposit insurance system contributes to bank fragility.[55]

Another source of instability came from the closure methods employed by the FDIC when banks fail. Between 1980 and 1990, 1010 banks failed and of these, 787 (77.9 percent) were closed using the purchase and assumption resolution method at the FDIC.[56] The purchase and assumption method is one in which the FDIC finds another bank to purchase the failed bank, after the FDIC has purchased the undesirable assets. In this way, the bank is not really allowed to fail; indeed most customers never know that their bank failed in a technical sense. The most famous example of the purchase and assumption use in this era was the Continental Illinois failure in 1984. Regulators claimed they had to find a purchaser for the bank because it was "too-big-to-fail" (TBTF) even though only ten percent of the bank's deposits were FDIC protected.[57] Scholars contend that this decision marked a clear policy shift towards TBTF.[58] The TBTF defense of not allowing the bank to fail is grounded in the belief that if the bank failed there would be systemic problems in the financial system; the payments system would be interrupted, other banks would fail, etc. However, the extensive use of the purchase and assumption method to resolve bank failures covers more than large banks. Indeed, close to 78 percent of all failures were resolved this way during the wave of failures in the 1980s and most were small. Further, the increasing use of the purchase and assumption method not only increased the willingness of bankers to assume much greater risk, it eliminated the need for uninsured depositors to monitor bank performance.[59] This lack of monitoring, in turn, reinforced the propensity for bankers to take on greater risk.

The moral hazard of increased risk taking brought about by the TBTF policy is hard to conclusively discern. Indeed, existing scholarship, while it tends to suggest a positive relationship between TBTF and increased risk, there is no consensus. Scholars find evidence that TBTF contributed to bank risk during the turbulent 1980s and the 1990s.[60] However, other scholars find that the relationship no longer holds in the 1992 through 2003 period.[61] In an environment where competition is increasing and the FDIC is not allowing troubled banks to truly fail, it seems likely that bankers will feel pressure, and have the incentive, to take on greater risk as a result of deposit insurance. Thus, while deposit insurance is certainly stabilizing in that it keeps bank runs at bay, it is more destabilizing during times of greater uncertainty, like the postwar era.

Interstate banking ban

The postwar banking era saw erosion in the ban on interstate banking. As shown in Table 6.1, particularly during the 1980s, an increasing number of states allowed for intrastate branching as well as interstate banking through regional agreements. Despite an opening for branching and banking at the state level, the national ban on interstate banking and branching remained in place during much of this era and certainly through the prolonged period of bank failures. Further, the system of interstate expansion provided by states is almost exclusively through bank holding company subsidiaries which are a significantly more expensive system than interstate banking and branching.[62] A separate subsidiary system requires duplicate costs in each state of operation. These costs include, for example, a separate board of directors, production of separate regulatory reports, and separate audit, budget, accounting and support personnel. Higher costs, all things equal, lower profitability and are consequently destabilizing. In addition, as in previous eras, particularly the 1930s, the ban on interstate banking was destabilizing as the evidence is overwhelming that competition enhances stability.[63]

Postwar era regulation

Existing regulation clearly added to the instability in banking; the provisions from the Banking Act of 1933 became increasingly destabilizing in the postwar era as market conditions changed significantly. Bank regulation also changed considerably in the postwar era so this new regulation must be evaluated in terms of its impact on bank stability as well.

Capital requirements

The rationale behind capital requirements is that they can reduce moral hazard of risk taking since a bank with sufficient capital stands to lose more in the event of failure. The Basel, or risk-weighted, capital requirements have been shown to not accurately reflect actual risk at banks. For example, the capital requirements stipulate that 100 percent capital be held on corporate loans (the highest risk weight). So, if a bank made two corporate loans; one to a corporation with a high credit rating and one to a corporation with a low credit rating, these are not of equal risk but do require equal capital holdings. The bank has the incentive to keep the high risk loan on the balance sheet and sell the low risk loan. In this way, the risk-weighted capital requirement may, contrary to its intended purpose, actually increase risk taking.[64] The perverse outcome of these capital requirements is that banks can assume greater risk without holding additional capital.

Community Reinvestment Act

The CRA requires that commercial banks extend loans to all of those in its community consistent with safe banking practices. During most of the postwar banking era, the CRA was not well understood by bankers nor well enforced by regulators. This changed when, in 1995, the act was amended to make clear the intent of the regulation and consequences of noncompliance. Given that this regulation was not given real teeth until 1995, which is subsequent to the instability of this era, its impact on bank stability is appropriately reserved for Chapter 7.

Depository Institutions Deregulation and Monetary Control Act

The most important provision of the DIDMCA was to phaseout regulation Q. By 1980, regulators realized the significant disintermediation caused by the interest rate ceilings. As mentioned earlier, not only did the ceilings lead to severe disintermediation, it increased the non-interest costs to bankers, and kept them from responding to market conditions. Unfortunately, the DIDMCA was insufficient in stopping the disintermediation because rather than eliminate the ceilings, the legislation called for a gradual reduction. The deregulation was a step in the right direction but the step was too small and too late. As shown in Figure 6.4, the most significant decline in time deposits at banks was throughout the late 1970s and 1980s. Further, as shown in Figure 6.3, the number of bank failures increased significantly in 1981 and the high failure rates continued until 1994. Empirical evidence indicates that disintermediation during the 1980s from existing regulation Q ceilings contributed to the high rate of bank failures. An empirical analysis that explains bank failures during this time frame finds that regulation Q was statistically significant in explaining bank failures.[65] It is clear that regulation Q had a significantly destabilizing impact on bank stability; it lead to disintermediation, kept banks from being able to compete for deposits, and contributed to the rate of bank failures in the postwar era.

Another provision of the DIDMCA that must be evaluated is the extension of reserve requirements as established by the Federal Reserve to nonmember banks. This provision made reserve requirements equal at national and state chartered banks, including those state banks that are not members of the Federal Reserve. The reserve requirements were essentially unchanged until the early 1990s when the Federal Reserve lowered reserve requirements twice (in 1990 and 1992). Empirical studies have indicated that these reductions saved bankers approximately $1.15 billion in forgone interest.[66] Another way of seeing this development is that lower reserve requirements reduce costs to banks because the requirements act as a tax on deposit accounts. This, in turn, will improve bank profits and stability. Of course, any increase in required reserves will have the opposite effect.

Finally, the DIDMCA also extended federal deposit insurance from $40,000 to $100,000. This provision will impact bank stability to the extent that deposit insurance is stabilizing or destabilizing.

Depository Institutions Act and the Competitive Equality in Banking Act

As disintermediation continued, legislators authorized commercial banks to offer money market deposit accounts. Such accounts are substitutes to money market mutual fund accounts and are not subject to regulation Q ceilings. Historical data that isolates money market deposit accounts from other deposits is not available. However, the FDIC categorizes money market deposit accounts as nontransaction accounts and as a percentage of total domestic deposits, the nontransaction accounts rose in 1982 but decline from 1983 through 1987 (see Figure 6.5). Despite the decline as a percent of total deposits, the dollar value of nontransactions deposits increased throughout the entire era. To the degree that these accounts were able to keep commercial bankers competitive for deposits, this regulatory changed improved bank stability.

A second important provision in terms of bank stability concerns the authority the DIA gave banks to acquire a failing bank in a different state, provided the failing bank had assets in excess of $500 million. Between 1980 and 1994, there were only 36 bank failures with assets that met the size criteria established in the DIA.[67] Consequently, there were few opportunities for this provision to actually be utilized during

Figure 6.5 Nontransaction Deposits as a Percent of Total Domestic Deposits: 1966–1999

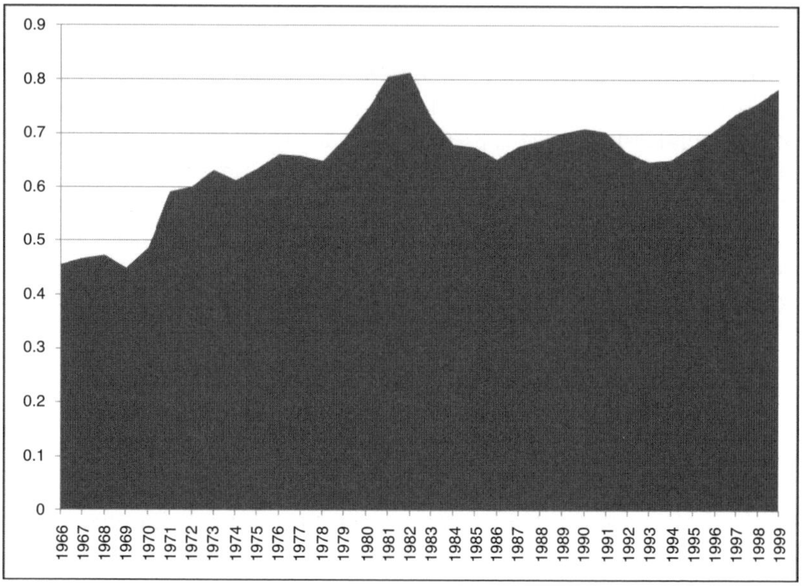

Source: www2.fdic.gov.

Note: Amount in thousands.

this banking crisis. However, the 1987 CEBA expanded on this DIA provision by allowing a healthy bank to acquire not only failing but weak banks across state lines. One may expect that the CEBA broadened the population of banks that could be acquired. To the extent that healthy banks went across state lines and were able to acquire these weaker banks and turn them around, the CEBA provision improved bank stability. Indeed, interstate acquisition could bring about geographic diversity, and in the process, improve bank stability.

Federal Deposit Insurance Corporation Improvement Act

The 1991 legislation was largely focused on recapitalizing a weakened deposit fund. Nonetheless, some of the provisions impact bank stability. For example, one provision required, subject to the regulator's discretion, that the FDIC use the least cost method of resolving bank failures. This is an attempt to limit the moral hazard of the purchase and assumption resolution described earlier in this chapter. Between 1992 and March 15, 2010, 83.1 percent of all failures have been resolved using the purchase and assumption method. This means that regulators have increasingly used the very policy the legislation sought to minimize.

FDICIA also ordered the FDIC to create risk-based deposit insurance. If deposit insurance increases risk taking, risk-based insurance may minimize that outcome. To the extent that the risk-based insurance formula reflects actual risk, this would reduce the moral hazard inherent in deposit insurance and improve bank stability. Indeed, scholars have argued that the FDICIA fails to make significant change to FDIC policy so we should not expect much change in TBTF policy.[68] At the same time, however, other scholars find that the post 1992 experience fails to produce evidence of moral hazard from TBTF policy.[69] This may suggest that the FDICIA was effective in removing the moral hazard problems associated with TBTF. However, as shown in Chapter 7, the problem resurfaced during the middle and late 2000s. This suggests that the FDICIA, at best, temporarily reduced moral hazard.

Finally, FDICIA limited brokered deposits for banks without sufficient capital and also limited state chartered bank activity for poorly capitalized banks. Tying activity to capital holdings may provide incentive to bankers to hold sufficient capital so as to earn the right to expand activities. In turn, holding capital may keep risk taking in check as the banker has more to lose with more capital holdings. In this way, these final two provisions of the FDICIA improved bank stability.

Riegle–Neal Interstate Banking and Branching Efficiency Act

Chapter 5 provides a detailed analysis of the costs of banning interstate banking. The IBBEA allows for interstate banking and consequently eliminates the costs associated with the ban. This is most certainly stabilizing. More specifically, allowing for interstate banking enhances bank stability through three channels: by expanding geographic diversity which reduces risk, by reducing costs associated with the subsidiary system earlier in this era, and by increasing competition so that banks improve their efficiency and improve profits.

The second primary provision of the IBBEA allows states to determine the extent to which there will be interstate branching. States may open their borders to free interstate branching or they may adopt up to four restrictions that make interstate branching more costly. Empirical research finds that banks in states that adopt more branching restrictions have more nonperforming loans and loan losses than banks in states with fewer branching provisions.[70] This suggests that greater freedoms to branch are associated with better performing loans and, as a result, greater stability. Thus, just as interstate banking is stabilizing, so is interstate branching.

Gramm–Leach–Bliley Act

Removing the separation between commercial and investment banking enhances stability just as Glass–Steagall reduced stability. Securities affiliates were profitable, which is why bankers were actively engaged in securities business prior to 1933. The separation of these two industries necessarily reduced the profitability to the commercial banker and, in doing so, made failure a greater possibility. Consequently, allowing commercial banks to engage in securities activity enhances profitability and stability. At the same time, as was shown in Chapter 5, banks were able to obtain some geographic diversity through their securities affiliates which made them less vulnerable to local economic downturns and shocks. This implies that the benefits of geographic expansion may be recaptured with the passage of the GLBA.

Concluding remarks

Reflecting on the postwar banking era, the experience is a clear illustration of the tension between static regulation and a dynamic market process. Recall that the Austrian perspective of economics envisions the market process as an evolving, dynamic interaction between market participants who respond to information created by the process itself. Regulation necessarily interrupts that process and, since it is not evolving, it necessarily becomes a destabilizing factor. The postwar era is replete with such examples.

Perhaps the most obvious is the disintermediation caused by regulation Q. Market interest rates increased to the point where interest rates became binding. Depositors responded by removing their funds from banks and seeking higher returns elsewhere. Because of static regulation, bankers were unable to respond until they found a way to partially avoid the regulation. Similarly, bankers were at a severe competitive disadvantage because much of the regulation during this era (e.g. Glass–Steagall, reserve requirements, limits in single loan amounts, etc.) made it increasingly costly for banks relative to nonbanks such as MMMFs, foreign banks, or finance companies who were not subject to the same regulation.

A second obvious example is that much of the regulation in this era was a reaction to market realities and not a new set of rules. For example: the DIDMCA made legal the use of NOW and ATS accounts because banks were already offering such accounts; the IBBEA allowed for interstate banking because 49 out of 50 states had already passed laws to allow for interstate banking; and the GLB of 1999 allowed commercial banks to engage in securities and insurance activity which many banks were already cleared to do through state law or decisions by courts and regulators. The point is that the markets had moved beyond the constraints of static regulation.

Similarly, it is clear from the postwar experience that policymakers recognized too late that the dynamic process had exposed the destabilizing impact of static regulation. Once this was realized, the process of deregulation began but it was too late; the damage had been done so the response to deregulation was to quickly repair the damage, often through high risk activity. More specifically, some have offered the perspective that the deregulation in wave 1 (Table 6.3) caused the bank failures of the 1980s and 1990s. While it is true that deregulation coincided with a period of increased bank failures, the deregulation did not cause the failures. Rather, as is shown in this chapter, policymakers waited until the fragility caused by regulation was exposed and then they began the process of deregulation. However, at that point the bankers were already far behind; profits were falling, disintermediation was in full swing, they faced increased competition from nonbanks, and many could not survive.

The postwar era revealed a potentially risk enhancing element to how bank failures are resolved by regulators. Deposit insurance, on its own, contributes to moral hazard problems of increased risk and this possibility is heightened under certain conditions. In addition, the element of moral hazard is exacerbated by the FDIC resolution policy (TBTF) to cover all, not just insured, deposits. Existing evidence indicates that the application of TBTF during the 1980s contributed to increase risk taking at banks. However, after 1991 and through 2003, the evidence shifts showing no increase in risk. But, as seen by its reappearance in the middle of the 2000s, it is clear that moral hazard has not been eliminated. Rather, this suggests that certain market conditions produce a greater likelihood of moral hazard related to deposit insurance and TBTF policy. TBTF removes the discipline of market outcomes, i.e. failures, and, in doing so, creates greater incentive to take risks particularly when the perceived risk is less.

During the 1980s, commercial bankers were under tremendous competitive pressure and were largely unable to respond in conventional ways. Existing static regulation kept banks from adapting to dynamic changes in the market. Consequently, the value of the bank charter deteriorated which, in turn, contributed to bank's willingness to assume greater risk under a regime of TBTF. Deregulation in the 1980s restored stability and charter values which explains why there is less evidence of moral hazard from TBTF in the 1990s and early 2000s. The postwar era experience with deposit insurance and the FDIC's resolution policy also illustrates the fundamental conflict established in Chapter 2 between static regulation and a dynamic market; the regulation may be stabilizing at a point in time (as was deposit insurance in 1933), but destabilizing at another. This is predicted by the Austrian vision of the market process in which the market continues to evolve and change as new information is revealed to participants. This appears to be a primary reason that bank regulation is largely destabilizing rather than stabilizing.

In addition to illustrating the destabilizing nature of bank regulation, the postwar era contains several illustrations of the extension of the federal safety net in banking. As mentioned above, the TBTF policy and its liberal application has serious implications for risk taking in commercial banking. However, economists and policymakers understood well before the 1980s the moral hazard dangers inherent in deposit insurance (see, for example, the discussion in Chapter 3 on state deposit insurance schemes). What is new to the postwar period is the extension of its use; this chapter clearly demonstrates that TBTF policy became the rule for resolving bank failures and not the exception. Another example of the expansion of the federal safety net is the Federal Reserve's assumption of Franklin National's foreign exchange liabilities; this was a clear extension of the central bank's lender of last resort function. In isolation perhaps this extension is not worth mentioning. However, it, along with the extensive use of TBTF, changes the appetite for government bailouts over market outcomes. As will be shown in Chapter 7, by the middle of the 2000s, not only were citizens not shocked at the level of the federal bailout, it was both expected and anticipated.

7
Banking and Crisis in the Twenty-First Century: 2000–2010

Introduction to a new millennium of banking

Most economic indicators show that, at the turn of the new century, the U.S. economy was flourishing. Despite significant challenges, such as the September 2001 terror attack on America, the economy grew. For the first eight and one half years, the unemployment rates were low, generally staying below six percent. RGDP growth was positive through 2007, and consumer prices held relatively steady during the same period. Between the beginning of 2003 and late into 2007, the Dow Jones Industrial Average generally increased, reaching a peak of over 14,000 in October of 2007. Thus, the economy during the first seven or so years of the twenty-first century may be described as healthy.

However, while there were earlier economic signs of decay, it was in the fall of 2008 that most Americans, and the world, learned that an asset bubble had burst and the general economy would pay a price.[1] The macroeconomic response was predictable: RGDP growth rates turned negative in 2008 and 2009. Expectedly, unemployment increased steadily beginning in April of 2008, reached over ten percent in October of 2009 and held close to ten percent for many months. The Dow Jones Industrial Average fell from its October 2007 high of over 14,000 to just under 6500 in March 2009: well over half of the index average had been lost. Between October 2007 and October 2008, eight trillion dollars in wealth was lost in the stock market.[2] The U.S. plunged into a severe recession.

In retrospect, we know that there was a housing bubble building during the first six or seven years of the new century. House prices rose far in excess of inflation. In some states, prices were rising, on average, over 25 percent a year (Hawaii, Arizona). In other states, house price inflation was much more modest, rising at most seven percent on average (Texas). The variability in house prices can be seen in panels A through C in Figure A.24. Several trends are observable. First, the Central regions (panel A) of the country saw home prices rise above the national average in the early years but prices peaked at below the national average. Panel B illustrates that the New England and Mid Atlantic regions lagged behind the national average during the initial upswing in prices but ended higher than average at the peak. The Pacific region experienced significant volatility peaking at above the national average and also plummeting much further than average (panel C). Interestingly, the West Central region in panel C witnessed house inflation below the national average but also enjoyed a smaller correction as prices fell. Taken together, these panels illustrate both the inflation and deflation in the housing market and also the high degree of variability in prices across different regions of the country.

As home prices fell and mortgage borrowers had increasing difficulty paying their loans, the vulnerability of banks was exposed. There were 267 bank failures between the turn of the century and June 1, 2010, and 88 percent of these were after the beginning of 2008. As shown in Table 7.1, some regions of the country were hit harder than others. The

Table 7.1 Number and Percent of Bank Failures by Region: 2000–June 1, 2010

Region	Number of Failures	Percent of Total Failures
Pacific	37	16.5%
Mountain	24	10.7%
West South Central	12	5.3 %
West North Central	29	12.9%
East North Central	46	20.5%
East South Central	5	2.2%
New England	2	0.9%
Middle Atlantic	5	2.2%
South Atlantic	64	28.6%

Source: www2.fdic.gov

Note: **Pacific** includes Hawaii, Alaska, Washington, Oregon, California; **Mountain** includes Montana, Idaho, Wyoming, Nevada, Utah, Colorado, Arizona, New Mexico; **West South Central** includes Oklahoma, Arkansas, Texas, Louisiana; **West North Central** includes North Dakota, South Dakota, Minnesota, Nebraska, Iowa, Kansas, Missouri; **East North Central** includes Michigan, Wisconsin, Illinois, Indiana, Ohio; **East South Central** includes Kentucky, Tennessee, Mississippi, Alabama; **New England** includes Maine, New Hampshire, Vermont, Massachusetts, Rhode Island, Connecticut; **Middle Atlantic** includes New York, New Jersey, Pennsylvania; **South Atlantic** includes Delaware, Maryland, DC, Virginia, West Virginia, North Carolina, South Carolina, Georgia, Florida.

South Atlantic region accounted for over 28 percent of all the bank failures during this period and just over 20 percent were in the East North Central region. Further, four states, Illinois, Florida, Georgia, and California, represented over 60 percent of all the commercial bank failures.

The housing bubble

The narrative which follows explains how the housing bubble was created, how it popped, and how it led to a bank crisis in the U.S. The unprecedented rise in home prices in the U.S. was the result of a mix of public policy, monetary policy, and regulation (see Table 7.2).[3] Blended together, the policies and regulation led to higher home prices by: significantly increasing the demand for homes and for mortgages to finance the home purchases; increasing the supply of mortgages, particularly for low-income home buyers; and restricting land use which created a scarcity of attractive new home sites. Once home prices crested and then began plummeting, the high risk nature of the mortgages was exposed. Unfortunately, by that time, the poor quality mortgages had proliferated throughout financial markets both domestically and internationally via new financial tools so that the impact of the housing bubble was widespread.

Public policy of homeownership

Beginning in the early 1990s, the U.S. federal government, through a series of regulatory, legislative, and policy directives, committed itself to the expansion of homeownership. On its own, none of the policies caused the run up in home prices but, collectively, they created a powerful set of conditions for the asset bubble. The percent of the population that owned homes had been relatively stable at just about 64 percent for much of the postwar era. However, it rose to 65.1 percent in 1995, reached 67.5 percent in 2000, and exceeded 69 percent in 2004.[4] By the end of 2009, 67.2 percent of the U.S. population owned homes.

To achieve this increase in ownership, public policy relied, in part, on Government Sponsored Enterprises (GSEs). In particular, the Federal National Mortgage Association (Fannie Mae) and the Federal Home Loan Mortgage Corporation (Freddie Mac), both GSEs under the regulatory supervision of the Office of the Federal Housing Enterprise Oversight (OFHEO) which, in turn, was housed in the Housing and Urban Development (HUD) agency, were required to undertake an affordable housing mission established by Congress. As GSEs, both Fannie Mae and

Table 7.2 Summary of Policies and Laws and the Impact on Home Prices in the Twenty-First Century

Policies/Laws	Description	How Policies/Laws Impact Home Prices
Housing Mandate at GSEs	• Mandate that the GSEs purchase subprime mortgages.	• Provided incentives for banks to make nonprime loans and sell them to the GSES. This increased the supply of mortgages and willingness of bankers to lend.
Ratings Agencies	• Inaccurately rated mortgage related securities as investment grade.	• Increased investor's demand for the securities and, in turn, the supply of mortgages, particularly nonprime mortgages.
Monetary Policy	• Held interest rates to historically low levels.	• Increased the demand for housing.
Mortgage Interest Deductibility	• Interest paid on mortgage loans is deductible from federal income tax.	• Increased the demand for housing.
Land Use Restrictions	• Many states use a variety of strategies to limit available land for housing development.	• Decreased the supply of land thereby increasing the price of home construction and existing homes.
Nonrecourse Loan Laws	• Many states allow mortgage holders to walk away from a mortgage loan without the debt of the loan.	• Increased demand for mortgage loans; increased demand for homes relative to rental property.

Notes: The first four policy/laws are at the federal level and the final two are state level laws. The first two policies are shaded to emphasize that these contributed to both the housing bubble as well as to the instability in banking. The impact of these policies on bank instability is found in Table 7.4.

Freddie Mac have a unique business model. Both GSEs are owned privately by shareholders but operate with a public mission, under a congressional charter, with a line of credit at the Treasury. Consequently, the GSEs are privately owned but publically operated with the backing of the U.S. Treasury.

Early on, Fannie Mae extended mortgage loans. However, in 1968, that function was moved out of Fannie Mae into a separate institution.[5] So, if the GSEs do not originate mortgage loans, how can they support an affordable housing mission? Banks, thrifts, or mortgage companies originate the mortgage loan and then turn around and sell the loans to the GSEs. This allows banks to convert long-term assets that had once been illiquid into cash so that they can make more loans. By purchasing these loans from banks, the GSEs facilitated mortgage credit to potential homebuyers. Further, since the GSEs stood willing and able to purchase mortgages loans, bankers knew they could quickly extend a loan and turn around and sell it; this substantially increased the supply of home mortgages in the United States.

Once Fannie and Freddie had purchased the mortgages they typically had two options. Either they would hold onto the mortgages and earn the interest on them or they would package up the mortgages and sell them off to investors. If they sold the mortgages off, this would free up funds to purchase even more mortgages from banks. Further, the GSEs guaranteed the investors that they would pay the interest and principal on the mortgages, even if the borrower could not.[6] Of course, this guarantee was attractive to the investors and was profitable for the GSEs because they charged a fee for the guarantee. However, this practice spreads the risk inherent in the mortgage loans to those investors purchasing the package of mortgages from the GSEs. By the second quarter of 2008, the GSEs were holding or guaranteeing over $5.5 trillion in home mortgages.[7] By comparison, commercial banks and savings banks held, in total, $3 trillion at time.[8] It is clear that the GSEs were major institutional players in the mortgage market.

The GSEs were purchasing many different types of mortgages but, given the affordable housing mission, many of the mortgages were subprime. There is no universal definition of a subprime loan, but generally speaking, a subprime loan is of higher credit risk than prime loans largely because of the risk characteristics of the borrower. Subprime borrowers, for example, may have poor credit histories, high debt burdens relative to their income, or little money for down payment. Since a subprime loan carries greater risk, the interest rate on these loans is higher than on prime mortgage loans. Another category of mortgage loans, known as Alt-A loans, carry risk between prime and subprime loans. The GSEs were committed to purchasing Alt-A and subprime loans as a part of their support for the affordable housing policy of the federal government. Consider that in 2006, 79.4 percent of all the private-label mortgage related securities retained at Freddie Mac were subprime or Alt-A; Fannie Mae retained 82.5 percent in the same year.[9] The commitment by the GSEs resulted in a significant expansion of this segment of the mortgage market. As evidence, consider that subprime and Alt-A mortgages were about eight percent of all mortgages in the U.S. in 2003 and approximately 22 percent three years later.[10] Further, the subprime mortgages increasingly made their way into mortgage backed securities and other securities. In 2002, 47 percent of subprime mortgages were securitized and by 2007 67.8 percent of all subprime mortgage loans were securitized.[11] Ultimately, by the middle of 2008, there were 27 million subprime and Alt-A mortgages in the U.S. Twelve million of these were held or guaranteed by the GSEs and 2.2 million were held at commercial banks.[12] By all measures, the subprime mortgages permeated the financial sector.

Monetary policy

Concurrent with the GSEs purchasing and reselling mortgage loans, the Federal Reserve was pursuing a policy of low interest rates. Figure A.25 contains the federal funds rate from January 2000 through March 2010 and shows that between the end of 2000 and the middle of 2004, interest rates fell to about one percent and held at this historically low level until rising to about three percent in the middle of 2005, and finally reaching just over five percent in the middle of 2006. Even at the peak of home prices, the federal funds rate did not significantly exceed this relatively low five percent rate. Low interest rates and the resulting reduced cost of borrowing fueled the increasing demand for mortgages. Indeed, the Federal Reserve has been criticized extensively for keeping interest rates low and, in doing so, contributing to the housing bubble.[13]

Laws and regulation

State laws and federal financial and tax regulation also played an important role in driving up home prices in the 2000s. More specifically, two state laws, one pertaining to land use and the other to the nature of mortgage loans are important elements in the inflation of home prices. State level laws and regulation differentiate one state from another. In other words, to understand why the housing bubble was more severe in some states (or regions) than others, we must look beyond federal policy since federal policy treats all states (or regions) the same. In contrast, differences in state level policy may help explain the regional variation of the housing bubble. At the federal level, financial regulation and the income tax code both also contributed to the run up in house prices. The amendment to the 1977 Community Reinvestment Act (introduced in Chapter 6) encouraged banks to extend mortgage loans to low-income borrowers while the deductibility of mortgage interest rates encouraged homeowners to purchase homes over other investments (or renting) and even take second mortgages which furthered the home inflation of the early 2000s.

A. *Land use regulation*

States and municipalities began, in the 1960s, passing land use restrictions. These may take several forms, from restricting how land may be used (e.g. the farmer who no longer wants to farm cannot sell the land for development), to mandated minimum lot-sizes (e.g. a home must be built on at least one acre of land), to limiting the annual number of building permits. Historically, these restrictions were confined to urban areas but growth-management and other laws gave cities control over rural areas as well. These policies and laws make land more scarce, and consequently, more expensive for home building. A study found that 23 of 26 urban areas around the world with land use restrictions are also designated to be areas that are "severely unaffordable".[14] Indeed, studies of home prices across the nation find that costs such as materials and labor are relatively equal but that the distinguishing cost is the land on which the home is built. One study found that in cities with land use restrictions in place for ten to 15 years, the price of the home is double what it would be without the restrictions.[15] By definition, these state and local laws reduce the supply of land and increase its price.

Statewide land use laws are not as common as local or municipal laws.[16] Nonetheless, the general trend has seen more states adopting growth-management land use laws. Hawaii did so in 1961 and two years later California law effectively gave cities control over all urban areas. Oregon followed in the 1970s and in the 1980s and 1990s many more states either passed statewide growth-management laws or followed the California model by giving cities control over rural development (see Table 7.3 for a list of those states).

B. *Nonrecourse mortgage loans*

In some states, when a borrower takes out a mortgage, the home is the only collateral behind the loan because the loan is linked to the home

Table 7.3 States with Land Use Restrictions and/or Nonrecourse Mortgages

State	Nonrecourse Loans	Land Use Restrictions	Average Annual Percent Change in Home Prices 2000–2006	Average Annual Percent Change in Home Prices 2007–2009	Number of Bank Failures (Percent of Total Bank Failures 2000–June 1, 2010)
Alaska	Yes	No	7.30%	0.77%	0
Arizona	Yes	Yes	12.05%	–12.41%	8 (2.88%)
California	Yes	Yes	15.02%	–14.88%	29 (10.86%)
Colorado	No	Yes	5.71%	–0.31%	3 (1.12%)
Connecticut	Yes	Yes	9.45%	–2.81%	1 (0.37%)
Florida	Yes	Yes	13.68%	–13.42%	29 (10.86%)
Georgia	No	Yes	4.98%	–2.99%	41 (15.3%)
Hawaii	No	Yes	14.37%	–3.47%	1 (0.37%)
Idaho	Yes	No	7.73%	–1.35%	1 (0.37%)
Maine	No	Yes	9.46%	–0.92%	3 (1.12%)
Maryland	No	Yes	13.18%	–5.17%	3 (1.12%)
Massachusetts	No	Yes	9.71%	–3.30%	1 (0.37%)
Minnesota	Yes	Yes	8.00%	–4.08%	14 (5.24%)
New Hampshire	No	Yes	10.04%	–3.65%	1 (0.37%)
New Jersey	No	Yes	12.13%	-3.72%	3 (1.12%)
North Carolina	Yes	No	4.68%	1.10%	2 (0.75%)
North Dakota	Yes	No	5.63%	2.92%	0
Oregon	No	Yes	9.03%	–2.61%	4 (1.49%)
Pennsylvania	No	Yes	8.17%	–0.31%	3 (1.12%)
Rhode Island	No	Yes	12.89%	–5.60%	0
Tennessee	No	Yes	4.61%	0.03%	1 (0.37%)
Texas	Yes	No	4.64%	2.23%	9 (3.37%)
Utah	Yes	No	6.02%	–0.38%	6 (2.24%)
Vermont	No	Yes	9.57%	0.56%	0
Washington	Yes	Yes	8.91%	–1.49%	9 (3.37%)
Wisconsin	No	Yes	5.69%	–0.99%	2 (0.75%)

Source: Nonrecourse mortgages laws comes from www.helcobasics.com, land use restrictions laws are from O'Toole (2007), home price indices are from www.fhfa.gov, and the bank failure data is from www2.fdic.gov.

Notes: Home Index data is through the fourth quarter of 2009. The land use laws vary from state to state and so some may be more restrictive than others. See O'Toole (2007) for more on the nature of these laws. The bank failure data is as of June 1, 2010.

and not the borrower. This means that, should the borrower stop paying the loan, the only recourse for the bank, or other lender, is the home. The borrower walks away unburdened by the debt from the loan. These are called nonrecourse mortgage loans. Twelve states have nonrecourse mortgage loan laws (see Table 7.3). Nonrecourse loans contribute to higher home prices by changing the incentives facing the borrower. That is, if the borrower can walk away from a loan without the debt of the loan, this increases the population of borrowers, particularly higher risk borrowers.

Table 7.3 lists all states that have land use restrictions in place and/or allow for nonrecourse mortgages. Shaded states have both land use restrictions and nonrecourse mortgages. This table also provides information on the average change in home prices from 2000–2006 and again from 2007–2009 as well as the number of bank failures from 2000 through June 1, 2010 and the percent of all bank failures that occurred in that state during the 2000–2010 period. This data reveals some interesting patterns. First, eight states had double digit house price inflation during the bubble and three of these were in states with both statewide land use restrictions and nonrecourse loans.[17] Further, two of the three states (California and Florida) with the largest increase in average prices were states with both state level laws. Second, three states have double digit average deflation; all three were states with both state level laws (Arizona, California, Florida). This suggests that such laws may contribute to the volatility of home prices and other research finds similarly.[18] Third, given the modest gains (16th highest from the list in Table 7.3), Minnesota had a relatively large correction (sixth largest). Minnesota is also a state with both growth-management laws and nonrecourse mortgages which may explain some of this volatility.

The final column in Table 7.3 indicates the number of bank failures in these selected states as well as the percent of all bank failures in each state. California and Florida each account for just under eleven percent of all banks failures in the country between 2000 and June 1, 2010. Minnesota accounts for the fourth highest percentage of total bank failures from this sample of states. All three of these states are shaded in the table; all allowed for nonrecourse mortgages and restricted land use throughout the state. At the same time, Georgia has more bank failures than any other state in the nation but did not witness extreme house price fluctuations. Consequently, there must be an alternative explanation for the situation in Georgia; this is considered later in the chapter.

C. Mortgage interest rate deductibility

While the nonrecourse and land use laws are at the state level, federal level tax law also influenced the financial crisis. The current federal tax code provides that interest paid on mortgages and home equity loans is deductible. This provision makes homeownership much more desirable than renting as the homeowner can deduct the interest payments and, in the process, reduce their federal income tax burden. In theory, this tax provision is desirable if it helps low-income families obtain homeownership. However, most low-income families do not pay federal income tax and so do not enjoy the benefits of the provision.

The deductibility of interest on home equity loans creates the incentive for borrowers to use the equity in their home to finance nonhome spending. That is, interest on other types of credit, from credit cards to auto loans, is not deductible. Rather than pay interest on these loans with no reduction in federal income tax burdens, borrowers take out a home equity loan and can spend that money freely and still enjoy a reduced tax burden. Increasing debt and reducing equity makes the housing market increasingly fragile and vulnerable to falling home prices.

D. Community Reinvestment Act

Also at the federal level, the Community Reinvestment Act exacerbated the financial crisis. As indicated in Chapter 6, the CRA was created in 1977 and requires that commercial banks extend loans to low-income borrowers, consistent with safe and sound banking practices. In 1995, the financial regulatory agencies collectively made amendments to the CRA which provided greater incentives to banks to follow CRA mandates. More specifically, the 1995 revision divided institutions into two classifications. Large institutions were those with $250 million or more in assets and small institutions were those with less than assets of $250 million. The size classification has been revised many times since 1995. As of December 2009, a small institution has assets of less than $1.098 billion for either of the prior two years and a large institution is defined as one with assets of at least $1.098 billion for both of the previous two years.[19] Large and small banks have different reporting requirements. While small banks are exempt from reporting information on CRA loans, large banks must report annual data on CRA loans, which includes small business, small farm, community development, and mortgage loans. Further, this large bank lending record is public information.

A CRA rating is assigned to each bank based on the results of a regulatory examination and analysis of their lending record.[20] Banks earn ratings that are "outstanding," "satisfactory," "needs to improve," or "substantial noncompliance." Between 1990 and 2007, 16.3 percent of the ratings were outstanding, 79.5 percent were satisfactory, 3.8 percent needed to improve and 0.4 percent fell into the substantial noncompliance rating.[21] The CRA ratings are public information for all sized banks. Certainly, the public nature of the rating may compel banks to extend low-income loans for fear of community backlash. However, perhaps more important in this regard, is what regulators do with the rating. The act compels regulators to consider the bank's CRA record and rating when the bank applies for a new branch, merger, or acquisition. Recall from Chapter 6 that in 1994, the IBBEA gives banks more freedom to branch, merge, and acquire other banks. Consequently, tying a bank's ability to pursue these activities to its CRA record and rating provides significant incentive for banks to comply with the CRA lending provisions. Further banks could meet their CRA obligations by extending loans to low-income borrowers and then turn around and sell the high risk mortgage loans to the GSEs with no further risk to the bank. In this way, the GSEs allowed banks to meet CRA lending standards but transferred some of the risk to the GSEs.

Thus far, the narrative of the housing bubble indicates that public policy impacted both the mortgage market and the housing market. The GSEs increased the supply of mortgages by standing ready to purchase mortgages from the banks and the CRA also increased the supply of mortgages by requiring that banks extend mortgages to a wider population. The Federal Reserve's low interest rate policy combined with nonrecourse loan laws both increased the demand for mortgages. In the housing market itself, land use laws decrease the supply of land thereby driving up home prices. Further, demand for housing increases with the mortgage deductibility provision in the federal income tax code. Taken together, public policies and laws significantly expanded the mortgage market by increasing both the supply and demand for mortgages and, at the same time, restricted land supply in many states and cities. The expansion of mortgages, of course, leads to an increase in the demand for homes so that in the housing market, supply is often restricted coupled with a growing demand and hence, higher home prices.

Wall Street

While public policy, regulation, and laws altered the mortgage and home markets, the private sector responded to the inflated home prices and to existing regulation by further expanding nontraditional segments of the market. As explain in Chapter 6, the postwar era saw an explosion in nonbank competition and witnessed banks increasingly rely on off-balance sheet activity. In the era of inflated home prices, these postwar era developments took on greater significance. Nonbank institutions including mutual funds, money market mutual funds and finance companies together with the off-balance sheet activity of commercial banks were growing alongside the formal financial sector and became described as the "shadow banking sector."

An important element of the shadow banking sector was the securitization of home mortgages. Securitization refers to the process of transforming illiquid assets into marketable, usually long-term, instruments. A bank may, for example, package up many of the home mortgages that it originated and sell them to another bank which is also packaging several thousand mortgages. This collection of mortgages is then divided into tranches which reflect varying degrees of risk. For example, the safest or lowest risk, tranche has the highest credit rating while a more risky collection of mortgages is in another tranche with a lower credit rating. If the households stop paying their mortgages, the owners of the securities in that tranche are not paid. This process creates a financial product known as mortgage backed securities (MBS).

Related to MBSs is another financial product known as collateralized-debt obligations (CDOs) which are a more complicated form of securitization than the MBSs. The original idea behind CDOs is to take previously securitized assets and package them to create an asset with even more diversified risk. As originally conceived, the CDOs were a package of a wide variety of securitized assets. However, during the housing bubble, Wall Street firms created CDOs from only mortgages. Just like MBSs, CDOs are also divided into tranches according to risk and pay interest rates that reflect the level of risk.

While the practice of securitization did not originate in the 2000s, it was made increasingly popular by inflated home prices and inflated credit ratings.[22] As described above, both MBSs and CDOs are financial innovations that are designed to spread and diversify risk. As such the innovations could be stabilizing to the financial sector. However, during the early 2000s, an unexpected development made investing in MBSs, CDOs and other derivatives extremely risky. That development was the inaccurate rating of these financial instruments.

Credit rating agencies, such as Moody's, Standard & Poor's, and Fitch, are private companies that analyze institutions including firms, banks, and governments, to evaluate their health and ability to repay debt. One output of the analysis is a rating on a financial product where the rating reflects the risk behind the product. Thus, if a firm wants to sell bonds, it hires a credit rating agency to assign a rating to the bond. If the firm hired Moody's, for example, an Aaa rating is the highest and is considered an exceptional security with very little risk while a Baa is considered to be an adequate security, and Caa extremely poor quality etc. The rating signals to potential buyers information about the health of the issuing firm. Provided the rating accurately reflects the risk of the bond, important information is disseminated in the market.

Problems arose, however, when the credit rating agencies were assigning investment grade (i.e., the highest) ratings to even the most risky tranches of MBSs, CDOs, and other financial derivatives. In other words, a MBS created from Baa rated mortgages was assigned an Aaa rating. Not surprisingly, this attracted investors from around the globe. An increase in demand for these derivatives fueled the origination of even more mortgages and, in this way, exacerbated the housing bubble.

It is easy to imagine how pressure from rival credit rating agencies could create incentives to inflate ratings. Indeed, it is well documented that when one agency attempted to lower the ratings on these mortgage backed derivatives, banks left that agency in favor of the remaining agencies that would provide the highest grade.[23] Since the issuers were paying for the ratings, they could shop around until they found an agency that would provide them with the desired rating. Unfortunately, these false grades created a substantial demand for the mortgage backed securities which fueled the housing bubble.

The bubble bursts

As is well understood in the financial crisis literature, and elsewhere, all good things must come to an end.[24] In most parts of the country, home prices started falling sometime in 2007. As expected, however, there were regional differences as to when house prices began declining (see Figure A.24). For example, in the West South Central region home prices did not deflate until the fourth quarter of 2008 while in the New England region, home prices starting falling in the third quarter of 2006. The subsequent increase in loan delinquencies suddenly made investors realize that their MBS and CDOs came with substantial risk. As evidence, consider that in August 2007 Moody's downgraded 691 MBSs in a single day because of poor performance.[25] As investors moved away from these financial instruments, their values declined. Declining values, in turn, eroded confidence. Investors questioned the reliability of the credit ratings and, by association, the value of the MBSs and CDOs. Investors not only ceased lending but they all wanted their money back. The contraction of credit, of course, reinforced the deflation in housing. House prices cannot increase as mortgage credit becomes scarce.

As home prices fell, borrowers found themselves increasingly unable to meet loan payments. When borrowers fail to make a payment, these loans are considered nonperforming to the bank. Figure 7.1 illustrates that by the middle of 2008, the percent of residential mortgages to total assets that were nonperforming increased substantially. Note also that the problem of nonperforming mortgage loans was much more acute at the largest commercial banks. Banks were forced to write-down their nonperforming loans and forced to increase capital holdings as they could not sell off mortgages; there were no buyers. As residential mortgage loan losses began to mount, many commercial banks became insolvent and failed. Figure 7.2 illustrates the bank failure problem; the number of bank failures has risen since 2007 with a significant spike in 2009 and as of the first of June, 2010 is on pace to exceed the failures of 2009. The number of failures is expected to continue to rise as the number of banks on the FDIC problem list at the beginning of June 2010

Figure 7.1 Nonperforming Loans Secured by 1–4 Family Residential Properties as a Percent of Total Assets: 2000–2009

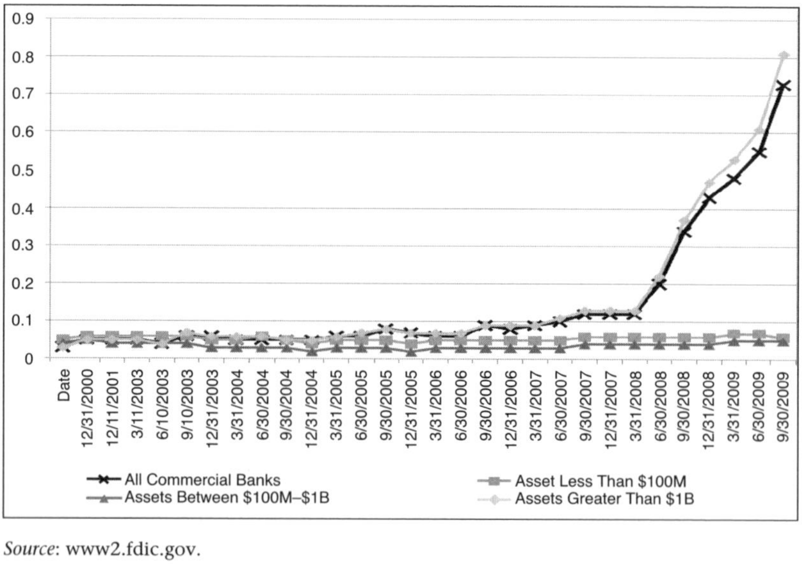

Source: www2.fdic.gov.

Note: These are loans past due 90 days or more for all commercial banks.

Figure 7.2 Total Number of Commercial Bank Failures: 2000–2010*

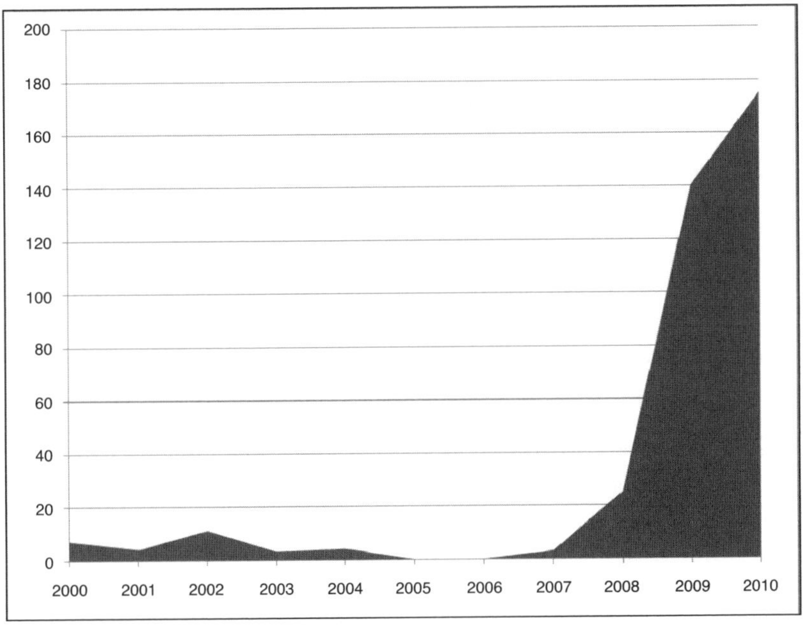

Source: www2.fdic.gov.

Note: *2010 is an estimate assuming the same rate of failures from the first five months through the end of the year.

was 829.[26] Further, though the financial crisis initially manifested in the residential mortgage market, the severe recession that followed has put significant pressure on the commercial real estate market. Consider, for example, that noncurrent construction and development loans were 1.29 percent of all loans at the end of 2007 and had climbed to 8.74 percent one year later.[27] Astonishingly, that figure almost doubled, to 16.15 percent by the end of 2009. Similar trends are also found in noncurrent commercial real estate loans.

Not surprisingly, as home prices fell and borrowers defaulted on their mortgage loans, the high risk portfolio of mortgages at the GSEs soured. In the middle of 2008, Fannie disclosed that at least 85 percent of their losses were related to subprime and high risk mortgages.[28] Certainly the declining value of their assets is destabilizing to the GSEs. However, the problems at both of these institutions were exacerbated by the fact that both Fannie and Freddie were severely undercapitalized. Consider that, in 2007, the GSEs had $83 billion in capital to cover its over $5 trillion in liabilities.[29] Not only were the capital requirements ineffective at the GSEs but, given the implicit backing of the government, investors were willing to ignore the fact that the GSEs were highly leveraged. In the end, the implicit backing became explicit as both GSEs were effectively nationalized.

Regulator response

As with the historical crises discussed in previous chapters, the immediate response to this crisis was an attempt to provide liquidity to the financial sector and to restore confidence more generally. Beginning in August 2007, the Federal Reserve initiated a fair number of new programs and actions.[30] These were intended to provide liquidity to banks and other financial firms. In addition to the programs, the Federal Reserve continued to cut the discount rate and to lower the targeted federal funds rate. Further, the Federal Reserve made direct loans to failing investment banks and insurance companies and also purchased hundreds of billions of dollars worth of MBSs from the GSEs.[31]

The Treasury also played a significant role in the immediate crisis period.[32] Like the Federal Reserve, the Treasury also purchased MBSs from the GSEs and in September of 2008, both Fannie and Freddie were placed under the control of the Federal Housing Finance Agency. Further, the Emergency Economic Stabilization Act (EESA) authorized the Treasury to use up to $700 billion to purchase troubled financial assets or to inject capital into financial institutions. Shortly after the passage of the EESA, the Treasury selected nine of the largest banks in the country and used $125 billion to purchase preferred shares in those banks. The Treasury did not disclose the criteria used to select the banks but some speculate that the Treasury was attempting to get the nine banks to acquire failing banks. Since so many banks were in financial trouble, if a stronger bank were to acquire a weaker bank, it would relieve the FDIC of the potential burden of the weak bank failing.

The Federal Reserve and the Treasury, together, created the largest safety net in U.S. banking history. Assets at the Federal Reserve grew from $880 billion in July of 2007 to $2.1 trillion at the end of November 2008.[33] The Treasury purchased preferred stock initially at nine banks but within a month purchased stock at almost fifty more banks.[34] The safety net was also extended with the aid of the FDIC who began finding strong banks to buy failing banks through the purchase and assumption method; virtually all bank failures during this crisis were resolved using the purchase and assumption method.

Assessment of regulation and stability

The first bank crisis of the twenty-first century is significant relative to historical experiences. Indeed, many have compared it in magnitude to the bank crises of the 1930s. In the late months of 2008 and early months of 2009, the comparisons to the Great Depression were difficult to miss.[35] As is evident from this chapter, blame for the crisis can be widely appointed. As with all the earlier episodes of crisis, the role of regulation as a contributing factor to the crisis is analyzed. Additionally, some have argued that this crisis was, in part, the result of deregulation from the 1990s. More specifically, the 1994 IBBEA and the 1999 GLB, discussed in Chapter 6, have been identified as culpable in the most recent financial crisis. Consequently, this analysis will assess the merits of that position as well. Finally, this crisis is unique from earlier crisis in that nonbank regulation contributed specifically to the instability in banking so that regulation is also considered. Table 7.4 summarizes the findings of the relationship between regulation and stability in commercial banking. The shaded areas of the table are distinguished as a reminder that this (shaded) regulation is outside of commercial bank regulation.

HUD mandate for the GSEs

The homeownership mission of the federal government put pressure on the GSEs to increasingly involve itself in the mortgage market, particularly that segment of the market targeting low-income borrowers. As part of that mission HUD increasingly required the GSEs to purchase mortgages made to low and moderate income families. In 1995, the mandate was set at 42 percent; at least this many of the mortgages or mortgage backed securities purchased by the GSEs were to come from the lower and moderate income demographic. This was increased to 50 percent in 2000 and increased over the years, reaching 58 percent in 2008.[36] This overpromotion of homeownership, in hindsight, proved costly as it legitimized and substantially increased the growth in securitized subprime mortgages. By purchasing trillions of dollars worth of subprime mortgages, the GSEs changed the incentives for loan originators. The banker knew that the GSEs would purchase the loan which removed the incentive for bankers to worry about the risk behind the loan. More high risk mortgage loans were extended because the banks knew that they could turn around and sell the loan to the GSEs. Indeed, empirical evidence indicates that the process of securitization adversely affects the lender's incentive to carefully screen applicants.[37]

Table 7.4 Summary of Bank Regulation and Its Impact on Commercial Bank Stability in the Twenty-First Century Banking Era

Regulation/Policy	Description	Channel(s) Through Which Regulation Impacts Bank Stability	Conclusion from the Evidence
Housing Mandate at HUD	• Mandate that the GSEs purchase subprime mortgages.	• Increase risk.	• Decrease stability by increasing the number of subprime loans (Barth et al. (2009)). • Decrease stability by reducing the quality of both subprime and prime loans (Figure 7.1, Wallison (2008), data in Barth et al. (2009)).
Ratings Agencies	• Provide securities rating for issuing firms/governments.	• Increase risk.	• Decrease stability by increasing the demand for subprime loans (Barth et al. (2009)).
Capital Regulation	• Risk-weighted capital standards for balance sheet and off-balance sheet activity.	• Increase risk.	• Decrease stability by providing incentives for bankers to take on more risk (Mishkin (2010), Norberg (2009), Kling (2010)).
CRA	• Required banks make loans to all members of the community with emphasis on low-income borrowers,	• Increase risk.	• Decrease stability by increasing the risk of bank assets (Gunther (1999), White (2008), Hendrickson and Nichols (2010)).

Table 7.4 Summary of Bank Regulation and Its Impact on Commercial Bank Stability in the Twenty-First Century Banking Era – *continued*

Regulation/Policy	Description	Channel(s) Through Which Regulation Impacts Bank Stability	Conclusion from the Evidence
IBBEA Interstate Branching Provisions	• Each state determines the extent to which there will be interstate branching across its borders. The analysis here pertains to states that adopted provisions that limit interstate branching.	• Decrease competition. • Increase risk by limiting geographic diversity. • Change bank structure by decreasing bank size. • Increase costs.	• Decrease stability by decreasing competition (Carlson and Mitchener (2005, 2009), Jayarathne and Strahan (1998), for example) and geographic diversity. • Decrease stability because small banks are more likely to fail (www2.fdic.gov). • Decrease stability by increasing costs associated with creating a new bank over branching (Mengle (1990)).
GLB	• Create financial firms that engage in banking, insurance, and securities underwriting.	• Decrease risk through diversification. • Increase competition.	• Increase stability by increasing competition (Flannery (1984)) and geographic diversity (White (1982, 1986)). • Increase stability by decreasing risk (Macey et al. (1991)).
Deposit Insurance	• Risk-based deposit insurance.	• Change risk.	• Increased stability by maintaining confidence in light of the large number of failures. • Decreased stability by reducing depositor-monitoring and increasing moral hazard (Stern and Feldman (2008)).

Notes: There are five identified channels through which regulation may impact stability; 1) change risk taking; 2) limit diversification; 3) change cost and revenue structure; 4) change the structure of the market; and 5) change the nature of competition. See Chapter 2 for a discussion of each. The first two policies are shaded to emphasize that these are not commercial bank regulation but, nonetheless, have a significant impact on bank stability.

Another unintended consequence of the HUD policy was the spillover of relaxed lending standards into the prime mortgage market. In order to get the subprime borrower qualified for a mortgage, it was often necessary to alter the terms of the loan or to lower the qualifying standards. It is well documented that many of the subprime mortgages made during this era were adjustable rate mortgages (ARMS) which are appealing to the borrower as they often carry an initial interest rate that is below a fixed rate loan. The percent of all mortgages that were ARMS increased from about ten percent in 2002 to over 21 percent by 2006; over 50 percent of all subprime loans were ARMS at the peak of the housing bubble.[38] In addition to the increased use of ARMS, interest-only loans, loans without documented income, hybrid loans (loans with both fixed and adjustable interest rates), and extremely low to no down payment loans, became the norm in order to get the low-income borrower qualified for the mortgage loan. As many scholars have identified, once the lending standards are reduced in the subprime market, the lower standards will spread to the prime market.[39] The banker will not hold the prime borrower to higher standards than the subprime borrower. Figure 7.1 illustrates the significant spike in nonperforming mortgage loans at commercial banks beginning in 2008. Nonperformance is a result, in part, of lower lending standards when the loans were originated.

Thus, the push by HUD to get mortgage loans to the low-income segment of the market contributed to commercial bank instability in two ways. First, it increased substantially the number of high risk mortgages that were originated by commercial banks. Second, lower subprime loans standards spread to the prime market so that even the prime loans became more risky.

Rating agencies

As indicated earlier in this chapter, the credit rating agencies played an important role in the expansion of securitized mortgage and, in the process, in the housing bubble itself. At the same time, the model that agencies use to sell their ratings also contributed to instability in commercial banking. The regulation of rating agencies falls under the purview of the Securities and Exchange Commission (SEC) and in the early 1970s the SEC determined that only Nationally Recognized Statistical Ratings Organizations (NRSRO) would be recognized agencies.[40] By excluding new entrants and recognizing only a small number of NRSROs, this created an oligopoly in the ratings industry. The ratings firms responded by moving away from selling their information to investors to a model in which their information was sold to the debt issuer. Many argue that had the SEC not created the oligopoly, the agencies would not have been able to change their model to sell to captive issuers. It is easy to see how selling ratings information to the firm that wants to issue debt is problematic; there exists an inherent conflict of interest as the issuer is paying the agency for a rating that will determine the perceived quality of the issue. From this perspective, the SEC's regulation of the ratings agencies created the conflict of interest that led to inflated ratings throughout the first seven years of the twenty-first century.

The inflated credit ratings fueled investor demand for MBSs, CDOs, and other securities backed by prime and subprime mortgage loans. As evidence of the extent to which the ratings were inflated, consider that 90 percent of the CDOs that were issued between 2005 and 2007 were downgraded by Standard and Poor's; 80 percent of them were downgraded below investment grade.[41] The loans to be securitized had to come from somewhere; they came from commercial banks and mortgage brokers. Had the ratings not been inflated, the demand for the securitized products would have been lower and banks may not have been as willing to continue extending mortgages, particularly those that were higher risk. The inflated ratings fed into the HUD mandate with the GSEs; both stimulated demand for more mortgages and often, more risky mortgages.

Bank regulation

While the HUD mandate to increase homeownership and the inflated credit ratings assigned by the primary credit rating agencies increased bank instability in the new millennium, commercial bank regulation also played an important role in destabilizing banking. Specifically, many of the regulatory developments from the postwar era contributed to bank instability as did deposit insurance and the too-big-to-fail policies of bank failure resolution.

A. Capital requirements

As described in Chapter 6, the Basel capital requirements are intended to reduce risk at banks but have had the unintended outcome of actually increasing risk. The risk-weighted capital requirements place a price on risk taking. Banks respond by taking risks that have the lowest price in terms of capital holdings. Many argue that the Basel capital requirements pushed banks to off-balance sheet activity and, at the same time, encouraged banks to make more mortgage loans as they had a lower capital requirement than, for example, commercial loans.[42]

Other scholars argue that the financial innovations of CDOs and other derivatives are the result of banks attempting to minimize the effects of capital requirements.[43] Without capital requirements that did not accurately recognize bank risk, these financial products may not have had widespread market penetration.

B. Community Reinvestment Act

Like capital requirements, the CRA changes the incentives at commercial banks by requiring that they extend loans to low-income borrowers. Noncompliance results in punishment. Many scholars have argued that, absent the CRA, bankers would not have made as many low-income and high risk mortgage loans.[44] Furthermore, the CRA is in direct conflict with capital requirements. The objective of the CRA is to cast a wider credit net while other regulation, capital requirements, for example, is designed to constrain risk taking. The conflict in this regulation may be illustrated by considering the CAMEL rating system with the CRA. CAMEL, which was put into place in 1979, requires that banks be evaluated in terms of their capital holdings, asset quality, management, earnings, and liquidity. The end result of the evaluation is known as the CAMEL safety and soundness rating. A separate rating is generated by the CRA regarding the lending record at the bank. Empirical analysis of these two opposing regulations finds that bank behavior, such as aggressive lending, improves the CRA rating but hurts the safety and soundness (CAMEL) ratings:

> ... evidence suggests that increases in the proportion of home-purchase mortgage volume extended to borrowers in low-income neighborhoods raise the chances of a problem CAMEL rating. The findings cast doubt on the typical claim made by CRA advocates that lending in low-income neighborhoods is relatively innocuous in terms of financial safety and soundness.[45]

Indeed, evidence prior to 2000 and the significant increase in home prices indicate that CRA loans had higher losses and higher cost than regular mortgage loans.[46] Further, there is evidence that many banks, in an attempt to meet CRA standards, purchased mortgage-backed securities that were largely backed by subprime mortgages which increased the banks' risk exposure.[47] That is, by purchasing these high risk MBSs, the banks were given credit towards their CRA rating. Unfortunately, when the housing bubble burst and the MBSs were downgraded, many banks began to fail and even more struggled to remain solvent.

Scholars at the Federal Reserve have argued that the CRA was not destabilizing because so few of the mortgage loans extended during the crisis were CRA loans.[48] The argument is that commercial bankers were not making enough of the high risk loans to have caused the crisis.[49] However, more recent research indicates that between 1993 and 2007, over $3.5 trillion in CRA loans were extended and, of these, ten percent where sold as MBSs.[50] Certainly the CRA did not cause the first bank crisis of the twenty-first century, but it did reward banks for making low-income bank loans and encouraged banks to invest in subprime MBSs. In this way, the CRA contributed to bank instability.

C. Interstate branching provisions from 1994 IBBEA

Recall from Chapter 6 that the 1994 passage of the IBBEA gave states the ability to customize the extent to which they would allow for interstate branching. Interestingly, the four states with the most bank failures during this crisis, California, Florida, Georgia, and Illinois all adopted four (the maximum) restrictive provisions in order to erect barriers to interstate branching. Illinois, in August 2004, reduced the number of restrictive barriers from four to two, making it friendlier to interstate branching than the other three high bank failure states. These results are not surprising as empirical research finds that banks perform better in states with more freedom for interstate branching in the post IBBEA era.[51]

Two states had substantially more bank failures than any other; Georgia and Illinois. Indeed, between 2000 and June 1, 2010, there were 41 failures in Georgia and 36 in Illinois. Consequently, a closer consideration of the bank failures in Georgia and Illinois is warranted. An analysis of characteristics of those banks that did fail reveals that the average size of the bank failure in Georgia had assets of approximately $570 million while the average size in Illinois was $783 million.[52] However, the average data may be misleading because of a few large failures. Indeed, 12 bank failures in both states had assets under 200 million. The average ratio of loan and lease losses to total assets was higher in Illinois (12.35 percent) than Georgia (7.85 percent) indicating more distressed loans in Illinois. Finally, 21 of the failed banks in Georgia were established since 1998 and were thus relatively young banks. In contrast, only seven of the Illinois bank failures were at banks established after 1998. Only one of the Illinois failures was established after the IBBEA change in 2004. This suggests that when Illinois opened its borders to more interstate branching, there were fewer new banks established. In contrast, in Georgia, many more of the bank failures were established in the new millennium. Perhaps the fact that Georgia erected barriers to interstate branching meant that the easiest way to enter the market was to establish a new bank. Creating a new bank is much more expensive than opening a branch across state lines. Further, the new bank, because it probably did not have branches across other state lines (many neighboring states require reciprocity for interstate branching), its assets were less diversified and more closely tied to the health of the city or county in which the bank was located.

D. Gramm–Leach–Bliley Act of 1999

In the fall of 2008, when most of America learned of the banking crisis, the popular press was quick to blame the 1999 deregulation of Glass–Steagall in the Gramm–Leach–Bliley Act. The argument was that the deregulation allowed banks to get too big, take on too much risk, and require bailouts. However, the evidence runs contrary. First, the big banks that had the greatest exposure to subprime mortgages (Merrill Lynch, Lehman Brothers, and Bear Stearns) were investment banks that had no affiliation with a commercial bank.[53] That is, these investment banks, and many others, did not respond to the 1999 deregulation; they remained investment banks without deposit functions. Further, as explained in this chapter, securitization is not new to banking; it did not result from GLB. This is an important misconception about the repeal of Glass–Steagall relative to this crisis. Banks were securitizing assets long before the turn of the century so that even if financial firms mixing commercial and investment banking were formed following deregulation the practice of securitization did not originate with that formation.

Further, rather than cause the crisis, the GLB has more recently been credited with stabilizing the financial sector during the crisis by providing regulators a resolution to the large investment bank troubles. Without GLB, J.P. Morgan Chase could not have purchased Bear Stearns and Bank of America could not have purchased Goldman Sachs. Both of these acquisitions added a stabilizing element to banking at the peak of the crisis.

E. Deposit insurance

As has been well established throughout this book, deposit insurance can be at times stabilizing and, at other times, destabilizing. The moral hazard of deposit insurance is that banks willingly take greater risks because of the safety net provided by the insurance. During the height of this crisis, one response was to increase deposit insurance from $100,000 per depositor to $250,000. Shortly thereafter, the Treasury Secretary admitted that this only encouraged banks to take on more risk.[54] The heightened risk taking also preceded the increase in deposit insurance because of the moral hazard inherent in the deposit insurance system.[55] Despite the propensity to increase risk at the bank, the deposit insurance certainly went a long way toward keeping bank runs at bay during this, and previous, bank crisis. Consequently, like all of commercial banking history, deposit insurance is both stabilizing and destabilizing.

Concluding remarks

At the heart of this crisis is the affordable housing directive of the federal government. This directive set in motion the foundation for the housing bubble and the instability in banking that followed. HUD created the policies at the GSEs which spread to the commercial banking sector and created the necessary conditions for an expansion of mortgage credit to both prime and subprime borrowers. Nonbank policy, e.g. the SECs policy with credit rating agencies, along with bank regulation, e.g. the CRA and capital requirements, fueled the expansion of credit. As is clearly illustrated in Table 7.4, regulation promoted risk taking through several channels. Indeed, this crisis is clear evidence that attempts to use regulation to limit risk taking (e.g. risk-based capital requirements and risk-based deposit insurance) have failed; risk taking increased as banks responded to the static regulation of the postwar period. Further, the risk assigned by the regulation did not accurately reflect the risk in the market. Regulators have incomplete information and so cannot create static regulation to capture behavior in the dynamic market.

At the same time, the resolution of the crisis marks a clear extension of the federal safety net, just as crises resolutions in the past have done. Two elements, in particular, stand out: the extension of lender of last resort at the Federal Reserve and the too-big-to-fail resolution of commercial banks and nonbanks. As clearly illustrated in this chapter, the Federal Reserve extended their safety net during this bank crisis. For example, it supported J. P. Morgan Chase's purchase of Bear Stearns and also opened the discount window to selected investment banks.[56] As in the 1980s, this was an extension of the lender of last resort functions of the Federal Reserve. Many scholars contend that the bigger the safety net, the more risk is shifted from the financial firms to taxpayers. This creates the moral hazard of increased risk taking and limits the incentives for monitoring.[57] This is the same moral hazard that scholars feared in the earliest history of U.S. commercial banking.

The federal safety net also expands when banks are not allowed to fail. During this crisis, the expansion of too-big-to-fail was extended to large nonbanks as well, including Fannie Mae and Freddie Mac, large insurance firms such as AIG, and investment banks such as Morgan Stanley and Goldman Sachs. All of these firms were rescued in one form or another. In commercial banking, there were 235 bank failures between 2008 and June 1, 2010 and 223 (94.8 percent) of these were resolved using the purchase and assumption method. Just as in the postwar era, this resolution policy creates significant moral hazard problems; bankers take on greater risk knowing that they will not fail and depositors no longer have an incentive to monitor or even carefully chose their bank. Indeed, the Chair of the Federal Reserve, Ben Bernanke, admitted in the aftermath of this crisis that the too-big-to-fail policy is one of the largest problems facing the entire country.[58]

8
Lessons from the History of U.S. Banking and Regulation

Since inception, commercial banking in the United States has been regulated. It began at the state level, progressively moved to the national level and then to increasing amounts of regulation at both the state and national level. Along with a steady growth in regulation has been the steady growth in the federal safety net. Yet, as this book clearly illustrates, banking has also become increasingly unstable over time. Indeed, perhaps the most stable time in banking history was the minimally regulated antebellum era; there were far fewer failures and crises were not systemic but, rather, largely isolated. Certainly, the world we live in today is much different from the antebellum era but we still must reconcile how banking has become both more regulated and more unstable. This chapter attempts to offer an explanation through the lens of history.

More specifically, this chapter first considers the evolution of increasing regulation and the tendency to increasingly rely on regulation as the response to each crisis. This is accomplished by comparing the nature of regulation from the antebellum era to the present. Second, a similar consideration is given to the increasing federal safety net in commercial banking. Third, this chapter attempts to shed some light on why, over time, there has been an increased appetite for regulatory responses to crises. Fourth, using the historical evidence from earlier chapters, this chapter illustrates the trend of increasing fragility in commercial banking and also offers a way to understand why the instability is increasing. Finally, this chapter offers a few closing thoughts on the implications for the future of commercial banking, given the tendency towards regulation induced instability in banking markets.

Increasing regulation throughout history

Since the antebellum era, there has been a significant growth in the scope of banking regulation. What began as state regulated enterprises are now regulated by multiple agencies that are at the state and/or federal level depending on the nature of the bank charter. Figure 8.1 illustrates the real expenditures federal regulators devoted to finance and banking regulation over the past 50 years. While expenditures do not always correlate with influence, it is interesting to note that since 1990, expenditures increased 45.5 percent and since 2000 they have risen over 18 percent.[1] Though there is not similar data for earlier periods, it is obvious that bank regulation has been expanding since the origin of U.S. banking almost 230 years ago.

Analysis across all periods

A more precise picture of the expansion of bank regulation is captured by comparing the summary regulation tables from Chapters 3 through 7 (Tables 3.3, 4.12, 5.13, 6.4, and 7.4). These tables provide a brief summary of the significant regulation for each banking era. As it was rare for deregulation to take place, one may largely think of these tables

Figure 8.1 Real Spending on Federal Finance and Banking Regulation: 1960–2010

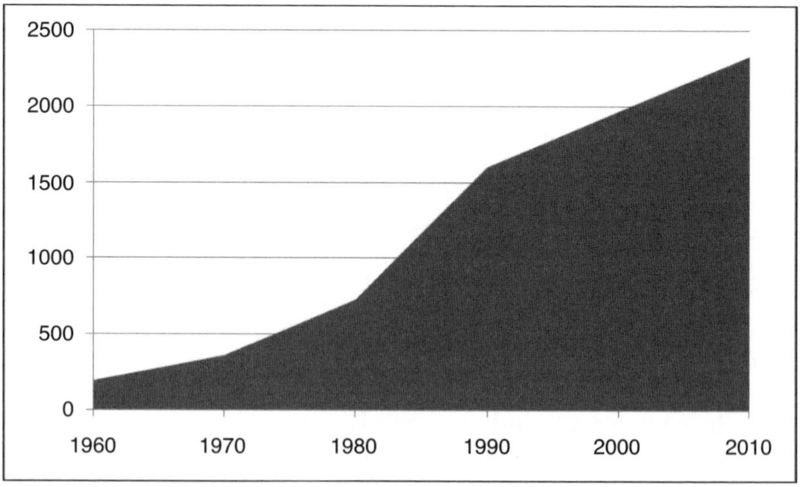

Source: Warren and de Rugy (2010).

Note: In millions of 2000 dollars. 2010 value estimated.

as the accumulation of regulation. It is interesting to note that two regulatory provisions are on all five tables; branching limits and deposit insurance. It is equally interesting to note that almost all banking regulation throughout U.S. history has influenced stability either by changing the risk taking at banks or by altering the competitive environment of banking. Both of these observations are discussed separately.

Until 1994, significant bank regulation throughout history sought to limit a banker's ability to branch. This despite the fact that scholars and regulators have known since the antebellum era that branching would stabilize banking. Recall from Chapter 2 that theories of regulation may help understand why regulation is established despite evidence that it will contribute to instability. Both the self-interest approach and the psychological attraction theory of financial regulation explain the history of the ban on branching in the U.S. Small, unit banks saw branching as a competitive threat so they worked hard and used their political clout to keep the ban on branching and interstate banking in place. They were self-interested. The psychological attraction theory holds that scapegoating is often used to justify additional regulation. In this case, the state banker argued that the national banker would limit credit to small borrowers; the national banker was the source of the problem so they must be kept from the market. Despite the fact that there was no evidence of such behavior, it depicted the national banker as a villain resulting in the preservation of the regulatory ban on branching. Even today interstate branching is not free as states have the ability to impose barriers to such branching and all have done so. As was shown throughout this book, the costs of this regulation have been extremely high. The limits on branching and interstate banking have contributed enormously to the instability in banking.

The other provision that spans all eras in banking is deposit insurance. State deposit insurance in the first two eras gave way to federal deposit insurance since 1933. Deposit insurance, as has been shown repeatedly in this book, can be at times stabilizing and at other times both stabilizing and destabilizing. All of the state deposit insurance schemes ultimately failed and there is little evidence to suggest that they were stabilizing while in operation. The federal deposit insurance program was perhaps most stabilizing at the point of its creation. More specifically, it is clear that consumer confidence increased and the number of bank failures decreased significantly following the passage of the Banking Act of 1933. While not the only factor, deposit insurance was surely instrumental in stopping bank runs and providing the incentive to get depositors to bank again. Since then, however, deposit insurance has also injected a destabilizing element to banking by changing the incentives for bank risk taking and the incentives for depositor monitoring. Bank runs are a thing of the past because of deposit insurance; is this necessarily stabilizing? There are no bank runs because depositors no longer care if their bank can repay the deposit since there is always the insurance to fall back on. Similarly, it matters less to the banker if they take greater risks as depositors will always be covered. In this way, deposit insurance removes an important element of market discipline from the intermediation process. Without the discipline, deposit insurance contributes to instability.

Further reflection on the summary regulation tables indicate that often the regulation discussed in this book impacted bank stability through two channels: 1) changes in risk taking; and 2) changes in the nature of competition. Commercial banking is risky business. The banker makes loans or investments based on the best available information and, in the end, assumes the risk that the loan or investment may or may not generate revenue. Attempts to regulate risk taking are, as history has shown, generally unsuccessful. At the same time however, bank regulation is frequently aimed at reducing risk (see, for example, Tables 3.3, 4.12, 5.13, 6.4, and 7.4). Such regulation generally fails because regulation changes the incentives for bank behavior in a way that leads to *more* risk taking. Capital holdings at commercial banks were higher before capital requirements were in place. For example, in the late nineteenth century, capital as a percent of total assets was 25 percent. This is considerably higher than has been held in the last one hundred years.[2] In contrast, consider the Basel capital requirements that have been in place since the late 1980s. As is shown in Chapters 6 and 7, this only served to encourage banks to keep more high risk assets on their books and to sell lower risk loans. Further, the lower risk weights placed on mortgage loans certainly contributed to the increased willingness of banks to extend mortgage credit over commercial credit. Attempts to control risk taking fail because banks are inherently risk-taking institutions and because attempts to identify risk only changes the behavior of the firm in ways that are unknowable to the regulators. Markets are a dynamic process and market participants continuously act upon new information that is generated by the process. This is information that cannot be known in advance, not by participants and certainly not by policymakers outside of the process. Attempts to control risk simply create new opportunities for future risk taking.

Historically, bank regulation has also attempted to alter bank stability by reducing competition. Perhaps this originates from the chartering process and the relationship formed between the state legislators and incumbent banks. Recall that the earliest banking in the U.S. required state charters from the legislator and that this resulted in rent seeking by regulators and provided a significant motivation for existing bankers to prevent further entrants in their market. It worked well for both groups to limit competition. Since then, much of bank regulation has been aimed at minimizing competition between banks as well as nonbanks. Indeed, the cornerstone of the Banking Act of 1933 was to limit competition because the belief was that competition for deposits was driving up interest rates (hence regulation Q), that there were too many banks (hence prohibition on branching), and that bankers should not be competing with securities firms (hence Glass–Steagall). The consequence of all of these attempts to limit competition has been to increase instability in banking. As has been shown throughout this book, the statistical and theoretical evidence overwhelmingly indicates that competition enhances *stability* not instability. Competition forces banks to reduce costs, improve efficiency, hold adequate capital, diversify their portfolios, take prudent risks, and perform profitably.

Like attempts to limit risk taking, attempts to limit competition are not successful. Market participants continue to seek out profitable opportunities and will, given enough time, work around the limits of regulation. The postwar era provides important evidence of the costs of being constrained by regulation and not being allowed to compete. It took some time and some hard lessons (e.g. bank failures) but bankers ultimately found ways around the regulation (see Chapter 6). In the end, numerous scholars provide evidence that the limits on competition throughout the years are the single most important reason that banking has been so unstable and vulnerable to crises and failure. The historical evolution of bank regulation in this book corroborates existing evidence.

Why does significant regulation follow significant crisis?

There can be no doubt: bank regulation in the U.S. continues to grow and, in the process, to cast a wider net. At the same time, significant regulation follows all significant bank crises. How can we reconcile this? Why, when regulation has shown to be destabilizing, is the response to a crisis always more regulation? Perhaps much of this may be explained in terms of the psychological attraction theory of financial regulation outlined in Chapter 2. This perspective argues that social and psychological processes underlie all financial regulation and so, to understand the regulation is to understand the processes.

Several social and psychological processes increase the demand for regulation and the willingness of regulators and legislators to offer regulation. All things equal, these tend to be heightened during periods of uncertainty or crisis. On the demand side, this theory argues that negative financial news that is attached to personal loss will provoke contempt for lenders, among others, and heighten the demand for regulation to punish those involved; bankers, securities traders, etc. As evidence, consider a May 1985 poll which found that 47 percent interviewed blamed the banker for the postwar bank failures while 14 percent blamed the federal government.[3]

On the supply side, overconfident regulators and legislators immediately seek to find blame in others. Indeed, scapegoating, as the finger pointing is called by psychologists, is predictably playing out in the aftermath of the most recent bank crisis. Regulators, particularly the Federal Reserve and the FDIC, are unwilling to shoulder any blame and the federal government is blaming greed on Wall Street. Indeed, just a week or so before the Senate passed a significant financial reform bill, Goldman Sachs was interrogated by Congress over their role in the crisis.[4] While no illegal activity was uncovered, it served the legislators well in two ways; first, it increases the demand for financial regulation and second, it provides a convenient scapegoat. As Chapter 7 indicates, the list of contributing factors in the most recent crisis is long and the role of public policy and regulation cannot be overstated. Yet, reform proposals do not address these contributing factors; to do so would be to forego scapegoating and would require a level of self-evaluation infrequently witnessed in U.S. regulatory and policymaking.

There is a historical precedent to investigating bankers in the wake of a crisis and then using the investigation to assign blame. After the crisis of 1907, the Comptroller of the Currency condemned bankers as lawbreakers and implied fraudulent banker behavior as banks attempted, during the latter crises in the national bank era, to deal with liquidity problems. As was demonstrated in Chapter 4, the primary source of bank problems was illiquidity caused by reserve pyramiding and the bond collateral requirements to banknotes. During crises, bankers would let their reserve requirements run low to meet the demand for specie. Further, they often used the Clearinghouse certificates and, in rare cases actually printed their own notes, in order to meet depositor withdrawals.[5] Regulation caused the problems but, in the face of crises, regulators blamed bankers. In 1908, after blaming bankers, the Comptroller called for increased regulation to solve the crises problem. A few years later, in 1912, a subcommittee to the House Committee on Banking and Currency investigated bankers for wrong doing and fraud as it related to the 1907 crisis. Just as in 2010, the bankers were not found to have done anything to cause the crisis, but the investigation sparked intense animosity towards bankers and created a scapegoat for regulators and policymakers.

In the wake of the 1933 crisis, once again, regulators blamed bankers for the crisis. A congressional committee alleged that bankers were speculating in the stock market, were engaged in fraudulent behavior and generally caused the crisis. These charges were never substantiated and, as was shown in Chapter 5, many financial historians agree that the role of the Federal Reserve in the crisis cannot be overlooked. Nonetheless, the committee hearings profoundly changed the public's perception of bankers; they were viewed as the cause of the deepest crisis in American history. This scapegoating paved the way for significant regulatory reform in the Banking Acts of 1933 and 1935.

The psychological attraction theory of financial regulation is a helpful framework for understanding why bank regulation is the predictable response to bank crisis. It may also explain the speed with which regulatory policy comes about. The two largest bank crises in this country were perhaps that in 1933 and the most recent. In both cases, a regulatory response was virtually immediate. President Roosevelt took office on March 4, 1933, he declared the national banking holiday on March 7, and the Banking Act of 1933 passed into law in June. There was little time for analysis or discussion regarding a landmark piece of banking legislation. Similarly, in September of 2008 most Americans learned of the fragility in the financial sector. That same month, three programs were established to inject liquidity into specific firms or the banking sector totaling up to over $846 billion and the GSEs were nationalized; two more programs were established in October to provide more than $2 trillion and the Emergency Economic Stabilization Act of 2008 was passed to allow the Treasury to purchase up to $700 billion in nonperforming assets at banks and other financial institutions.[6] As predicted by the psychological attraction theory of financial regulation, demand for government regulation is particularly strong during crisis which explains the timing of regulatory developments.

Increasing federal safety net throughout history

A second observation from the history of commercial banking is the trend of an increasing federal safety net. The lender of last resort function at the Federal Reserve and the FDIC failure resolution policy combine to create the safety net in commercial banking. Each is discussed.

Lender of last resort

In the classic definition, lender of last resort (LOLR) refers to the central bank's mission to keep the money supply from contracting during runs and crises.[7] Maintaining the money supply allows banks to satisfy liquidity demands during fragile periods. Scholars, including Humphrey (2010), contend that the Federal Reserve's LOLR has so deviated from the classical definition that it is almost inappropriate to continue to call the central bank action LOLR. Despite Humphrey's critique, this analysis continues to refer to the Federal Reserve action as LOLR.

An early example of the Federal Reserve extending its LOLR function was in 1974 when it purchased foreign-exchange liabilities at Franklin National. The most recent bank crisis is replete with examples of the extension of classic LOLR functions. The classic doctrine requires that central banks make loans to banks on good collateral. However, in 2008, the Federal Reserve purchased nonperforming MBSs from Bear Stearns, purchased debt from the GSEs and lent to American International Group absent quality collateral. Classic LOLR doctrine also is strictly a monetary function with commercial banks and not nonbanks. In the wake of the most recent crisis the Federal Reserve established many new lending facilities to extend credit to investment banks, insurance companies, and securities dealers.[8] This is a clear departure from traditional LOLR that focuses on the money supply and towards the extension of credit and unfreezing credit markets.

This extension of LOLR has important implications for the stability of banking because of the systemic moral hazard created by LOLR policy.[9] LOLR application, particularly in its expanded form, creates expectations for bankers and other financial market participants that they too will be rescued. This is clearly illustrated in the most recent crisis. Bear Stearns was rescued in March of 2008 through a combination of LOLR and Treasury action. As a result, other troubled financial firms (Lehman Brothers, Merrill Lynch, Morgan-Stanley and Goldman Sachs) did little to raise capital or to make themselves more stable. It was only after Lehman Brothers was *not* rescued in September of 2008 that these investment banks either converted to BHCs so that they would enjoy LOLR benefits or were acquired.[10] One account of Lehman's attempt to find a buyer for itself suggests that potential buyers were waiting for government to bailout Lehman, the "Bear Stearns precedent", before making an offer to purchase.[11]

FDIC resolution policy

The policy at the FDIC for resolving failing banks is the second element of the increasing federal safety net. The FDIC, when handling a troubled bank, can provide assistance to the bank or allow the bank to fail and then resolve the failure. As defined in this book, the too-big-to-fail (TBTF) policy is when the FDIC resolves the failure using the purchase and assumption method or when it assists a large bank simply because it is large. As explained in Chapters 6 and 7, the FDIC increasingly uses the purchase and assumption method for resolving bank failures. In doing so, the FDIC does not really let these banks fail; the failing bank is purchased by a healthy bank after the FDIC purchases the bad assets. All deposits, insured and uninsured, are covered. Between the beginning of 2008 through June 1, 2010, 94.8 percent of all failures were resolved using the purchase and assumption method.[12]

Another aspect of TBTF is when the FDIC steps in and assists banks that are considered too big. The TBTF application has always been motivated by the belief that the failure of a large bank will be contagious; other banks and the financial system will suffer as a result.[13] Of all the bank failures and assistances during the past few years, the two largest by a significant margin were both treated as TBTF because of their size. At the same time, because most banks are getting larger, every year more banks become eligible for TBTF. Scholars have investigated whether there is value to large banks of reaching some threshold size so that they could receive the regulatory subsidy of the TBTF treatment. If so, large banks should be willing to pay a premium to achieve that threshold size. Recent scholarship that empirically investigates this issue during the 1990s finds that there is evidence that banks will pay more during mergers and acquisitions to achieve TBTF status.[14]

Between 1984 and 2008, the average size of a commercial bank in the U.S. has increased five-fold in real terms.[15] This is a concern for the application of TBTF. Changing regulation such as the 1994 IBBEA and the 1999 GLBA, among others, coupled with technological advances have changed the optimal bank size. More specifically, earlier work on scale economies in banking found that scale economies were exhausted at $100 to $200 million in total assets. However, more contemporary scholarship finds that most U.S. banks experience increasing returns to scale.[16] The implication is that, increasingly, more banks will qualify for the TBTF rescue of the FDIC, particularly in, but not limited to, times of crisis. The moral hazard of TBTF is much more acute during crisis. Scholars have found empirical evidence of this during the 1980s.[17] Further, the aggressive application of TBTF has again been applied during the most recent crisis demonstrating that it has not been contained by postwar regulation.[18] Of course, this simply exacerbates the moral hazard problems of risk taking and monitoring. Scholars almost universally recognize the moral hazard of TBTF as one of the most destabilizing element in banking today.

Together, the LOLR at the Federal Reserve and the TBTF at the FDIC create the federal safety net in U.S. commercial banking. Rather than stabilize banking, the safety net has been destabilizing. As evidence, consider that the severity of bank crises has been magnified as the safety net has widened.

Increasing appetite for regulation

Bank regulation and the federal safety net have expanded historically, in part, because America has gradually shifted away from a system of limited government. Government played a relatively minor role in the U.S. economy in eighteenth and nineteenth centuries.[19] However, that changed at the end of the 1800s. During the early years of the United States, the prevailing view was that limited government, as established in the Constitution, best served the nation. However, a complex set of developments in the late nineteenth century created a shift away from limited government. It began in 1887 with the federal regulation of railroads and was compounded by two additional developments. First, following the passage of the Sixteenth Amendment to the Constitution, the federal government successfully implemented a national income tax. Scholars contend that the primary reason for bigger government (in terms of spending, regulation, and intervention in the market) may be traced back to the Sixteenth Amendment because it provided the federal government with a revenue source unlike any they had known previously.[20] Second, a shift in political ideology towards greater government stemmed from a changing set of voter preferences. Part of the philosophical shift followed from the work of social commentators who stressed the important role of government in eliminating repression of the working class inherent, in their view, in capitalism. Political groups developed, such as the Progressive Movement, and called for an increased role for government. Further, at the turn of the century, the economy was developing such that some firms were able to capture an increasing market share. Progressives, and others, called for government to put an end to so-called monopolies and voters were increasingly sympathetic to the ideology of government intervention and control in the economy. In the end, the revenue from the national income tax, coupled with a voter preference for bigger government manifested itself in the form of more regulation, government spending, and intervention in the private market.

Polling data is often a useful way to gage voter preferences. Unfortunately, reliable polling data in the U.S. is not available until after the Great Depression. For earlier eras, it is sometimes useful to consider voting data or sources of the day such as major newspapers or trade journals. During the antebellum era, much of the news on the bank crises was focused on alerting the public about the condition of banks. There was little demand for government to take control of the problem. Rather, many of the articles provided detailed information on the banks that were in trouble and those that were healthy and offered suggestions for banking during the crisis. For example, a September 19, 1857 article in the *Saturday Evening Post* reminded readers of the 1837 crisis and drew parallels with the crisis 20 years later.[21] Further, like many articles during this time frame, it encouraged the public to hoard specie in their homes until the banks were stronger. During the national bank era, articles in primary papers offered similar analysis and advice. For example, during the 1907 crisis, there were many articles that drew parallels to the 1884 crisis. The theme seems to be one of admiration and hope; in 1907 the writers were impressed with the composure in which the 1884 crisis was handled and resolved privately and felt confident that the same recovery would be forthcoming.[22] Solutions were sought from within banking during these earliest eras and not by outside policymakers.

Polling data since the late 1930s certainly provides evidence to suggest a preference towards government regulation in banking. For example, 64 percent of those polled in 1938 thought banks were safe because government made them safe; 23 percent saw bank safety as a reflection of bank management. During the height of postwar bank failures another poll, in 1985, asked if subjecting banks to fewer government controls was good or bad for consumers; 42 percent replied that it would hurt consumers while 41 percent thought it was beneficial to consumers. Toward the end of the postwar period, in 1990, 80 percent of poll respondents wanted more regulation on thrifts and commercial banks. The pattern continues during the most recent crisis: a May 2010 poll asked if government should implement more or less regulation in response to financial crisis and 53 percent replied that government should regulate more while only 37 percent replied to regulate less.

It is clear from the evidence that most Americans do want regulation and government intervention in response to bank crises. This confirms the perspective put forth in the psychological attraction theory of financial regulation that both the demand for and supply of regulation is particularly acute near crises.

Increasing instability throughout history

The increasing scale and scope of banking regulation along with the increasing federal safety net have produced a crisis prone banking system. The four crises in the antebellum era were relatively small and the limited failure data indicates that bank failures were few. Of the five crises from the national bank era, the final two were the most systemic and serious. Indeed, Table 4.7 contains the failure data for the national bank era and it indicates that the 1893 crisis was most severe with 326 failures or approximately five percent of all banks failing. By 1907, there were significantly more banks in the country (see Tables 4.2 and 4.4) so that the 156 failures were less than one percent of all banks. Nonetheless, the national bank era, when measured in crises and failures, was more unstable than the antebellum era.

Certainly, the 1933 crisis was more severe with thousands of bank runs and failures and the temporary closing of all commercial banks in the country. Tables 5.5 through 5.7 illustrate the significant number of bank failures during the Great Depression. In 1933 alone, 3887 banks failed which represented over 17 percent of all banks. When compared to the national bank era, the 1930s were a much more unstable time in commercial banking history.

The postwar era exposed the destabilizing elements of the 1933 regulation as hundreds of banks, a few of them very large, failed. Between 1983 and 1993, 2292 banks and thrifts failed and another 532 required FDIC assistance. While the postwar era was not as significant as the Great Depression bank crises, it was more significant than the initial two banking eras.

The first crisis of the twenty-first century, when compared to historical crises, is certainly considerable. Two hundred and thirty-five commercial banks have failed between 2008 and June 1, 2010 and trillions of dollars have been spent attempting to contain the crisis. Further, as explained in Chapter 7, the expectations are for many more failures as the amount of nonperforming commercial and other loans continue to grow. Indeed, as of the first of June, 2010 is on pace to outnumber 2009 in terms of the total number of failures (see Figure 7.2). By most accounts, the first crisis of the twenty-first century rivals that of the Great Depression. Collectively, the bank crises in the United States form a historic pattern of deeper and more systemic crises.

Historically, the problem was too many small undiversified banks were failing. Indeed, throughout history, the propensity is for smaller banks to fail more often than larger banks and that remains true today.

This reflects, in part, the fact that there have always been more small banks in the U.S. than large banks and part of this structural reality reflect the many regulations discussed in this book. Nonetheless, in the 2000s, the failures have spanned the range of bank size, with greater emphasis placed on the larger banks because of their too-big-to-fail costs. As mentioned earlier, this may reflect the increasing returns to scale in banking so that, as a general rule, banks are getting larger. Given the instability caused by regulation and the propensity to use the federal safety net, particularly in crisis, larger banks may face even more instability moving forward.

Role of knowledge and markets

How can more regulation leading to more instability be reconciled? Why is banking subject to more severe crises now than in the past? These are the very questions laid out on page one of Chapter 1. The answer lies in the knowledge discrepancy between those actually in the market and those making regulatory and legislative decisions. As introduced in Chapter 2, knowledge is highly dispersed and specialized. Each individual has a specialized knowledge set that is both limited and changing. Economic knowledge comes from the dynamic market process. Engaging in the market process reveals new information to the participants. Those outside of the process do not and cannot know that information. On July 10, 2008, the Treasury Secretary indicated that the GSEs regulator made clear that Fannie and Freddie were adequately capitalized.[23] Three days later, the Treasury Secretary announced that the GSEs would require a massive bailout. The Treasury Secretary did not know on the tenth about the state of capital adequacy at the GSEs. He did learn a few days later when market conditions exposed this information to him. This is true of all market participants, not just regulators and policymakers. Information is generated by the interaction of market participants and the information to be revealed tomorrow, or next month, or next year, is not known today.

Because the future information (or knowledge) from the market process is not known, to think that the future can be improved upon through regulation requires the belief that the future *is* knowable today. This is why attempts to regulate banking fail. Regulators and policymakers have less information than those in the financial markets to begin with. For example, during the national bank era, legislators taxed all state banknotes in an attempt to make state banking unprofitable. Legislators and regulators underestimated the degree to which banks were accepting deposits so the tax was easily avoided. Further, all participants and regulators lack the information that will develop from the markets in the future.

Regulation interrupts the market process and changes the opportunities that are available to market participants and entrepreneurs. However, the market is dynamic; it takes the regulation into account as it moves forward. The history of commercial banking is full of examples. During the national bank era, in response to the ten percent tax on banknotes, banks increasingly relied on deposits. Banks also used security affiliates to avoid the ban on branching and higher capital requirements at national banks provided incentive for national bankers to convert to state charters. Another example is found in the years prior to the Great Depression when national banks used the merging process established in 1918 to create branch units. The postwar period is replete with examples as banks responded to rapidly changing market conditions that made the 1933 regulation more onerous. In response to a binding regulation Q, banks created negotiable orders of withdraw accounts and automatic transfer system accounts, and began aggressively using brokered deposits to fight disintermediation. Banks responded to the Basel capital requirements by extending more mortgages and fewer commercial loans because mortgages were given a lower risk weight. Finally, bankers increasingly developed off-balance sheet activities in an effort to remain profitable in light of the regulatory constraints that kept them from competing in the new environment of the postwar period.

Austrian scholars such as Hayek (1937), Mises (1949), and Kirzner (1984, 1992) have long recognized the market process and the asymmetry of knowledge. More recently, scholars argue that knowledge is becoming increasingly more specialized and asymmetric.[24] As the world becomes more complex and integrated, knowledge is increasingly specialized. Kling (2010) offers an array of examples that illustrate different ways in which knowledge is becoming increasingly dispersed: the vast specialties in medicine, academia, the law, and job classifications represent a few. Indeed, it is exceptionally rare to know someone today with a broad skill set across several fields. In the aftermath of the most recent crisis, email and other documents have surfaced which illustrate the dispersed nature of knowledge. For example, an employee at Standard & Poor's credit rating agency wrote "Let's hope we are all wealthy and retired by the time this house of cards falters."[25] Knowledge is specialized; a small set of individuals knew the true risk of the securitized mortgages but most did not. Defending their role in the crisis, the manager in the MBSs division at Moody's indicated "We aren't loan officers. Our expertise is as statisticians on an aggregate basis."[26]

While it may be argued that the pace at which specialized knowledge is narrowing has hastened through technology, it is equally true that knowledge has progressively become more specialized really since the founding of the nation. For example, consider the incredible transformation in skill sets during the antebellum era when life moved, for many, from the farm to the factory. Machines created significant divisions of labor and knowledge became more specialized. The same can be written about the national bank era; entrepreneurial ingenuity changed the production process and final goods and services at an amazing pace. During the postwar era Read (1958) wrote an essay entitled "I, Pencil". This classic essay describes the life of a simple, wooden pencil and the many people, machines, and materials from across the globe used in its production. The point of the essay is to let the reader know that not a single person on earth knows how to make the pencil; there are too many hands, too many machines, too many trucks, and too many resources involved for one person to have all of the knowledge. As the nation has advanced economically, each individual has been required to know more specific details and tasks and so knowledge has been increasingly specialized over time. If we cannot know how to make a wooden pencil, how can we expect regulatory policymakers to know how banks are operating today and how they will operate tomorrow?

The point is that the gap between knowledge in the market and knowledge of policymakers is widening. Consider the most recent crisis. No one had all the information; if they did, perhaps we could have avoided the crisis. Certainly there were signs and experts who warned of pending problems, but no one saw all of the pieces put together. Indeed, it is impossible to have that knowledge since it is revealed on a daily basis through the interaction and exchange in the market. For this very reason, many believe that the seeds for the next financial crisis are planted in plans to further regulate the banking system in response to the most recent crisis.[27]

Future implications

Can you imagine what the U.S. commercial banking system would look like today had it not been so highly regulated? What would U.S. bank history look like? What if, at the beginning, banks were free to enter markets? What if banks had always been free to branch? Certainly, no industry evolving with the market process would have turned out as it did. Competition and the market process would have determined the historical path. As the history detailed in this book has shown, the intervention of government in financial markets makes them less stable and not more. Indeed, many believe that without government intervention, banks would hold more capital, and invest more in money markets where they can quickly turn their assets into liquidity.[28] Indeed, the historical evidence is that this is what banks did when less regulated.

In what may be described as an ironic development given what we know about U.S. commercial bank history, many countries, including the U.S., are considering policy changes to limit the size of commercial banks.[29] Limiting bank size, as the U.S. experience clearly illustrates, is destabilizing by limiting competition and reducing geographic diversification. The evolution of commercial banking is largely one of bankers attempting to circumvent regulation aimed at keeping them small. If policymakers have their way on this point, it is certain that history will repeat itself.

An economist observed: "If there is anything more tragic than our current banking crisis, it is that the crisis is being blamed on the wrong group, on the bankers, instead of the primary culprit, government intervention."[30] This was in reference to the postwar era bank failures and instability but could accurately describe many of the U.S. episodes of bank crisis. Unfortunately, the scapegoating has serious consequences as it results in policy responses that do not, and cannot, make banking more stable in the future. Congress is currently discussing bills to make significant regulatory change in banking and these reforms will create more instability moving forward for two reasons. First, all proposals fail to account for the role of public policy in the crisis. That is, neither the GSEs, the CRA, monetary policy, nor the federal affordable housing mandate, is addressed. Rather, all blame is placed on the greed on Wall Street. The second, and perhaps most important reason that regulatory reform will fail to stabilize banking is because regulation itself, as this history has shown, is destabilizing. Regulation is necessarily destabilizing because it interrupts the market process and because it assumes knowledge about the future that cannot be known. Scholars predict that legislative reform is likely to try and extend capital and other regulation to the shadow banking sector. History indicates this will not work because the market will respond by finding ways to avoid or minimize the new regulation. As one economist summarizes the problem of regulation: "(t)his regulatory arbitraging is why regulation can never be proactive – the rule maker will never get ahead of the rule evaders."[31] Of course, rule makers (regulators) are always behind the rule evaders (bankers, in this case) because they have less information.

In the end, this means that the regulatory response to the most recent banking crisis will create the conditions for the next bank crisis. This is true regardless of the specifics of the regulation. Indeed, the historic pattern of crisis followed by regulation, and increasing amounts of regulation at that, is a clear indication that regulation is not the answer. While it is beyond the scope of this book to offer options outside of regulation, it appears that market solutions may offer more relief from bank crises. This is simply because the market process generates the information and knowledge from the interaction of market participants to discipline and guide decisions. History offers an insightful perspective on bank regulation. Policymakers would be well served to learn from that history before formulating more regulation for the future.

Data Appendix

Figure A.1 Real Gross National Product During the Antebellum Era: 1834–1859

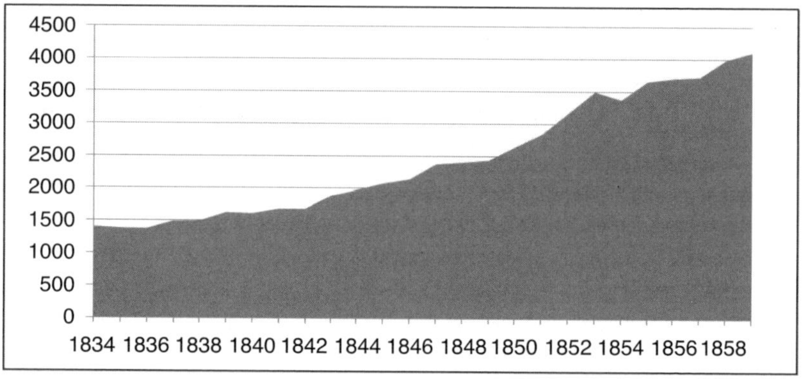

Source: Historical Statistics, Series Ca219.

Figure A.2 Selected U.S. Male Occupations: Selected Years, 1800–1960

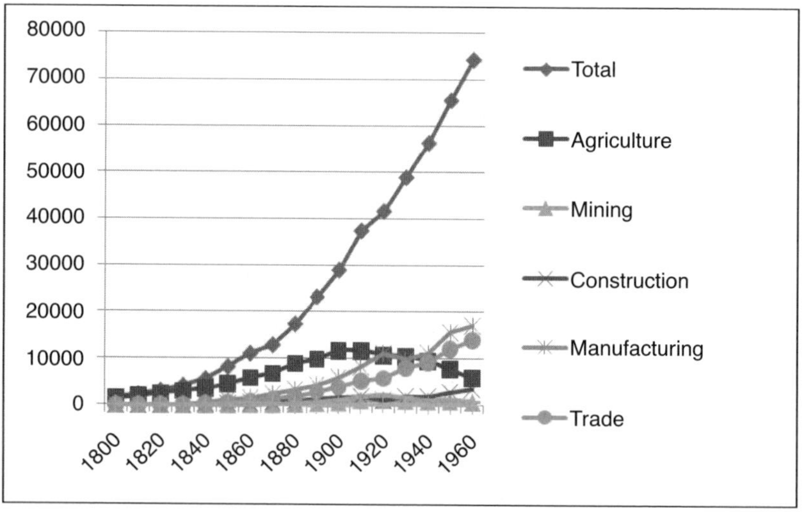

Source: Historical Statistics, Series Ba814, Ba817, Ba819, Ba820, BA821, Ba824, Ba825, Ba826.

Note: In thousands.

Figure A.3 Stock Index During the Antebellum Era: 1802–1870

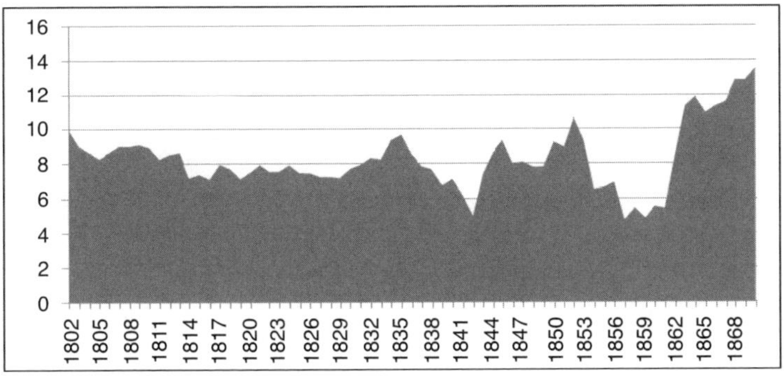

Source: Historical Statistics, Series Cj979.

Note: This is the Schwert's Index of Common Stock.

Figure A.4 Total Number of U.S. Business Failures: 1857–1997

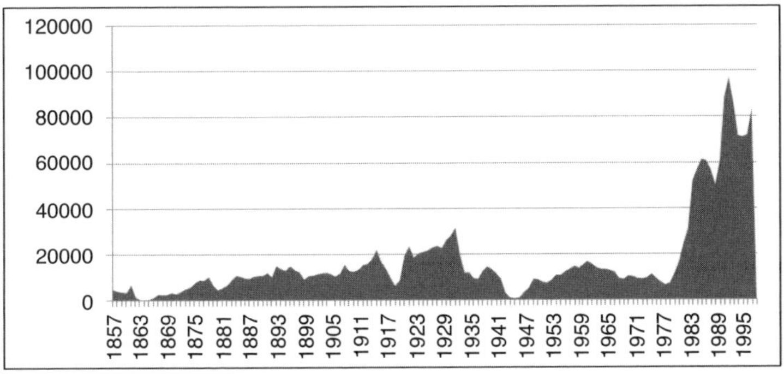

Source: Historical Statistics, Series Ch411.

Figure A.5 U.S. Population for Selected Years: 1790–1990

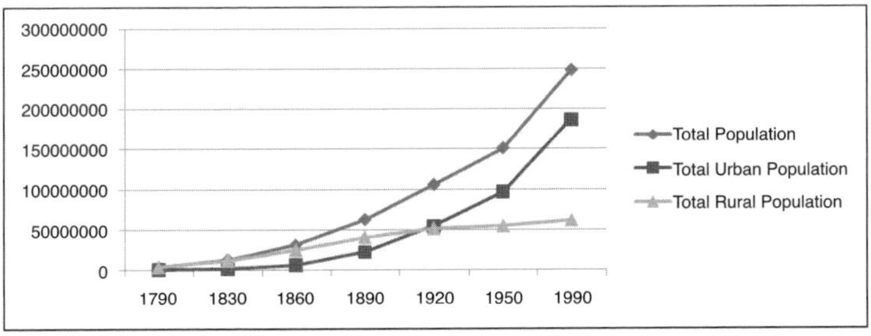

Source: Historical Statistics, Series Aa36, Aa46, Aa56.

Figure A.6 Number of Passenger Cars Sold: 1900–1996

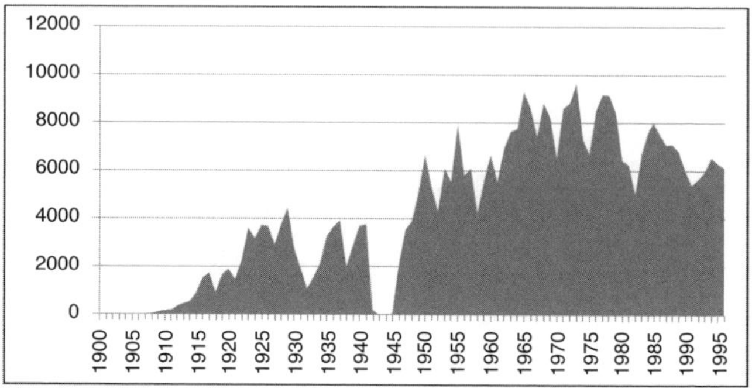

Source: Historical Statistics, Series Df343.

Figure A.7 Real Gross National Product During the National Banking Era and up to the Great Depression: 1869–1929

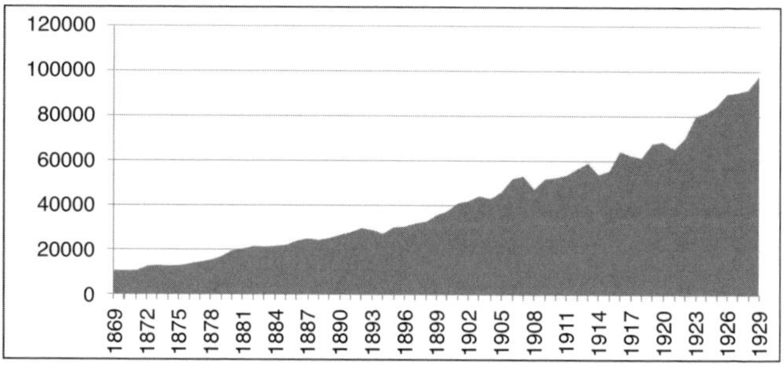

Source: Historical Statistics, Series Ca208.

Note: This data is from Gallman-Kuznets estimation and is in 1929 dollars.

Figure A.8 Stock Index During the National Banking Era: 1871–1914

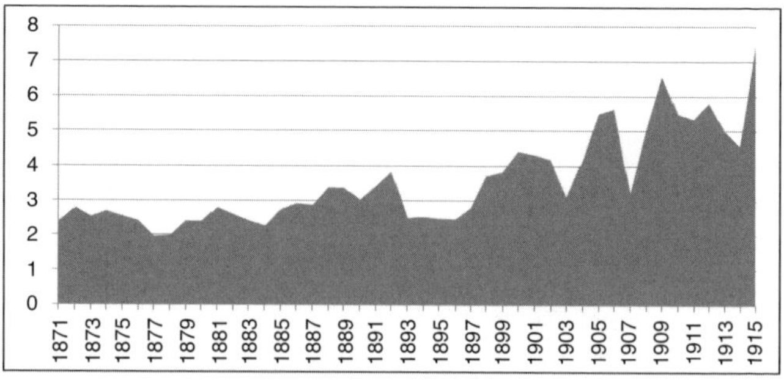

Source: Historical Statistics, Series Cj801.

Note: This is the Industrials Index.

Figure A.9 Total Number of Business Failures per 10,000 Businesses: 1870–1997

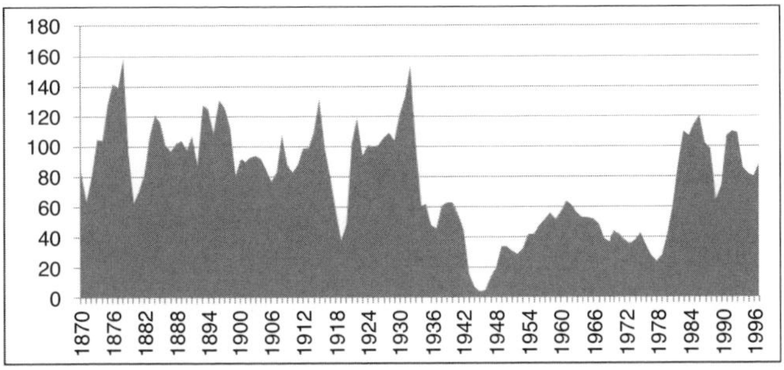

Source: Historical Statistics, Series Ch412.

Figure A.10 Average Annual Yield on U.S. Government Bonds: 1842–1899

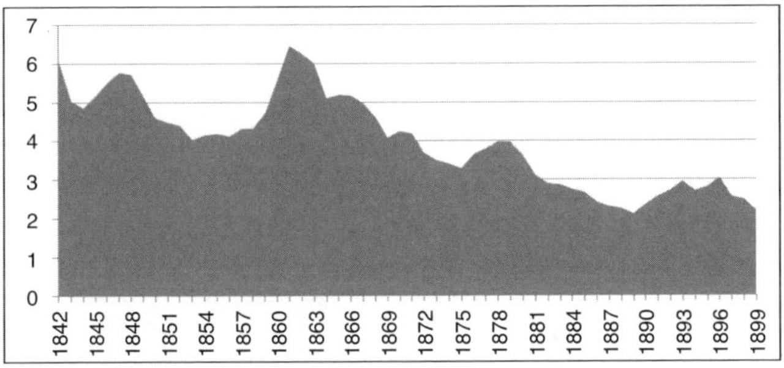

Source: Historical Statistics, Series Cj1192.

Figure A.11 Real Gross Domestic Product: 1929–1940

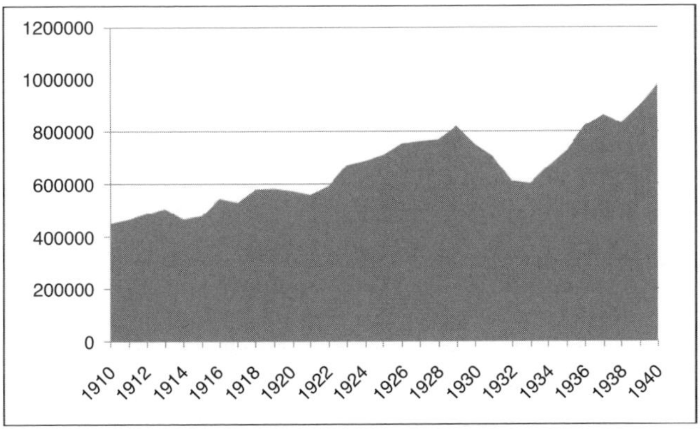

Source: Historical Statistics, Series Ca9.

Note: In millions of 1996 dollars.

Figure A.12 U.S. Unemployment Rate: 1890–2009

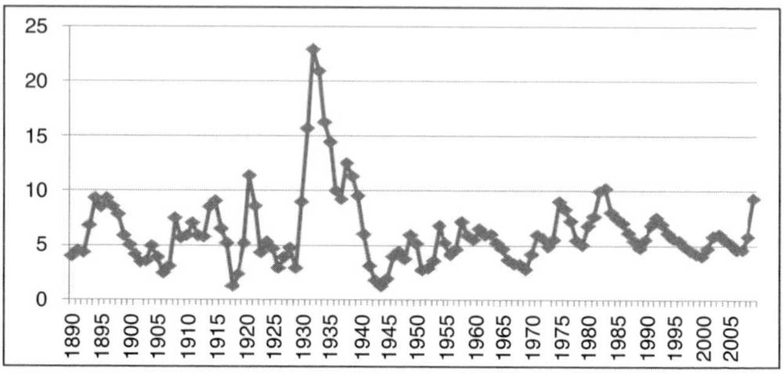

Source: Historical Statistics, Series Ba475.

Figure A.13 Private Sector Earnings: 1929–1940

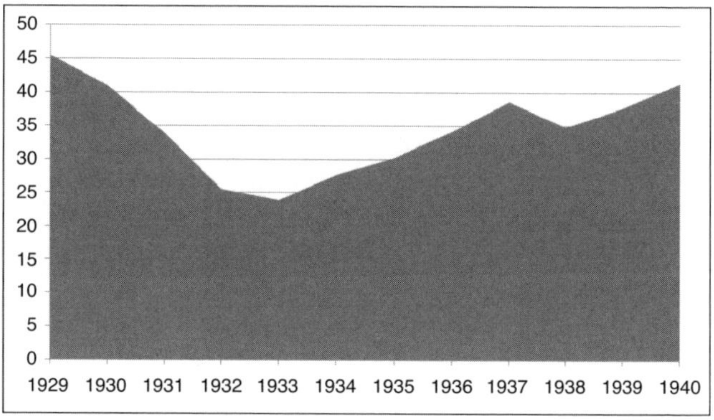

Source: Historical Statistics, Series Ca55.

Note: In billions of dollars.

Figure A.14 Dow Jones Industrial Average Index: 1910–1940

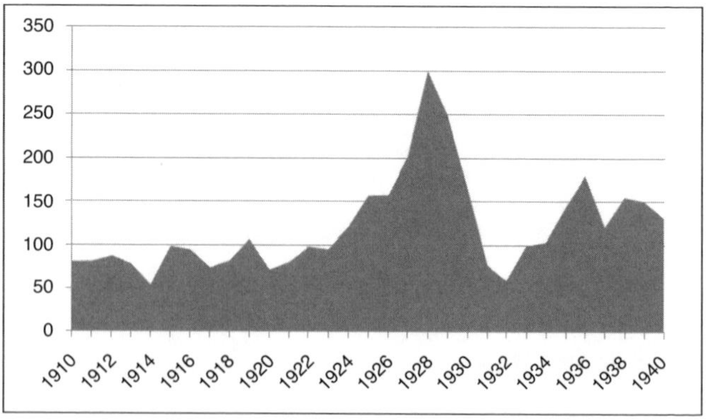

Source: Historical Statistics, Series Cj804.

Figure A.15 Farm Prices for Selected Commodities: 1900–1940

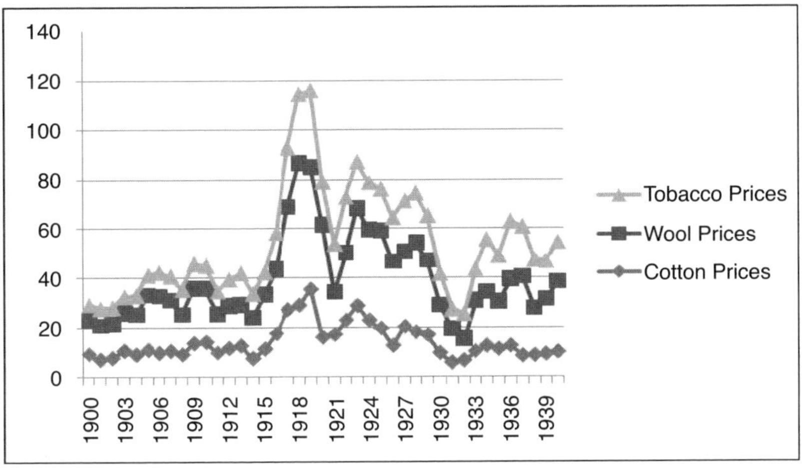

Source: Historical Statistics, Series Da757, Da762, Da765.

Figure A.16 Net Farm Income: 1910–1950

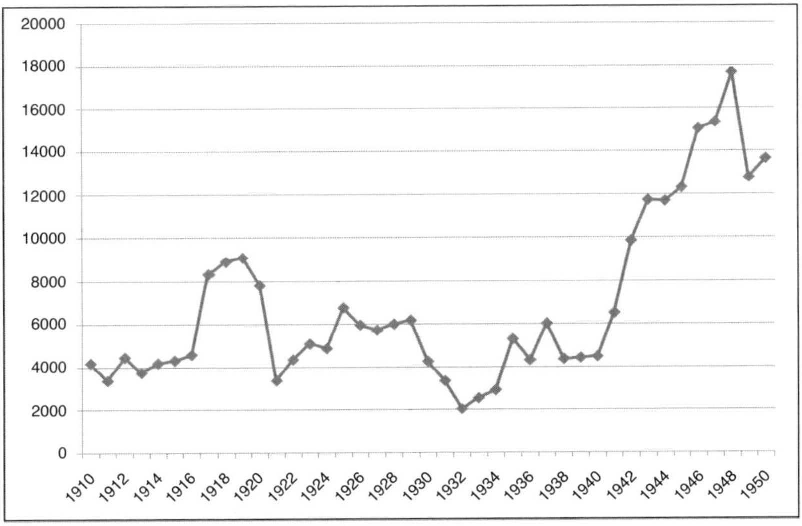

Source: Historical Statistics, Series Da1295.

Note: All prices are cents per pound in millions of dollars.

Figure A.17 Number of Individuals Employed in Farming: 1910–1950

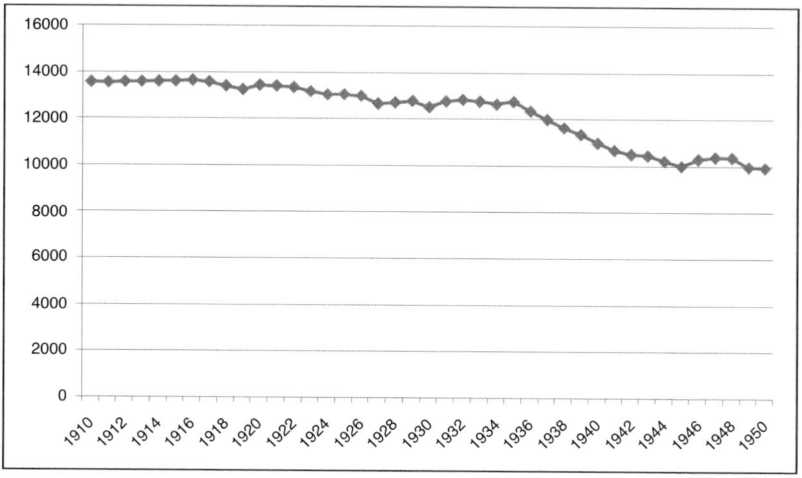

Source: Historical Statistics, Series Da612.

Note: In thousands.

Figure A.18 Annual Average Rate of Inflation: 1960–1999

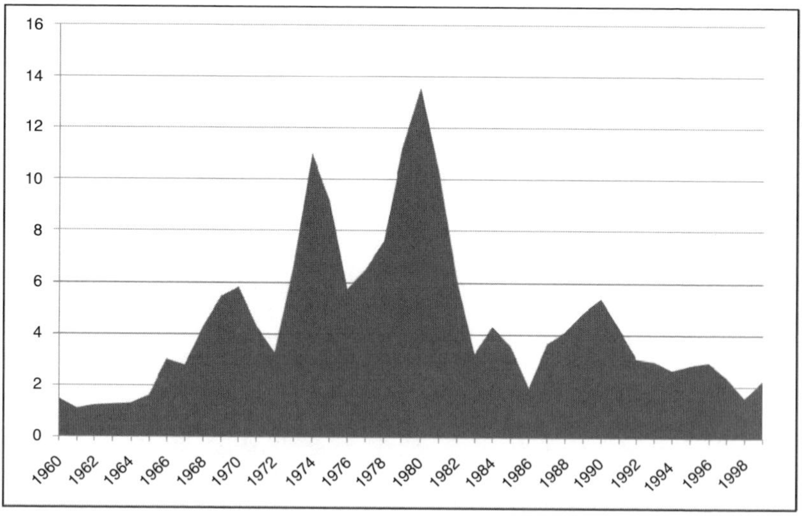

Source: Calculated from CPI(U) data at BLS.gov.

Figure A.19 Major Currencies Dollar Index: Monthly 1973–1981

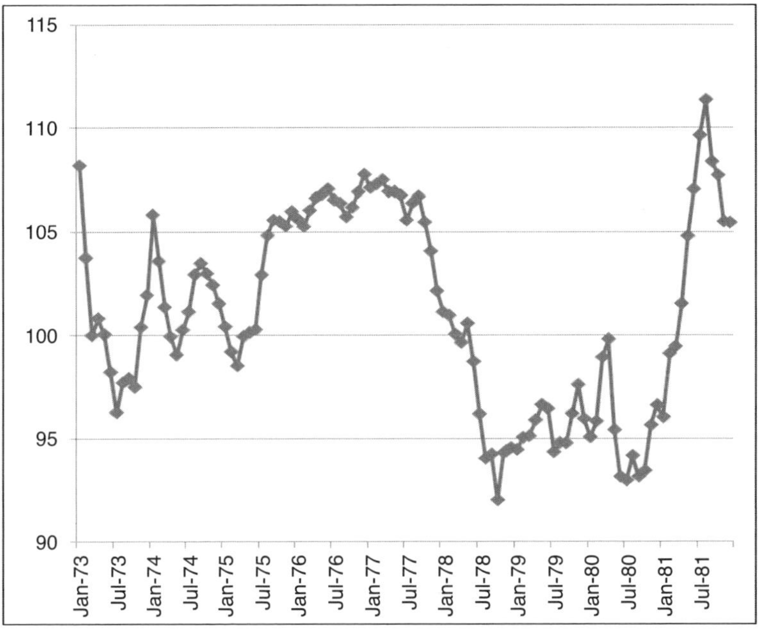

Source: Federalreserve.gov/releases/h10/summary/indexn_m.txt.

Figure A.20 Three Month Treasury-Bill Rate: 1931–1997

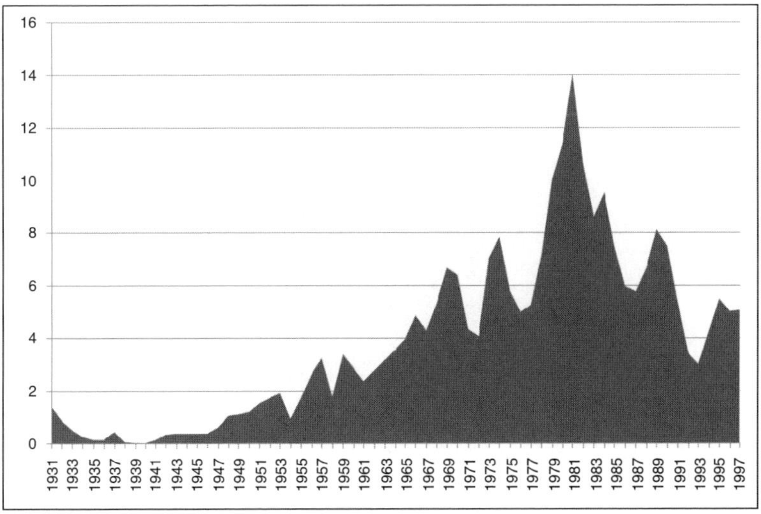

Source: Historical Statistics, Series Cj1232.

Figure A.21 Nonfinancial Corporation's Reliance on Commercial Paper: 1955–2009

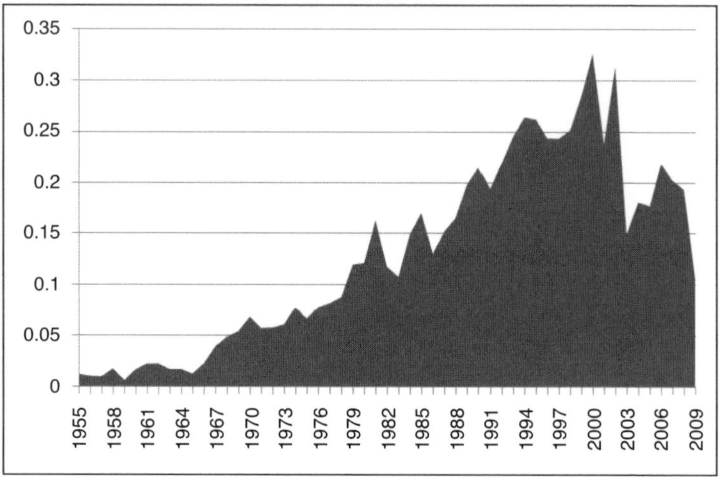

Source: Federal Reserve Flow of Funds, http://www.federalreserve.gov/releases/z1/current/data.htm.

Note: This is the ratio of commercial paper issued to bank loans at nonfinancial, nonfarm corporations.

Figure A.22 Role of Finance Companies in Providing Business Credit: 1955–2009

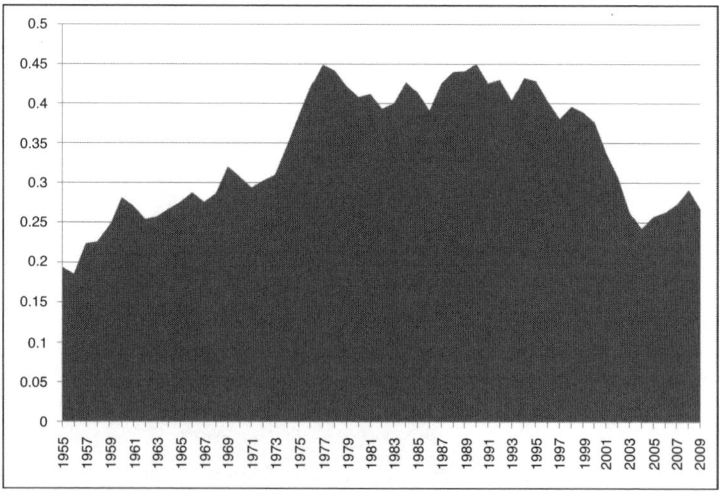

Source: Federal Reserve Flow of Funds, http://www.federalreserve.gov/releases/z1/current/data.htm.

Note: This is the ratio of short-term loans to total assets at finance companies.

Figure A.23 Asset Growth at Mutual Funds and Money Market Mutual Funds: 1955–2009

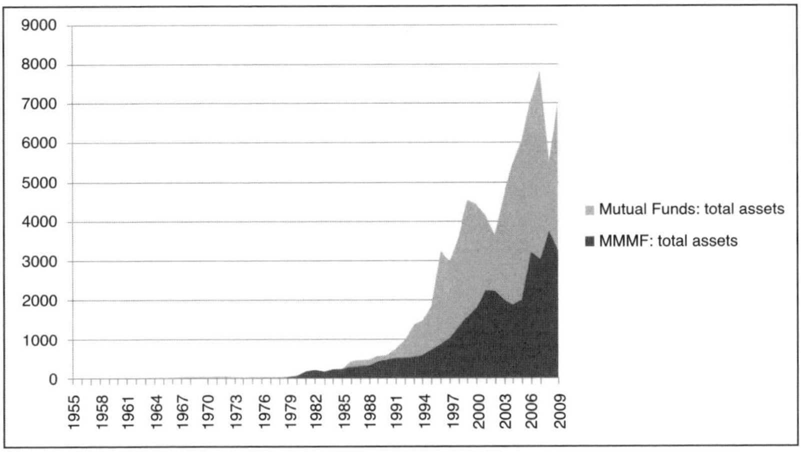

Source: Federal Reserve Flow of Funds, http://www.federalreserve.gov/releases/z1/current/data.htm.

Note: Dollars in billions.

Figure A.24 Regional Four-Quarter Change in FHFA House Price Indices: Panels A–C

Panel A

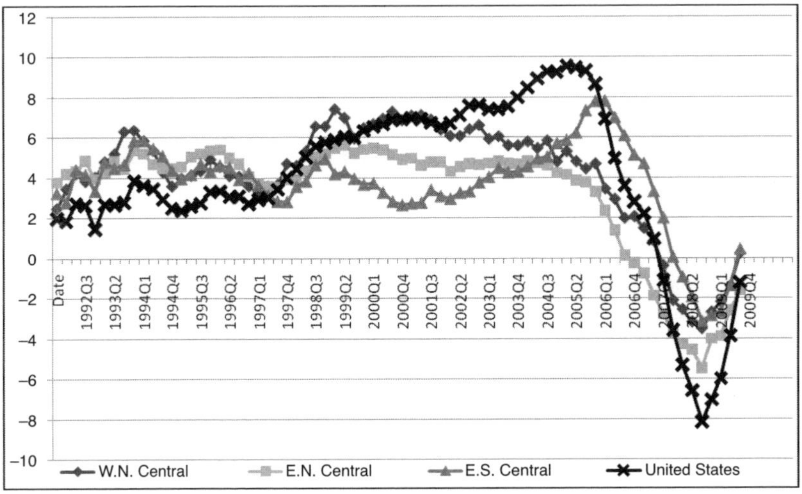

Panel B

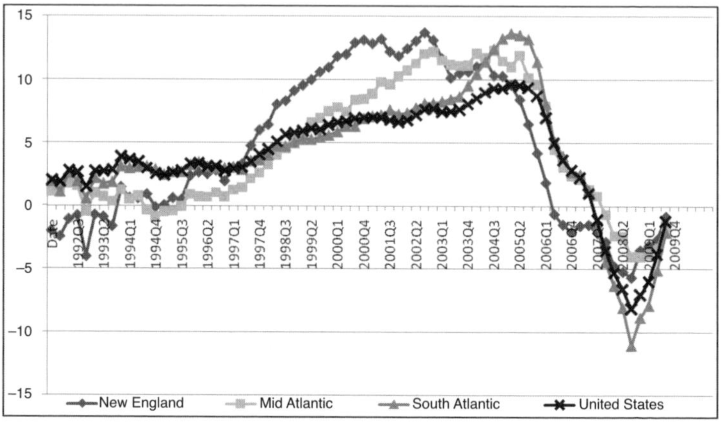

Panel C

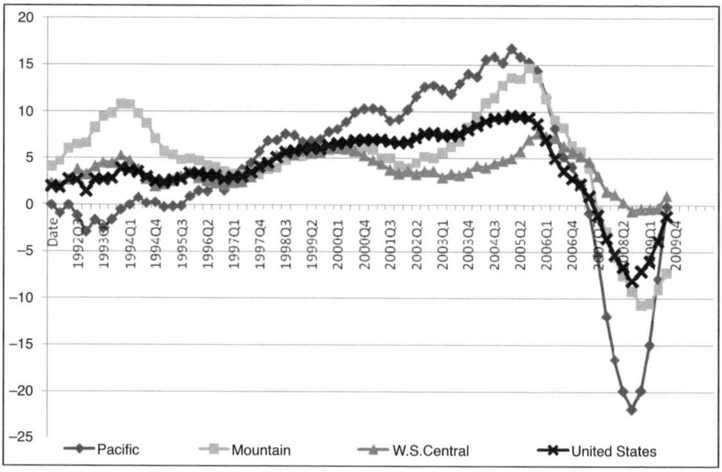

Source: www.fhfa.gov.

Note: **Pacific** includes Hawaii, Alaska, Washington, Oregon, California; **Mountain** includes Montana, Idaho, Wyoming, Nevada, Utah, Colorado, Arizona, New Mexico; **West South Central** includes Oklahoma, Arkansas, Texas, Louisiana; **West North Central** includes North Dakota, South Dakota, Minnesota, Nebraska, Iowa, Kansas, Missouri; **East North Central** includes Michigan, Wisconsin, Illinois, Indiana, Ohio; **East South Central** includes Kentucky, Tennessee, Mississippi, Alabama; **New England** includes Maine, New Hampshire, Vermont, Massachusetts, Rhode Island, Connecticut; **Middle Atlantic** includes New York, New Jersey, Pennsylvania; **South Atlantic** includes Delaware, Maryland, DC, Virginia, West Virginia, North Carolina, South Carolina, Georgia, Florida.

Figure A.25 Federal Funds Rate: January 2000–March 2010

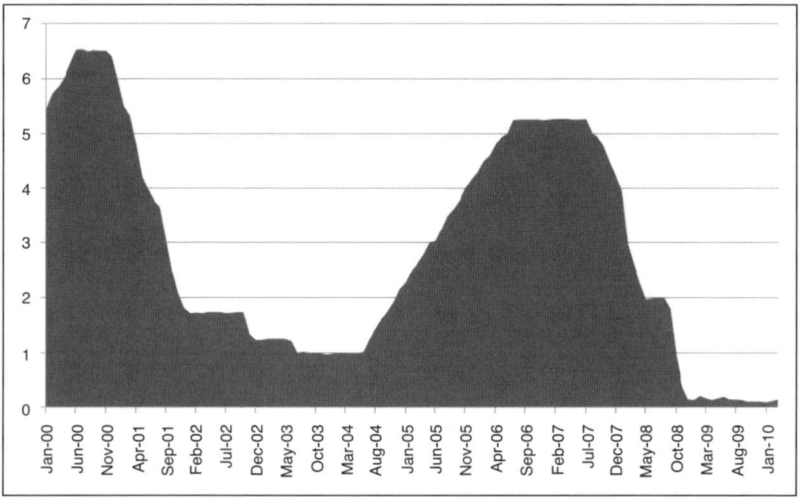

Source: http://www.federalreserve.gov/releases/h15/data/Monthly/H15_FF_O.txt.

Notes

Chapter 1 Commercial Bank Instability

1 Definitions of bank crisis and financial stability are found later in this chapter.
2 Much of this discussion draws from Grossman (1994).
3 Grossman's (1994) analysis is during the Great Depression and considers the performance of many nations during this period.
4 These three perspectives are not necessarily mutually exclusive. For example, Bordo and James (2009) find more than one perspective to be important in understanding the cause of bank crises.
5 See, for example, Hayek (1937), Kirzner (1992), Mises (1949).
6 The term "bank crisis" is synonymous with "bank panic" in this work. The earliest episodes are often referred to as panics and later episodes are often characterized as crises. However, the author does not find a discernible difference in the meaning of these word choices.
7 For an example of the many different scholarly perspectives and definitions, see Wolfson (1994), Gorton (1985, 1988), Wicker (1996), Schwartz (1986), Kindleberger and Aliber (2005), Mishkin (1991).
8 It would be more feasible to form a more precise definition if the time frame under consideration was smaller (e.g. if this book only considered a single era in commercial banking). However, over time banking markets evolve and regulation becomes more burdensome both of which change the elements of the crisis. Consequently, a broader definition is constructed to capture only the elements that prevail over the entire history of commercial banking.

Chapter 2 Theories of Bank Regulation

1 McChesney (1997).
2 See, for example, Litan and Nordhaus (1983).
3 See, for example, Stigler (1971) and Peltzman (1976).
4 See, for example, McChesney (1987).
5 This literature review does not claim to be exhaustive of all bank regulation literature. Rather, it is meant to introduce the reader to different perspectives.
6 See, for example, Benston (2000, 1986) who argues that these very reasons for historically supporting regulation are largely invalid today. Litan (1987) discusses how bank regulation was consistent with the public-interest approach. Spong (1992) and Dewatripont and Tirole (1993) also argue that one of the primary objectives of bank regulation is to protect depositors.
7 Edwards and Scott (1979) argue that bank regulation, first and foremost, is designed to protect the solvency of bank institutions. Benston (2000, 1986) enumerates several self-interested reasons for bank regulation in the United States. Kane (1989) argues that bankers and regulators were primarily concerned with maximizing their own revenue during the 1980s thrift crisis.
8 See Chapter 3 for more details on antebellum branching.

9 Hendrickson (2010).
10 This discussion is largely from Hirshleifer (2008).
11 Benston (1991) identified the first three channels and the author added the final two.
12 See, for example, Nichols and Hendrickson (1997).
13 Allen and Gale (2004). See also Boyd et al. (2004) who use a theoretical model to test whether a competitive or monopolistic banking system is most likely associated with bank crises. The Boyd et al. (2004) model does not control for regulatory intervention, but does find that the probability of a banking crisis may be higher under monopoly or competitive systems; it depends on the rate of inflation.
14 Carlson and Mitchener (2005).
15 Calomiris (1993), Jayaratne and Strahan (1998), Flannery (1984).
16 Note that throughout this book, the author views the world through this Austrian lens or understanding of markets. However, this does not mean that all Austrian scholars would embrace the analysis or findings of this work. Rather, the author borrows critical concepts from the Austrian school to create a vision of how markets work and then utilizes this vision to understand the evolution of banks and bank regulation in the United States.
17 See Hayek (1937).

Chapter 3 Antebellum Banking: 1781–1863

1 All figures that are not directly banking statistics are labeled with an "A" and are found in the Data Appendix at the back of the book.
2 Engerman and Gallman (1983: 10).
3 Engerman and Gallman (1983: 12).
4 Bodenhorn (2000: 2).
5 Ferrie (1997).
6 Ferrie (1997).
7 For example, Hammond (1963) produced a manuscript entitled *Banking Before the Civil War* and in it devotes one sentence to the private banker. In contrast, Sylla (1976) makes a compelling case that the private banker was a viable member of the financial sector during antebellum America.
8 See the section *Experiments in Federal Banking* later in this chapter for more explanation on these federal banks.
9 Helderman (1931).
10 Following Bodenhorn (2000: 101) merchants included shoe dealers, grocers, jewelers, etc. Manufacturers included blacksmiths, distillers, cabinet makers, etc. Services included attorneys, dentists, doctors, teachers, etc.
11 Fenstermaker (1965).
12 Fenstermaker (1965).
13 These banknotes were often referred to as horse blankets because of their large size.
14 Fenstermaker (1965: 39).
15 Fenstermaker (1965: 43).
16 Fenstermaker (1965).

17 Actually, commercial banking varied from state to state but such an analysis is beyond the scope this book.
18 Lamoreaux (1986, 1994).
19 See, for example, Bodenhorn (2000), Trivoli (1979).
20 Calomiris and Kahn (1996: 15).
21 See, for example, Rolnick, Smith, and Weber (2000), Weber (2010), Trivoli (1979), Calomiris and Kahn (1996). For evidence of the System's contribution to stability, see the subheading *Performance* later in this chapter.
22 Bodenhorn (2000: 35–8) provides details of how the state of Pennsylvania benefited from the charters they extended.
23 For an extensive look at southern banking during this period, see Schweikart (1987).
24 Fenstermaker (1965: 84, 86).
25 See Bodenhorn (2000: 42–4) for a discussion of the Louisiana situation.
26 Gorton (1985: 278) argues that Clearinghouses emerged with the rise in demand deposits as an important liability to the commercial banker. Since demand deposits are not traded in a secondary market, important information asymmetries form which, in part, Clearinghouses can overcome. In contrast, Dowd (1994) argues that the emergence of clearinghouses in the United States was the result of restrictive bank regulation, significantly the prohibition on branch banking, which made banks more susceptible to runs and problems. Another perspective argues that Clearinghouses were formed first and foremost to help in the clearing of checks. Rather than send checks back to each separate bank for redemption, a member bank would simply send all member checks to the Clearinghouse for collection (see, for example, Dwyer and Gilbert (1989)).
27 During the national bank era, depositors were converting demand deposits into currency.
28 Timberlake (1984), Moen and Tallman (2000), Kroszner (2000).
29 Bodenhorn (1993).
30 Fenstermaker (1965: 20).
31 The extent to which some states relied on bank regulation is evidenced by the fact that Massachusetts and Delaware, for example, received most of their state revenue from the regulation of banks during the nineteenth century (Sylla et al., 1987).
32 For example, Louisiana banks were required to extend loans for hotel construction and operation, and Massachusetts and Pennsylvania banks made compulsory loans to agriculture and manufacturing (Fenstermaker, 1965).
33 Much of this discussion draws from Calomiris (1989) and Weber (2010).
34 For a detailed consideration of failed insured banks in New York, see Root (1895) who indicates that 17.2 percent of all insured antebellum banks failed in this state.
35 Weber (2010).
36 Weber (2010).
37 Ideally, a discussion of the macroeconomic impact of these crises could also accompany the description of the crises itself, as is done is later chapters. However, reliable macroeconomic data does not exist, though Calomiris and Gorton (1991: 114) do have data identifying business cycles peaks. From that data, it is clear that the crises of 1837, 1857 and of 1860 coincided with the

business cycle peaks but their data does not extend back far enough to comment on the 1792 crisis.

38 Rothbard (1962).
39 Sylla et al. (2009).
40 See, for example, Hammond (1957).
41 Sylla (2001).
42 See, for example, Temin (1969).
43 Rolnick, Smith, and Weber (2000: 4).
44 See, for example, Timberlake (1960).
45 Rolnick, Smith, and Weber (2000).
46 Without the Suffolk System, if a bank was repaid a loan there was no way the bank could be sure that the notes used to pay the loan were its own. The loan could be paid off using "foreign" banknotes. In this scenario, the bank has not been able to reduce its own notes outstanding. Under the Suffolk System, the bank could deposit the "foreign" notes at the Suffolk Bank and receive any of its own notes that had been deposited with the System.
47 Weber (2010).
48 Calomiris and Kahn (1996).
49 See, for example, Trivoli (1979: 17).
50 See, for example, Tivoli (1979: 25). Rolnick, Smith, and Weber (1998) explain how another note clearing bank was formed in Boston in 1855 to compete with Suffolk and this bank found support from other New England banks as almost half were shareholders in the new bank when it opened in 1858.
51 Calomiris and Kahn (1996) find that Boston banks were not more profitable than others in Massachusetts nor those in other regions. However, Rolnick, Smith, and Weber (1998) argue that the Suffolk Bank was more profitable, after 1833, than other Massachusetts banks.
52 This account of the crisis of 1857 draws heavily from Calomiris and Schweikart (1991).
53 See Calomiris and Schweikart (1991) for evidence of this claim.
54 Calomiris and Schweikart (1991).
55 Swanson (1908: 218).
56 This analysis of the crisis of 1860 and the role of the clearinghouse draws from Swanson (1908).
57 For example, Redlich (1947) thought the private banker to be insignificant.
58 See Bodenhorn (2000a) for a discussion of the role of the private banking in real sector development. Klebaner (1990: 14) comments that "... these (private) banks were especially significant in the antebellum economy."
59 From Jay Cooke's *Memoirs* quoted in Bodenhorn (1997: 516).
60 Klebaner (1990).
61 Bodenhorn (1997).
62 Klebaner (1990) and Sylla (1976) both make this point.
63 Bodenhorn (1997).
64 Sylla (1976).
65 For example, Massachusetts, New Hampshire, Maryland, and Ohio prohibited unincorporated banks while Florida, Missouri, and North Carolina prohibited private note issuance.
66 Sylla (1976: 177).

67 Cowen (2000).
68 Cowen (2000).
69 Cowen (2000: 1046).
70 Sylla et al. (2009).
71 Quoted in Sumner (1896: 52). The concern over foreign influence came from the fact that of the Bank's 25,000 shares, 18,000 were owned abroad though these shares had no voting rights associated with them (Sumner, 1896: 53).
72 The technical name of this bank was The President and Directors of the Bank of the United States. However, historians typically refer to this as the Second Bank of the United States. This book follows that convention.
73 See, for example, Hammond (1963), Fenstermaker (1965), Krooss and Blyn (1971).
74 Fenstermaker and Filer (1986).
75 Though the discussion of free banking laws reached wider public arenas near 1836 with the closure of the Second Bank, this was not the beginning of the free banking discussion in America. Scholars and economists knew of free banking theoretically from the work of Adam Smith and others. Further, they knew of other nation's experiences with free banking such as that in Scotland and Great Britain. See Redlich (1947) for an interesting discussion of the theoretical and practical history of free banking ideas. See Dowd (1992) for discussions of worldwide free banking experiences.
76 Dowd (1993) also argues that this provision was an important source of state revenue by creating a captive audience for the purchase of state debt. Thus, this provision raised revenue for the state in a similar manner that the earlier legislative system raised state revenue by selling charters.
77 Ng (1988) argues that New York did experience growth from the free banking era but finds that outside of New York, growth was not as robust. From this, Ng argues that free banking did not significantly lower barriers to entry.
78 Rolnick and Weber (1982).
79 Rolnick and Weber (1982).
80 See, for example, Dwyer (1996) and Hassan and Dwyer (1994). Note that national banks came into existence in 1863 with the passage of the National Currency Act so that by 1865 there were state banks, free banks, and national banks operating side by side. A complete discussion of national banking is found in Chapter 4.
81 The author is grateful to George Selgin for a conversation he and I had on how the free banks were ruined by the Revenue Act tax when the state chartered banks were not.
82 Hammond (1963).
83 Benston (1986), Kaufman (1988).
84 Roussakis (1997) and Klebaner (1990).
85 Dowd (1993).
86 Dowd (1993) and others make this case.
87 Schweikart (1987).
88 Chapman and Westerfield (1942).
89 Chapman and Westerfield (1942: 41).
90 Fenstermaker (1965: 2).

91 Fenstermaker and Filer (1986).
92 A similar point is made by Krooss and Blyn (1971).
93 Quoted in Krooss and Blyn (1971: 45).
94 Rockoff (1974).
95 Rolnick and Weber (1982).
96 See, for example, Hammond (1963).
97 Rolnick and Weber (1984).
98 Rolnick and Weber (1984).
99 Rolnick and Weber (1986).
100 Rolnick and Weber (1986).
101 Rolnick and Weber (1986: 884).
102 Dowd (1993), L. White (1986).
103 Rockoff (1985).

Chapter 4 National Banking Era: 1864–1912

1 The recession data comes from the National Bureau of Economic Research and the unemployment number is from Garrett et al. (2010).
2 Schweikart and Allen (2004: 434).
3 McPherson (1982) in Schweikart and Allen (2004).
4 *Annual Report of the Comptroller of the Currency* (1910: 371–401).
5 Throughout this book, the date 1864 and title "National Bank Act" is used to mean the 1863 and 1864 Acts which collectively created nationally chartered banks and their initial regulation. This is a common practice among commercial bank historians.
6 Hammond (1957).
7 Sylla (1972: 254).
8 Sylla (1972: 255).
9 Banks in designated central reserve cities could not extend mortgage loans. However, other national banks could extend mortgage loans that were no greater than five years in maturity and no more than 50 percent of the appraised value of the land. Further, these national banks could not have mortgage loans exceed 25 percent of their capital holdings (White (1983: 23)).
10 In 1874, the law was changed so that reserve requirements were only on deposits and no longer applied to banknotes.
11 White (1983: 14).
12 Klebaner (1990: 68).
13 Klebaner (1990: 75).
14 See, for example, Sprague (1910), Friedman and Schwartz (1963), Wicker (2000), and Chari (1989).
15 Wilson, Sylla and Jones (1990) address the relationship between stock market volatility and bank crises during the national banking era.
16 In 1862, Congress passed the Pacific Railway Act which helped to finance the building of the transcontinental railroad to connect California with the rest of the nation. Due to the war effort and lack of additional financial backing, the project did not get underway until 1866. Yet, the first of five transcontinental railways was complete in May of 1869. The completion of the first rail was an important spark behind the enthusiasm for further construction.

17 See Wicker (2000: 19–26) for a discussion of specific bank experiences and losses.
18 Wicker (2000: 21).
19 See Wicker (2000: 35–6) for more details on these failures.
20 Wicker (2000: 40).
21 For an interesting and contemporary analysis of the 1893 crisis, see Stevens (1894).
22 The bankruptcy data comes from Mishkin (1991).
23 Markham (2002).
24 Wicker (2000: 56).
25 Carlson (2005).
26 Stevens (1894).
27 Stevens (1894).
28 Wicker (2000: 87).
29 For a detailed explanation of the development of the trust problems and runs during the 1907 crisis see Moen and Tallman (1992, 2000) or Wicker (2000).
30 Prior to 1906, the New York trust did not have reserve requirements but the state implemented a 15 percent requirement in 1906 (Moen and Tallman (1992)). Note that even this reserve requirement was substantially less that the 25 percent placed on all national banks.
31 Trust companies of New York cancelled their Clearinghouse membership in 1903 when the Clearinghouse decided that trusts would be subject to the same reserve requirements as member commercial banks.
32 A detailed analysis of the performance of Clearinghouses is found later in the chapter.
33 White (1981: 537) makes a similar claim.
34 At the national level, William Jennings Bryan proposed the first bill for deposit insurance in 1893 after the panic of that same year.
35 See White (1981) for the empirical model and results.
36 See Hendrickson (2010).
37 Oklahoma, Texas, Kansas, Nebraska, and South Dakota established state deposit insurance during the national banking era and North Dakota, Washington, and Mississippi established deposit insurance following the creation of the Federal Reserve System.
38 See White (1981) or Calomiris (1989) for a detailed discussion of the provisions and performance of those deposit insurance programs in Oklahoma, Kansas, Nebraska, and Texas.
39 See, for example, Livingston (1986) for a political economy analysis. For a banking and Clearinghouse performance perspective see, for example, Timberlake (1984), Moen and Tallman (1999).
40 This essentially describes the proposed Aldrich-Vreeland Act of 1908.
41 This argument is elaborated on in the next section of this chapter.
42 It is worth noting that many accounts of the Federal Reserve's creation perpetuate the myth that the 1907 crisis was the most severe of those during the national banking era. Perhaps one reason the 1907 crisis is often erroneously characterized as the largest crisis of this era is because the stock market did have one of its largest declines in the fall of 1907. For interesting data on stock market performance during this era, see Wilson et al. (1990).

43 The data in Table 4.11 indicate the growth of the trust company between 1896 and 1907 and is evidence that the rise in the trust company with its riskier behavior could contribute significantly to the potential fragility of the banking sector.
44 Moen and Tallman (2000).
45 Moen and Tallman (1999) make this argument.
46 *Annual Report of the Comptroller of the Currency* (1914: 37).
47 Calomiris and Mason (2008).
48 For data comparing state and national bank capital requirements, see White (1983: 18–21).
49 Davis (1965).
50 Bordo et al. (1992: 212–13).
51 Stock market data during this era may be found in Calomiris and Gorton (1991) and Wilson et al. (1990). See also Figure A.8.
52 Chapman and Westerfield (1942).
53 Hendrickson (2010).
54 Goldenweiser (1931).
55 Stability in the wider economic community has also been linked to branch banking. Specifically, Dehejia and Lleras-Muney (2007) find that between 1919 and 1940, states with branch banking enjoyed faster economic rates of growth. Ramirez (2009) finds the same results for the 1900–1930 period.
56 Calomiris and Gorton (1991: 116).
57 See Selgin (2000: Table 1) for more data.
58 It is believed the no free banks survived the Civil War. Discussions separately with George Selgin and Arthur Rolnick support this belief.
59 See, for example, Selgin (2000), Dowd (1993).
60 Selgin (2000).
61 Selgin (2000).
62 Selgin (2000).
63 Greenback is the popular name given to paper currency issued by the federal government during the Civil War to finance war expenses. A February 1862 law authorized the federal government to issue the currency up to $150 million though this amount was revised upward in July of 1862 and again in March of 1863.
64 *Annual Report of the Comptroller of the Currency* (1910: 63).
65 White (1981: 556).
66 Dehejia and Lleras-Muney (2007) find slower rates of growth in state income in states with deposit insurance between 1919 and 1930.
67 Gorton (1985) makes a similar argument.
68 Krozsner (2000: 159).
69 Moen and Tallman (2000).
70 See, for example, Gorton (1985) and Chari (1989).
71 This currency issue changed with the passage of the Aldrich-Vreeland Act of 1908 which allowed Associations of national banks to legally issue temporary currency (Dwyer and Gilbert (1989: 52)).
72 See, for example, Krozsner (2000).
73 See, for example, Krozsner (2000) and Calomiris and Gorton (1991: 119).
74 E. White (2008) also makes this point and the author borrowers the term "competition in laxity" from White.

Chapter 5 Era of Instability and Change: 1913–1944

1 Schweikart and Allen (2004: 539).
2 Schweikart and Allen (2004: 543).
3 The next section of this chapter explains more about the central bank in the United States.
4 Friedman and Schwartz (1963).
5 Schweikart and Allen (2004).
6 See, for example, Schweikart and Allen (2004), Aldrich (1933), White (2009), Shlaes (2007), who discuss the role of the Smoot-Hawley Tariff in the economic contraction.
7 Wanniski (1989).
8 Klebaner (1990: 115).
9 The eight states characterized as the Midwest include Ohio, Indiana, Illinois, Michigan, Wisconsin, Minnesota, Iowa and Missouri.
10 The central western region includes North Dakota, South Dakota, Nebraska, Kansas, Montana, Wyoming, Colorado, New Mexico and Oklahoma.
11 *Federal Reserve Committee on Branch, Group, and Chain Banking* (1932).
12 Abrams and Settle (1993).
13 The total number of bank failures peaked in 1933 with 4000 failures. The next year, there were 57 failures and the number remained low for many years thereafter (Board of Governors, 1943).
14 See, for example, Kennedy (1973: 219).
15 White (1985).
16 See, for example, Klebaner (1990: 132) and White (1985).
17 Klebaner (1990: 126).
18 E. White (1986).
19 White (1985).
20 White (1985).
21 In a city with a population between 25,000 and 50,000, one branch could be established; in a city with a population over 50,000 but less than 100,000, two branches could be established, and if the population exceeded 100,000, the Comptroller of the Currency could determine the maximum number of branches (*Federal Reserve Committee on Branch, Group, and Chain Banking* (1932)).
22 *Federal Reserve Committee on Branch, Group, and Chain Banking* (1932).
23 Investment grade securities generally referred to bonds and notes (Markham (2002)).
24 All data from the *Federal Reserve Bulletin* (1937: 866) is technically bank suspensions (versus bank failures). A bank suspension is defined as "… all banks closed to the public either temporarily or permanently by supervisory authorities or by the banks' board of directors on account of financial difficulties… If a bank closed under a special holiday declared by civil authorities and remained closed only during such holiday or part thereof, it has not been counted as a bank failure."
25 The ten states with a state bank failure rate in excess of ten percent in 1930 are North Carolina, South Carolina, Florida, Alabama, Mississippi, Arkansas, Indiana, North Dakota, South Dakota, and Arizona.
26 Wicker (1996) also makes this point.

27 Wicker (1996).
28 Temin (1976).
29 Olson (1977).
30 Mason (2001).
31 See Kennedy (1973) for a history of the situation in Michigan. Wicker (1996) also has an analysis of role of the Michigan holiday in the larger bank crisis.
32 *Federal Reserve Bulletin* (1937).
33 See, for example, Westerfield (1933). The leaders of the National Monetary Commission that was assembled after the 1907 crisis were convinced that the advantages of branching were so great that it would quickly drive unit banks out of business (*Federal Reserve Committee on Branch, Group, and Chain Banking* (1932)).
34 See, for example, Preston (1933) or Eccles (1982).
35 See, for example, Cox (1966) or Haywood and Linke (1968).
36 The Federal Reserve set the ceiling at 3 percent on November 1, 1933 and on February 1, 1935, lowered it to 2.5 percent (Gilbert (1986)).
37 For more information on the investigation and allegation into the banker/broker dealings during this time see Anderson (1949), Carosso (1970), Hendrickson (2001) or Barth et al. (2000).
38 See, for example, E. White (1986) or Schweikart and Allen (2004).
39 A bank, for example, may have the incentive to underwrite securities for a firm that owes the bank money so that the proceeds from the securities can repay the bank (Kroszner and Rajan (1994)). Empirical evidence finds that banks with security affiliates actually were underwriting securities of higher quality than independent investment banks so there is no evidence of a conflict of interest (Kroszner and Rajan (1994)).
40 Symons and White (1984).
41 There were other provisions in the Banking Act of 1935 that may interest the reader but that are not relevant to the arguments of this book. See, for example, Krooss and Blyn (1971).
42 L. White (1986) also makes this point.
43 American Bankers' Association (1935).
44 Board of Governors (1943).
45 Bradley (2000).
46 Olson (1977) and Ebersole (1933).
47 Kennedy (1973) and Preston (1933).
48 Kennedy (1973).
49 Even prominent members of Congress, including Senator Glass, opposed deposit insurance because of the poor experience states had with it during the first two banking eras and because of moral hazard concerns (O'Connor, 1933).
50 Board of Governors (1943).
51 See, for example, Carlson and Mitchener (2005, 2009), Westerfield (1933, 1939), Calomiris (1993, 2000), Calomiris and Gorton (1991) or Schweikart (1991).
52 Preston (1924), Sprague (1903), Westerfield (1939).
53 Preston (1924), Westerfield (1939).
54 Gilbert (1986).
55 Kilcollin and Hanweck (1981).

56 Gilbert (1986) indicates that the average interest rate paid by member banks on time and savings deposits were below the effective ceiling rate until the mid-1960s.
57 E. White (1986).
58 White (1982, 1986).
59 Kroszner and Rajan (1994).
60 E. White (1986).
61 E. White (1986).
62 See, for example, Allen and Gale (2004), Carlson and Mitchener (2005, 2009), Calomiris (1993), Jayarathne and Strahan (1998), Flannery (1984).
63 Bradley (2000).

Chapter 6 Postwar Banking Era and Regulatory Response: 1945–1999

1 See Berger et al. (1995) for a detailed description of the U.S. banking industry for much of this era.
2 Hanc (1995).
3 Commercial paper is a bond with a maturity of less than one year that is issued by corporations, banks, finance companies, etc. (Ball (2009)).
4 See D'Arista and Schelsinger (1994) for a detailed explanation of the regulatory competitive disadvantage facing commercial bankers.
5 Much of this discussion of the expansion of the commercial paper market following the 1966 credit crunch is from Wolfson (1994).
6 According to Woelfel (1994) disintermediation is defined as "an excess of withdrawals from a depository institution's interest-bearing accounts."
7 Eurodollars are deposits from accounts in the U.S. that are transferred to a bank outside of the U.S. but kept in dollars (i.e. are not converted to another currency) (Mishkin (2010)). Most are kept as time deposits.
8 See Becketti and Morris (1992) for more on finance companies.
9 D'Arista and Schlesinger (1994).
10 Unless noted otherwise, data on foreign banks is from http://www.allcountries.org/uscensus/804_u_s_banking_offices_of_foreign.html.
11 Macey et al. (1991).
12 Calomiris and Carey (1994).
13 Rouwenhorts (2004).
14 A closed-ended mutual fund raises funds once through an initial offering and then the fund shares are sold to investors.
15 Unless otherwise noted, the mutual fund data comes from McWinney (2010). An open-ended fund does not have restrictions on the number of shares that will be issued. This is the most common fund type today.
16 A no-load fund is a mutual fund that does not charge commission or a sales charge for the purchase of shares.
17 The data on the number of mutual fund shareholder accounts comes from the *Investment Company Institute Mutual Fund Factbook* found at http://www.icifactbook.org/fb_data.html.
18 See Buljevich and Park (1999: 79) for a detailed list of all type of off-balance sheet activities.

19 A derivative is a security whose value is determined by fluctuations in the price of an underlying asset. Sinkey and Carter (1994) indicate that banks are relatively newer users of derivatives and that, during this era in banking, a small population of banks were participating in derivative markets.
20 Berger et al. (1995).
21 Boyd and Gertler (1994a) also make this point.
22 A bank holding company is a corporate structure that owns one or more banks and may also own nonbanks such as security or insurance companies.
23 Table 6.1. indicates the year that each state allowed for some interstate banking in these regional agreements.
24 Boyd and Gertler (1994a).
25 Berger et al. (1995).
26 Data on the location and number of bank failures is found at http://www2.fdic.gov/hsob/hsobRpt.asp. According to the USDA, the top five agricultural states are California, Iowa, Illinois, Texas, Nebraska.
27 The savings and loan (thrift) crisis was concurrent to the 1980s commercial banking crisis. For details on the thrift crisis see, for example, Federal Deposit Insurance Corporation (1997: Chapter 9) or Barth (1991).
28 Much of this discussion on the 1966 credit crunch draws from Wolfson (1994).
29 Wolfson (1994).
30 Owens and Schreft (1995).
31 Much of this discussion about the Franklin National experience draws from Wolfson (1994).
32 See Berger et al. (1995: 179–80) for a brief description of capital regulation in the 1950s by the Federal Reserve.
33 Mishkin (2010).
34 Much of this discussion on the Penn Square failure is from Wolfson (1994).
35 Gilbert (1986: 29).
36 Berger et al. (1995).
37 Federal Deposit Insurance Corporation (1997: 95).
38 Federal Deposit Insurance Corporation (1997: 94).
39 Much of this discussion of the Continental Illinois failure is from Wolfson (1994).
40 Federal Deposit Insurance Corporation (1997: 88).
41 Moral hazard is the risk that, after a transaction, one party will engage in activities that are undesirable (i.e. immoral).
42 This discussion draws from the Federal Deposit Insurance Corporation (1997: 104).
43 Johnson and Rice (2007).
44 See Hendrickson (2001) for a discussion of the history of attempts to repeal the Glass–Steagall provisions.
45 See Hendrickson (2001) and Macey et al. (1991) for more on the court and regulator decisions that eroded the Glass–Steagall provisions prior to the 1999 act.
46 Saulsbury (1987).
47 See Cook (1978) for further evidence of disintermediation.
48 Kilcollin and Hanweck (1981).
49 Cebula and Saltz (1994).

50 See, for example, Allen and Gale (2004), Carlson and Mitchener (2005, 2009), Calomiris (1993), Jayarathne and Strahan (1998), Flannery (1984).
51 Hetzel (1991).
52 Benston (1989) also finds that the evidence does not support the hypothesis that banks would take on more risk if allowed to engage in securities activity.
53 Keeley (1990).
54 Risk-based deposit insurance became effective initially in 1994 as mandated by the FDICIA in 1991.
55 Hanc (1995).
56 Failure and failure resolution data is calculated from the FDIC report on bank and thrift failures (Table BF01 at www2.fdic.gov).
57 Hetzel (1991).
58 Boyd and Gertler (1994a).
59 Hanc (1995), among many others, also makes this point.
60 See Boyd and Gertler (1994) for an analysis of the 1980s and Kane (2000) for an analysis of the 1990s.
61 Ennis and Malek (2005).
62 See Mengle (1990) for a detailed explanation of additional costs.
63 See, for example, Carlson and Mitchener (2005 and 2009), Calomiris (1993, and 2000), Calomiris and Gorton (1991), Jayarathne and Strahan (1998), Mengle (1990).
64 Michkin (2010: 261) also suggests that the Basel capital requirements may increase risk taking.
65 Ostrosky (1997).
66 Feinman (1993).
67 The data for this calculation is from the FDIC list of failed and assisted banks (Table BF01 at www2.fdic.gov).
68 Stern and Feldman (2004). Prescott (2002) attempts to address whether risk-based deposit insurance can control moral hazard. The fact that Prescott is analyzing this issue in 2002 is clearly suggestive that moral hazard was not brought under control with the 1991 regulation.
69 Ennis and Malek (2005).
70 Hendrickson and Nichols (2011).

Chapter 7 Banking and Crisis in the Twenty-First Century: 2000–2010

1 Demyanyk and Van Hemert (2008) find evidence that loan quality, particularly subprime loan quality, had been deteriorating since 2001.
2 Brunnermeier (2009).
3 Many scholars offer a similar explanation including, for example, Calabria (2009), Ely (2009), L. White (2008), Wallison (2008 and 2009), Wallison and Calomiris (2008), Norberg (2009), Barth et al. (2009), among others.
4 U.S. Census Bureau, "Housing Vacancies and Homeownership."
5 Norberg (2009).
6 Norberg (2009), Kling (2010).
7 Barth et al. (2009).
8 Barth et al. (2009).

9 Barth et al. (2009).
10 Wallison and Calomiris (2008).
11 Barth et al. (2009).
12 Wallison (2010).
13 See, for example, L. White (2008), Taylor (2009a and 2009), Diamond and Rajan (2009), and O'Driscoll (2009).
14 Sowell (2009).
15 Sowell (2009).
16 The state level data comes from O'Toole (2007).
17 Scholars argue that the inflation in Nevada reflects the fact that almost 90 percent of all the land is owned by the federal government and prior to 2000, much of this land was sold to developers but that federal land sales fell off significantly in 2001 (O'Toole (2009)).
18 Glaeser (2006).
19 This data and the history of changes to the CRA institutional size definitions may be found at http://www.ffiec.gov/cra/examinations.htm.
20 Four regulatory bodies conduct CRA examinations: The Federal Reserve Board, the Office of Thrift Supervision, The Federal Deposit Insurance Corporation, and the Office of the Comptroller of the Currency.
21 Taylor and Silver (2008).
22 Securitization of home mortgages began in 1970 when a GSE, the Government National Mortgage Association, started bundling and selling off their mortgages. Fannie Mae and Freddie Mac began securitizing mortgages in 1982 (Norberg (2009)).
23 See Norberg (2009) for several examples.
24 See, for example, Kindleberger and Aliber (2005) and Minsky (1982).
25 Barr (2007).
26 The number of banks on the problem list was retrieved September 2, 2010 from fdic.gov/new/new/press/2010/pr10201.html.
27 All noncurrent loan data are from www2.fdic.gov in their Statistics on Depository Institutions tables.
28 Wallison and Calomiris (2008).
29 Norberg (2009).
30 See Table 6.6 in Barth et al. (2009) which contains a detailed summary of all of the regulatory responses to the crisis, including the new programs and actions of the Federal Reserve.
31 For example, in March of 2008, the Federal Reserve provided funds to Bear Stearns and in September of that year, loans were extended to American International Group (AIG) and to Goldman Sachs and Morgan Stanley both of whom had just converted from investment banks to bank holding companies (Barth et al. (2009)).
32 The Treasury and Congress played a much larger role in the aftermath of the crisis than is described here. However, to describe all of the bailouts goes beyond the scope of this book. See Barth et al. (2009) or Wheelock (2010) for more information.
33 Federal Reserve balance sheet data is from Table H.4.1 at www.federal reserve.gov.
34 Barth et al. (2009).
35 See, for example, Hilsenrath et al. (2008) or, more recently, Wheelock (2010).

36 Barth et al. (2009).
37 Keys et al. (2010).
38 Barth et al. (2009).
39 Wallison (2008).
40 This discussion draws from Calabria (2009).
41 White (2010).
42 Norberg (2009), Ely (2009).
43 Kling (2010).
44 See, for example, L. White (2008), Wallison and Calomiris (2008), Wallison (2009), Norberg (2009), or Husock (2008).
45 Gunther (1999).
46 Avery et al. (2000).
47 L. White (2008).
48 See, for example, Kroszner (2008) or Canner and Bhutta (2008).
49 Hendrickson and Nichols (2010) find evidence that banks closed branches in low-income areas in order to avoid CRA lending. This may explain why, as a percent of total loans, CRA lending was not as important in the crisis.
50 Pinto (2008).
51 Further, both Georgia and Illinois have anti-predatory lending laws in place. Recent empirical studies show that banks in states with anti-predatory lending laws perform worse than states operating in laws without the laws (Hendrickson and Nichols (2011)).
52 Calculated from institutional level data at www2.fdic.org.
53 The same argument is made in Norberg (2009) and Barth et al. (2009). See also Ely (2009).
54 Norberg (2009).
55 Ely (2009), Stern and Feldman (2004).
56 See Wheelock (2010) for more details on the extension of lender of last resort.
57 Stern and Feldman (2008), Norberg (2009).
58 Bernanke (2010).

Chapter 8 Lessons from the History of U.S. Banking and Regulation

1 De Rugy and Warren (2009).
2 Salsman (1993).
3 All polling data in this chapter is from the Roper Center retrieved May 27, 2010 from http://www.ropercenter.uconn.edu.
4 McKinnon and Craig (2010).
5 Salsman (1993).
6 Barth et al. (2009).
7 For a thorough discussion of the classical definition of LOLR, see Humphrey (2010).
8 See Barth et al. (2009) for details on these new lending facilities.
9 See also Wheelock (2010).
10 Calomiris (2009) makes this same case for the moral hazard of LOLR in the most recent crisis.

11 Norberg (2009: 82).
12 Failure data from Table BF02 at www2.fdic.gov.
13 Kaufman (1994) reviews the literature and fails to find evidence of bank failure contagion.
14 Brewer and Jagtiani (2007).
15 Wheelock and Wilson (2009).
16 Wheelock and Wilson (2009).
17 Boyd and Gertler (1994a).
18 Stern and Feldman (2008).
19 The historical evolution of the role of government draws from Garrett et al. (2010).
20 Holcombe and Lacombe (1998).
21 "The Money Panic" page 2 of the *Saturday Evening Post* on September 19, 1857.
22 See, for example, "New York Bank Panic," on page 8 of *The Manchester Guardian*, November 12, 1907.
23 Norberg (2009: 78).
24 See, for example, Kling (2010).
25 Norberg (2009: 62).
26 Norberg (2009: 65).
27 See, for example, Ely (2009).
28 See, for example, Wolf (2008).
29 Dermine and Schoenmaker (2009).
30 Salsman (1993: 81). Kaufman (1996) also argues that regulation is the primary destabilizing influence on commercial banking.
31 Ely (2009: 102).

References

Abrams, Burton A., and Russell F. Settle (1993) "Pressure-Group Influence and Institutional Change: Branch-Banking Legislation During the Great Depression," *Public Choice*, Vol. 77: 687–705.

Aldrich, Winthrop W. (1933) "The Causes of the Present Depression and Possible Remedies," retrieved January 19, 2010 from http://fraser.stlouisfed.org/publications.

Allen, Franklin, and Douglas Gale (2004) "Competition and Financial Stability," *Journal of Money, Credit and Banking*, Vol. 36, No. 3: 453–80.

American Bankers' Association (1935) *The Bank Chartering History and Policies of the United States*, American Bankers' Association, New York, New York.

American Bankers' Association (1936) *Changes in Bank Earning Assets*, American Bankers' Association, New York, New York.

Anderson, B. (1949) *Economics and the Public Welfare: Financial and Economic History of the United States, 1914–1946*, D. Van Nostrand, New Jersey.

Avery, Robert B., Raphael W. Bostic, and Glenn B. Canner (2000) "The Performance and Profitability of CRA-Related Lending," *Federal Reserve Bank of Cleveland Economic Commentary*, November, retrieved December 22, 2009 from www.clevelandfed.org/research/Commentary/2000/1100.htm.

Ball, Lawrence M. (2009) *Money, Banking, and Financial Markets*, Worth Publishers, New York.

Barnett, Kinley (1911) *State Banks and Trust Companies Since the Passage of the National-Bank Act*, National Monetary Commission, Government Printing Office, Washington D.C.

Barr, Alistair (2007) "Moody's Downgrades 691 Mortgage-Backed Securities," August 16, retrieved March 11, 2010 from www.marketwatch.com.

Barth, James R., Tong Li, and Wenling Lu (2009) *The Rise and Fall of the U.S. Mortgage and Credit Markets: A Comprehensive Analysis of the Market Meltdown*, Wiley, Hoboken, New Jersey.

Barth, James R., R. Dan Brumbaugh Junior, and James A. Wilcox (2000) "Policy Watch: The Repeal of Glass–Steagall and the Advent of Broad Banking," *Journal of Economic Perspectives*, Vol. 14, No. 2: 191–204.

Barth, James R. (1991) *The Great Savings and Loan Debacle*, The American Enterprise Institute, Washington, D.C.

Becketti, Sean, and Charles Morris (1992) "Are Bank Loans Still Special?" *Federal Reserve Bank of Kansas City Economic Review*, Vol. 3: 71–84.

Benston, George J. (2000) "Is Government Regulation of Banks Necessary?" *Journal of Financial Services Research*, Vol. 18, No. 2: 185–202.

Benston, George J. (1991) "Does Bank Regulation Produce Stability? Lessons from the United States," in *Unregulated Banking: Chaos or Order?*, eds. Forrest Capie and Geoffrey E. Woods, St. Martin's Press, New York: 207–32.

Benston, George J. (1989) "The Federal 'Safety Net' and the Repeal of the Glass–Steagall Act's Separation of Commercial and Investment Banking," *Journal of Financial Services Research*, Vol. 2, No. 4: 287–305.

Benston, George J. (1986) "Federal Regulation of Banking: Historical Overview," in *Deregulating Financial Services: Public Policy in Flux*, eds. George G. Kaufman and Roger C. Kormendi, Ballinger Publishing Company, Cambridge, MA: 1–47.

Berger, Allen N., Anil K. Kashyap, Joseph M. Scalise, Mark Gertler, and Benjamin M. Friedman (1995) "The Transformation of the U.S. Banking Industry: What a Long, Strange Trip It's Been," *Brooking Papers on Economic Activity*, Vol. 26, No. 2: 55–218.

Bernanke, Ben (2010) "Person of the Year," *Time*, December 28, 2009–January 4, 2010: 76.

Board of Governors (1943) *Banking and Monetary Statistics, 1914–1941*, retrieved from http://fraser.stlouisfed.org/publications/bms/issue/61/download/128/section8.pdf.

Board of Governors of the Federal Reserve (1959) *All-Banks Statistics: U.S. 1896–1955*, Washington D.C.

Bodenhorn, Howard (2000a) *A History in Banking in Antebellum America*, Cambridge University Press, New York, New York.

Bodenhorn, Howard (2000) "A History of Banking in Antebellum America: Financial Markets and Economic Development in an Era of Nation-Building," *Studies in Macroeconomic History*, Cambridge University Press, New York, New York.

Bodenhorn, Howard (1997) "Private Banking in Antebellum Virginia: Thomas Branch & Sons of Petersburg," *Business History Review*, Vol. 71, No. 4: 513–42.

Bodenhorn, Howard (1993) "Small-Denomination Banknotes in Antebellum America," *Journal of Money, Credit, and Banking*, Vol. 25, No. 4: 812–27.

Bordo, Michael D., and Harold James (2009) "The Great Depression Analogy" NBER Working Paper 15584, retrieved January 27, 2010 from www.nber.org/papers/w15584.

Bordo, Michael D., Peter Rappoport, and Anna J. Schwartz (1992) "Money Versus Credit Rationing: Evidence for the National Banking Era, 1880–1914," in *Strategic Factors in Nineteenth Century American Economic History*, University of Chicago Press, Chicago, IL: 189–223.

Boyd, John H., Gianni De Nicolo, and Bruce D. Smith (2004) "Crises in Competitive versus Monopolistic Banking Systems," *Journal of Money, Credit and Banking*, Vol. 36, No. 3 (June, part 2): 487–506.

Boyd, John H., and Mark Gertler (1994a) "Are Banks Dead? Or, Are the Reports Greatly Exaggerated?" *The Declining Role of Banking: Proceedings of the 30th Annual Conference on Bank Structure and Competition*, Federal Reserve Bank of Chicago: 85–113.

Boyd, John H., and Mark Gertler (1994) "The Role of Large Bank in the Recent U.S. Banking Crisis," *Federal Reserve Bank of Minneapolis Quarterly Review*, Winter: 319–68.

Bradley, Christine M. (2000) "A Historical Perspective on Deposit Insurance Coverage," *FDIC Banking Review*, Vol. 13, No. 2: 1–15.

Brewer, Elijah III, and Julapa Jagtiani (2007) "How Much Would Banks Be Willing to Pay to Become 'Too-Big-to-Fail' and to Capture Other Benefits?" *Federal Reserve Bank of Kansas City Research Working Paper*: 07-05.

Brumbaugh, R. Dan Jr. (1993) *The Collapse of Federally Insured Depositories: The Savings and Loan as Precursor*, Garland Publishing, Inc., New York, New York.

Brunnermeier, Markus K. (2009) "Deciphering the Liquidity and Credit Crunch 2007–2008," *Journal of Economic Perspectives*, Vol. 23, No. 1: 77–100.

Buljevich, Esteban C., and Yoon S. Park (1999) *Project Financing and the International Financial Markets*, Kluwer Academic Publishers, Boston, MA.
Calabria, Mark A. (2009) "Did Deregulation Cause the Financial Crisis?" *Cato Policy Report*, Vol. 31, No. 4: 5–8.
Calomiris, Charles (2009) "Financial Innovation, Regulation, and Reform," *Cato Journal*, Vol. 29, No. 1: 65–91.
Calomiris, Charles (2000) *U.S. Bank Deregulation in Historical Perspective*, Cambridge University Press, New York, New York.
Calomiris, Charles (1993) "Regulation, Industrial Structure and Instability in U.S. Banking: A Historical Perspective," in *Structural Change in Banking*, eds. Michael Klausner and Lawrence J. White, New York University Salomon Center, Business One Irwin, Homewood, IL.
Calomiris, Charles (1989) "Deposit Insurance: Lessons From the Record," *Economic Perspectives*, Federal Reserve Bank of Chicago, Vol. XIII, No. 3: 10–30.
Calomiris, Charles, and Joseph R. Mason (2008) "Resolving the Puzzle of the Underissuance of National Bank Notes," *Explorations in Economic History*, Vol. 45, No. 4: 327–55.
Calomiris, Charles, and Charles Kahn (1996) "The Efficiency of Self-Regulated Payments Systems: Learning from the Suffolk System," *National Bureau of Economic Research Working Paper: 5442*.
Calomiris, Charles, and Gary Gorton (1991) "The Origins of Banking Panics: Models, Facts, and Bank Regulation," in *Financial Markets and Financial Crises*, ed. Glenn R. Hubbard, University of Chicago Press: 109–73.
Calomiris, Charles, and Larry Schweikart (1991) "The Panic of 1857: Origins, Transmission, and Containment," *Journal of Economic History*, Vol. 51, No. 4: 807–34.
Calomiris, Charles, and Mark Carey (1994) "Loan Market Competition Between Foreign and U.S. Banks: Some Facts About Loans and Borrowers," *The Declining Role of Banking: Proceedings of the 30th Annual Conference on Bank Structure and Competition*, Federal Reserve Bank of Chicago: 331–51.
Canner, Glenn, and Neil Bhutta (2008) *Staff Analysis of the Relationship Between the CRA and the Subprime Crisis*, Board of Governors of the Federal Reserve System, retrieved April 17, 2009 from http://www.federalreserve.gov/newsevents/speech/20081203_analysis.pdf.
Carlson, Mark (2005) "Causes of Bank Suspensions in the Panic of 1893," *Explorations in Economic History*, Vol. 42, No. 1: 56–80.
Carlson, Mark, and Kris James Mitchener (2009) "Branch Banking as a Devise for Discipline: Competition and Bank Survivorship During the Great Depression," *Journal of Political Economy*, Vol. 117, No. 2: 165–210.
Carlson, Mark, and Kris James Mitchener (2005) "Branch Banking, Bank Competition, and Financial Stability, *NBER Working Paper 11291*, retrieved February 14, 2010 from http://www.nber.org/papers/w11291.
Carosso, Vincent P. (1970) *Investment Banking in America: A History*, Harvard University Press, Cambridge, MA.
Cebula, Richard J., and Ira S. Saltz (1994) "On Regulation Q and the Bank Failure Rate in the United States," *Rivista Internazionale di Economiche e Commerciali*, Vol. 41, No. 2: 185–91.
Chapman, John M. (1934) *Concentration in Banking*, Columbia University Press, New York, New York.

Chapman, John M., and Ray B. Westerfield (1942) *Branch Banking: Its Historical and Theoretical Position in America and Abroad*, Harper & Brothers Publishers, New York, New York.

Chari, V. V. (1989) "Banking Without Deposit Insurance or Bank Panics: Lessons From a Model of the U.S. National Banking System," *Federal Reserve Bank of Minneapolis Quarterly Review*, Vol. 13, No. 3: 3–19.

Cook, Timothy Q. (1978) "Regulation Q and the Behavior of Savings and Small Time Deposits at Commercial Banks and Thrift Institutions," *Federal Reserve Bank of Richmond Economic Review*, November/December: 14–28.

Cowen, David J. (2000) "The First Bank of the United States and the Securities Market Crash of 1792," *Journal of Economic History*, Vol. 60, No. 4: 1041–60.

Cox, Alfred (1966) *Regulation of Interest Rates on Bank Deposits*, University of Michigan, Ann Arbor, MI.

D'Arista, Jane W., and Tom Schlesinger (1994) "The Parallel Banking System," *The Declining Role of Banking: Proceedings of the 30th Annual Conference on Bank Structure and Competition*, Federal Reserve Bank of Chicago: 288–309.

Davis, Lance E. (1965) "The Investment Market, 1870–1914: The Evolution of a National Market," *Journal of Economic History*, Vol. 25, No. 3: 355–99.

Dehejia, Rajeev, and Adriana Lleras-Muney (2007) "Financial Development and Pathways of Growth: State Branching and Deposit Insurance Laws in the United States, 1900–1940," *Journal of Law and Economics*, Vol. 50, No. 2: 239–72.

Demyanyk, Yuliya S. and Van Hemert, Otto (2008) *Understanding the Subprime Mortgage Crisis*, December 5, retrieved June 28, 2010 from http://ssrn.com/abstract=1020396.

Dermine, Jean and Dirk Schoenmaker (2009) "In Banking, Is Small Beautiful?" *Financial Markets, Institutions & Instruments*, Vol. 19, No. 1: 1–19.

De Rugy, Veronique, and Melinda Warren (2009) *Expansion of Regulatory Budgets and Staffing Continues in the New Administration, Fiscal Year 2010 Annual Report of the Regulators' Budget*, retrieved May 24, 2010 from http://mercatus.org/publication/regulators-budget-report.

Dewatripont, Mathias, and Jean Tirole (1993) *The Prudential Regulation of Banks*, The MIT Press, Cambridge, MA.

Dhawan, Juhi (1996) *Branch Banking, Holding Companies and Universal Banking in the US*, Doctoral Thesis, Brown University Press, Providence, RI.

Diamond, Douglas W. and Raghuram G. Rajan (2009) "The Credit Crisis: Conjectures about Causes and Remedies," *American Economic Review*, Vol. 99, No. 2: 606–10.

Dowd, Kevin (1994) "Competitive Banking, Bankers' Clubs, and Bank Regulation," *Journal of Money, Credit, and Banking*, Vol. 26, No. 2: 289–308.

Dowd, Kevin (1993) *Laissez-Faire Banking*, Routledge, New York, New York.

Dowd, Kevin (1992) *The Experience of Free Banking*, Routledge, New York, New York.

Dywer, Gerald P. (1996) "Wildcat Banking, Banking Panics, and Free Banking in the United States," *Federal Reserve Bank of Atlanta Economic Review*, December: 1–20.

Dywer, Gerald P., and Alton Gilbert (1989) "Bank Runs and Private Remedies," *Federal Reserve Bank of St. Louis Review*, Vol. 71, No. 3: 43–61.

Ebersole, Franklin J. (1933) "One Year of the Reconstruction Finance Corporation," *Quarterly Journal of Economics*, Vol. 47, No. 3: 464–92.

Eccles, George (1982) *The Politics of Banking*, University of Utah, Salt Lake City, Utah.

Edwards, Franklin R., and James Scott (1979) "Regulating Solvency of Depository Institutions: A Perspective for Deregulation," in *Issues in Financial Regulation*, ed. Franklin Edwards, McGraw-Hill Book Company: 65–105.

Ely, Bert (2009) "Bad Rules Produce Bad Outcomes: Underlying Public-Policy Causes of the U.S. Financial Crisis," *Cato Journal*, Vol. 29, No. 1: 93–114.

Engerman, Stanley L., and Robert E. Gallman (1983) "U.S. Economic Growth, 1783–1860," in *Research in Economic History*, ed. Paul Uselding, JAI Press Inc., Greenwich, CT: 1–46.

Ennis, Huberto M., and H.S. Malek (2005) "Bank Risk of Failure and the Too-Big-To-Fail Policy," *Federal Reserve Bank of Richmond Economic Quarterly*, Vol. 91, No. 2: 21–44.

Federal Deposit Insurance Corporation (1997) *History of the Eighties – Lessons for the Future* retrieved April 22, 2010 from http://fdic.gov/bank/historical/history/vol1.html.

Federal Reserve (various years) *Federal Reserve Bulletin*, Board of Governors of the Federal Reserve System, Washington, D.C.

Federal Reserve (1943) *Banking and Monetary Statistics, 1914–1941*, Board of Governors of the Federal Reserve System, Washington, D.C.

Federal Reserve Committee on Branch, Group, and Chain Banking (1932) *Branch Banking in the United States*, retrieved January 14, 2010 from http://fraser.stlouisfed.org/historicaldocs/1073/download/37824/branch_banking_us.pdf.

Feinman, Joshua N. (1993) "Reserve Requirements: History, Current Practice, and Potential Reform," *Federal Reserve Bulletin*, Vol. 79, No. 6: 569–89.

Fenstermaker, J. Van (1965) *The Development of American Commercial Banking: 1782–1837*, Kent State University Press, Kent, OH.

Fenstermaker, J. Van, and John E. Filer (1986) "Impact of the First and Second Banks of the United States and the Suffolk System on New England Bank Money, 1791–1837," *Journal of Money, Credit, and Banking*, Vol. 18, No. 1: 28–40.

Ferrie, Joseph P. (1997) "The Entry of Antebellum European Immigrants Into the U.S. Labor Market, 1840–60," *Explorations in Economic History*, Vol. 34, No. 3: 295–330.

Flannery, Mark J. (1984) "The Social Cost of Unit Banking Restrictions," *Journal of Monetary Economics*, Vol. 13, No. 2: 237–49.

Friedman, Milton, and Anna Schwartz (1963) *A Monetary History of the United States, 1867–1960*, National Bureau of Economic Research, New York, New York.

Garrett, Thomas A., Andrew F. Kozak, and Russel M. Rhine (2010) "Institutions and Government Growth: A Comparison of the 1890s and the 1930s," *Federal Reserve Bank of St. Louis Review*, March/April: 109–19.

Gilbert, R. Alton (1986) "Requiem for Regulation Q: What it Did and Why it Passed Away," *Federal Reserve Bank of St. Louis Economic Review*, February: 22–37.

Glaeser, Edward L. (2006) "The Economic Impact of Restricting Housing Supply," *Rappaport Policy Briefs*, May, retrieved April 29, 2010 from www.americandream-coalition.org/housing/housing_final.pdf.

Goldenweiser, E. A. (1931) "Branch Banking in California," *Federal Reserve Committee on Branch, Group, and Chain Banking*, retrieved May 18, 2010 from http://fraser.stlouisfed.org/historicaldocs/frbgc/download/37825/branch_banking_california.pdf.

Gorton, Gary (1988) "Banking Panics and Business Cycles," *Oxford Economic Papers*, Vol. 40, No. 4: 751–81.
Gorton, Gary (1985) "Clearinghouses and the Origin of Central Banking in the United States," *Journal of Economic History*, Vol. 45, No. 2: 277–83.
Grossman, Richard S. (1994) "The Shoe That Didn't Drop: Explaining Banking Stability During the Great Depression," *Journal of Economic History*, Vol. 54, No. 3: 654–82.
Gunther, Jeffrey W. (1999) "Should CRA Stand for Community Redundancy Act?" *Regulation*, Vol. 23, No. 3: 56–60.
Hammond, Bray (1963) "Banking Before the Civil War," in Deane Carson, ed., *Banking and Monetary Studies*, Richard D. Irwin, Inc., IL: 1–15.
Hammond, Bray (1957) *Banks and Politics in America, from the Revolution to the Civil War*, Princeton University Press, Princeton, NJ.
Hanc, George (1995) "The Banking Crises of the 1980s and Early 1990s: Summary and Implications," *FDIC Banking Review*: 1–55.
Hassan, Iftekhar, and Gerald Dwyer (1994) "Bank Runs in the Free Banking Period," *Journal of Money, Banking, and Credit*, Vol. 26, No. 2: 271–88.
Hayek, Friedrich A. (1937) "Economics and Knowledge," *Economica*, Vol. 4: 33–54.
Hayes, S.L. III, Spence, A.M., and Marks, D. (1983) *Competition in the Investment Banking Industry*, Harvard University Press, Cambridge, MA.
Haywood, Charles, and Charles Link (1968) *The Regulation of Deposit Interest Rates*, Association of Reserve City Bankers, Chicago, IL.
Helderman, Leonard (1931) *National and State Banks*, Houghton Mifflin, Boston, MA.
Hendrickson, Jill M., and Mark W. Nichols (2010) "Did Commercial Banks Close Branches in Low-Income Neighborhoods in Response to the CRA? Implications for Understanding the 2007–2008 Financial Crisis," *Journal of Legal, Ethical and Regulatory Issues*, Vol. 13, No. 1: 17–38.
Hendrickson, Jill M., and Mark W. Nichols (2011) "How Do Predatory Lending Laws Impact Bank Performance?" *Academy of Banking Studies Journal*, Vol. 10, No. 1: 1–22.
Hendrickson, Jill M. (2010) "The Interstate Banking Debate: A Historical Perspective," *Academy of Banking Studies Journal*, Vol. 9, No. 2: 95–130.
Hendrickson, Jill M. (2001) "The Long and Bumpy Road to Glass-Steagall Reform," *The American Journal of Economics and Sociology*, Vol. 60, No. 4: 849–79.
Hetzel, Robert L. (1991) "Too Big to Fail: Origins, Consequences, and Outlook," *Federal Reserve Bank of Richmond Economic Review*, November/December: 3–15.
High, Jack (1991) "Regulation as a Process: On the Theory, History, and Doctrine of Government Regulation," in *Austrian Economics*, ed. Richard M. Ebeling, Hillsdale College Press, Hillsdale, MI: 261–80.
Hilsenrath, Jon, Serena Ng, and Damian Paletta (2008) "Worst Crisis Since '30s, With No End Yet in Sight," *Wall Street Journal*, September 18, retrieved October 19, 2009 from http://online.wsj.com/article/SB122169431617549947.html.
Hirshleifer, David (2008) "Psychological Bias as a Driver of Financial Regulation," *European Financial Management*, Vol. 14, No. 5: 856–74.
Holcombe, Randall G., and Donald J. Lacombe (1998) "Interest Versus Ideology in the Ratification of the 16th and 17th Amendments," *Economics and Politics*, Vol. 19, No. 2: 143–59.

Humphrey Thomas, M. (2010) "Lender of Last Resort: What It Is, Whence It Came, and Why the Fed Isn't It," *Cato Journal*, Vol. 30, No. 2: 333–64.

Husock, Howard (2008) "The Financial Crisis and the CRA," *The City Journal*, October 30, retrieved April 16, 2009 from http://www.city-journal.org/2008/eon1030hh.html.

Investment Company Institute Mutual Fund Factbook (2010) retrieved March 11, 2010 from http://www.icifactbook.org/fb_data.html.

Jayaratne, Jith, and Philip E. Strahan (1998) "Entry Restrictions, Industry Evolution and Dynamic Efficiency: Evidence from Commercial Banking," *Journal of Law and Economics*, Vol. 41, No. 1: 239–74.

Johnson, Christian, and Tara Rice (2007) "Assessing a Decade of Interstate Bank Branching," *Federal Reserve Bank of Chicago Working Paper 2007–03*.

Kane, Edward (2000) "Incentives for Banking Megamergers: What Motives Might Regulators Infer From Event-Study Evidence?" *Journal of Money, Credit and Banking*, Vol. 32, No. 3: 671–701.

Kane, Edward J. (1989) "Changing Incentives Facing Regulators," *Journal of Financial Services Research*, Vol. 2, No. 3: 265–74.

Kaufman, George G. (1996) "Bank Failures, System Risk, and Bank Regulation," *Cato Journal*, Vol. 16, No. 1: 17–45, retrieved April 22, 2010 from www.cato.org/pubs/journal.

Kaufman, George G. (1994) "Bank Contagion: A Review of the Theory and Evidence," *Journal of Financial Services Research*, Vol. 8, No. 2: 123–50.

Kaufman, George G. (1988) "Bank Runs: Causes, Benefits and Costs," *Cato Journal*, Vol. 7: 559–87.

Keeley, Michael C. (1990) "Deposit Insurance, Risk, and Market Power in Banking," *American Economic Review*, Vol. 80, No. 5: 1183–200.

Kennedy, S.E. (1973) *The Banking Crisis of 1933*, Kentucky University Press, Lexington, KY.

Keys, Benjamin, J., Tanmoy Mukherjee, Amit Seru, and Vikrant Vig (2010) "Did Securitization Lead to Lax Screening? Evidence From Subprime Loans," *The Quarterly Journal of Economics*, Vol. 125, No. 1: 307–62.

Kilcollin, Thomas Eric, and Gerald A. Hanweck (1981) "Regulation Q and Commercial Bank Profitability," *Research Papers in Banking and Financial Economics*, Board of Governors of the Federal Reserve, No. 46.

Kindleberger, Charles, and Robert Aliber (2005) *Manias, Panics, and Crashes*, Fifth Edition, Wiley & Sons, Inc., New Jersey.

Kirzner, Israel M. (1992) *The Meaning of Market Process*, Routledge, New York, NY.

Kirzner, Israel M. (1984) "The Perils of Regulation: A Market-Process Approach," *Austrian Economics: A Reader*, ed. Richard M. Ebeling, Hillsdale College Press, Hillsdale, MI: 618–54.

Klebaner, Benjamin J. (1990) *American Commercial Banking: A History*, Twayne Publishers, Boston, MA.

Kling, Arnold (2010) *Unchecked and Unbalanced: How the Discrepancy Between Knowledge and Power Caused the Financial Crisis and Threatens Democracy*, Hoover Studies in Politics, Economics, and the Society, Stanford, CA.

Knox, John Jay (1903) *A History of Banking in the United States*, Bradford Rhodes & Co., New York.

Krooss, Herman E., and Martin R. Blyn (1971) *A History of Financial Intermediaries*, Random House, New York.

Kroszner, Randall S. (2008) "The Community Reinvestment Act and the Recent Mortgage Crisis," *Confronting Concentrated Poverty Policy Forum*, Board of Governors of the Federal Reserve System, December, 3, retrieved April 15, 2009 from http://www.federalreserve.gov/newsevent/speech/kroszner20081203a.htm.

Kroszner, Randall S. (2000) "Lessons from Financial Crises: The Role of Clearinghouses," *Journal of Financial Services Research*, Vol. 18, No. 2/3: 157–71.

Kroszner, Randall S., and Raghuram G. Rajan (1994) "Is the Glass–Steagall Act Justified? A Study of the U.S. Experience with Universal Banking Before 1933," *The American Economic Review*, Vol. 84, No. 4: 810–32.

Lamoreaux, Naomi R. (1994) *Insider Lending*, Cambridge University Press, Cambridge, MA.

Lamoreaux, Naomi R. (1986) "Banks, Kinship, and Economic Development: The New England Case," *Journal of Economic History*, Vol. 46, No. 3: 653–8.

Litan, Robert E. (1987) *What Should Banks Do*? Brookings Institution, Washington, D.C.

Litan, Robert E., and William Nordhaus (1983) *Reforming Federal Regulation*, Yale University Press, New Haven, CT.

Livingston, James (1986) *Origins of the Federal Reserve System: Money, Class, and Corporate Capitalism, 1890–1913*, Cornell University Press, Ithaca, New York.

Macey, Jonathan R., M. Wayne Marr, and S. David Young (1991) "The Glass–Steagall Act and the Riskiness of Financial Intermediaries," *Research in Law and Economics*, Vol. 14: 19–30.

Markham, Jerry (2002) *A Financial History of the United States*, Vol. 1, ME Sharpe Armonk, New York.

Mason, Joseph R. (2001) "Do Lender of Last Resort Policies Matter? The Effects of Reconstruction Finance Corporation Assistance to Banks During the Great Depression," *Journal of Financial Services Research*, Vol. 20, No. 1: 77–95.

McChesney, Fred S. (1997) *Money for Nothing: Politicians, Rent Extraction, and Political Extortion*, Harvard University Press, Cambridge, MA.

McChesney, Fred S. (1987) "Rent Extraction and Rent Creation in the Economic Theory of Regulation," *Journal of Legal Studies*, Vol. XVI: 101–18.

McKinnon, John D., and Susanne Craig (2010) "Goldman is Bruised, Defiant in Senate," *Wall Street Journal*, retrieved April 29, 2010 from online.wsj.com.

McWinney, James E. (2010) "A Brief History of the Mutual Fund," retrieved April 10, 2010 from http://www.investopedia.com/articles/mutualfund/05/MF-history.asp.

Mengle, David L. (1990) "The Case for Interstate Branch Banking," *Federal Reserve Bank of Richmond Economic Review*, November/December: 3–17.

Minskey, Hyman (1982) *Can "It" Happen Again*?, M.E. Sharp, New York.

Mises, Ludwig von (1949) *Human Action*, Yale University Press, New Haven.

Mishkin, Frederic S. (2010) *The Economics of Money, Banking, and Financial Markets*, 9th edition, Pearson Publishing, New York.

Mishkin, Frederic S. (1991) "Asymmetric Information and Financial Crises: A Historical Perspective," in *Financial Markets and Financial Crises*, ed. Glenn R. Hubbard, University of Chicago Press: 69–108.

Moen, Jon, and Ellis Tallman (2000) "Clearinghouse Membership and Deposit Contraction During the Panic of 1907," *Journal of Economic History*, Vol. 60, No. 1: 145–63.

Moen, Jon, and Ellis Tallman (1999) "Why Didn't the United States Establish a Central Bank Until After the Panic of 1907?" Federal Reserve Bank of Atlanta, *Working Paper 99-16*.

Moen, Jon, and Ellis Tallman (1992) "The Bank Panic of 1907: The Role of Trust Companies," *Journal of Economic History*, Vol. 52, No. 3: 611–30.

National Bureau of Economic Research, *Historic Recession Dates*, retrieved April 21, 2010 from www.nber.org/cycles.html.

Ng, Kenneth (1988) "Free Banking Laws and Barriers to Entry in Banking, 1838–1860," *Journal of Economic History*, Vol. XLVIII, No. 4: 877–89.

Nichols, Mark W., and Jill M. Hendrickson (1997) "Profit Differentials Between Canadian and U.S. Banks: The Role of Regulation," *Journal of Economic History*, Vol. 57, No. 3: 674–96.

Norberg, Johan (2009) *Financial Fiasco*, The Cato Institute, Washington, D.C.

O'Connor, James Francis (1933) "The Glass and Steagall Bills, *American Bankers' Association Journal*, June: 22.

O'Driscoll, Gerald P. Jr. (2009) "What Savings Glut?" *Wall Street Journal*, March 26, retrieved March 30, 2009 at http://online.wsj.com/article/ SB123811-225716453243.html.

Olson, James Stuart (1977) *Herbert Hoover and the Reconstruction Finance Corporation: 1931–1933*, The Iowa State University Press, Ames, Iowa.

Ostrosky, Anthony L. (1997) "Bank Failures in the U.S.: A Note on Regulation Q," *International Advances in Economic Research*, Vol. 3, No. 2, May: 176–80.

O'Toole, Randal (2009) "Housing Policy," *Cato Handbook for Policymakers*, 7th Edition, Cato Institute, Washington, D.C.: 241–7.

O'Toole, Randal (2007) "The Planning Tax: The Case Against Regional Growth-Management Planning," *Policy Analysis*, No. 606, Cato Institute, Washington, D.C.

Owens, Raymond, and Stacey L. Schreft (1995) "Identifying Credit Crunches," *Contemporary Economic Policy*, Vol. 13, No. 2: 63–77.

Peltzman, Sam (1976) "Towards a More General Theory of Regulation," *Journal of Law and Economics*, Vol. 19: 211–40.

Pinto, Edward (2008) "Sizing Total Exposure to Subprime and Alt-A Loans in U.S. First Mortgage Market as of 6.30.08," *Memorandum*, retrieved May 14, 2010 from www.aei.org/docLib/Pinto-Sizing-Total-Exposure.pdf.

Prescott, Edward Simpson (2002) "Can Risk-Based Deposit Insurance Premiums Control Moral Hazard?" *Federal Reserve Bank of Richmond Economic Quarterly*, Vol. 88, No. 2: 87–100.

Preston, Howard H. (1924) "Recent Developments in Branch Banking," *American Economic Review*, Vol. 14, No. 3: 443–62.

Preston, Howard H. (1933) "The Banking Act of 1933," *The American Economic Review*, Vol. XXIII, No. 4: 585–607.

Ramirez, Carlos D. (2009) "Bank Fragility, 'Money Under the Mattress', and Long-Run Growth: US Evidence from the 'Perfect' Panic of 1893," *Journal of Banking & Finance*, Vol. 33, No. 12: 2185–98.

Read, Leonard (1958) "I, Pencil," *The Freeman*, retrieved June 1, 2010 from http://www.thefreemanonline.org/featured/i-pencil/#.

Redlich, Fritz (1947) *The Molding of American Banking: Men and Ideas*, Hafner, New York.

Rockoff, Hugh (1985) "New Evidence on Free Banking in the United States," *American Economic Review*, Vol. 75, No. 4: 886–9.

Rockoff, Hugh (1975) *The Free Banking Era: A Re-Examination*, Arno Press, New York.

Rockoff, Hugh (1974) "The Free Banking Era," *Journal of Money, Credit, and Banking*, Vol. 6, No. 2: 141–67.

Rolnick, Arthur J., Bruce D. Smith, and Warren E. Weber (2000) "The Suffolk Bank and Panic of 1837," *Federal Reserve Bank of Minneapolis Quarterly Review*, Vol. 24, No. 2: 3–13.

Rolnick, Arthur J., Bruce D. Smith, and Warren E. Weber (1998) "Lessons From a Laissez-Faire Payments System: The Suffolk Banking System (1825–58)," *Federal Reserve Bank of Minneapolis Quarterly Review*, Vol. 22, No. 3: 11–21.

Rolnick, Arthur J., and Warren E. Weber (1986) "Inherent Instability in Banking: The Free Banking Experience," *Cato Journal*, Vol. 5: 877–90.

Rolnick, Arthur J., and Warren E. Weber (1984) "The Causes of Free Bank Failures," *Journal of Monetary Economics*, Vol. 14, No. 3: 267–91.

Rolnick, Arthur J., and Warren E. Weber (1983) "New Evidence on the Free Banking Era," *American Economic Review*, Vol. 73, No. 5: 1080–91.

Rolnick, Arthur J., and Warren E. Weber (1982) "Free Banking, Wildcat Banking, and Shinplasters," *Federal Reserve Bank of Minneapolis Quarterly Review*, Vol. 6: 10–19.

Root, L. Carroll (1895) "New York Bank Currency," *Sound Currency*, Sound Currency Committee of the Reform Club, New York, New York: 285–309.

Rothbard, Murray N. (1962) *The Panic of 1819: Reactions and Policies*, Columbia University Press, New York, online edition, 2002, Ludwig Von Mises Institute, retrieved June 25, 2010 from http://mises.org/rothbard/panic1819.pdf.

Roussakis, Emmanuel N. (1997) *Commercial Banking in an Era of Deregulation*, Praeger Press, New York.

Rouwenhorst, K. Geert (2004) "The Origins of Mutual Funds," *Yale ICF Working Paper No. 04-48*, retrieved April 13, 2010 from http://papers.ssrn.com/sol3/papers.cfm?abstract_id=636146.

Salsman, Richard M. (1993) "Bankers as Scapegoats for Government-Created Banking Crises in U.S. History," in *The Crisis in American Banking*, ed. Lawrence H. White, New York University Press, New York: 81–118.

Saulsbury, Victor L. (1987) "State Banking Powers: Where Are We Now?" *Regulatory Review*, April/March: 1–17.

Schwartz, Anna J. (1986) "Real and Pseudo-Financial Crises," *in Financial Crises and the World Banking System*, eds. Forrest Capie and Geoffrey Wood, St. Martin's Press, New York.

Schweikart, Larry, and Michael Allen (2004) *A Patriot's History of the United States*, Sentinel Penguin Group, New York.

Schweikart, Larry (1991) "U.S. Commercial Banking: A Historiographical Survey," *Business History Review*, Vol. 65, No. 3: 606–61.

Schweikart, Larry (1987) *Banking in the American South from the Age of Jackson to Reconstruction*, Louisiana State University Press, Baton Rouge, LA.

Selgin, George A. (2000) "The Suppression of State Banknotes: A Reconsideration," *Economic Inquiry*, Vol. 38, No. 4: 600–15.

Shlaes, Amity (2007) *The Forgotten Man: A New History of the Great Depression*, HarperCollins Publisher, New York, New York.

Sinkey, Joseph F. Jr., and David Carter (1994) "The Derivatives Activities of U.S. Commercial Banks," *The Declining Role of Banking: Proceedings of the*

30th Annual Conference on Bank Structure and Competition, Federal Reserve Bank of Chicago.

Sowell, Thomas (2009) *The Housing Boom and Bust*, Basic Books, New York.

Spong, Kenneth (1992) "History of Banking Regulation," *Bank Management and Regulation: A Book of Readings*, ed. A. Saunders, G. Udell, and L. White, Bristlecone Books, Mayfield Publishing Co., Mountain View, CA: 17–24.

Sprague, O. M. W. (1903) "Branch Banking in the United States," *Quarterly Journal of Economics*, Vol. 27: 242–60.

Sprague, O. M. W. (1910) *History of Crises Under the National Banking System*, Government Printing Office, Washington, D.C.

Stern, Gary H., and Ron J. Feldman (2008) "Managing the Expanded Safety Net," *Federal Reserve Bank of Minneapolis The Region*, retrieved April 20, 2010 from www.minneapolisfed.org/pubs/region.

Stern, Gary H., and Ron J. Feldman (2004) *Too Big To Fail: The Hazards of Bank Bailouts*, Brookings Institution Press, Washington, D.C.

Stevens, Albert C. (1894) "Analysis of the Phenomena of the Panic in the United States in 1893," *Quarterly Journal of Economics*, Vol. 8, No. 2: 117–48.

Stigler, George (1971) "The Theory of Economic Regulation," *The Bell Journal of Economics and Management Science*, Vol. 2, No. 1: 3–21.

Sumner, William Graham (1896) *History of Banking in the United States*, Augustus M. Kelley, New York.

Swanson, William Walker (1908) "The Crisis of 1860 and the First Issue of Clearing-House Certificates," *Journal of Political Economy*, Vol. 16, No. 2 and 4: 65–75 and 212–26.

Sylla, Richard (2001) "Review of Peter Temin: The Jacksonian Economy," *Economic History Services*, August 17, retrieved February 4, 2009 from www.eh.net/bookreviews/library/sylla.shtml.

Sylla, Richard (1976) "Forgotten Men of Money: Private Bankers in Early U.S. History," *Journal of Economic History*, Vol. 36, No. 1: 173–88.

Sylla, Richard (1972) "The United States 1863–1913," in *Banking and Economic Development: Some Lessons of History*, ed. Rondo Cameron, Oxford University Press, New York: 232–62.

Sylla, Richard, Robert E. Wright, and David J. Cowen (2009) "Alexander Hamilton, Central Banker: Crisis Management during the U.S. Financial Panic of 1792," *Business History Review*, Vol. 83, No. 2: 61–86.

Sylla, Richard, John Legler, and John Wallis (1987) "Banks and State Public Finance in the New Republic: The United States, 1790–1860," *Journal of Economic History*, Vol. 47, No. 2: 391–403.

Symons, Edward L. Jr., and James J. White (1984) *Banking Law*, West Publishing, St. Paul, MN.

Taylor, John B. (2009a) "The Financial Crisis and the Policy Responses: An Empirical Analysis of What Went Wrong," *NBER Working Paper Series*, retrieved March 11, 2009 from http://www.nber.org/papers/w14631.

Taylor, John B. (2009) "How Government Created the Financial Crisis," *Wall Street Journal*, February 9, retrieved March 11, 2009 from http://online.wsj.com/article/SB123414310280561945.html.

Talor, John, and Josh Silver (2008) "The Community Reinvestment Act: 30 Years of Wealth Building and What We Must Do to Finish the Job," *Revisiting the CRA: Perspectives on the Future of the Community Reinvestment Act*, retrieved

June 10, 2009 from http://www.frbsf.org/publications/community/cra/cra_30_years_wealth_building.pdf.
Temin, Peter (1976) *Did Monetary Forces Cause the Great Depression?* W.W. Norton, New York.
Temin, Peter (1969) *The Jacksonian Economy*, W.W. Norton, New York.
Timberlake, Richard (1984) "The Central Banking Role of Clearinghouse Associations," *Journal of Money, Credit, and Banking*, Vol. 16, No. 1: 279–93.
Timberlake, Richard (1960) "The Species Circular and Distribution of the Surplus," *Journal of Political Economy*, Vol. 68, No. 2: 109–17.
Trivoli, George (1979) *The Suffolk Bank: A Study of a Free-Enterprise Clearing System*, Adam Smith Institute, London.
U.S. Comptroller of the Currency (various years) *Annual Report of the Comptroller of the Currency*, Government Printing Office, Washington, D.C.
United States Department of Commerce (1976) *Historical Statistics of the United States Colonial Times to 1970*, Part 2.
Wallison, Peter J. (2010) "Government Housing Policy and the Financial Crisis," *Cato Journal*, Vol. 30, No. 2: 397–406.
Wallison, Peter J. (2009) "The True Origins of this Financial Crisis," *Financial Services Outlook*, retrieved December 3, 2009 from http://www.aei.org/include/pub_print.asp?pubID=29372.
Wallison, Peter J. (2008) "Cause and Effect: Government Policies and the Financial Crisis," *Financial Services Outlook*, November, retrieved February 15, 2009 from http://www.aei.org/publications/filter.,pubID.29015/pub_detail.asp.
Wallison, Peter J., and Charles W. Calomiris (2008) "The Last Trillion-Dollar Commitment: The Destruction of Fannie Mae and Freddie Mac," *Financial Services Outlook*, September, retrieved January 3, 2009 from http://www.aei.org/publications/filter.all,pubID.28704/pub_detail.asp.
Wanniski, Jude (1989) *The Way the World Works*, Regnery Publishing Inc., 3rd edition, Washington, D.C.
Weber, Warren E. (2010) "Bank Liability Insurance Schemes Before 1865," *Federal Reserve Bank of Minneapolis Working Paper 679*.
Weber, Warren E. (2006) "Early State Banks in the United States: How Many Were There and Where Did They Exist?" *Federal Reserve Bank of Minneapolis Quarterly Review*, Vol. 30, No. 2: 28–40.
Westerfield, Ray B. (1939) *Historical Survey of Branch Banking in the United States*, American Economists Council for the study of Branch Banking, reprinted by Arno Press, New York, 1980.
Westerfield, Ray B. (1933) "The Banking Act of 1933," *The Journal of Political Economy*, Vol. 41, No. 6: 721–49.
Wheelock, David C. (2010) "Lessons Learned? Comparing the Federal Reserve's Responses to the Crises of 1929–1933 and 2007–2009," *Federal Reserve Bank of St. Louis Review*, March/April: 89–107.
Wheelock, David C., and Paul W. Wilson (2009) "Are U.S. Banks Too Large?" *Federal Reserve Bank of St. Louis Working Paper 2009-054B*, retrieved April 13, 2010 from http://research.stlouisfed.org/wp/2009/2009-054.pdf.
White, Eugene Nelson (2009) "Lessons From the Great American Real Estate Boom and Bust of the 1920s," *NBER Working Paper 15573*, retrieved January 22, 2010 from http://www.nber.org/papers/w15573.

White, Eugene Nelson (2008) "Lessons From the History of Bank Examination and Supervision in the United States, 1863–2008," Unpublished Manuscript presented at the Conference on Financial Market Regulation After Financial Crises: The Historical Experience, April 16–17, Banca d'Italia.

White, Eugene Nelson (1986) "Before the Glass–Steagall Act: An Analysis of the Investment Banking Activities of National Banks," *Explorations in Economic History*, Vol. 23, 33–55.

White, Eugene Nelson (1985) "The Merger Movement in Banking, 1919–1933," *Journal of Economic History*, Vol. 45, No. 2: 285–91.

White, Eugene Nelson (1983) *The Regulation and Reform of the American Banking System, 1900–1929*, Princeton University Press, Princeton, New Jersey.

White, Eugene Nelson (1982) "The Membership Problem of the National Banking System," *Explorations in Economic History*, Vol. 19, No. 2: 110–27.

White, Eugene Nelson (1981) "State-Sponsored Insurance of Bank Deposits in the United States, 1907–1929," *Journal of Economic History*, Vol. 41, No. 3: 537–57.

White, Lawrence J. (2010) "The Credit Rating Agencies," *Journal of Economic Perspectives*, Vol. 24, No. 2: 211–26.

White, Lawrence (2008) "How Did We Get Into This Financial Mess?" *Cato Briefing Papers*, November 18, retrieved November 29, 2008 from http://www.cato.org/pub_display.php?pub_id=9788.

White, Lawrence (1986) "Regulatory Sources of Instability in Banking," *Cato Journal*, Vol. 5, No. 4: 891–7.

Wicker, Elmus (2000) *Banking Panics of the Gilded Age*, Cambridge University Press, New York, New York.

Wicker, Elmus (1996) *The Banking Panics of the Great Depression*, Cambridge University Press, New York, New York.

Wilson, Jack W., Richard E. Sylla, and Charles P. Jones (1990) "Financial Market Panics and Volatility in the Long Run, 1830–1988," in *Crashes and Panic: The Lessons from History*, ed. Eugene N. White, Dow Jones-Irwin, Homewood, IL: 85–125.

Woelfel, Charles J. (1994) *Encyclopedia of Banking and Finance*, 10th edition, Infobase Press, New York.

Wolf, Martin (2008) *Fixing Global Finance*, John Hopkins University Press, Baltimore, MD.

Wolfson, Martin (1994) *Financial Crises*, M.E. Sharpe, Armonk, New York.

Index